Story and Art by Arina Tanemura

SAKURA HIME

The Legend of Princess Sakura

9

Characters

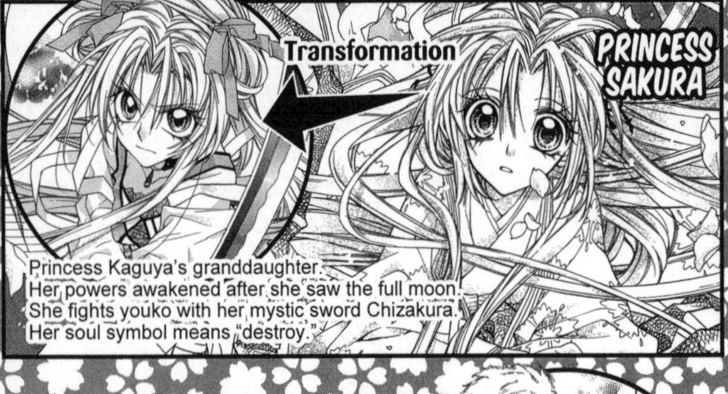
Transformation
PRINCESS SAKURA
Princess Kaguya's granddaughter.
Her powers awakened after she saw the full moon.
She fights youko with her mystic sword Chizakura.
Her soul symbol means "destroy."

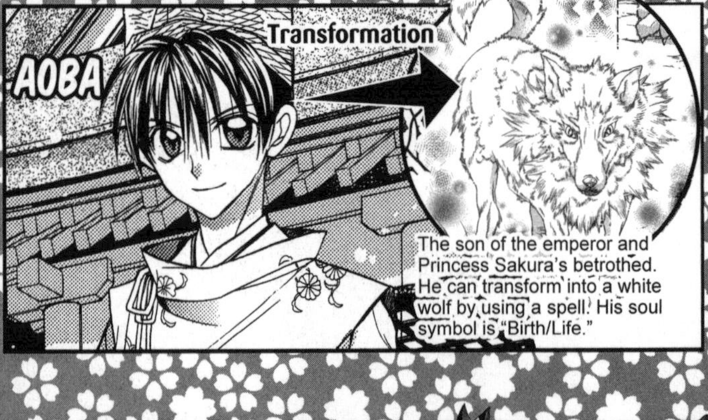
Transformation
AOBA
The son of the emperor and Princess Sakura's betrothed. He can transform into a white wolf by using a spell. His soul symbol is "Birth/Life."

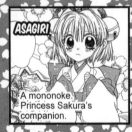

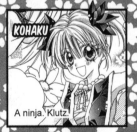

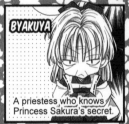

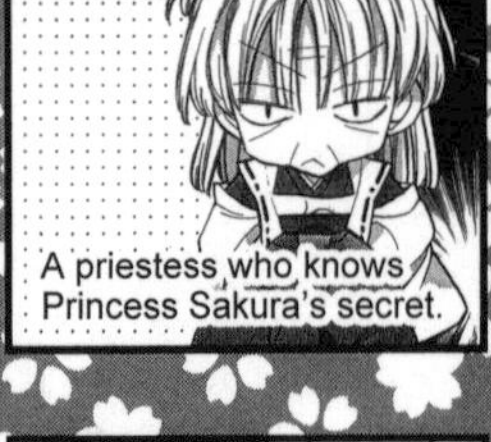
BYAKUYA
A priestess who knows Princess Sakura's secret.

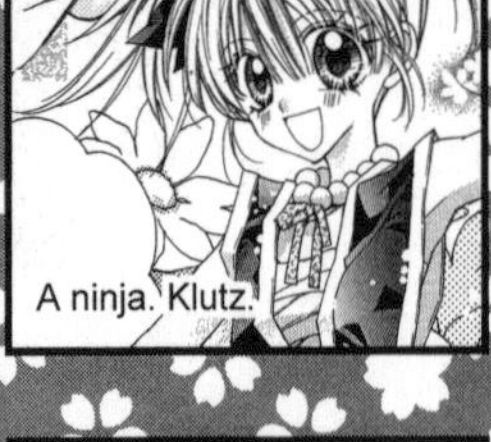
KOHAKU
A ninja. Klutz.

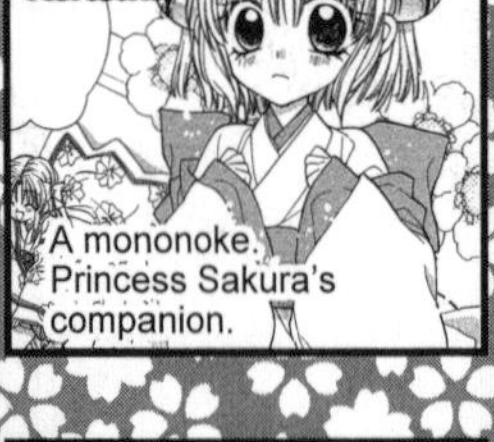
ASAGIRI
A mononoke. Princess Sakura's companion.

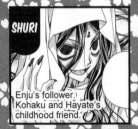

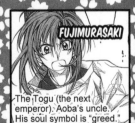

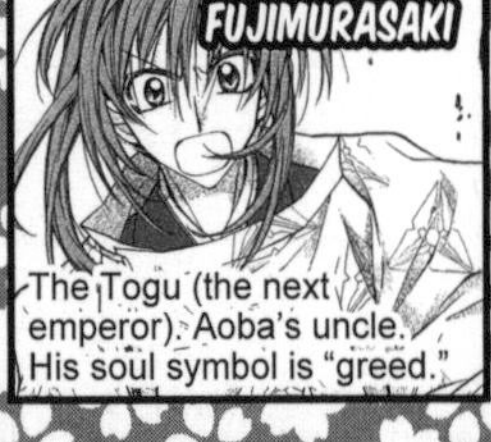
FUJIMURASAKI
The Togu (the next emperor). Aoba's uncle. His soul symbol is "greed."

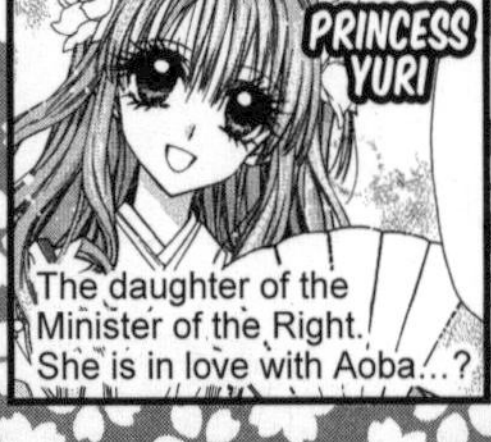
PRINCESS YURI
The daughter of the Minister of the Right. She is in love with Aoba...?

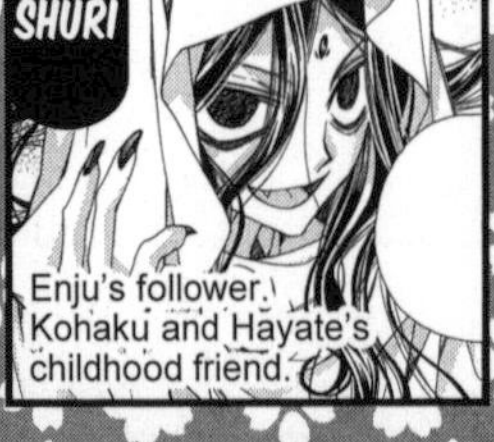
SHURI
Enju's follower. Kohaku and Hayate's childhood friend.

ENJU

Princess Sakura's older brother. He used to be kind, but he hates humans now and hopes to reinstate the moon kingdom.

HAYATE

Kohaku's childhood friend. He can return to human form when there's a full moon.

RURIJO

Enju's follower. She hates Princess Sakura.

SAKURA HIME
The Legend of Princess Sakura

Story Thus Far

Heian era. Princess Sakura, granddaughter to Princess Kaguya, has the power to wield the mystic sword Chizakura. Under orders from the emperor, she must hunt down youko with Aoba, her betrothed.

Enju, whom she thought dead, kidnaps her and takes her to Shura Yugenden. While under Enju's control, Sakura kills Ukyo with her sword Chizakura. Sakura also learns of Enju's plans to resurrect Princess Kaguya and decides to part ways with him. She escapes Shura Yugenden with the help of Aoba, Fujimurasaki, and her other allies who came to save her.

Sakura and Aoba return to their daily lives, but then the emperor orders Aoba to take Princess Yuri as a second wife. Sakura fights with Aoba after he spends the night at Princess Yuri's place. Sakura runs off to stay with Fujimurasaki.

Aoba arrives at Fujimurasaki's estate in search of Sakura. Fujimurasaki lies to him and tells him she's not there. Fujimurasaki confesses to Sakura, "You are the first person I have ever desired to have for myself." Now Sakura does not know what to do...

SAKURA HIME
The Legend of Princess Sakura

CONTENTS

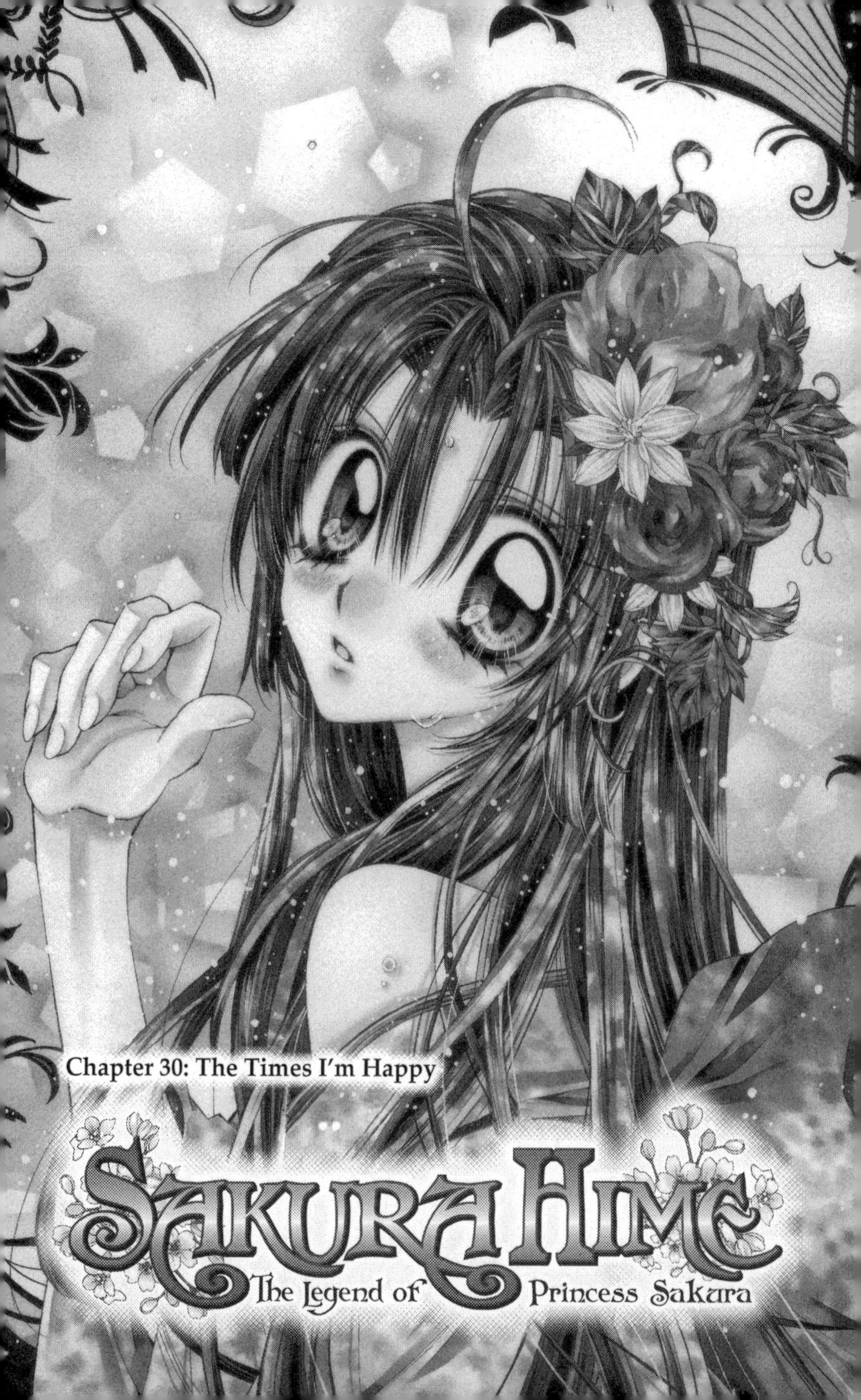
Chapter 30: The Times I'm Happy
SAKURA HIME
The Legend of Princess Sakura

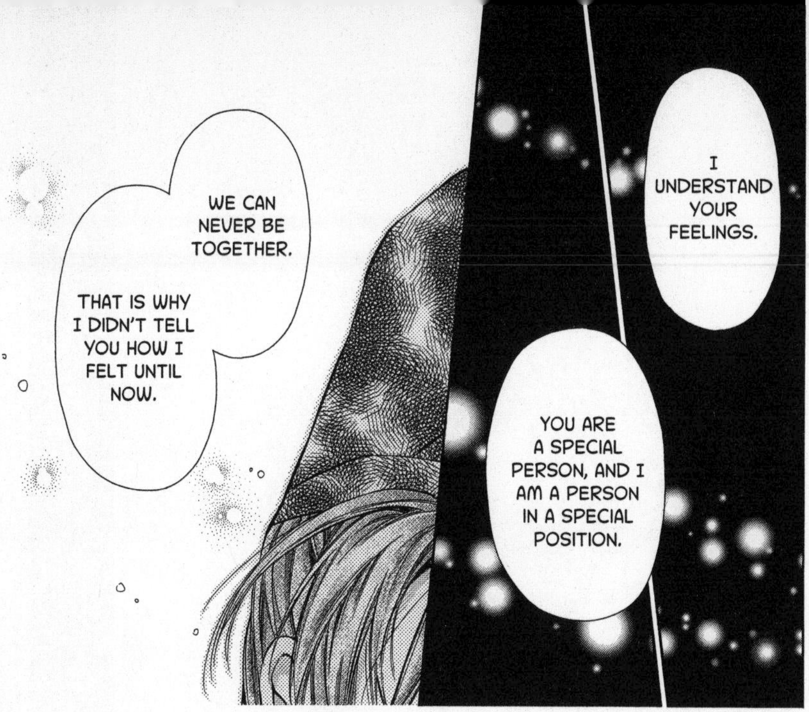
I UNDERSTAND YOUR FEELINGS.
YOU ARE A SPECIAL PERSON, AND I AM A PERSON IN A SPECIAL POSITION.
WE CAN NEVER BE TOGETHER.
THAT IS WHY I DIDN'T TELL YOU HOW I FELT UNTIL NOW.

Chapter 30: The Times I'm Happy

※ I'm giving away the story.

This is the final chapter of the Princess Yuri introduction arc. When volume 8 came out, Princess Yuri was very unpopular when she first appeared, but I think some people started to like her after this chapter. I've never been a person with "girl skills," so I like women like Yuri who are very girly. I can never be like them. (laugh) I'm too sloppy...

This chapter is filled with kissing scenes, but drawing them is difficult. I can remember feeling like crying when I was working on this chapter. I drew the rough draft saying, "I don't have any new angles left for those kissing scenes."

Just for record, the most popular panel in this chapter according to fan mail was the scene in which Yuri keeps taking quick glimpses at Sakura. Yuri will leave the story for the time being, but she will come back again to interact with a different character, so please look forward to volume 10.

By the way, it's very easy to draw her in the rough draft, but she takes twice as much time as the other characters to ink. How strange...

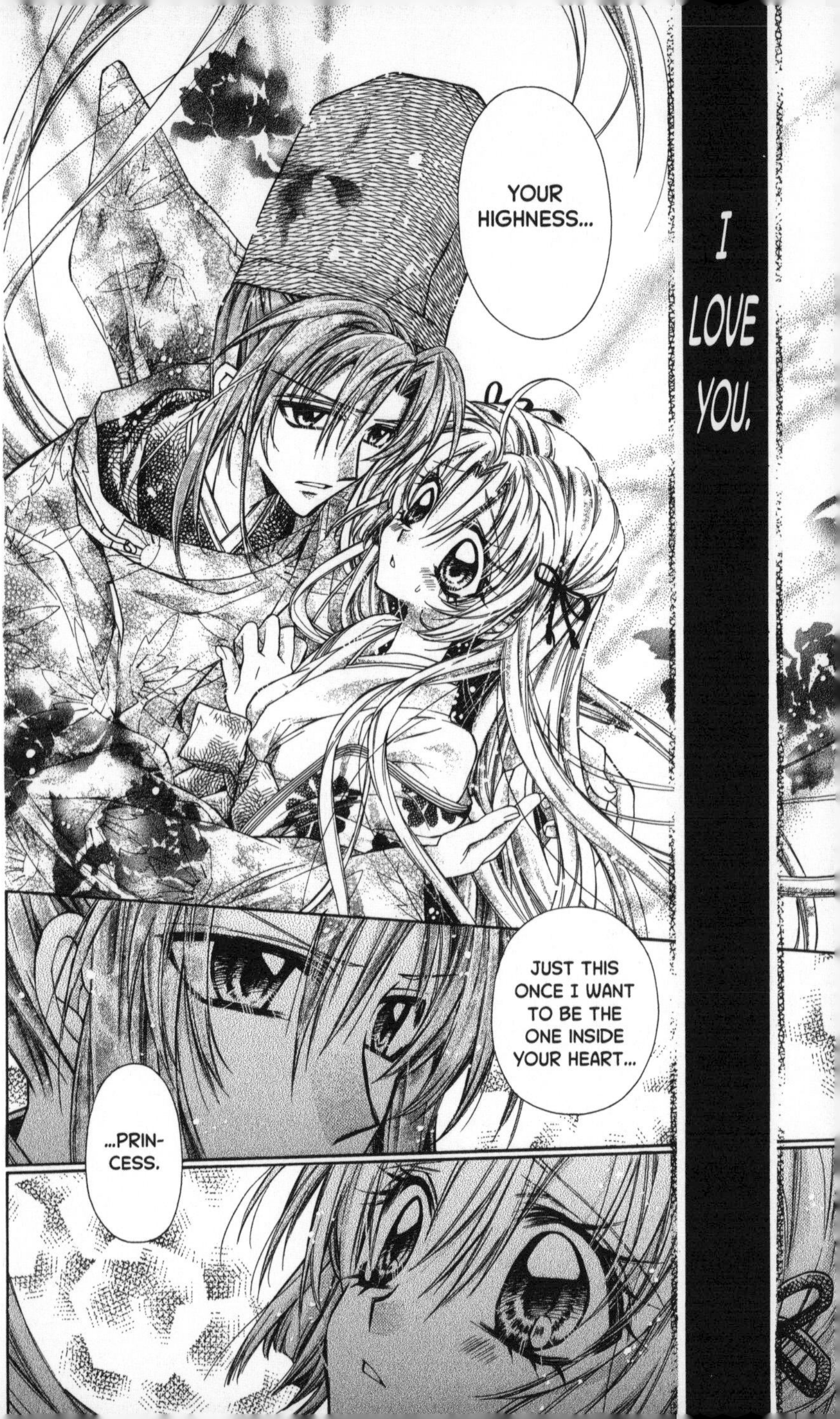
I LOVE YOU.
YOUR HIGHNESS...
JUST THIS ONCE I WANT TO BE THE ONE INSIDE YOUR HEART...
...PRIN- CESS.

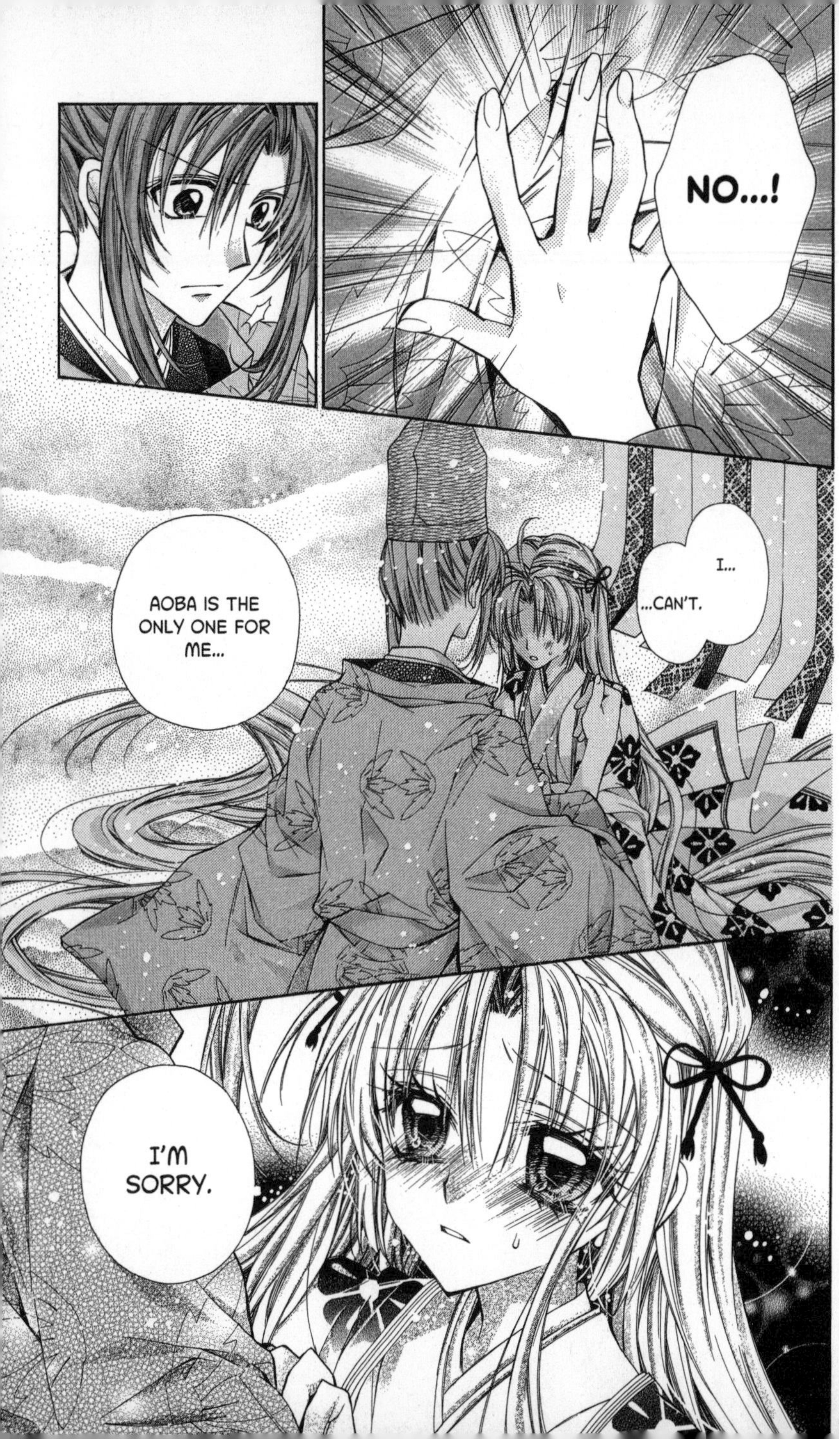
NO...!
I...
...CAN'T.
AOBA IS THE ONLY ONE FOR ME...
I'M SORRY.

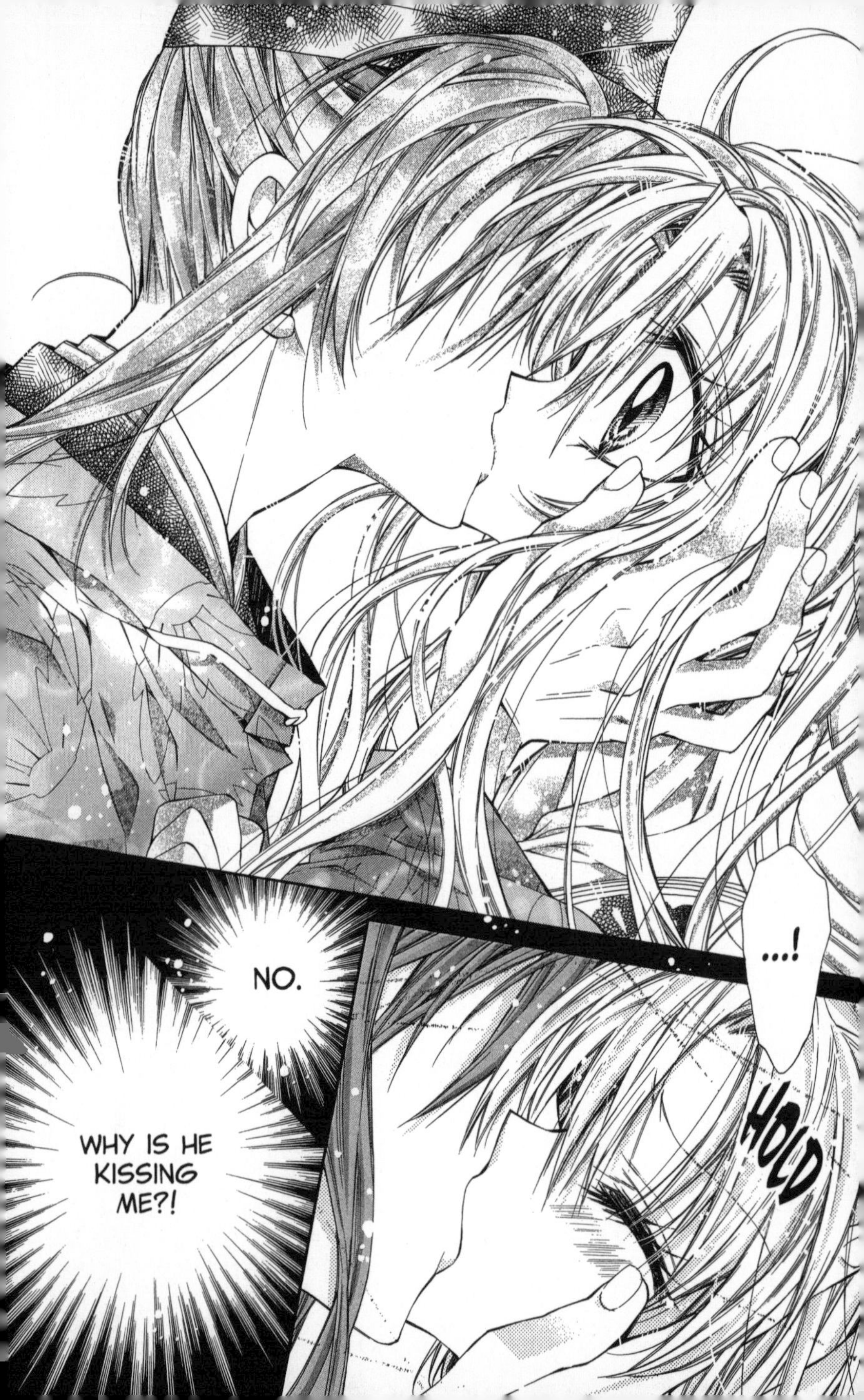
...!
NO.
HOLD
WHY IS HE KISSING ME?!

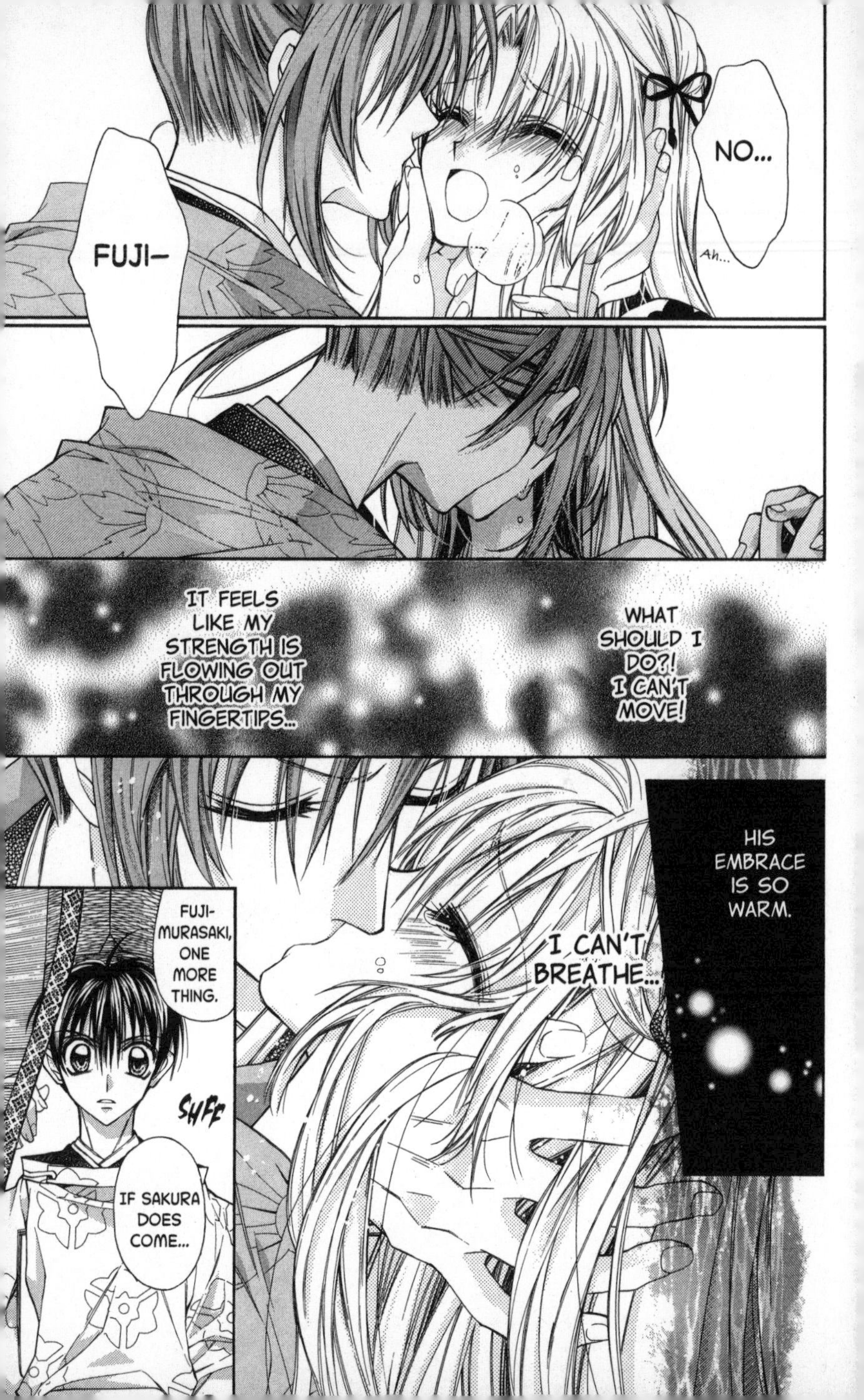
NO...
Ah...
FUJI–
WHAT SHOULD I DO?! I CAN'T MOVE!
IT FEELS LIKE MY STRENGTH IS FLOWING OUT THROUGH MY FINGERTIPS...
HIS EMBRACE IS SO WARM.
I CAN'T BREATHE...
FUJI-MURASAKI, ONE MORE THING.
SHFF
IF SAKURA DOES COME...

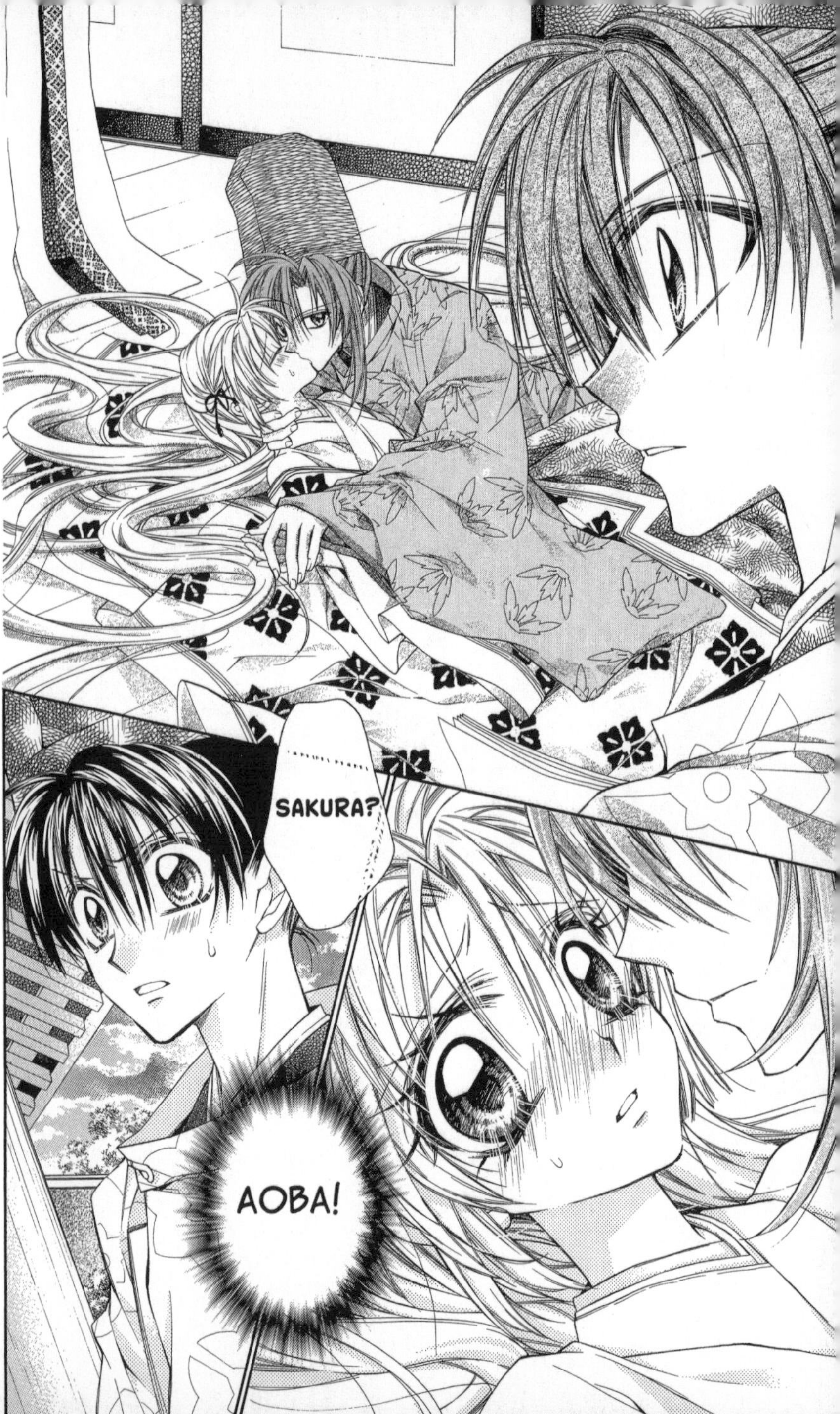
SAKURA?
AOBA!

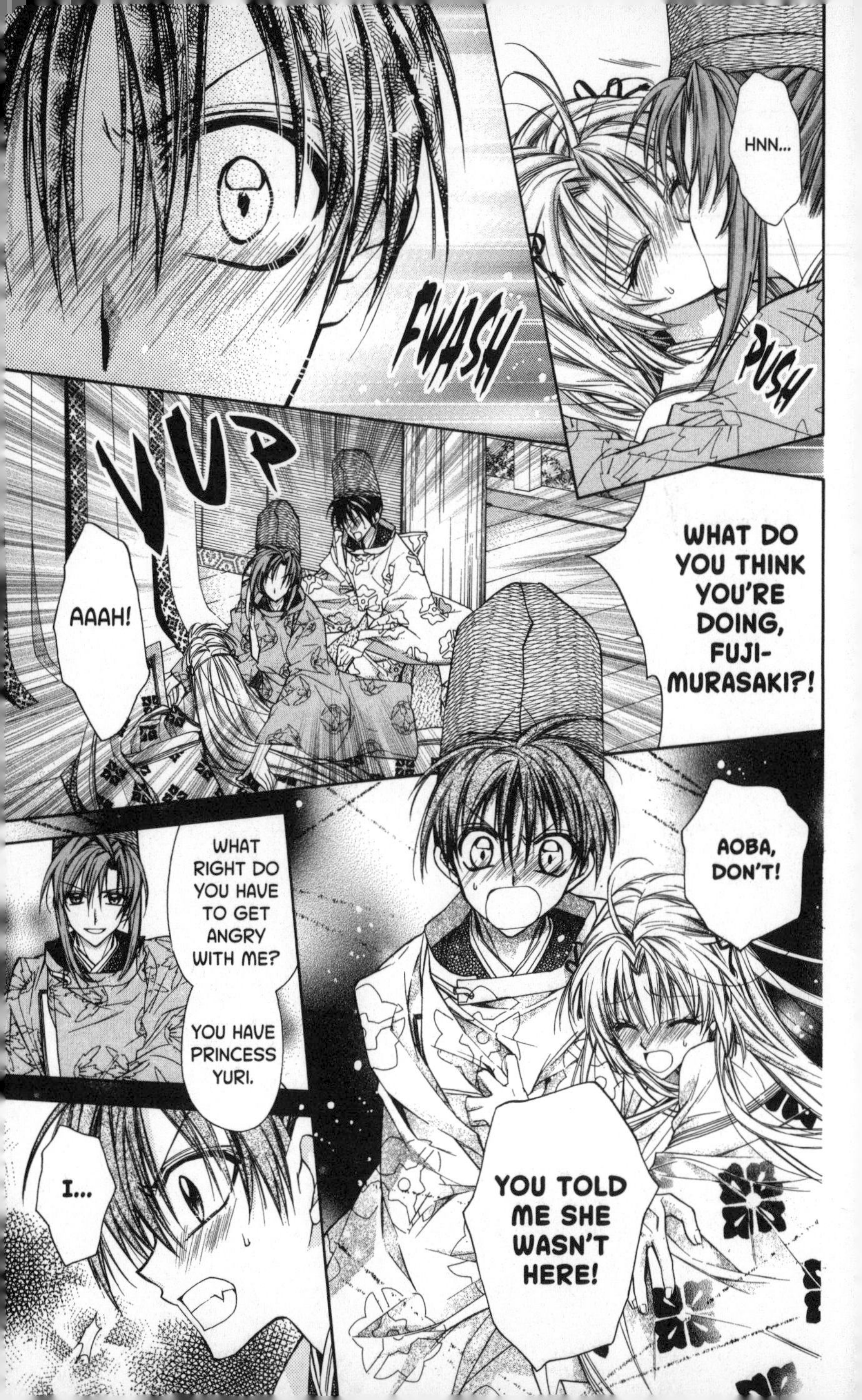
HNN...
PUSH
FWASH
WHAT DO YOU THINK YOU'RE DOING, FUJI-MURASAKI?!
VUP
AAAH!
AOBA, DON'T!
YOU TOLD ME SHE WASN'T HERE!
WHAT RIGHT DO YOU HAVE TO GET ANGRY WITH ME?
YOU HAVE PRINCESS YURI.
I...

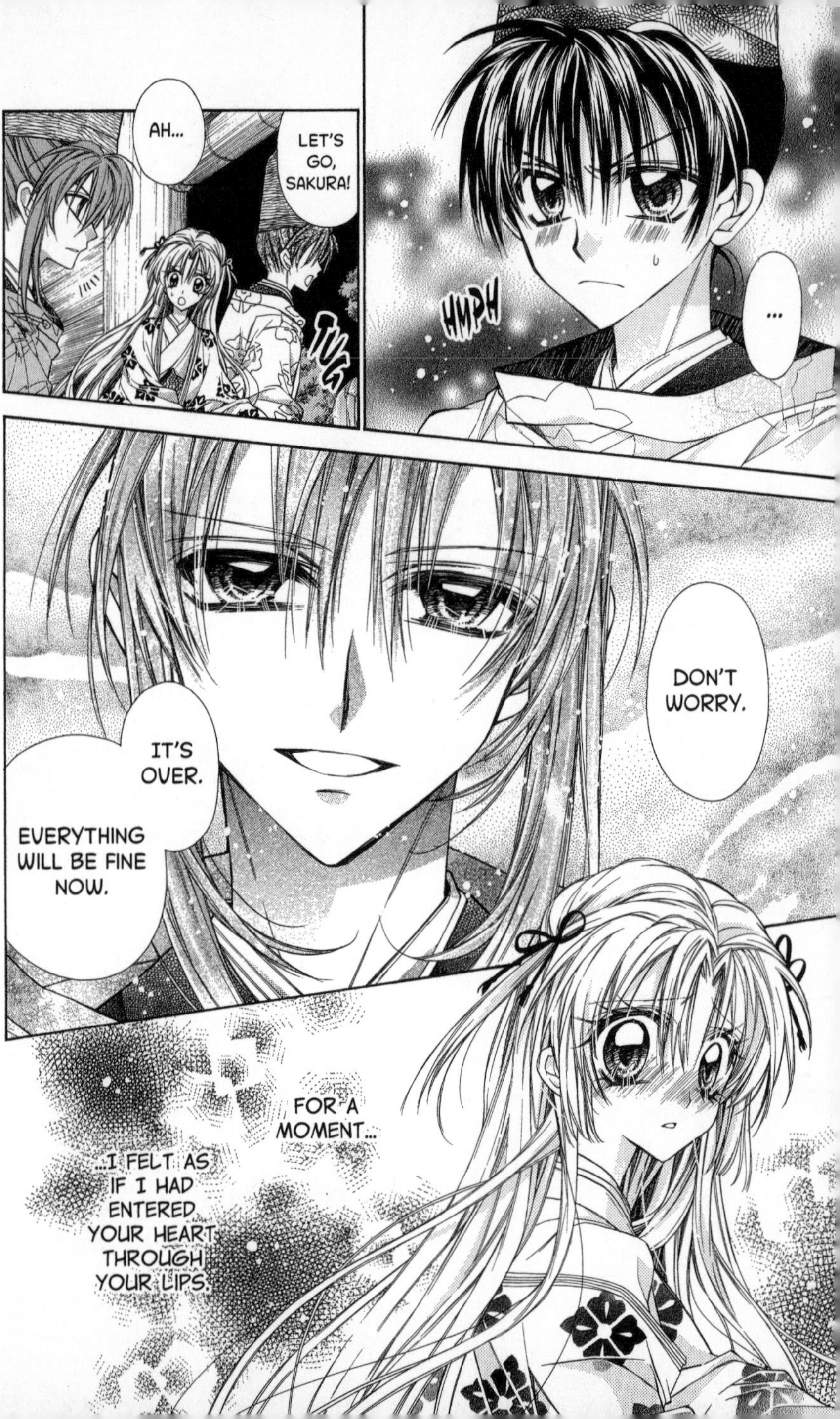
...
HMPH
LET'S GO, SAKURA!
AH...
TUG
DON'T WORRY.
IT'S OVER.
EVERYTHING WILL BE FINE NOW.
FOR A MOMENT...
...I FELT AS IF I HAD ENTERED YOUR HEART THROUGH YOUR LIPS.

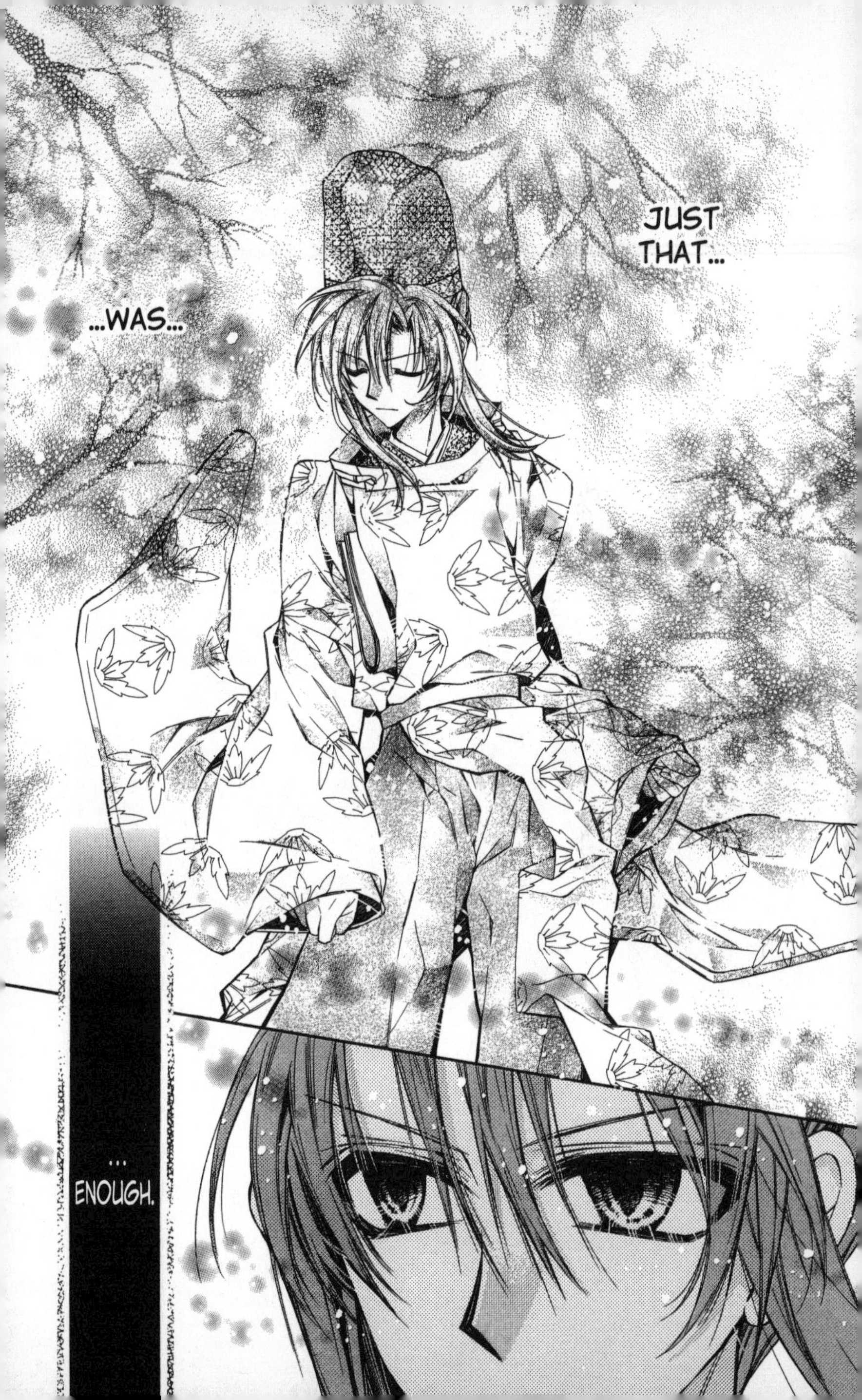
JUST THAT...
...WAS...
... ENOUGH.

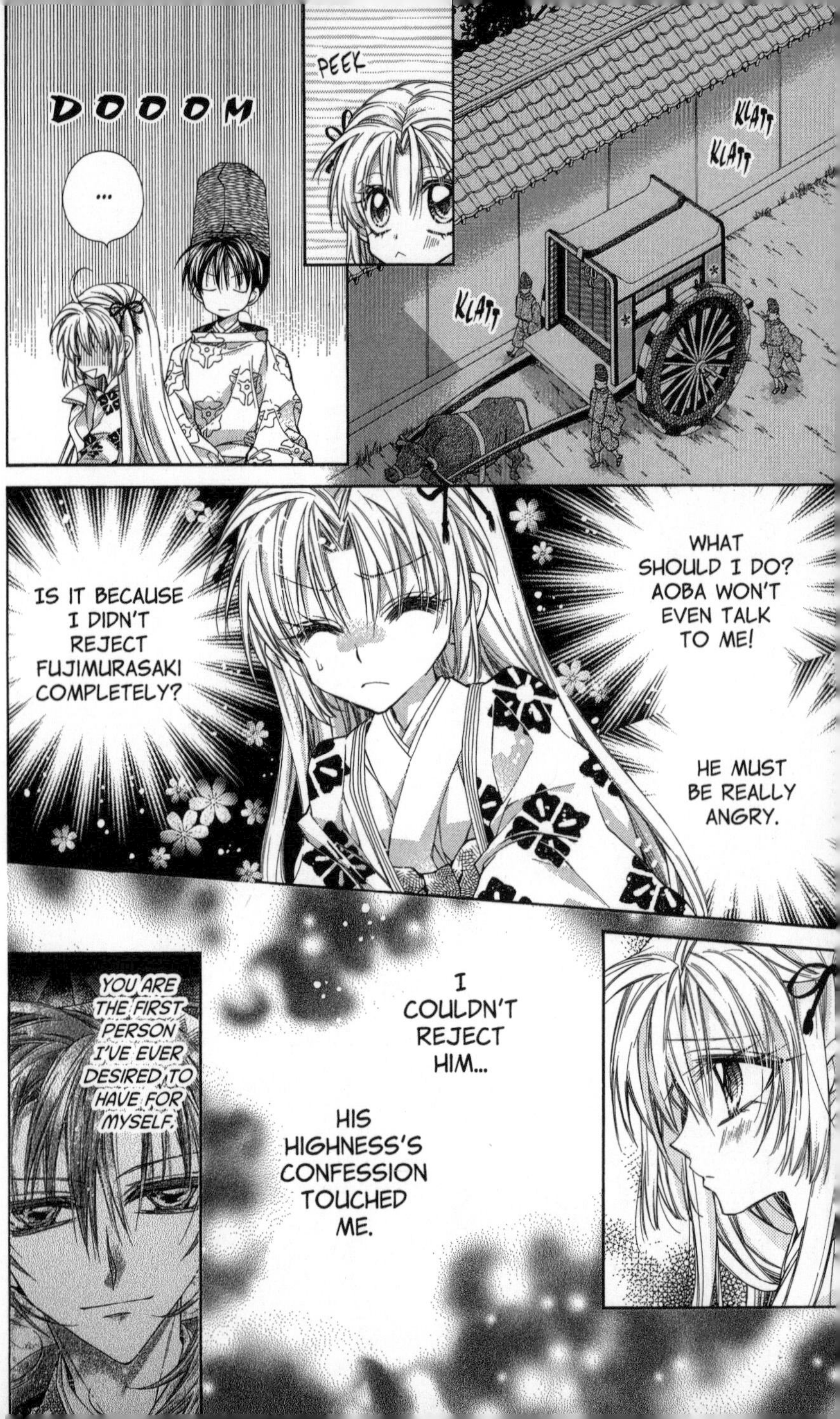
KLATT
KLATT
KLATT
PEEK
DOOOM
...
WHAT SHOULD I DO? AOBA WON'T EVEN TALK TO ME!
HE MUST BE REALLY ANGRY.
IS IT BECAUSE I DIDN'T REJECT FUJIMURASAKI COMPLETELY?
I COULDN'T REJECT HIM...
HIS HIGHNESS'S CONFESSION TOUCHED ME.
YOU ARE THE FIRST PERSON I'VE EVER DESIRED TO HAVE FOR MYSELF.

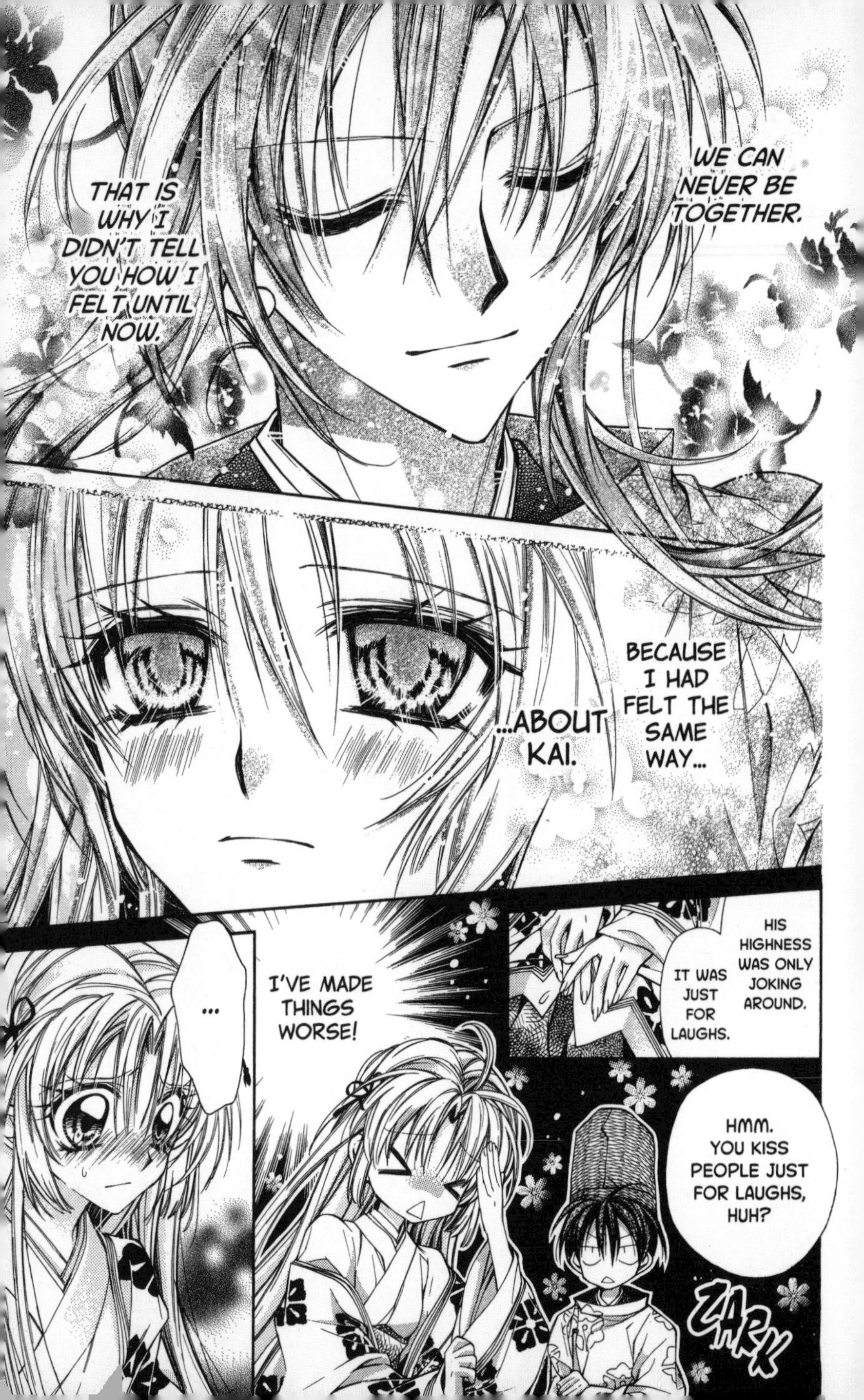
WE CAN NEVER BE TOGETHER.
THAT IS WHY I DIDN'T TELL YOU HOW I FELT UNTIL NOW.
BECAUSE I HAD FELT THE SAME WAY...
...ABOUT KAI.
HIS HIGHNESS WAS ONLY JOKING AROUND.
IT WAS JUST FOR LAUGHS.
HMM. YOU KISS PEOPLE JUST FOR LAUGHS, HUH?
ZARK
I'VE MADE THINGS WORSE!
...

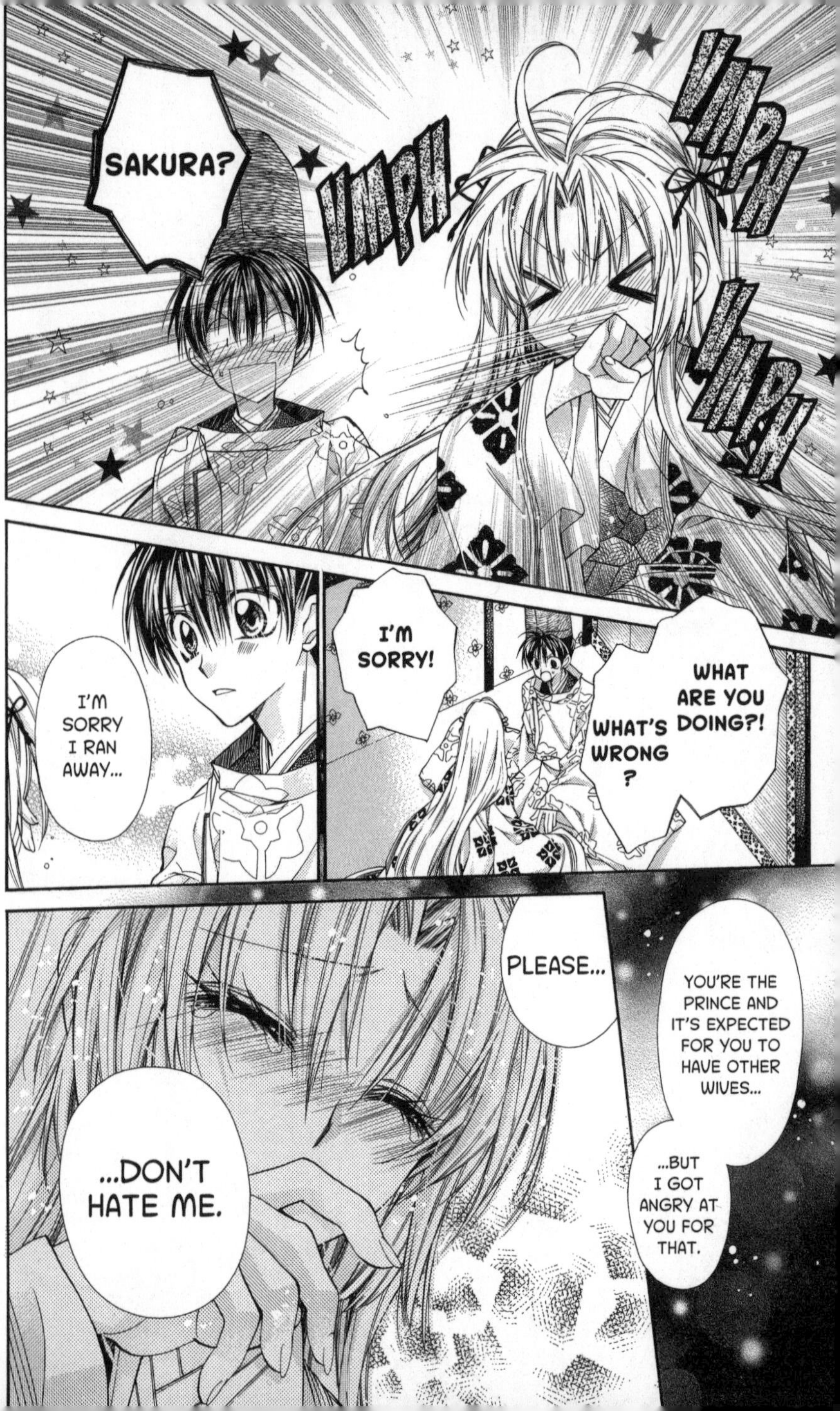
UMPH
UMPH
UMPH
SAKURA?
WHAT ARE YOU DOING?!
WHAT'S WRONG?
I'M SORRY!
I'M SORRY I RAN AWAY...
YOU'RE THE PRINCE AND IT'S EXPECTED FOR YOU TO HAVE OTHER WIVES...
...BUT I GOT ANGRY AT YOU FOR THAT.
PLEASE...
...DON'T HATE ME.

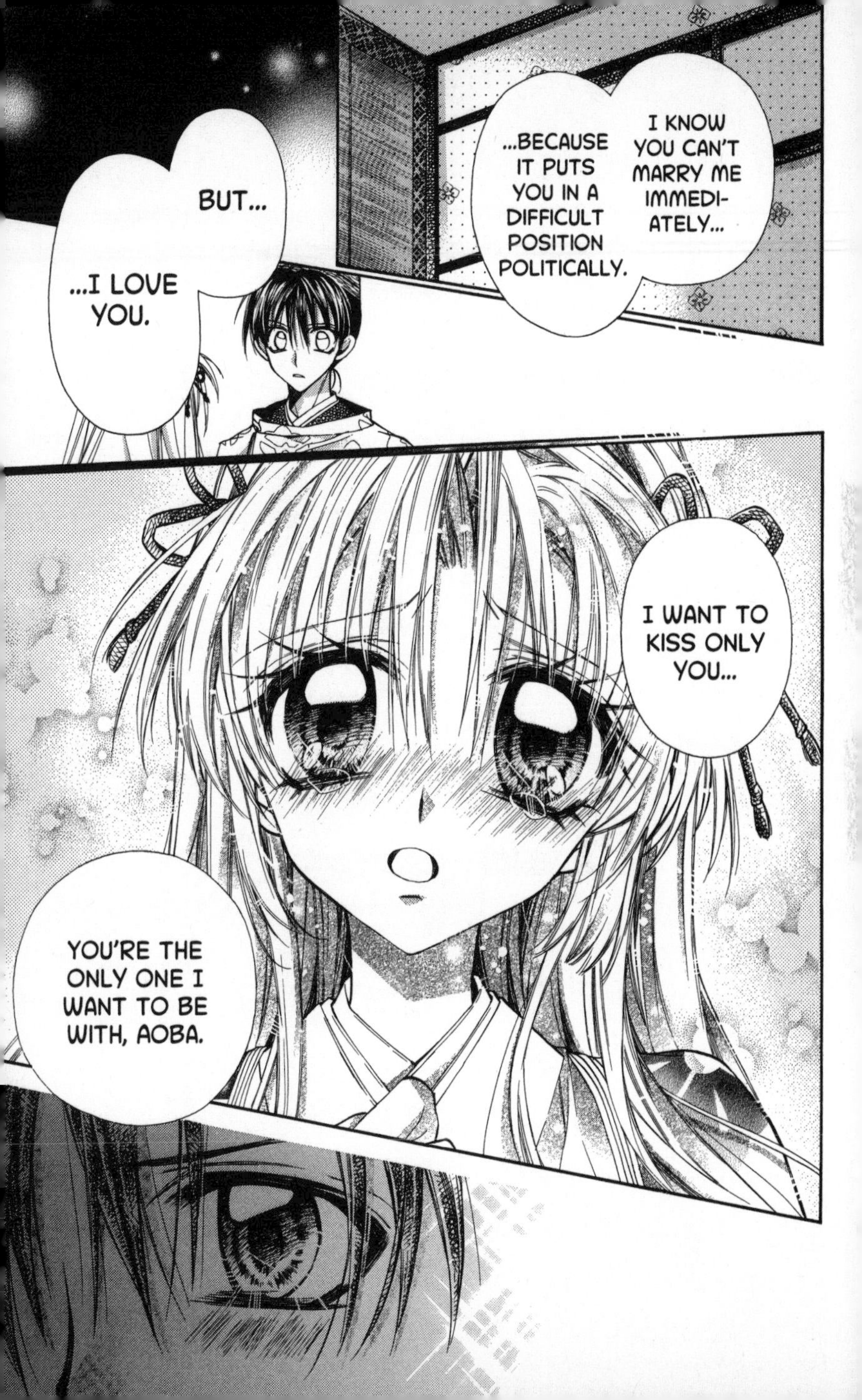
I KNOW YOU CAN'T MARRY ME IMMEDI-ATELY...
...BECAUSE IT PUTS YOU IN A DIFFICULT POSITION POLITICALLY.
BUT...
...I LOVE YOU.
I WANT TO KISS ONLY YOU...
YOU'RE THE ONLY ONE I WANT TO BE WITH, AOBA.

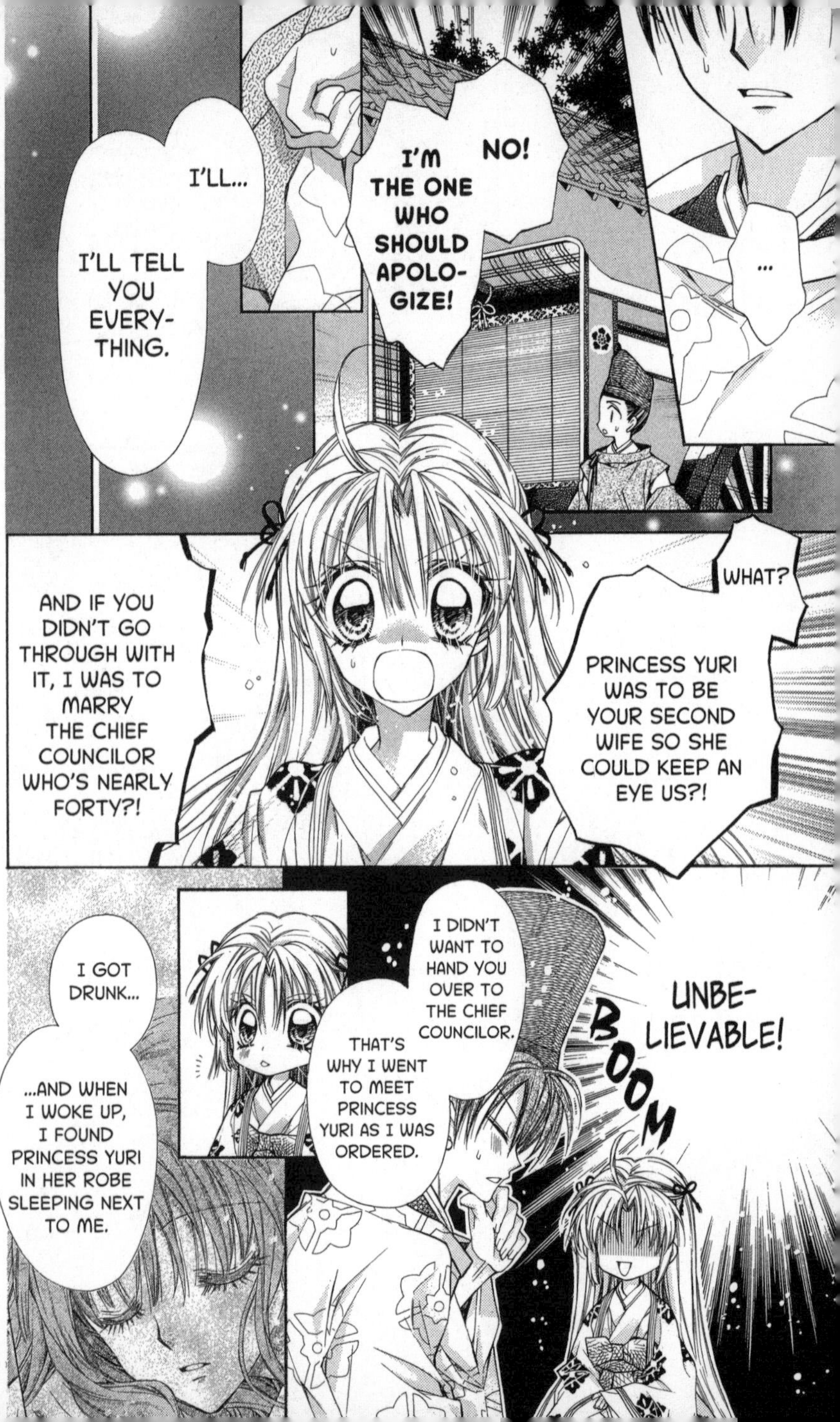
...
NO!
I'M THE ONE WHO SHOULD APOLO-GIZE!
I'LL...
I'LL TELL YOU EVERY-THING.
WHAT?
PRINCESS YURI WAS TO BE YOUR SECOND WIFE SO SHE COULD KEEP AN EYE US?!
AND IF YOU DIDN'T GO THROUGH WITH IT, I WAS TO MARRY THE CHIEF COUNCILOR WHO'S NEARLY FORTY?!
UNBE-LIEVABLE!
BOOM
I DIDN'T WANT TO HAND YOU OVER TO THE CHIEF COUNCILOR.
THAT'S WHY I WENT TO MEET PRINCESS YURI AS I WAS ORDERED.
I GOT DRUNK...
...AND WHEN I WOKE UP, I FOUND PRINCESS YURI IN HER ROBE SLEEPING NEXT TO ME.

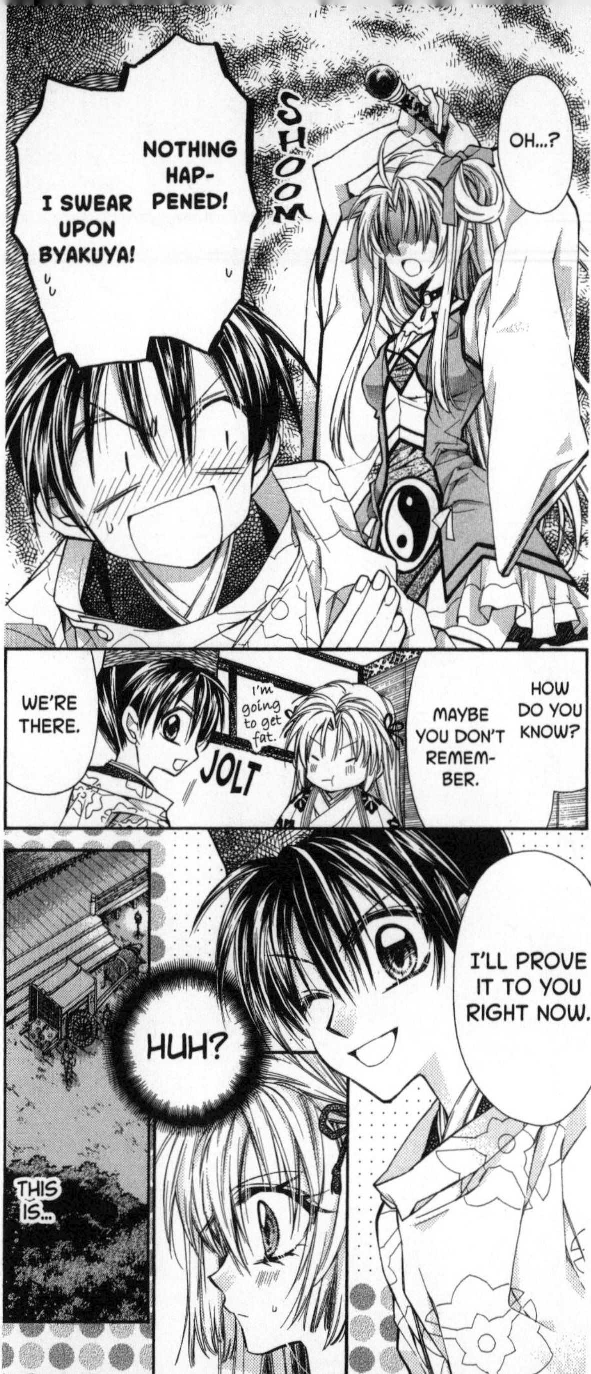
OH...?
SHOOOM
NOTHING HAP-PENED! I SWEAR UPON BYAKUYA!
HOW DO YOU KNOW?
MAYBE YOU DON'T REMEM-BER.
I'm going to get fat.
JOLT
WE'RE THERE.
I'LL PROVE IT TO YOU RIGHT NOW.
HUH?
THIS IS...

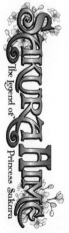

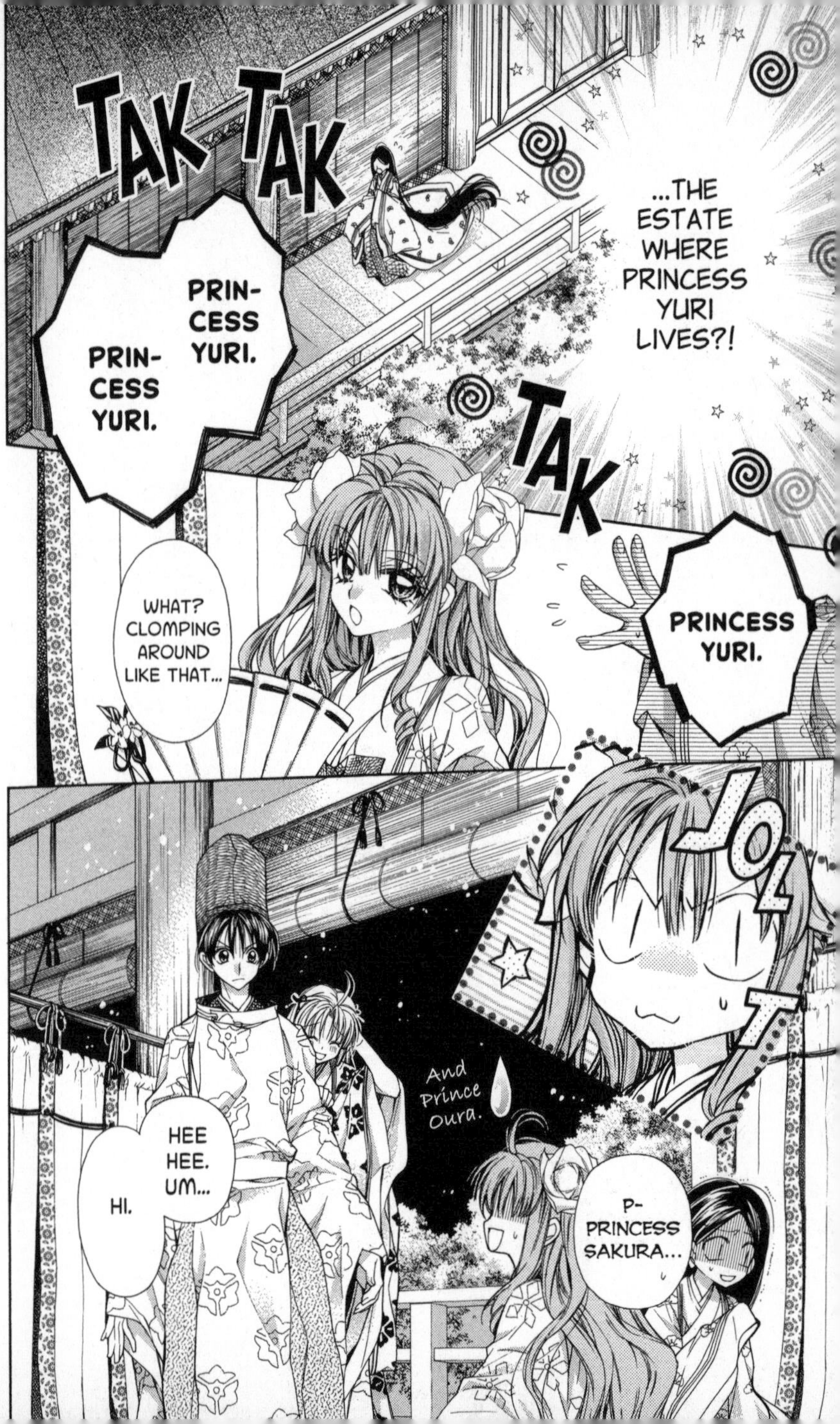
...THE ESTATE WHERE PRINCESS YURI LIVES?!
TAK TAK
PRIN-CESS YURI.
PRIN-CESS YURI.
TAK
PRINCESS YURI.
WHAT? CLOMPING AROUND LIKE THAT...
JOLT
P-PRINCESS SAKURA...
And Prince Oura.
HEE HEE. UM...
HI.

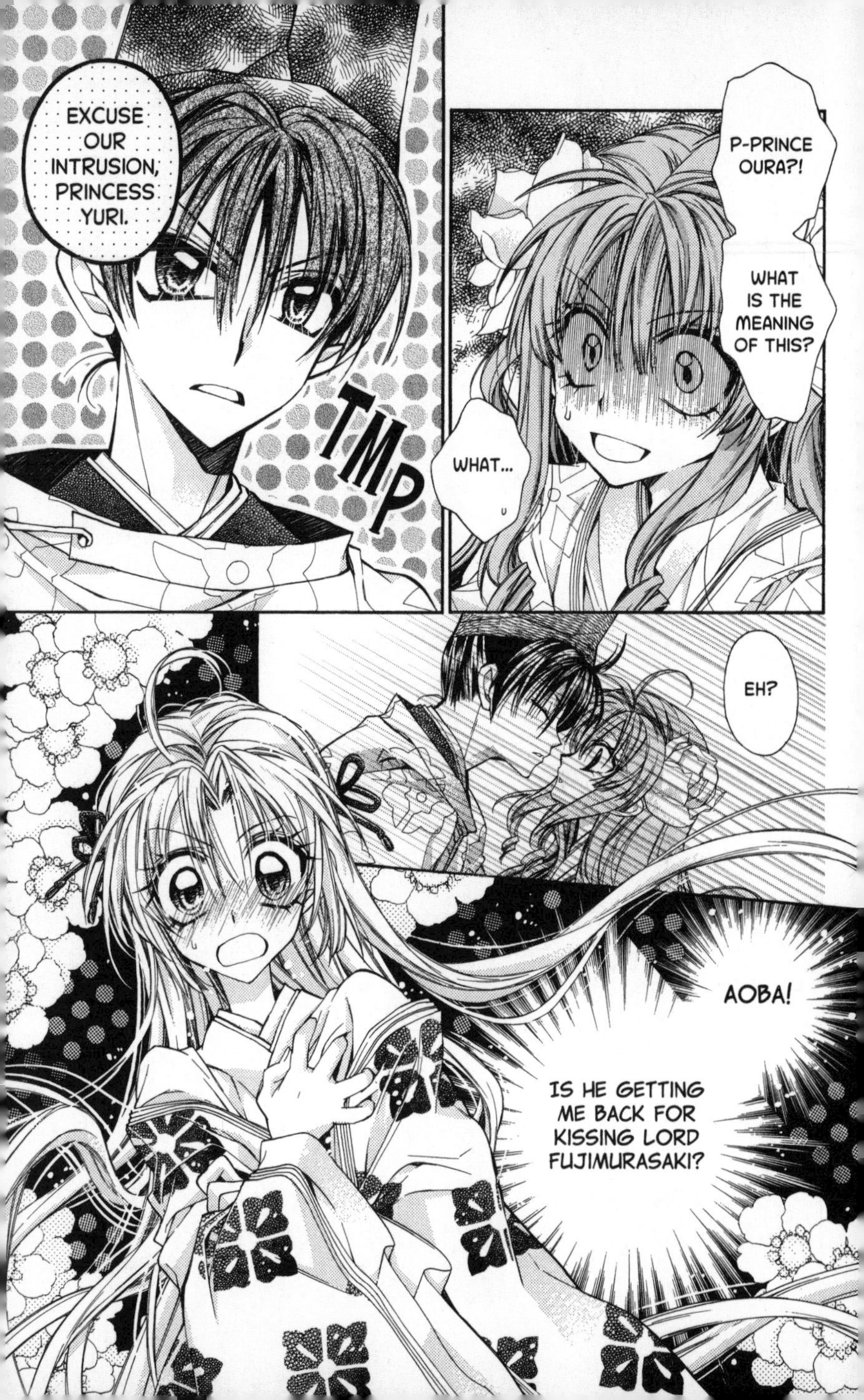
P-PRINCE OURA?!
WHAT IS THE MEANING OF THIS?
WHAT...
EXCUSE OUR INTRUSION, PRINCESS YURI.
TMP
EH?
AOBA!
IS HE GETTING ME BACK FOR KISSING LORD FUJIMURASAKI?

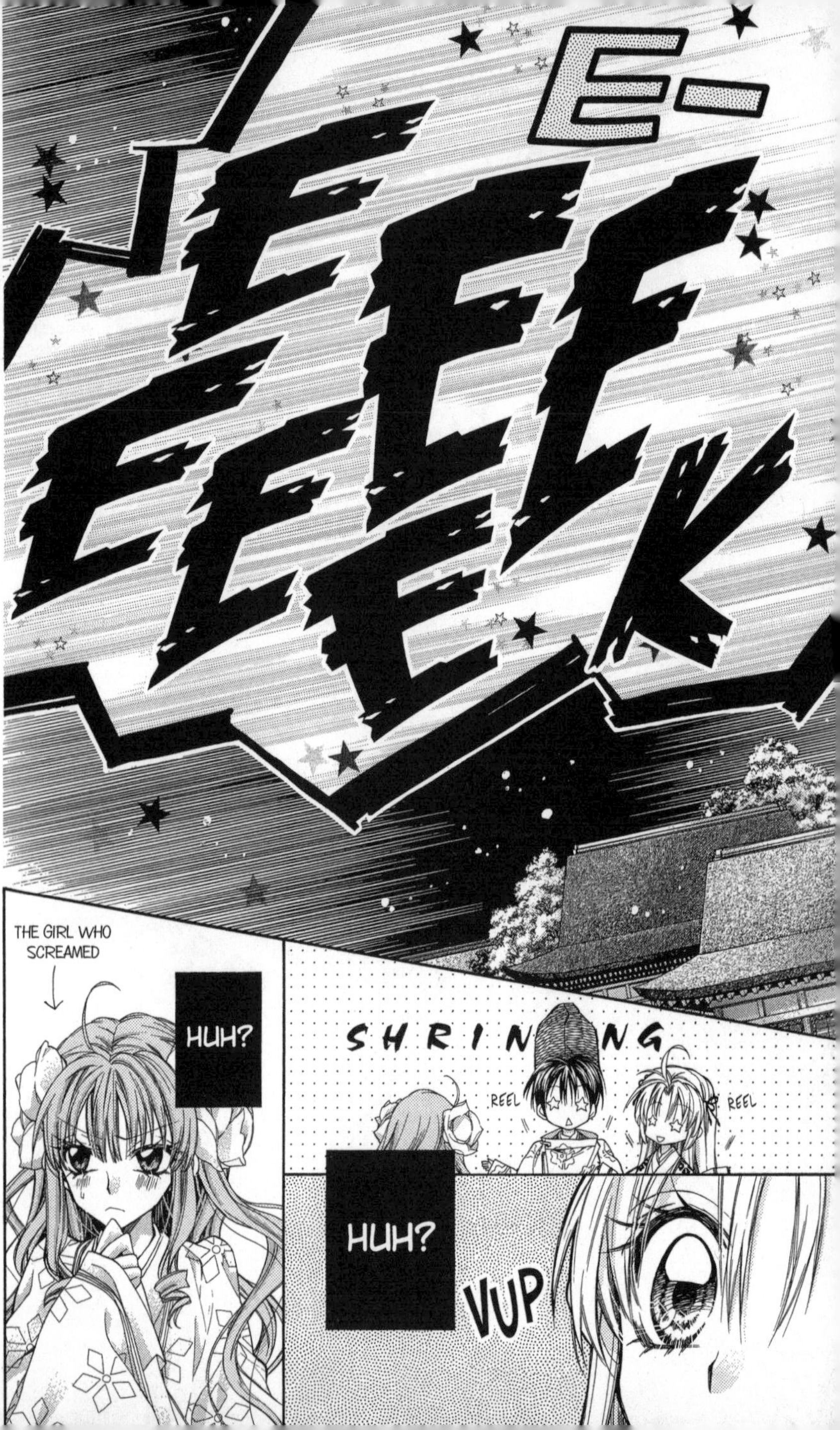
E-EEEEEEK
SHRIN NG
REEL
REEL
HUH?
VUP
THE GIRL WHO SCREAMED
HUH?

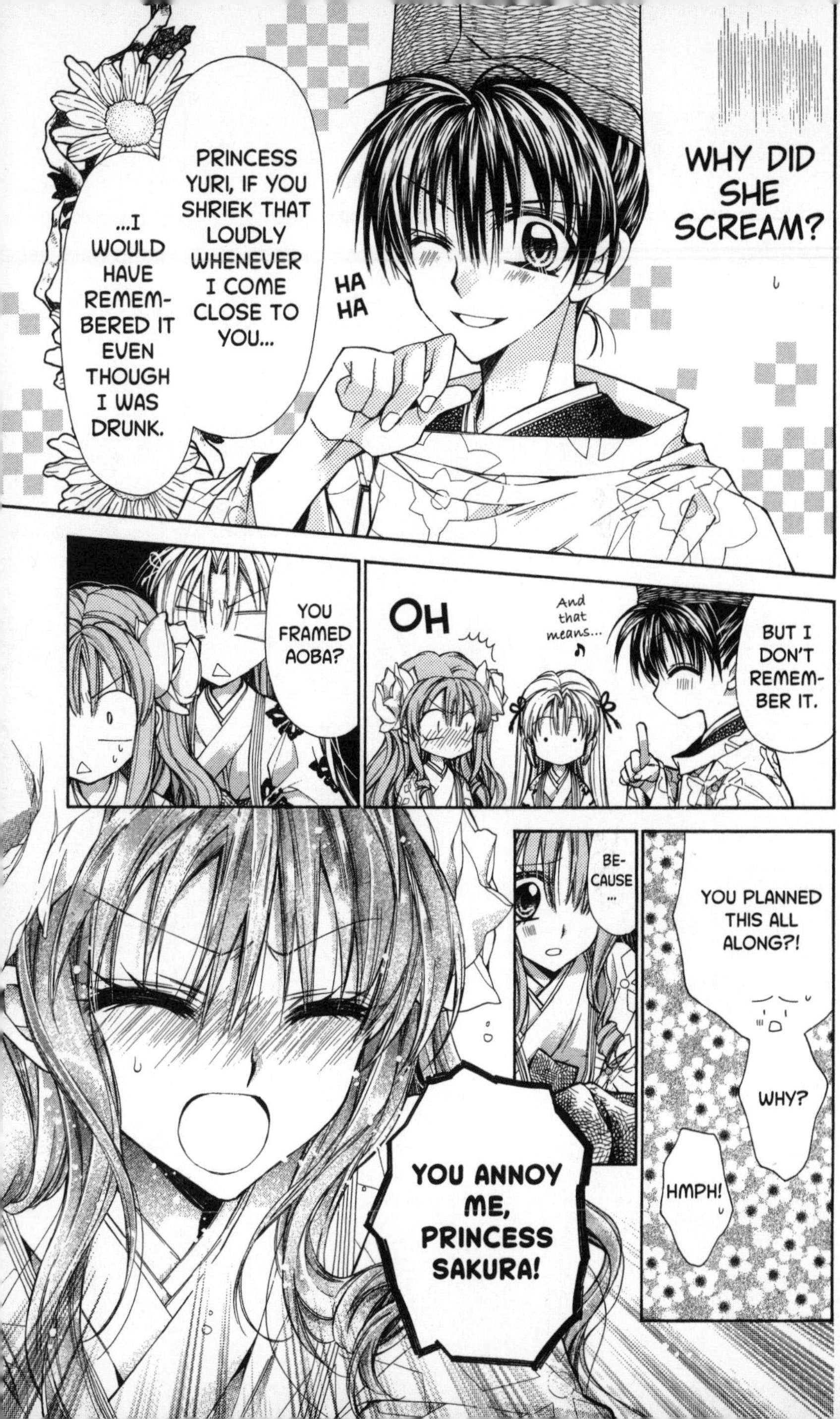
WHY DID SHE SCREAM?
HA HA
PRINCESS YURI, IF YOU SHRIEK THAT LOUDLY WHENEVER I COME CLOSE TO YOU...
...I WOULD HAVE REMEMBERED IT EVEN THOUGH I WAS DRUNK.
BUT I DON'T REMEMBER IT.
And that means... ♪
OH
YOU FRAMED AOBA?
YOU PLANNED THIS ALL ALONG?!
WHY?
HMPH!
BECAUSE...
YOU ANNOY ME, PRINCESS SAKURA!

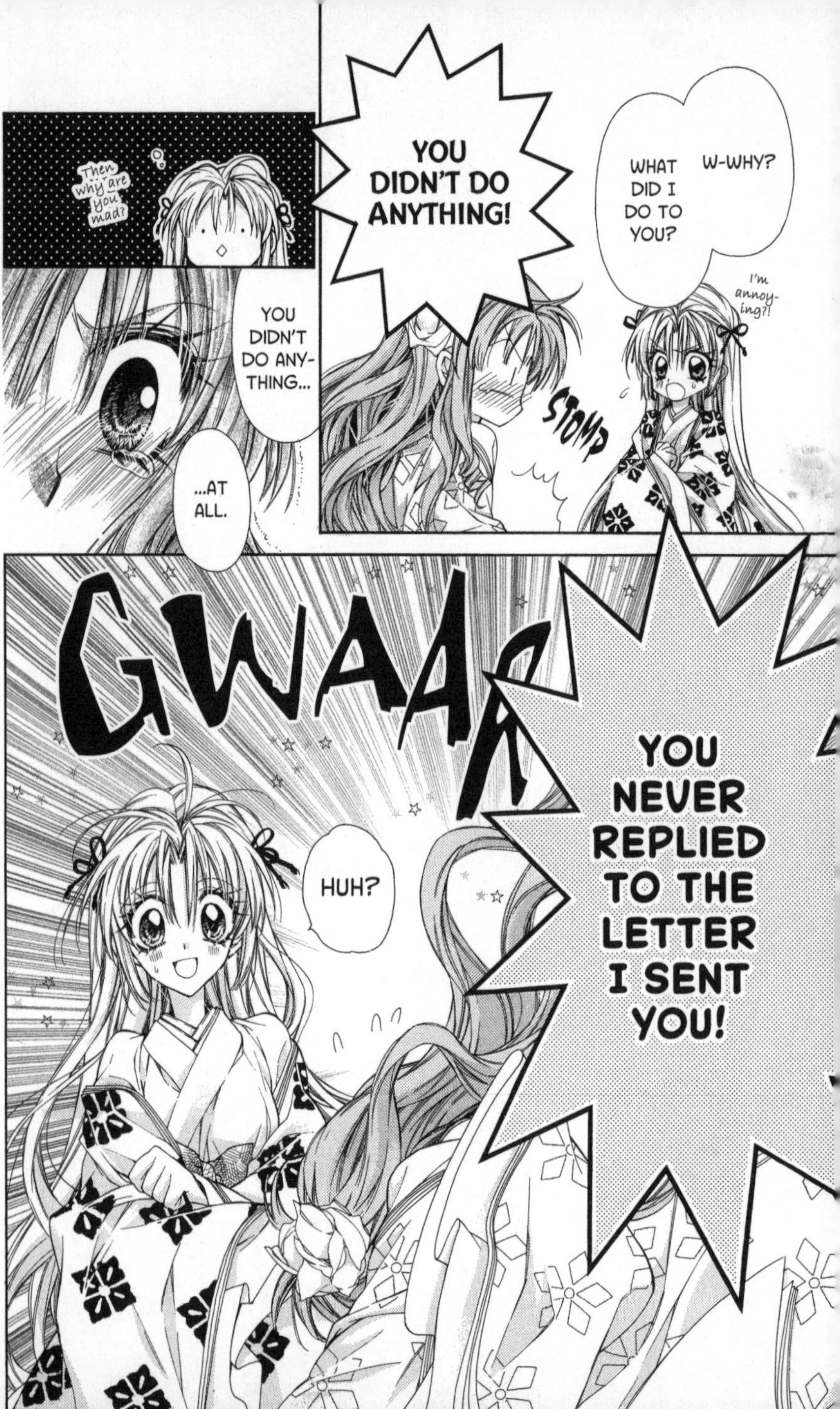
W-WHY? WHAT DID I DO TO YOU?
YOU DIDN'T DO ANYTHING!
I'm annoying?!
STOMP
Then why are you mad?
YOU DIDN'T DO ANYTHING...
...AT ALL.
YOU NEVER REPLIED TO THE LETTER I SENT YOU!
GWAAR
HUH?

HELLO

Hi! This is Arina Tanemura. I bring to you volume 9 of *Sakura Hime*.

It has been nine months since volume 8 was published. I'm sorry. Many things are involved in publishing a manga volume, so that is why you had to wait for such a long time.

But I'm happy you were waiting for me... I was worried no one would. I'm still putting all my effort into this series!

Volume 9 just came out, but 10 will be coming out next month in Japan (for those who are reading this in real time). I have a feeling you're all going to say, "You made us wait nine months, and now there are two volumes out at once? Balance it out, Tanemura!" But it is coming out!

I would like to introduce various books that will be released in Japan in the near future.

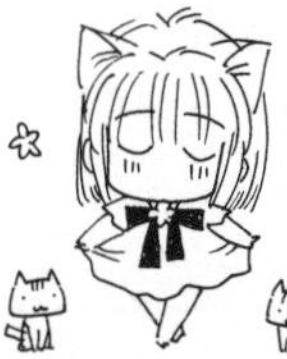
CURTSEY

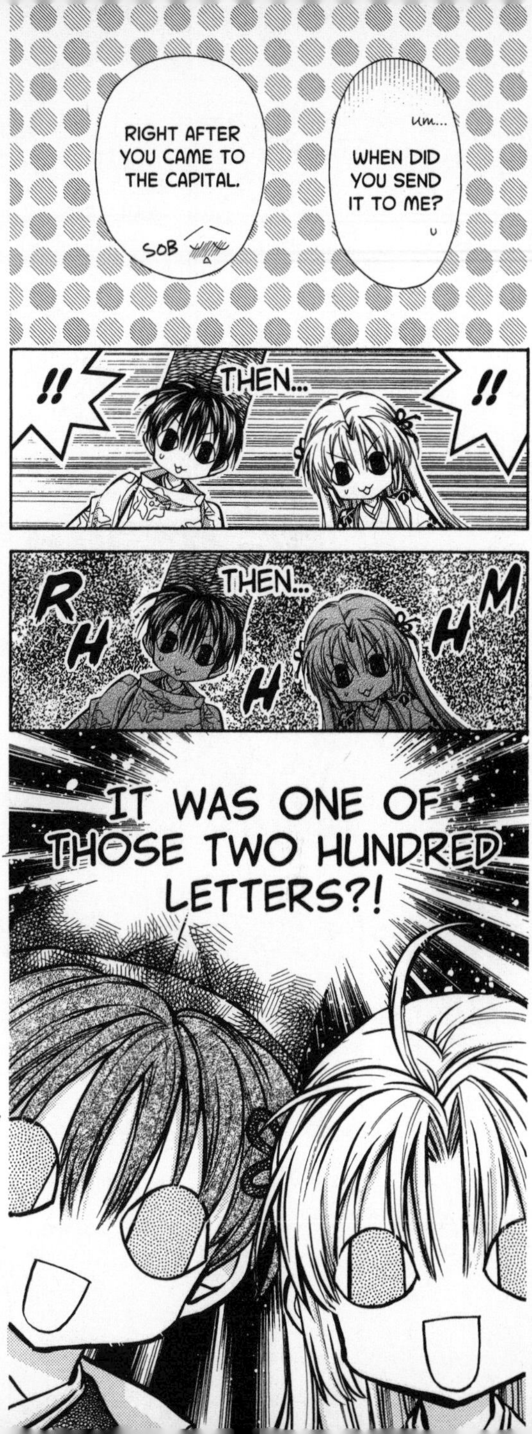
UM...
WHEN DID YOU SEND IT TO ME?
RIGHT AFTER YOU CAME TO THE CAPITAL.
SOB
!!
THEN...
!!
THEN...
RHHHHM
IT WAS ONE OF THOSE TWO HUNDRED LETTERS?!

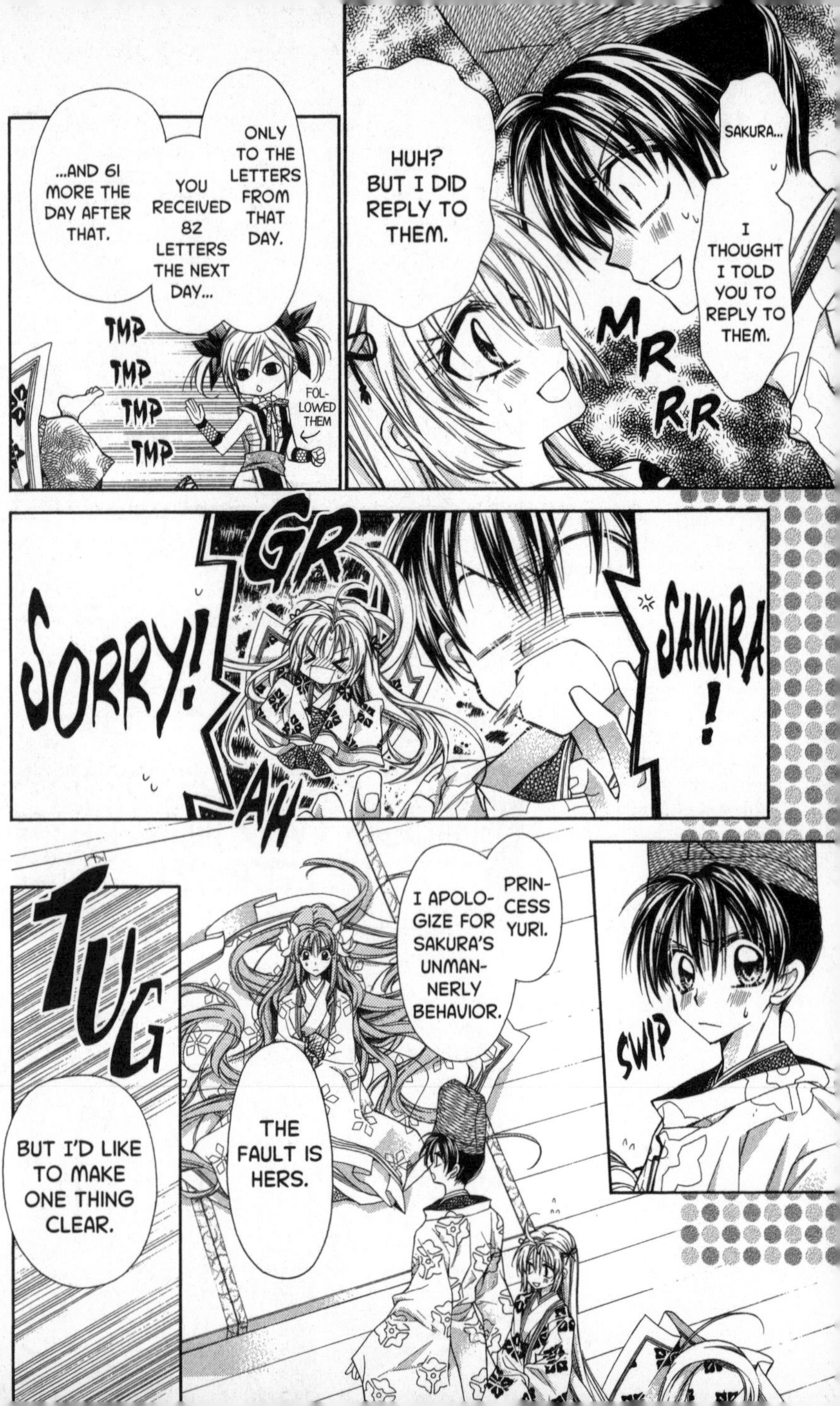
SAKURA...
I THOUGHT I TOLD YOU TO REPLY TO THEM.
MRRRR
HUH? BUT I DID REPLY TO THEM.
ONLY TO THE LETTERS FROM THAT DAY.
YOU RECEIVED 82 LETTERS THE NEXT DAY...
...AND 61 MORE THE DAY AFTER THAT.
TMP TMP TMP TMP
FOL-LOWED THEM
SAKURA!
GR
SORRY!
AH
SWIP
PRIN-CESS YURI.
I APOLO-GIZE FOR SAKURA'S UNMAN-NERLY BEHAVIOR.
THE FAULT IS HERS.
BUT I'D LIKE TO MAKE ONE THING CLEAR.
TUG

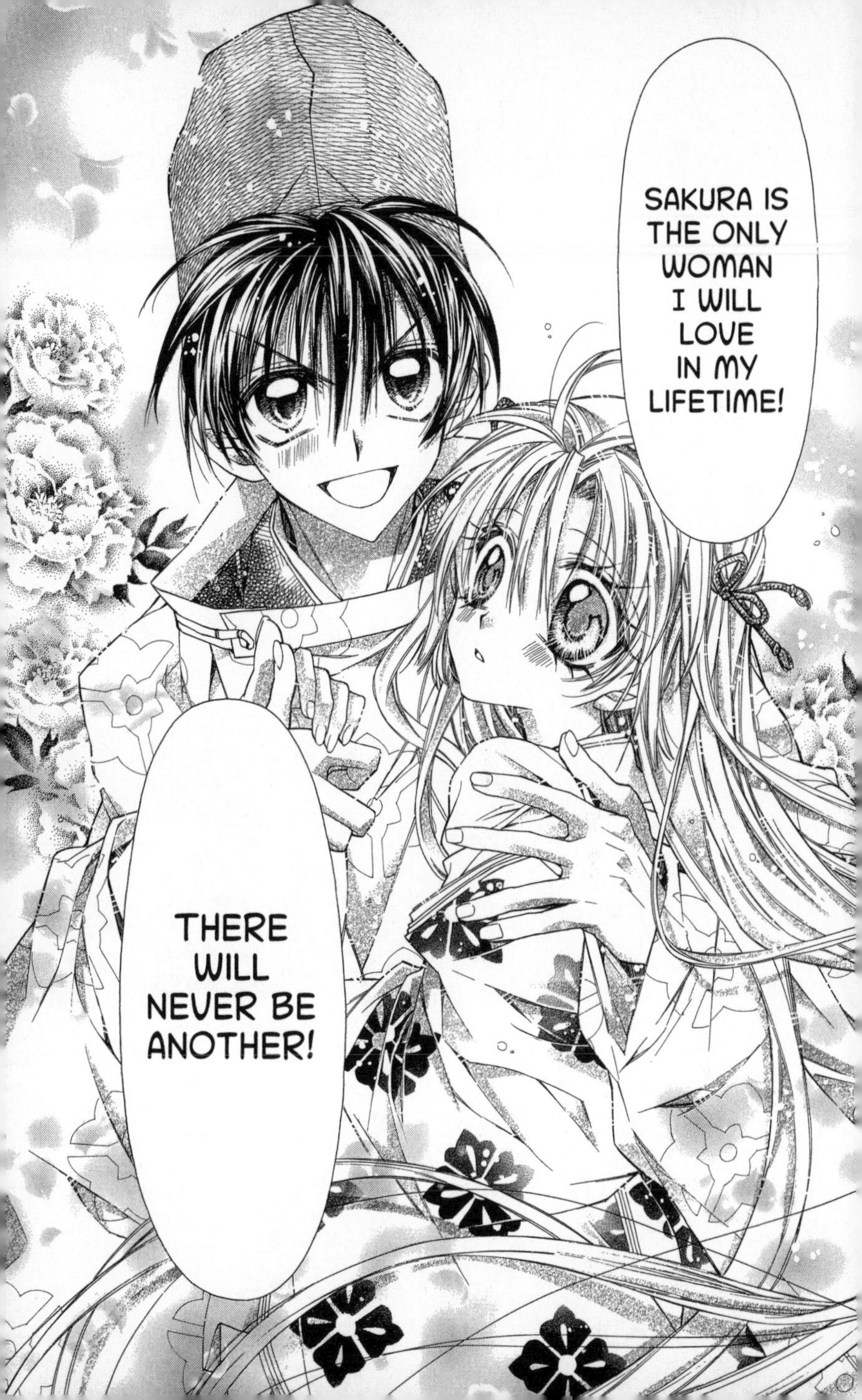
SAKURA IS THE ONLY WOMAN I WILL LOVE IN MY LIFETIME!
THERE WILL NEVER BE ANOTHER!

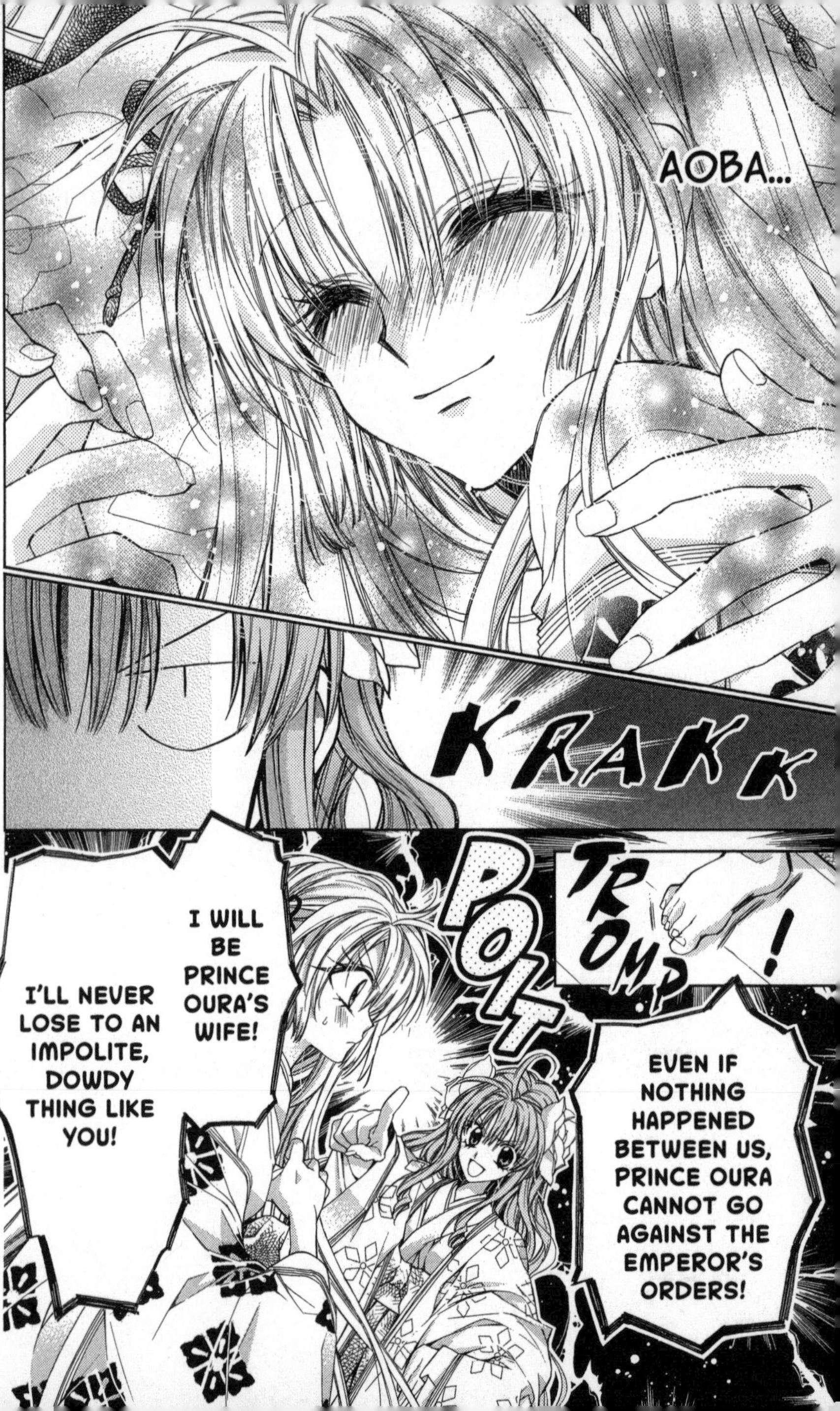
AOBA...
KRAKK
TROMP!
POIT
EVEN IF NOTHING HAPPENED BETWEEN US, PRINCE OURA CANNOT GO AGAINST THE EMPEROR'S ORDERS!
I WILL BE PRINCE OURA'S WIFE!
I'LL NEVER LOSE TO AN IMPOLITE, DOWDY THING LIKE YOU!

8 BOOKS

So after a long wait, these books will come out in 20012. (Huh? I've written one "0" too many.) They will come out in January and February of 2012 in Japan!

January

- *Sakura Hime: The Legend of Princess Sakura* vol. 9
- *Arina's Seed* (Essay Manga)
- *Full Moon* reissue vols. 1 and 2

February

- *Sakura Hime: The Legend of Princess Sakura* vol. 10
- *Fudanjuku Story*
- *Full Moon* reissue vols. 3 and 4

There are too many of them!! (Really) Even I have never known an author who has had eight books released in two months (unless the books were all reissues.)

Full Moon has finally been released as a bunkoubon. I've drawn new illustrations for the covers. Please take a look at them.

Fudanjuku Story will be published as a complete edition. Color illustrations and interviews with the members have been included too. They are one of my favorite idol groups. Please take a look at the book and listen to their live performances.

Arina's Seed will come out at the same time as volume 9. Please sit back and read it at your leisure.

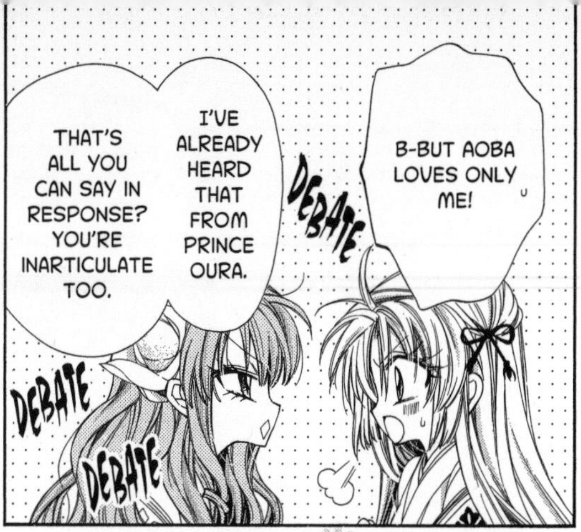
B-BUT AOBA LOVES ONLY ME!
DEBATE
I'VE ALREADY HEARD THAT FROM PRINCE OURA.
THAT'S ALL YOU CAN SAY IN RESPONSE? YOU'RE INARTICULATE TOO.
DEBATE
DEBATE

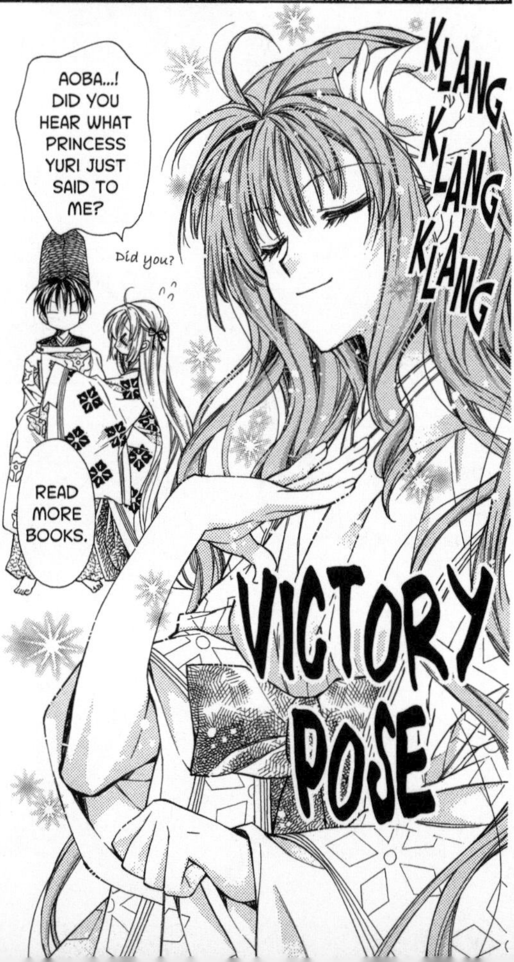
KLANG KLANG KLANG KLANG
AOBA...! DID YOU HEAR WHAT PRINCESS YURI JUST SAID TO ME?
Did you?
READ MORE BOOKS.
VICTORY POSE

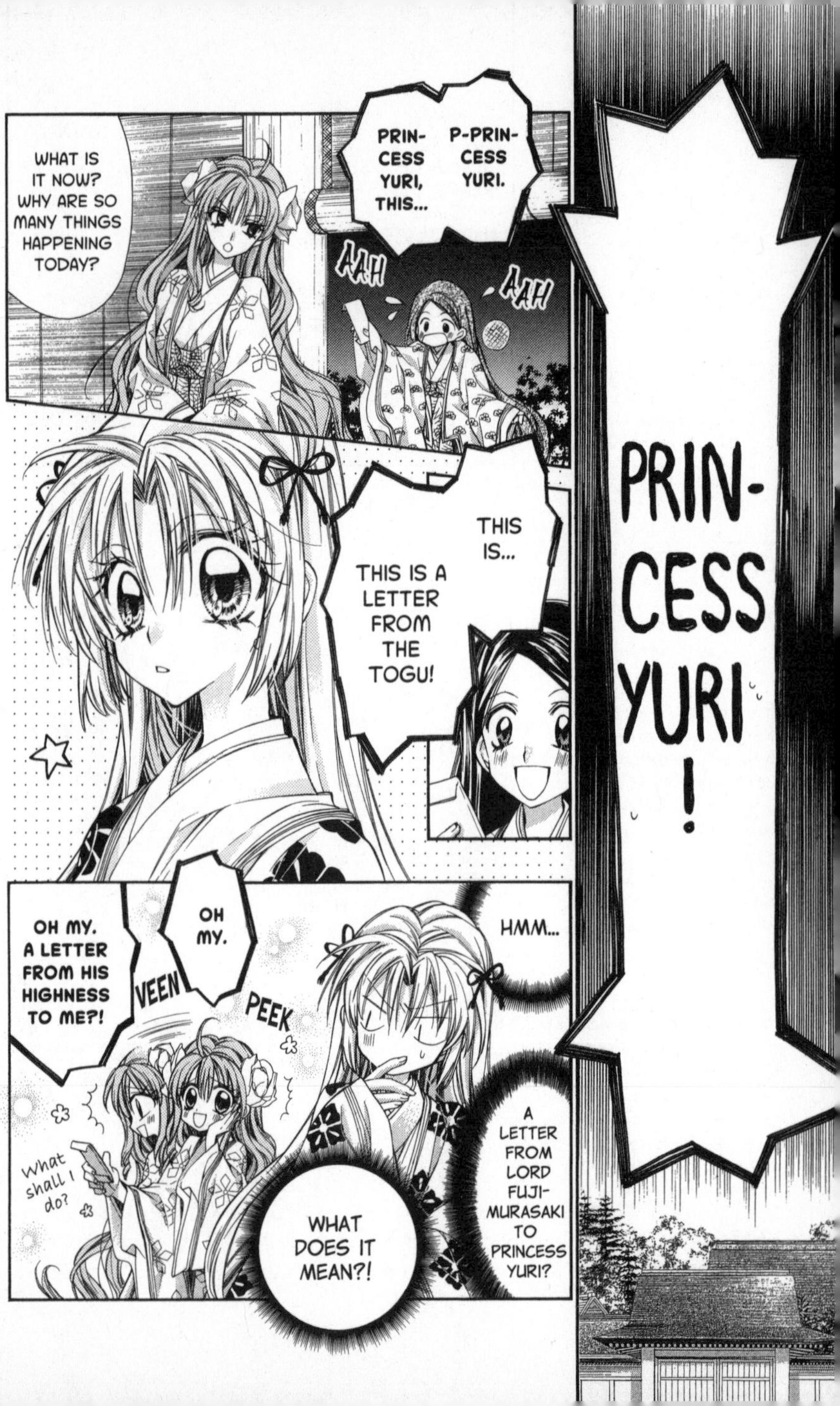
PRIN-CESS YURI!
P-PRIN-CESS YURI.
PRIN-CESS YURI, THIS...
AAH
AAH
WHAT IS IT NOW? WHY ARE SO MANY THINGS HAPPENING TODAY?
THIS IS...
THIS IS A LETTER FROM THE TOGU!
HMM...
OH MY.
OH MY. A LETTER FROM HIS HIGHNESS TO ME?!
VEEN
PEEK
A LETTER FROM LORD FUJI-MURASAKI TO PRINCESS YURI?
WHAT DOES IT MEAN?!
What shall I do?

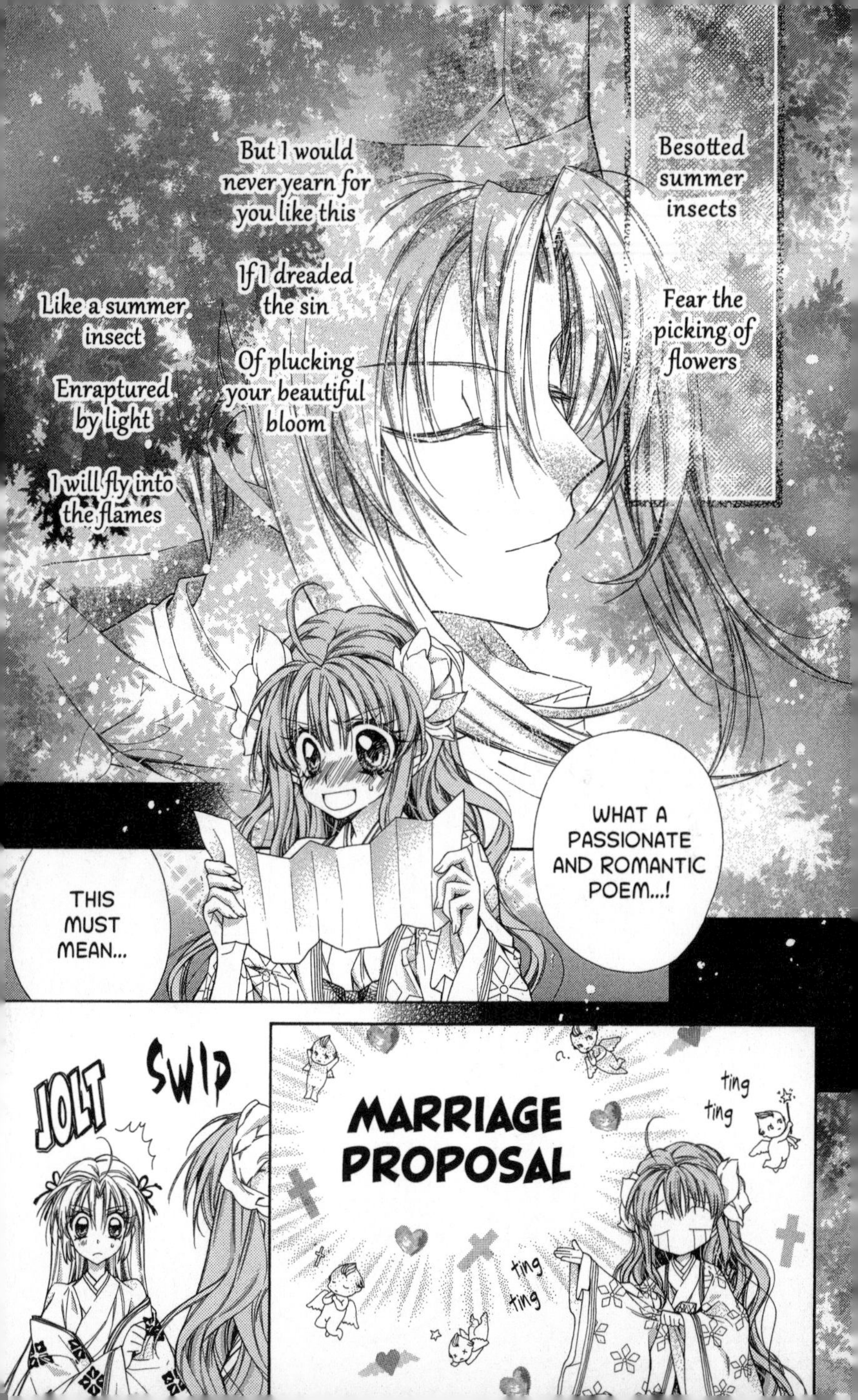
Besotted summer insects
Fear the picking of flowers
But I would never yearn for you like this
If I dreaded the sin
Of plucking your beautiful bloom
Like a summer insect
Enraptured by light
I will fly into the flames
WHAT A PASSIONATE AND ROMANTIC POEM...!
THIS MUST MEAN...
ting ting
MARRIAGE PROPOSAL
ting ting
SWIP
JOLT

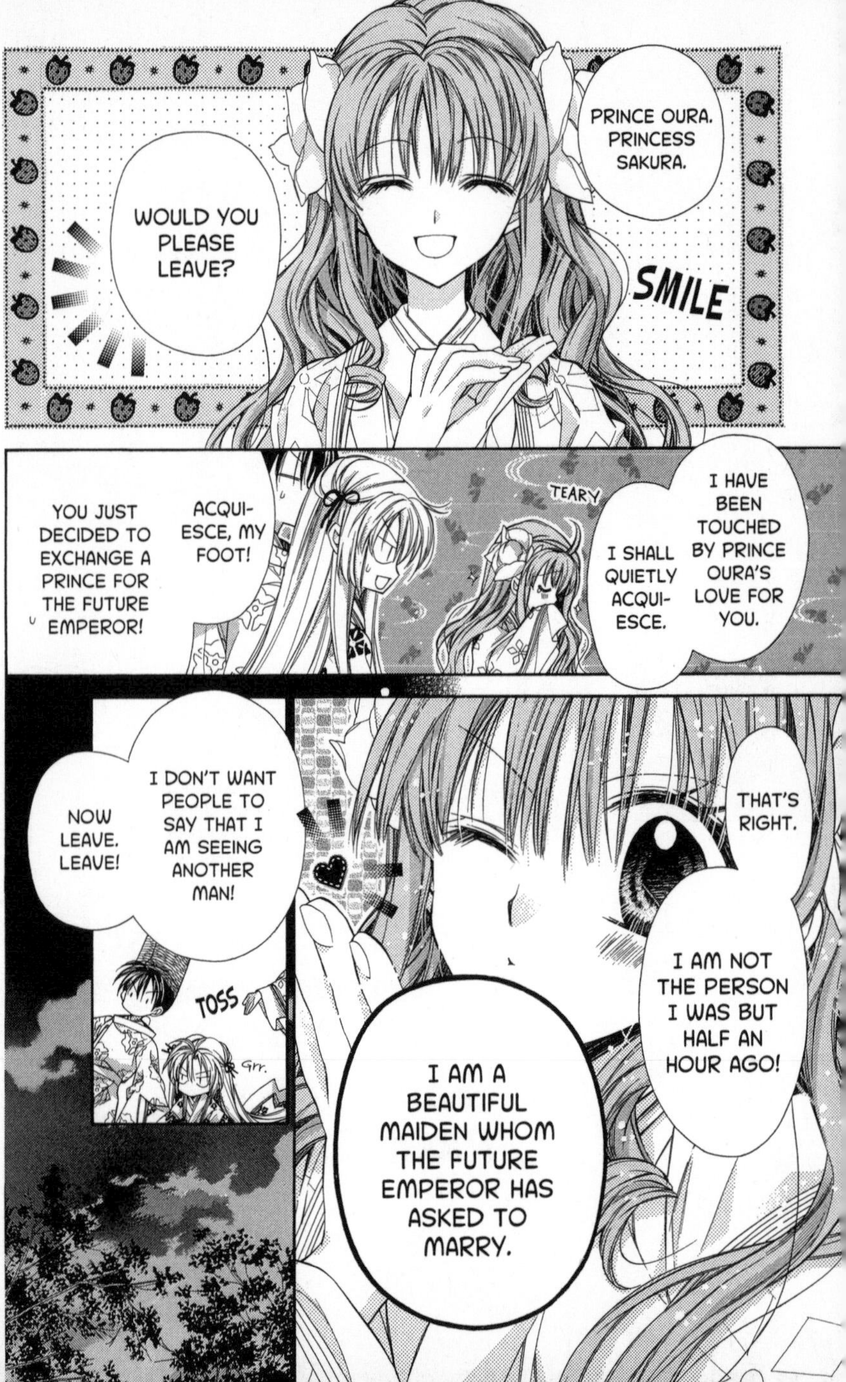
PRINCE OURA. PRINCESS SAKURA.
SMILE
WOULD YOU PLEASE LEAVE?
I HAVE BEEN TOUCHED BY PRINCE OURA'S LOVE FOR YOU.
I SHALL QUIETLY ACQUI-ESCE.
TEARY
ACQUI-ESCE, MY FOOT!
YOU JUST DECIDED TO EXCHANGE A PRINCE FOR THE FUTURE EMPEROR!
THAT'S RIGHT.
I AM NOT THE PERSON I WAS BUT HALF AN HOUR AGO!
I AM A BEAUTIFUL MAIDEN WHOM THE FUTURE EMPEROR HAS ASKED TO MARRY.
I DON'T WANT PEOPLE TO SAY THAT I AM SEEING ANOTHER MAN!
NOW LEAVE. LEAVE!
TOSS
Grr.

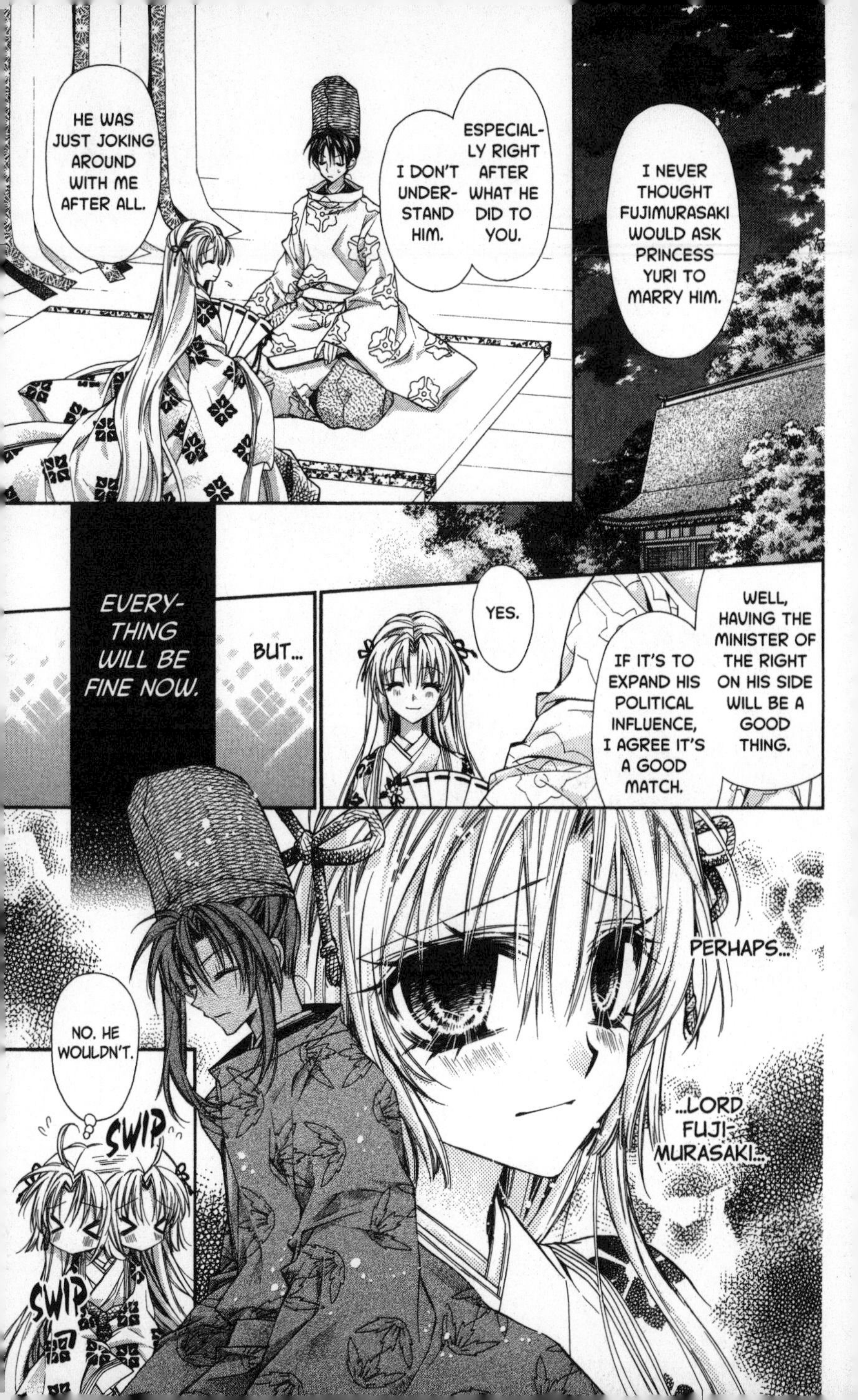
I NEVER THOUGHT FUJIMURASAKI WOULD ASK PRINCESS YURI TO MARRY HIM.
I DON'T UNDERSTAND HIM. ESPECIAL-LY RIGHT AFTER WHAT HE DID TO YOU.
HE WAS JUST JOKING AROUND WITH ME AFTER ALL.
WELL, HAVING THE MINISTER OF THE RIGHT ON HIS SIDE WILL BE A GOOD THING.
IF IT'S TO EXPAND HIS POLITICAL INFLUENCE, I AGREE IT'S A GOOD MATCH.
YES.
BUT...
EVERY-THING WILL BE FINE NOW.
PERHAPS...
...LORD FUJI-MURASAKI...
NO. HE WOULDN'T.
SWIP
SWIP

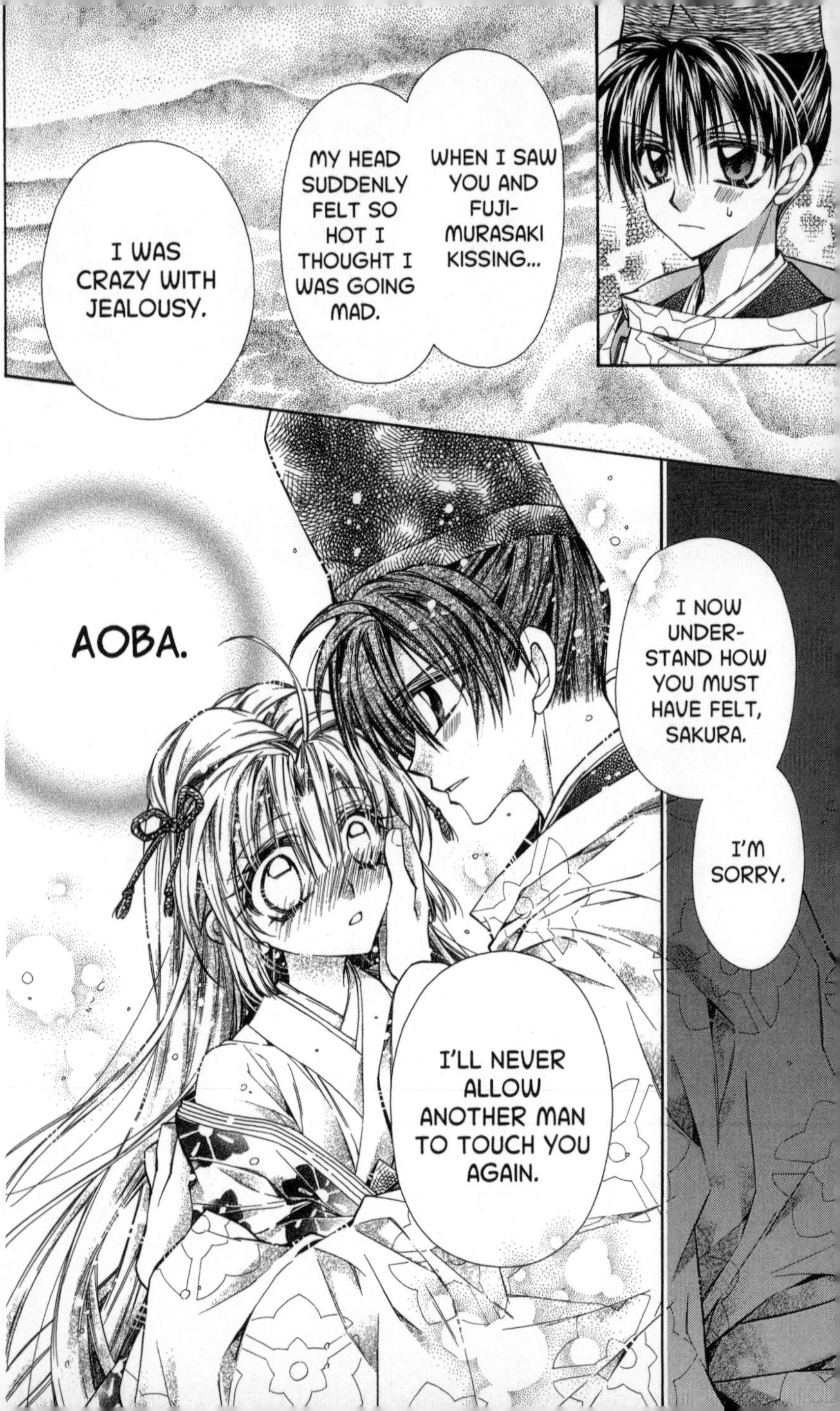
WHEN I SAW YOU AND FUJI-MURASAKI KISSING...
MY HEAD SUDDENLY FELT SO HOT I THOUGHT I WAS GOING MAD.
I WAS CRAZY WITH JEALOUSY.
I NOW UNDERSTAND HOW YOU MUST HAVE FELT, SAKURA.
I'M SORRY.
AOBA.
I'LL NEVER ALLOW ANOTHER MAN TO TOUCH YOU AGAIN.

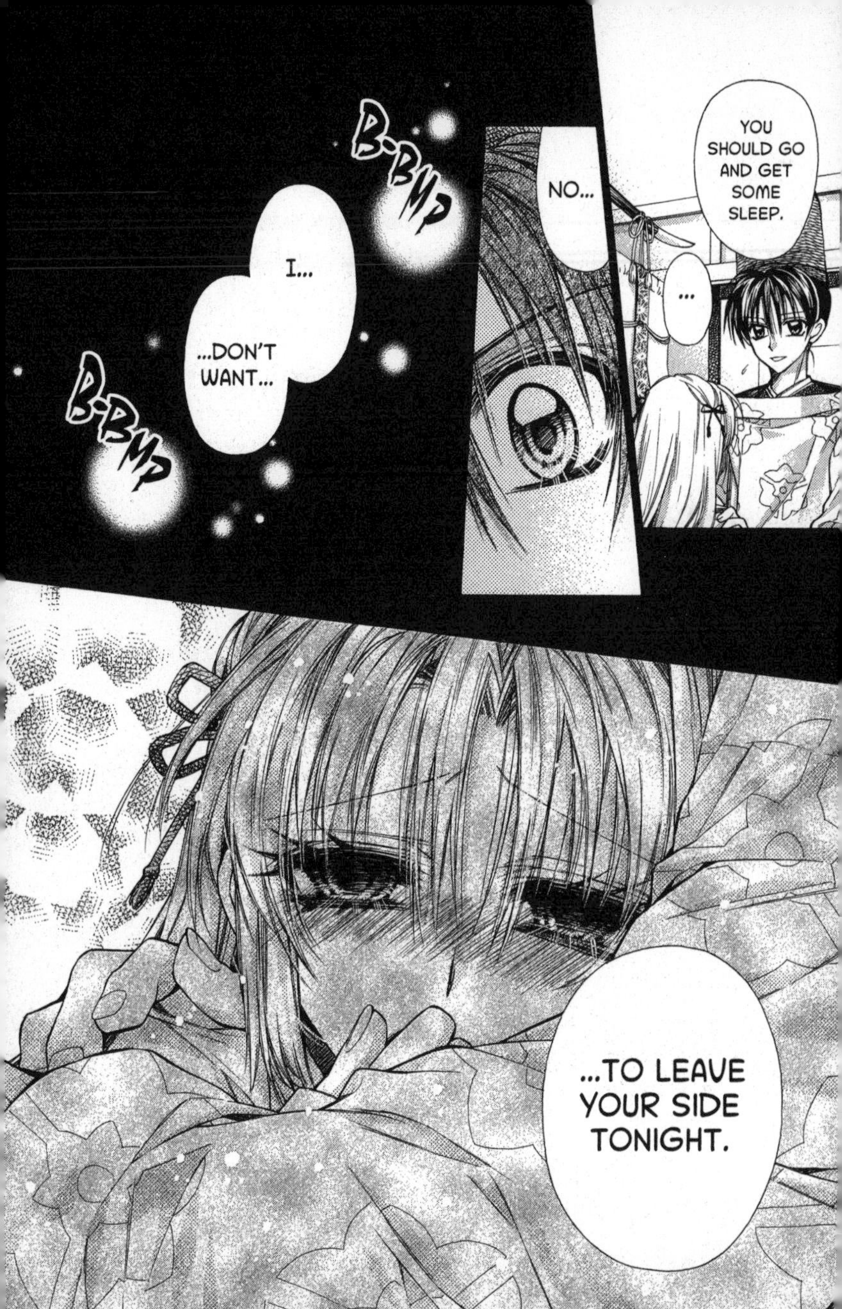
YOU SHOULD GO AND GET SOME SLEEP.
...
NO...
B-BMP
I...
...DON'T WANT...
B-BMP
...TO LEAVE YOUR SIDE TONIGHT.

I DON'T WANT TO LEAVE YOUR SIDE TO-NIGHT.

Chapter 31: Aoba's Secret

✻ I'm giving away the story.

Aoba is the main character in this chapter. Aoba is in such a hurry to live... He loves Sakura but is unable to open up to her... Here we learn why. It's also how he knew he hadn't done anything with Princess Yuri (as well as harm her). In this series, drinking the blood of a mononoke means → Obtaining the power of another creature → Life will burn out twice as fast → A short life.

Sakura is mixed blood from birth, so she is different from the others who have obtained a mononoke's power by other means.

I'd feel so shocked if I were Sakura. She's immortal and can use her powers as much as she needs to—even if she transforms—but the more the others use their powers to protect her, the more their own lives will be shortened. Maybe that's what "destroy" means in her soul symbol.

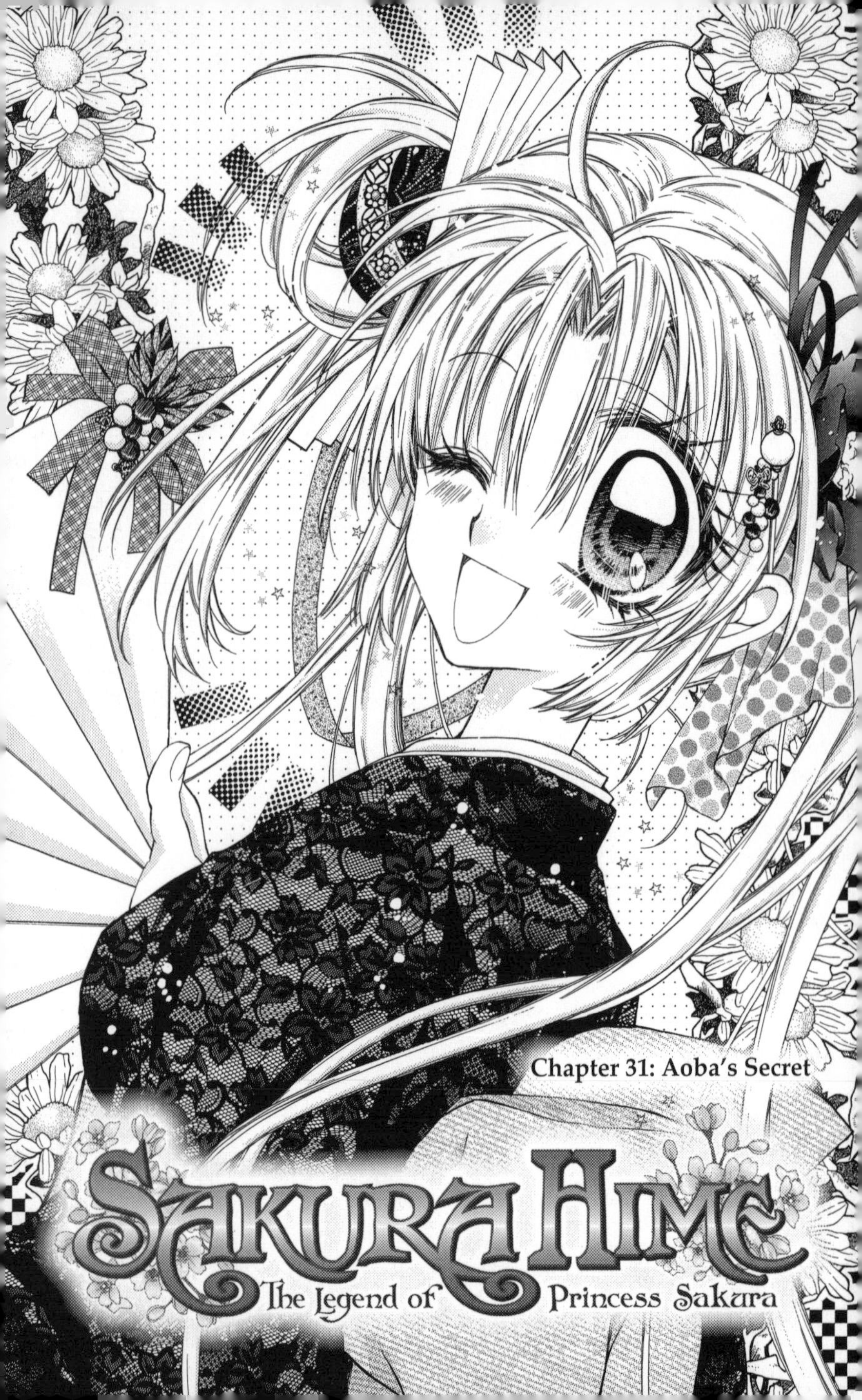
Chapter 31: Aoba's Secret
SAKURA HIME
The Legend of Princess Sakura

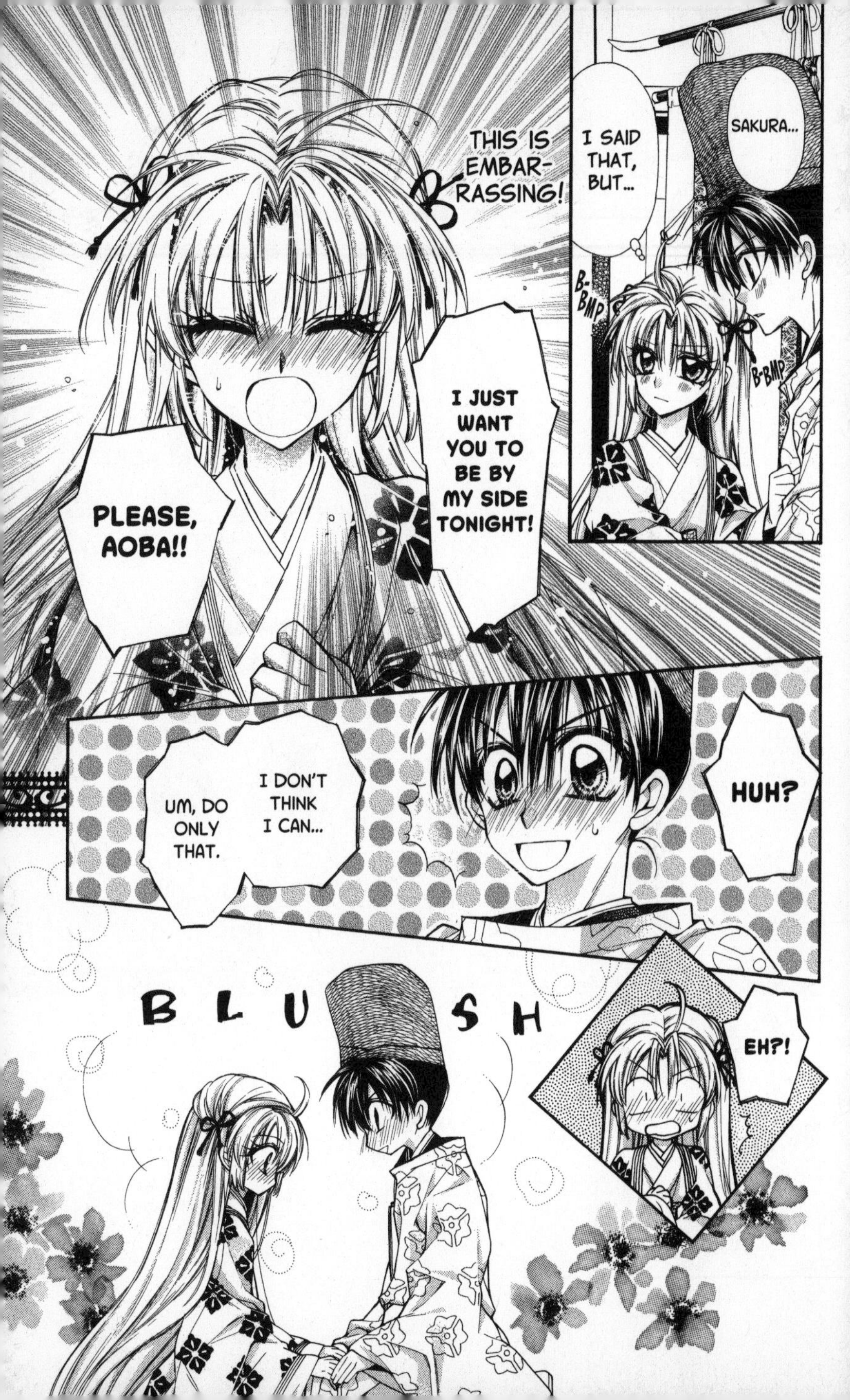
SAKURA...
B-BMP
B-BMP
I SAID THAT, BUT...
THIS IS EMBAR-RASSING!
I JUST WANT YOU TO BE BY MY SIDE TONIGHT!
PLEASE, AOBA!!
HUH?
I DON'T THINK I CAN...
UM, DO ONLY THAT.
EH?!
BLUSH

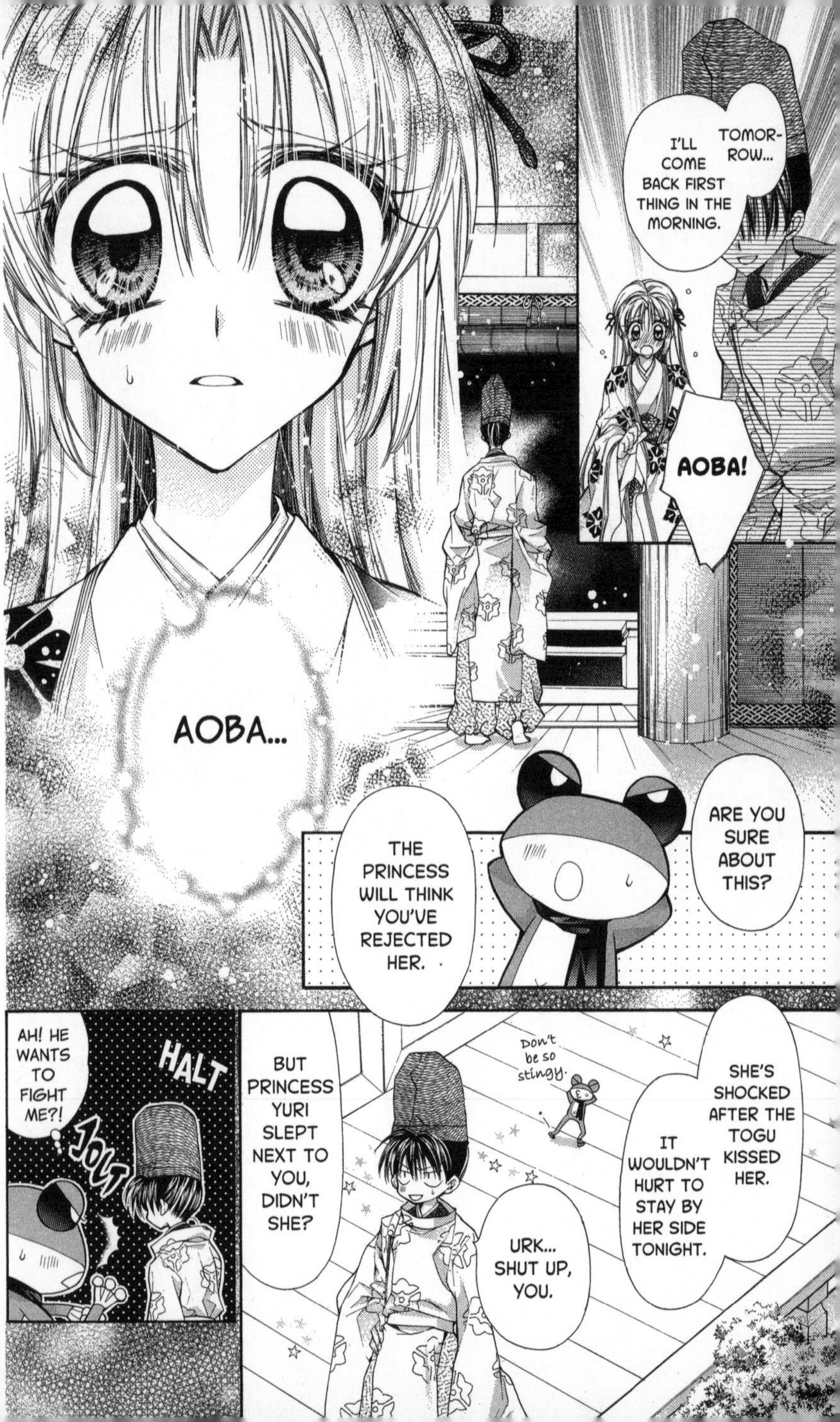
TOMORROW... I'LL COME BACK FIRST THING IN THE MORNING.
AOBA!
ARE YOU SURE ABOUT THIS?
THE PRINCESS WILL THINK YOU'VE REJECTED HER.
AOBA...
SHE'S SHOCKED AFTER THE TOGU KISSED HER.
IT WOULDN'T HURT TO STAY BY HER SIDE TONIGHT.
URK... SHUT UP, YOU.
Don't be so stingy.
BUT PRINCESS YURI SLEPT NEXT TO YOU, DIDN'T SHE?
HALT
JOLT
AH! HE WANTS TO FIGHT ME?!

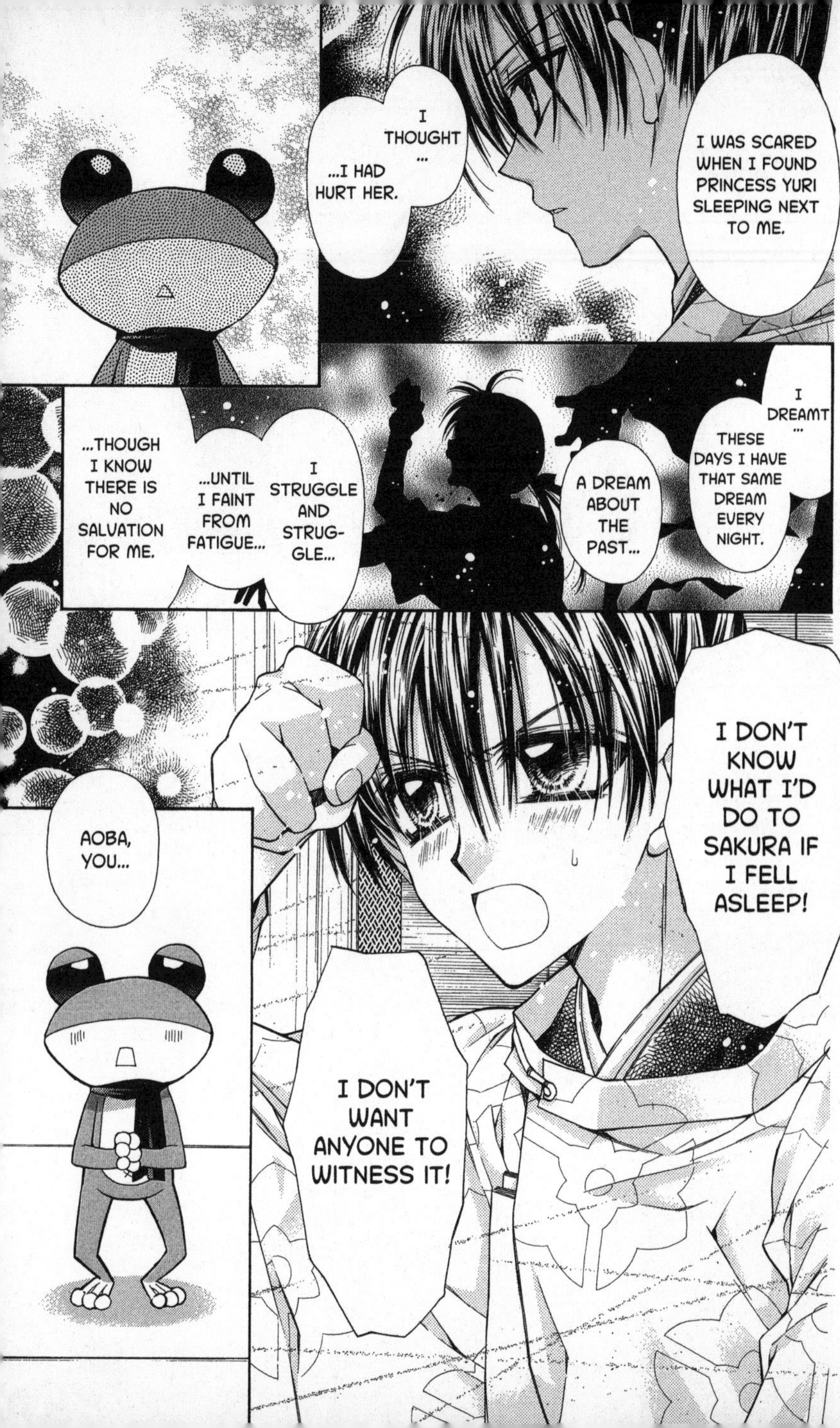
I WAS SCARED WHEN I FOUND PRINCESS YURI SLEEPING NEXT TO ME.
I THOUGHT... ...I HAD HURT HER.
I DREAMT...
THESE DAYS I HAVE THAT SAME DREAM EVERY NIGHT.
A DREAM ABOUT THE PAST...
I STRUGGLE AND STRUG-GLE...
...UNTIL I FAINT FROM FATIGUE...
...THOUGH I KNOW THERE IS NO SALVATION FOR ME.
I DON'T KNOW WHAT I'D DO TO SAKURA IF I FELL ASLEEP!
I DON'T WANT ANYONE TO WITNESS IT!
AOBA, YOU...

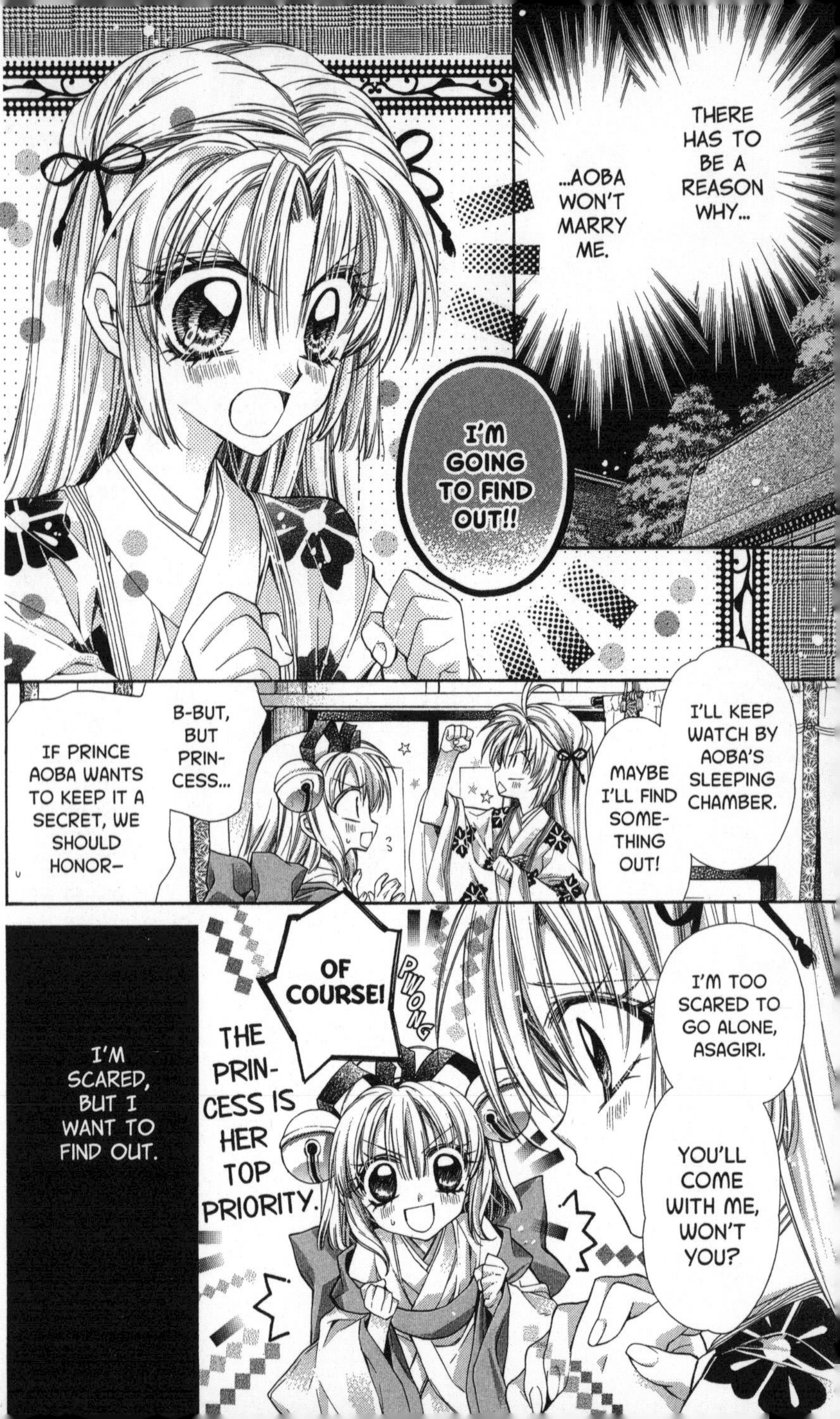
THERE HAS TO BE A REASON WHY...
...AOBA WON'T MARRY ME.
I'M GOING TO FIND OUT!!
I'LL KEEP WATCH BY AOBA'S SLEEPING CHAMBER.
MAYBE I'LL FIND SOME-THING OUT!
B-BUT, BUT PRIN-CESS...
IF PRINCE AOBA WANTS TO KEEP IT A SECRET, WE SHOULD HONOR–
I'M TOO SCARED TO GO ALONE, ASAGIRI.
YOU'LL COME WITH ME, WON'T YOU?
OF COURSE!
PWONG
THE PRIN-CESS IS HER TOP PRIORITY.
I'M SCARED, BUT I WANT TO FIND OUT.

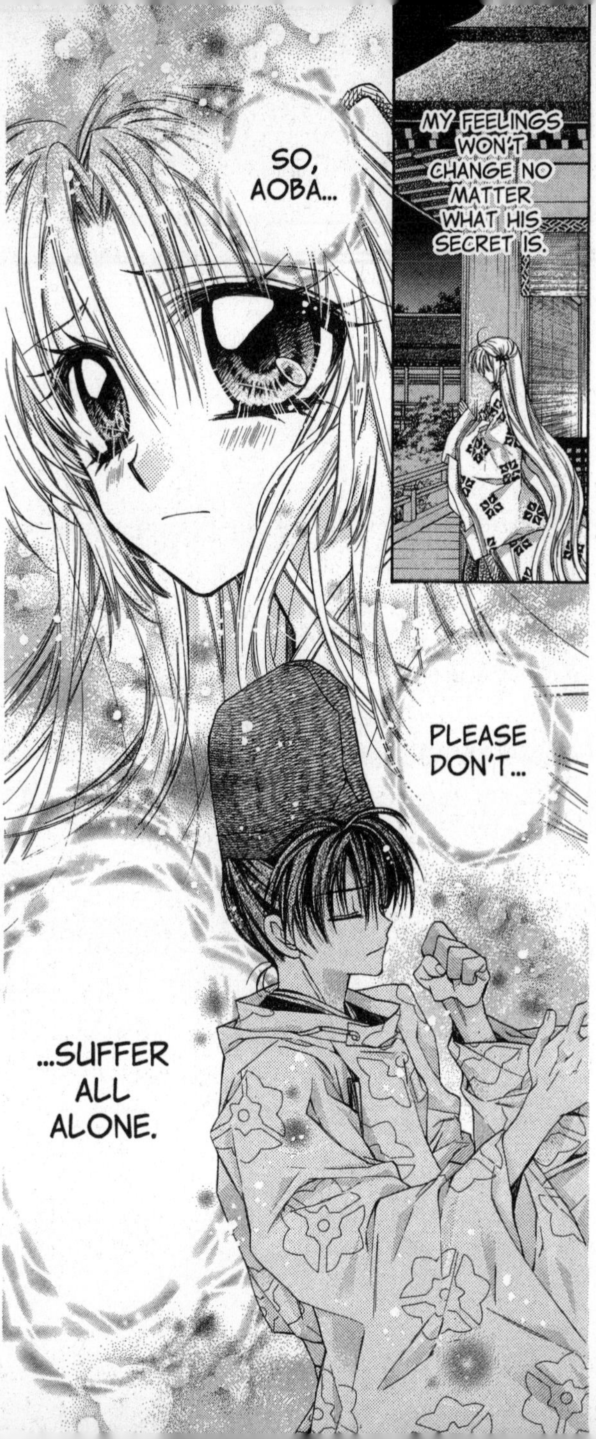
MY FEELINGS WON'T CHANGE NO MATTER WHAT HIS SECRET IS.
SO, AOBA...
PLEASE DON'T...
...SUFFER ALL ALONE.

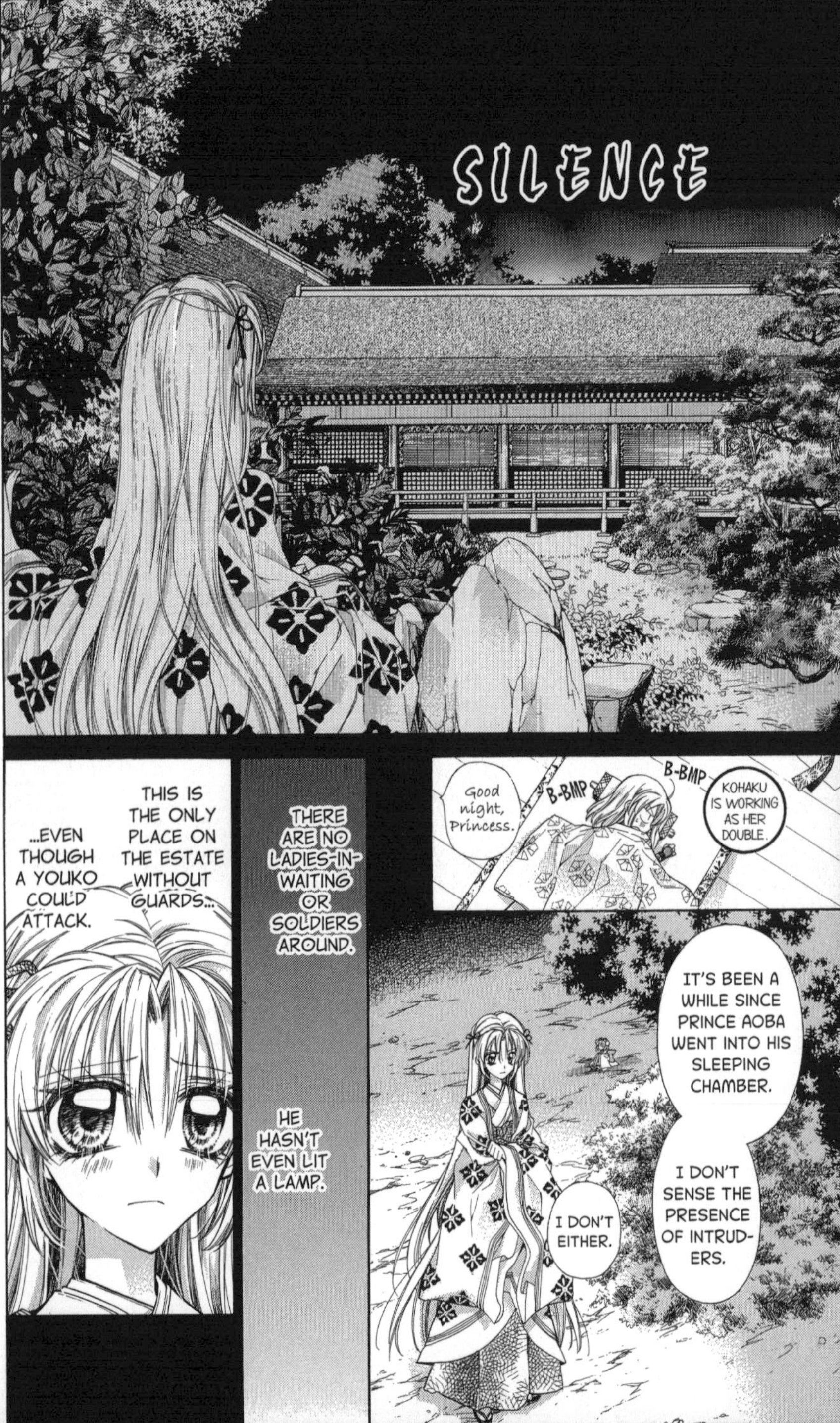
SILENCE
KOHAKU IS WORKING AS HER DOUBLE.
B-BMP
B-BMP
Good night, Princess.
IT'S BEEN A WHILE SINCE PRINCE AOBA WENT INTO HIS SLEEPING CHAMBER.
I DON'T SENSE THE PRESENCE OF INTRUD-ERS.
I DON'T EITHER.
THERE ARE NO LADIES-IN-WAITING OR SOLDIERS AROUND.
HE HASN'T EVEN LIT A LAMP.
THIS IS THE ONLY PLACE ON THE ESTATE WITHOUT GUARDS...
...EVEN THOUGH A YOUKO COULD ATTACK.

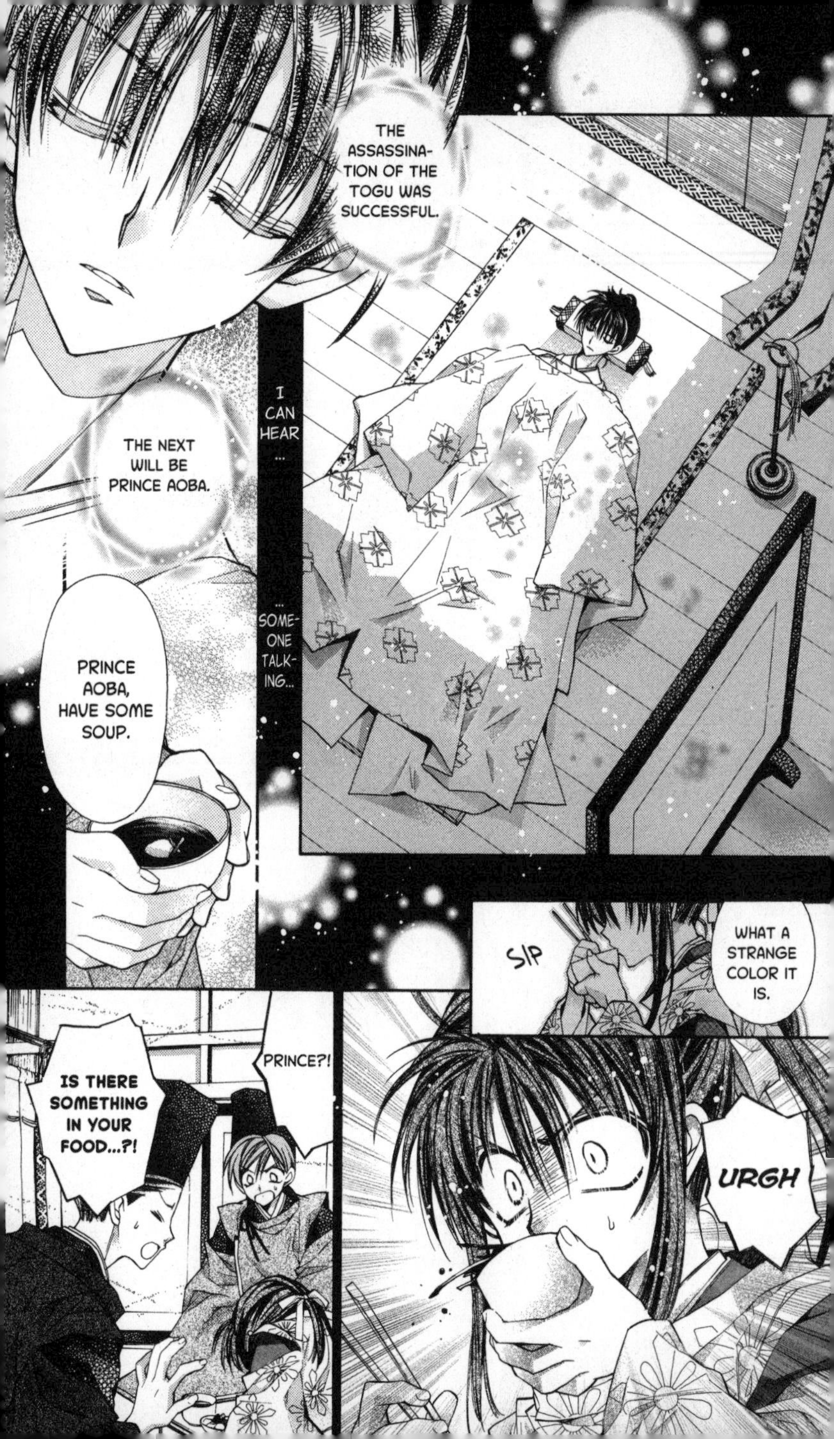
THE ASSASSINATION OF THE TOGU WAS SUCCESSFUL.
I CAN HEAR ...
... SOMEONE TALKING...
THE NEXT WILL BE PRINCE AOBA.
PRINCE AOBA, HAVE SOME SOUP.
WHAT A STRANGE COLOR IT IS.
SIP
URGH
PRINCE?!
IS THERE SOMETHING IN YOUR FOOD...?!

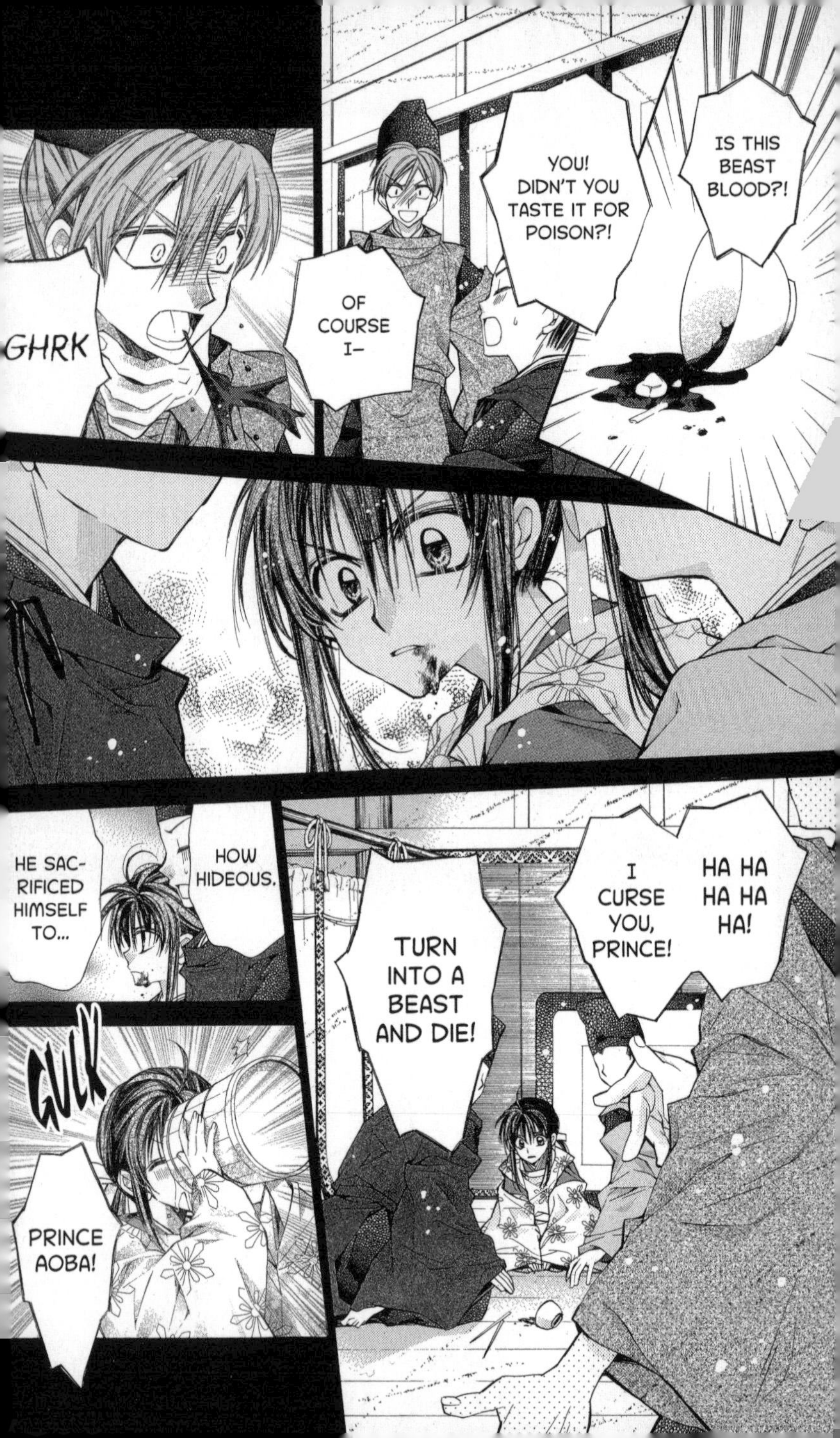
IS THIS BEAST BLOOD?!
YOU! DIDN'T YOU TASTE IT FOR POISON?!
OF COURSE I–
GHRK
HA HA HA HA HA!
I CURSE YOU, PRINCE!
TURN INTO A BEAST AND DIE!
HOW HIDEOUS.
HE SACRIFICED HIMSELF TO...
GULK
PRINCE AOBA!

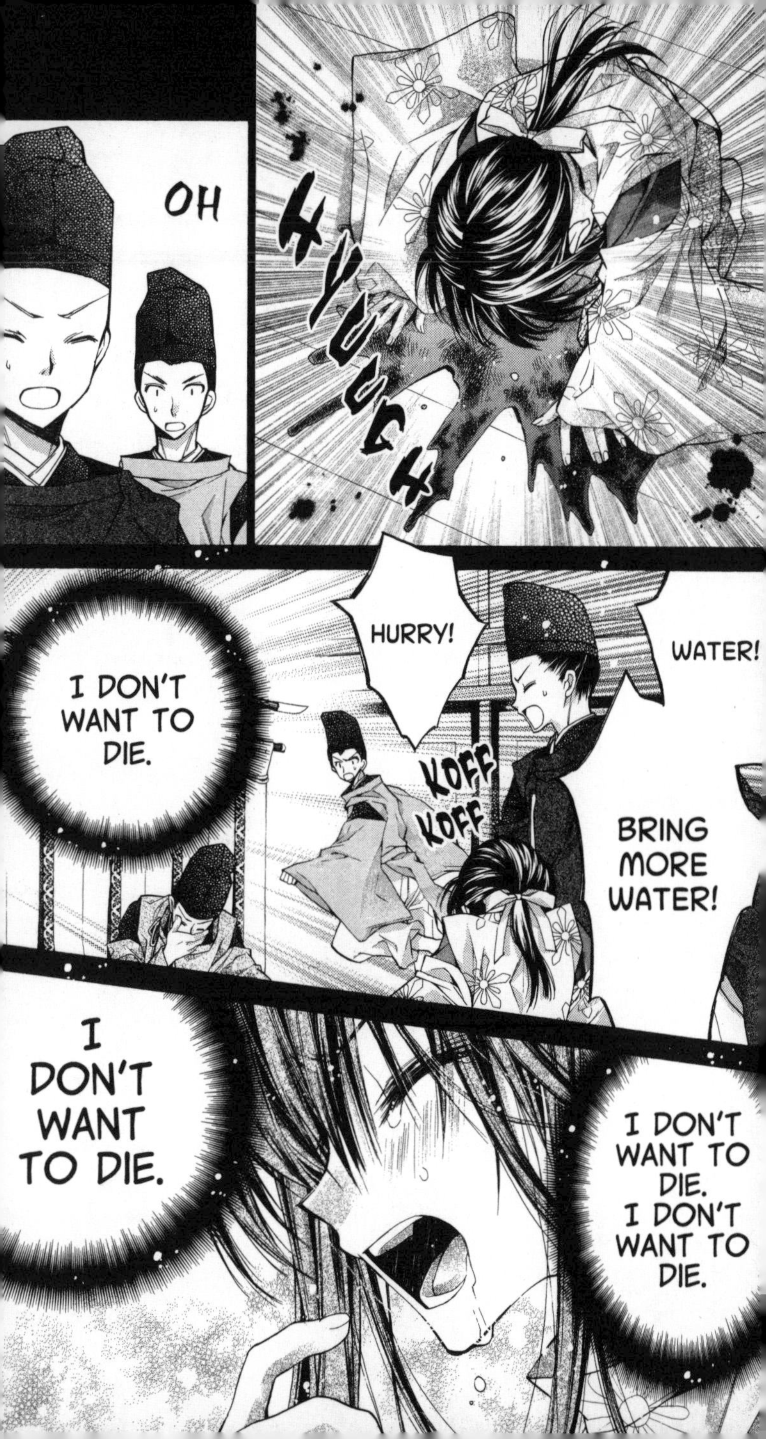
HYUUGH
OH
WATER!
HURRY!
BRING MORE WATER!
KOFF KOFF
I DON'T WANT TO DIE.
I DON'T WANT TO DIE. I DON'T WANT TO DIE.
I DON'T WANT TO DIE.

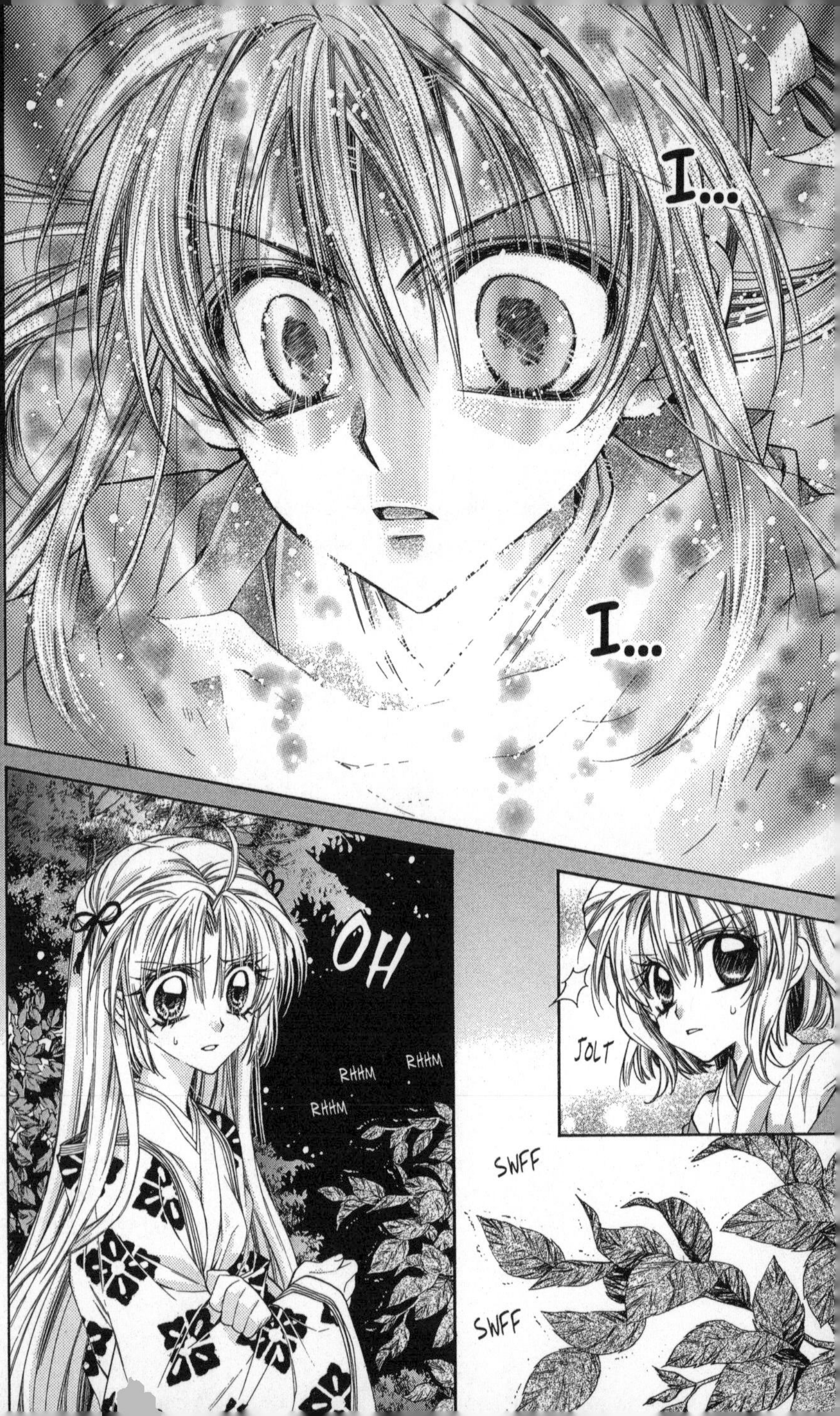
I...
I...
JOLT
OH
RHHM
RHHM
RHHM
SWFF
SWFF

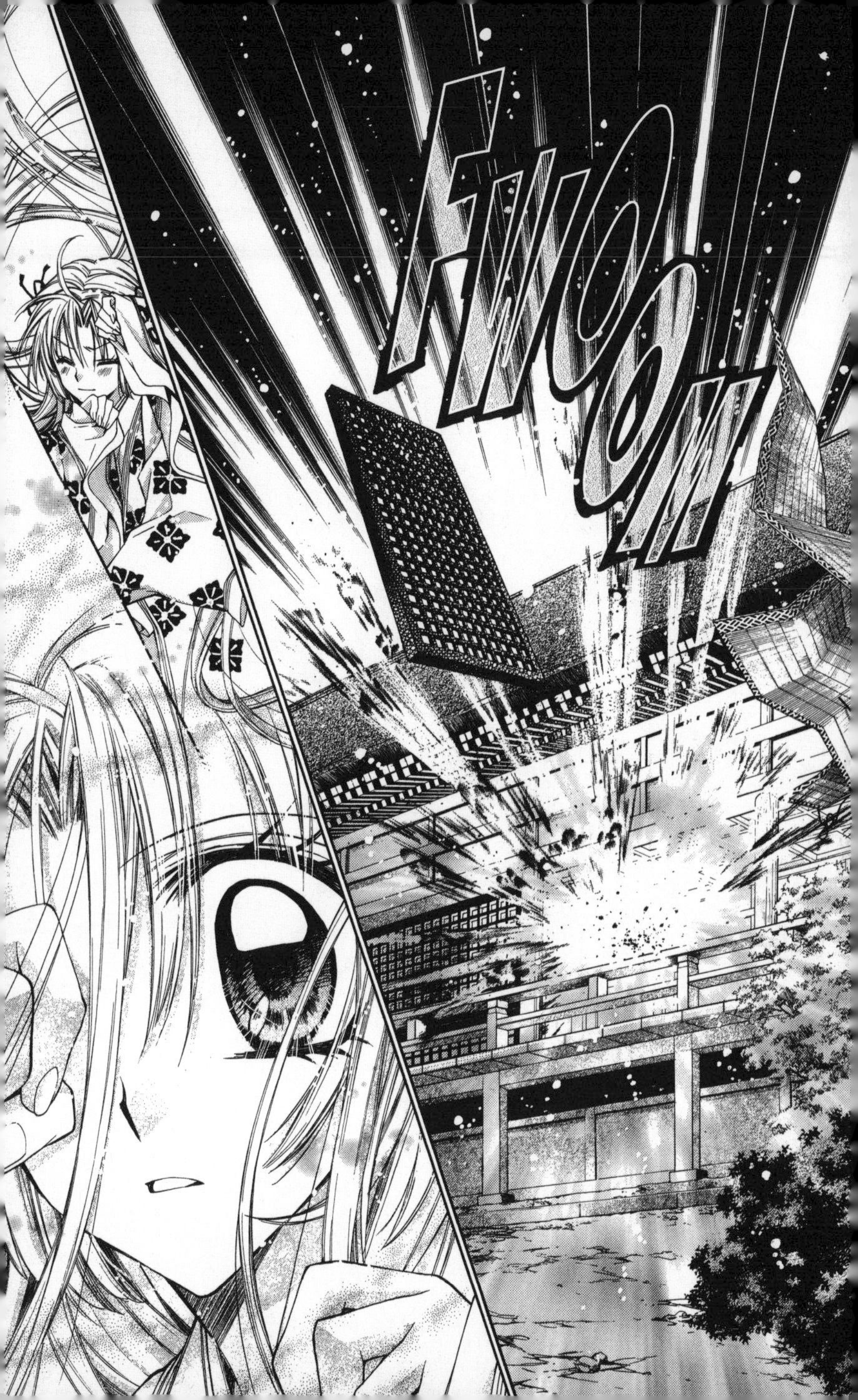
FWOOM

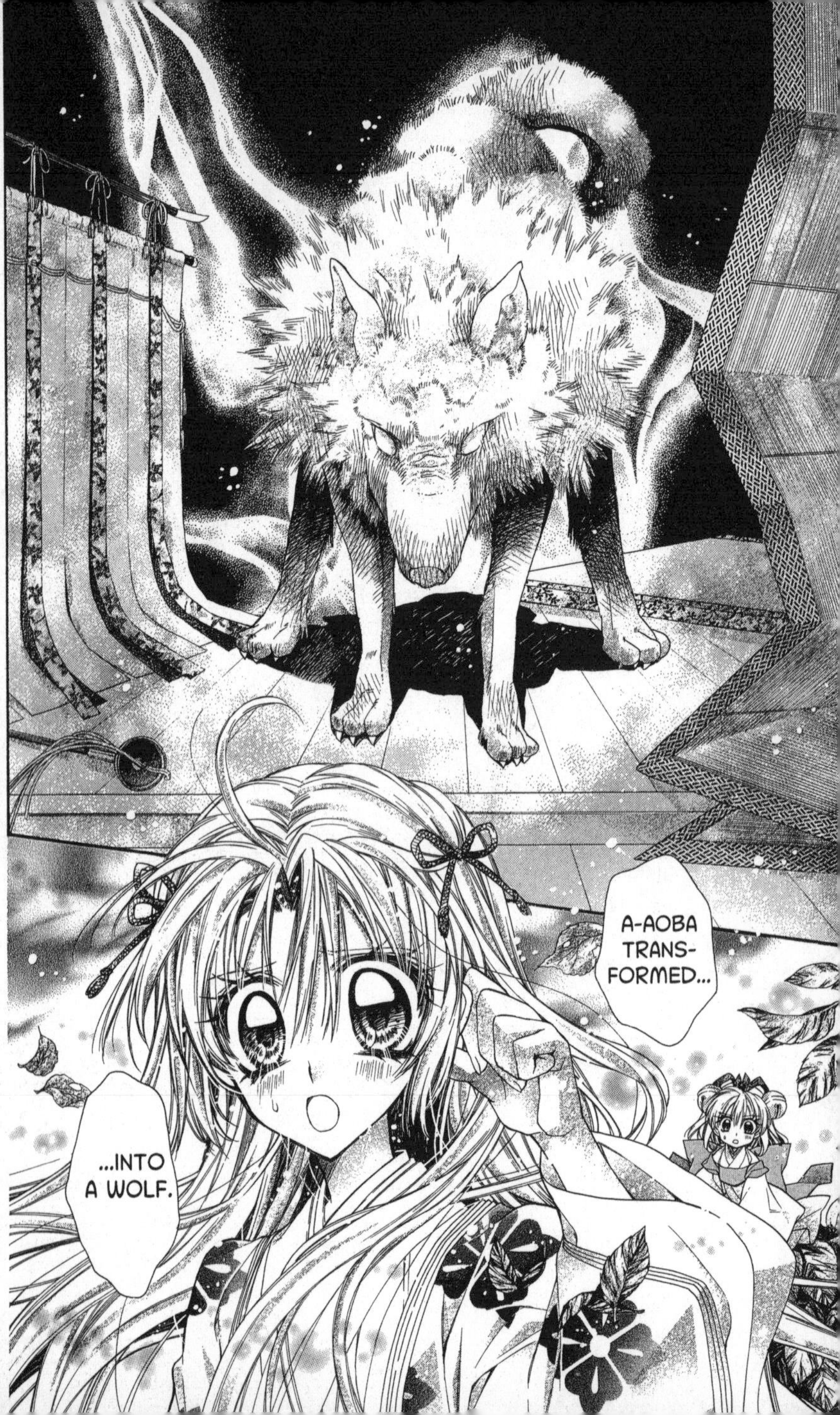
A-AOBA TRANS-FORMED...
...INTO A WOLF.

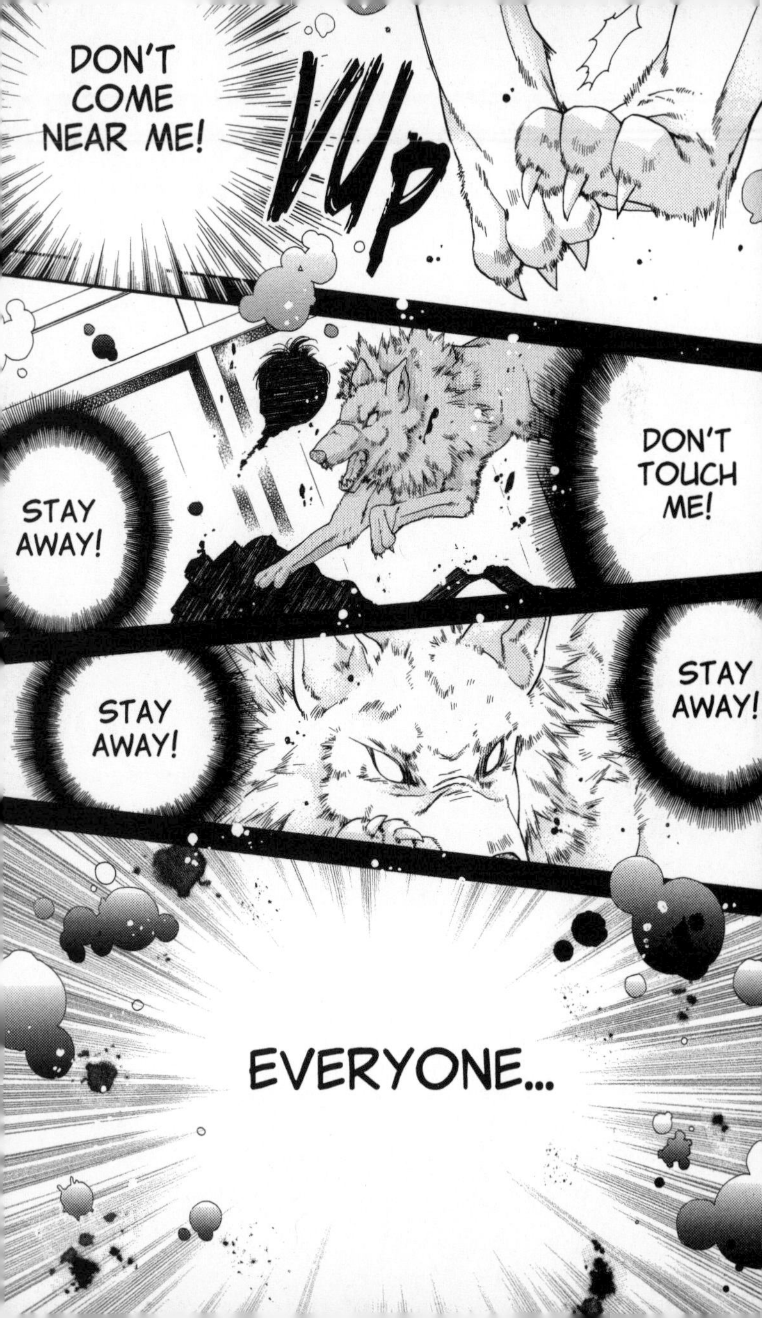
VUP
DON'T COME NEAR ME!
DON'T TOUCH ME!
STAY AWAY!
STAY AWAY!
STAY AWAY!
EVERYONE...

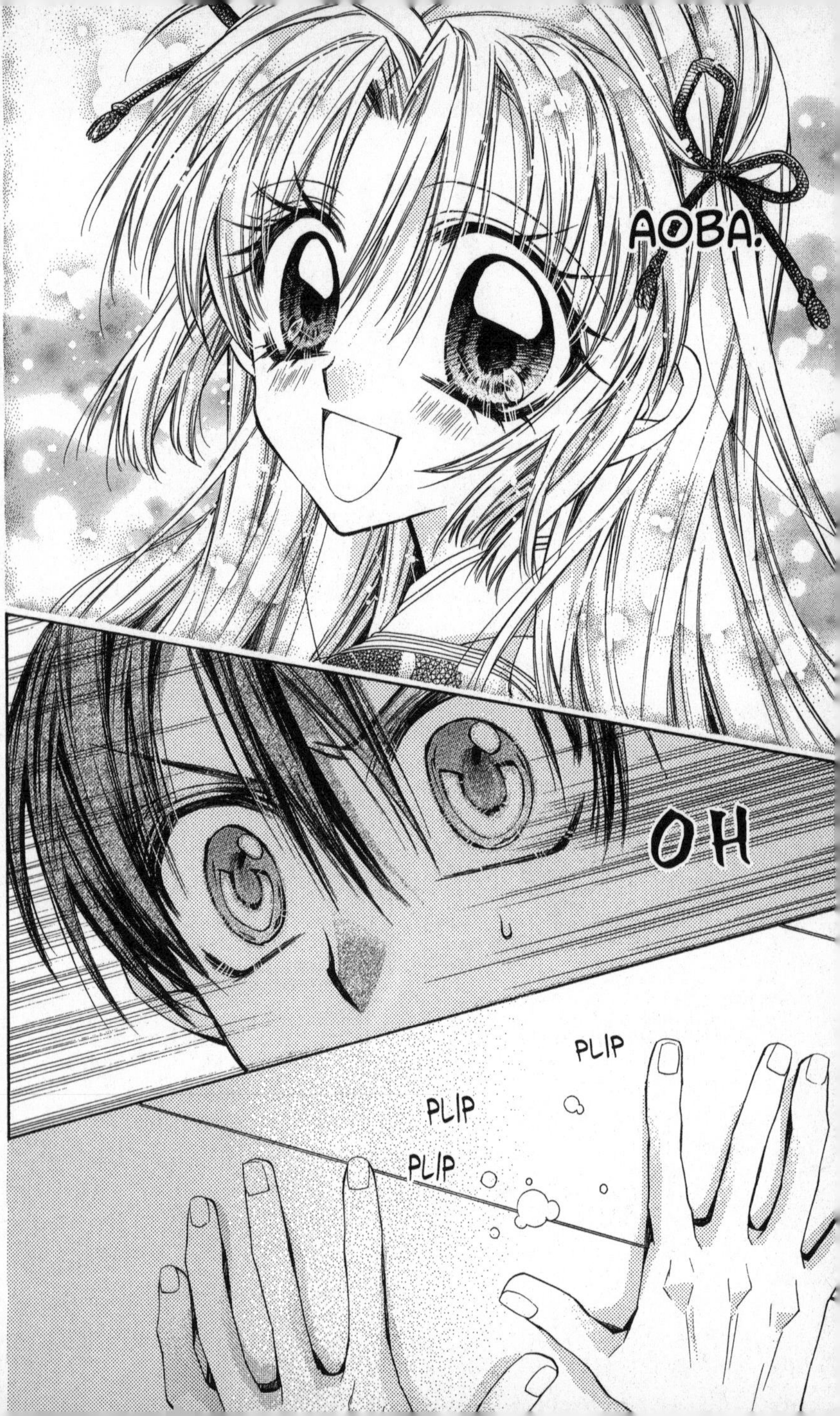
AOBA.
OH
PLIP
PLIP
PLIP

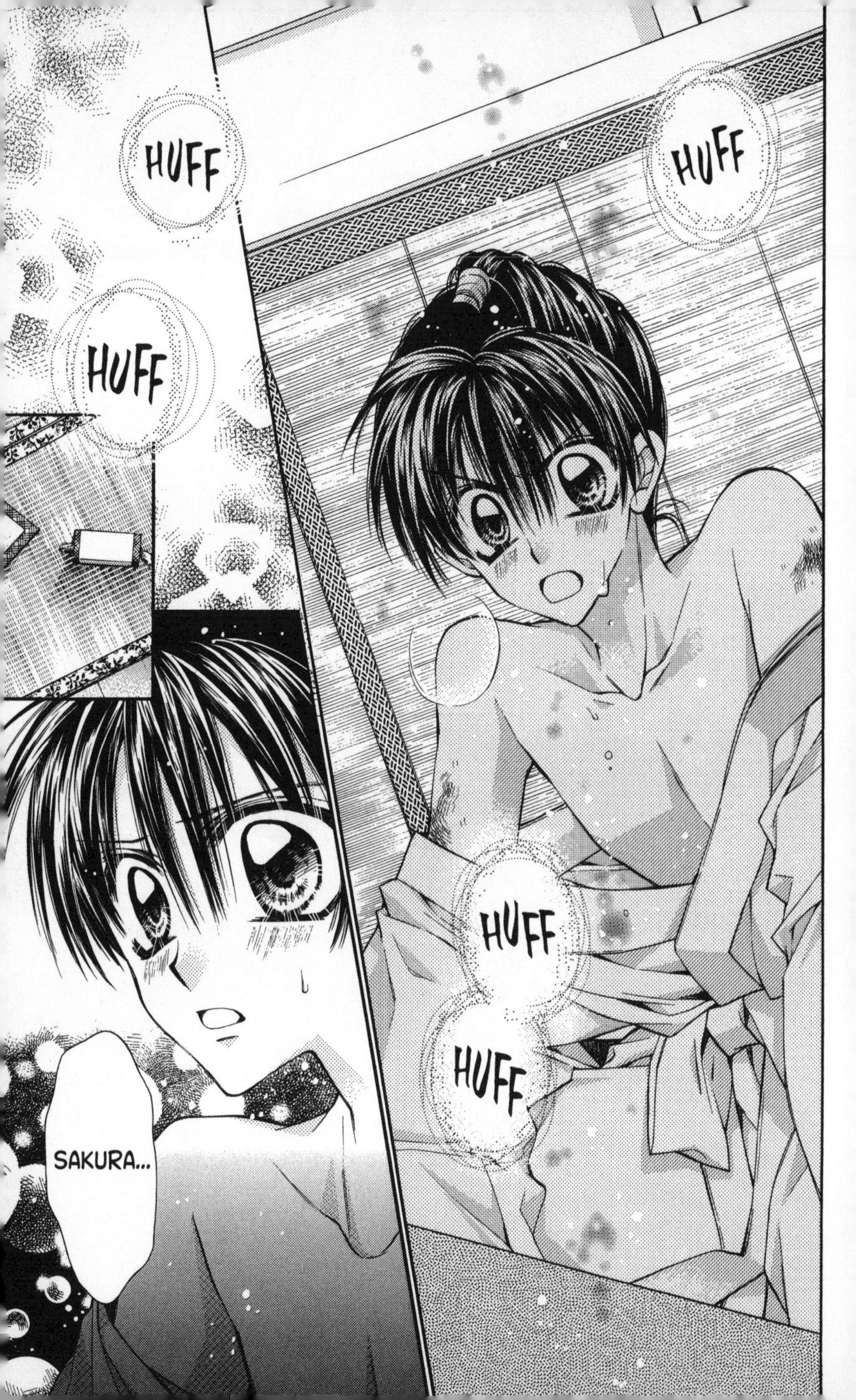
HUFF
HUFF
HUFF
HUFF
HUFF
SAKURA...

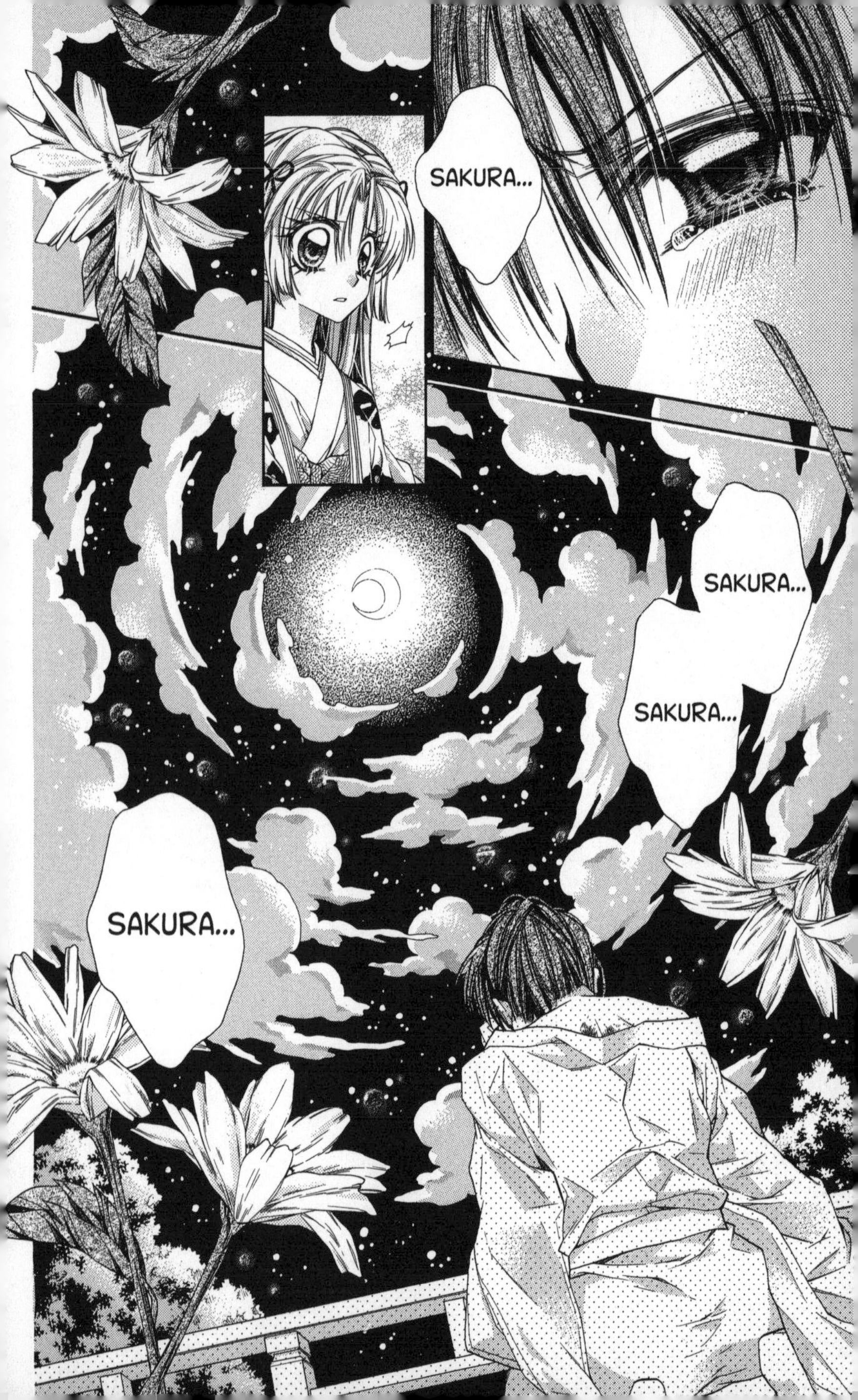
SAKURA...
SAKURA...
SAKURA...
SAKURA...

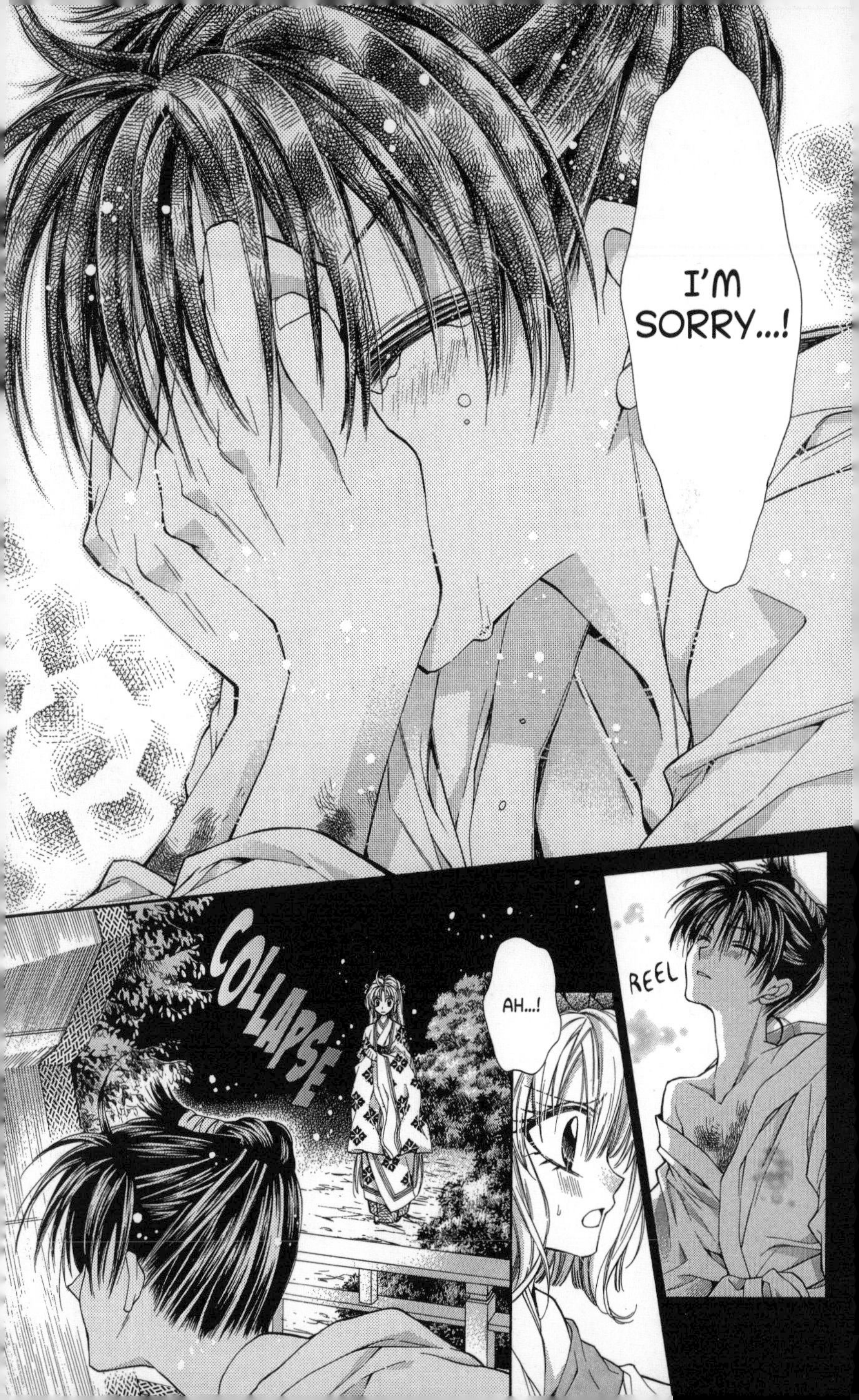
I'M SORRY...!
REEL
AH...!
COLLAPSE

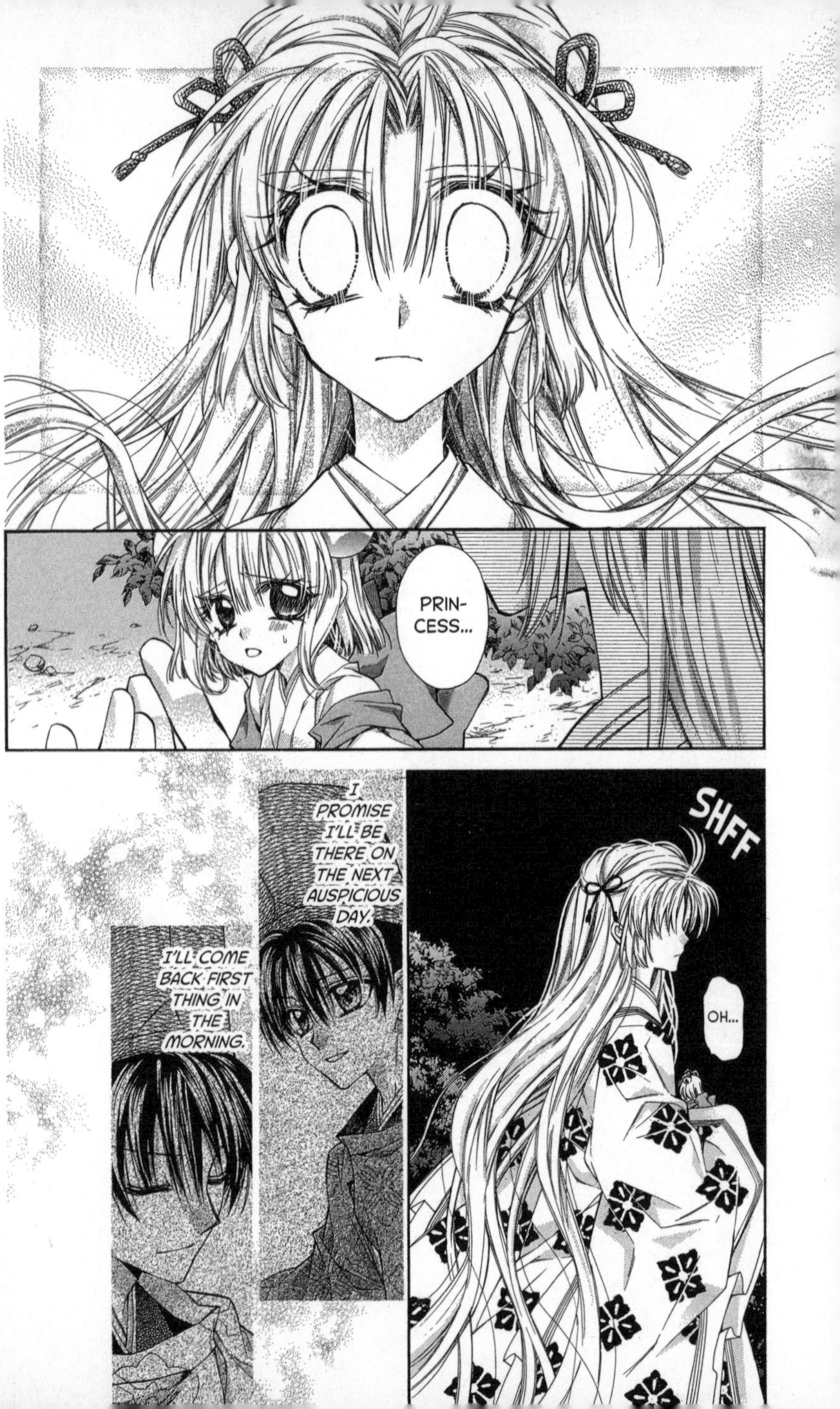
PRIN-CESS...
SHFF
OH...
I PROMISE I'LL BE THERE ON THE NEXT AUSPICIOUS DAY.
I'LL COME BACK FIRST THING IN THE MORNING.

FUDANJUKU

I've been working on *Fudanjuku Story* in *Margaret* magazine. I liked Fudanjuku from the start, but I've fallen in love with the members even more now! My love✧ has grown since I started drawing them. They changed the spelling of the group's name from 腐男塾 to 風男塾. [The character meaning "rotten" (as in *fujoshi*) was changed to "wind." -Ed.]

So how did I work on that and *Sakura Hime*?! To tell you the truth, the due dates were...

✿ *Margaret*
Due around the 5th
Due around the 20th

✿ *Ribon*
Due around the 15th

Huh? The second due date for *Margaret* and the due date for *Ribon* were that close?! I was panting pretty hard when the 20th of each month neared. (laugh) I had my interviews with the Fudanjuku members as well, so I staggered around on those four days before the deadline. (laugh) But my love✧ managed to get me through it all! (Love plus everyone's incredible support...)

I consider myself bad at one-shots, but I didn't have much trouble drawing the Fudanjuku members because their personalities were all so easy to capture! I want all the Fudanjuku fans as well as those who do not know them yet to read it.✿ (I have drawn it in a way that makes it read just like a regular shojo manga).

Thank you. ♥

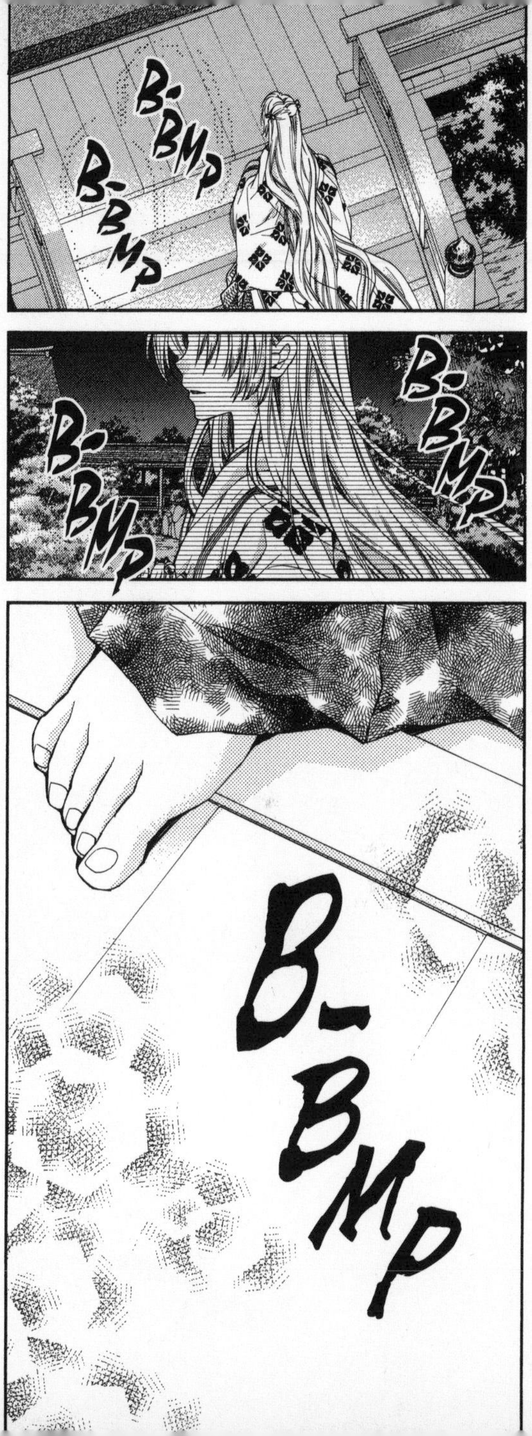

B-BMP
B-BMP
B-BMP
B-BMP
B-BMP

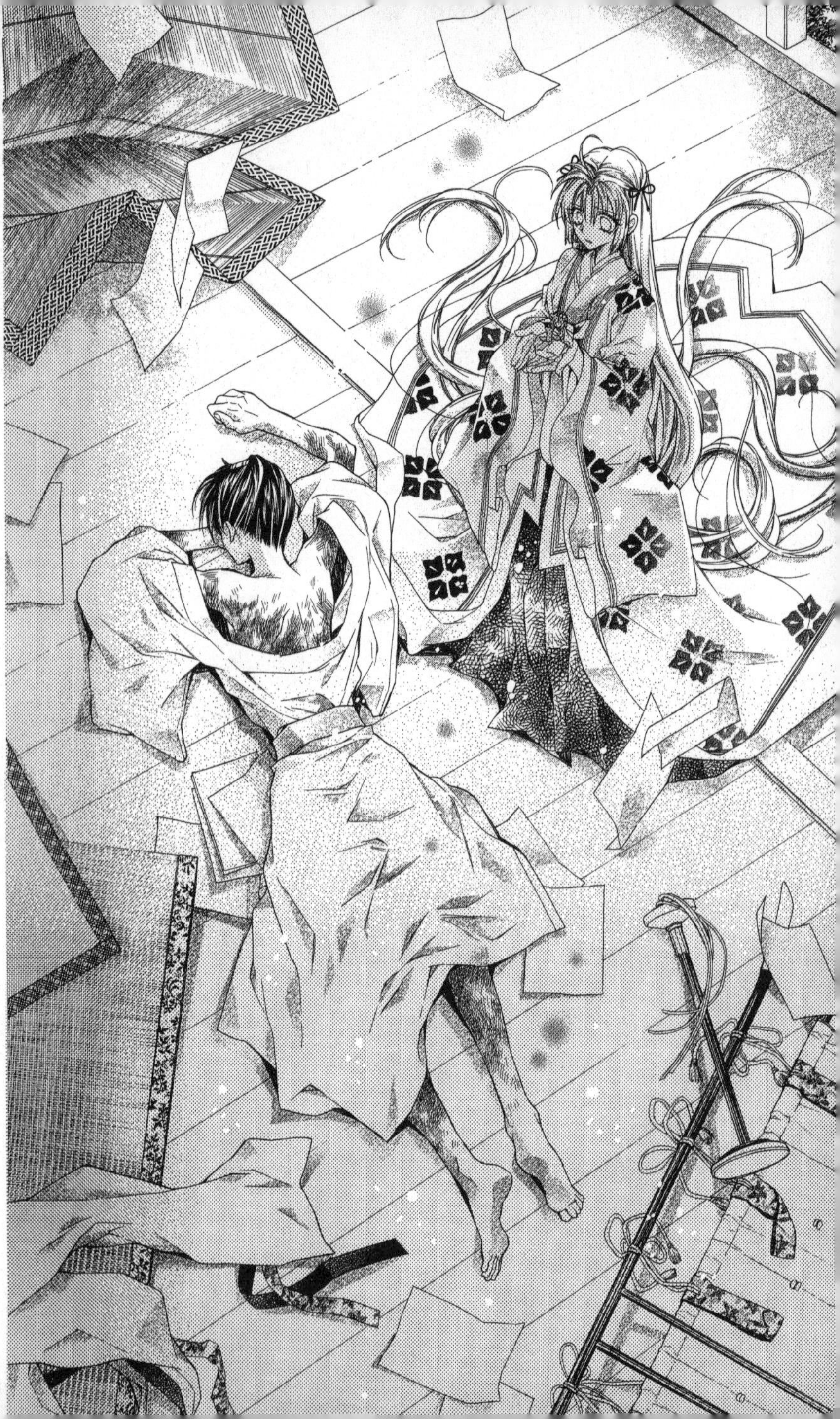

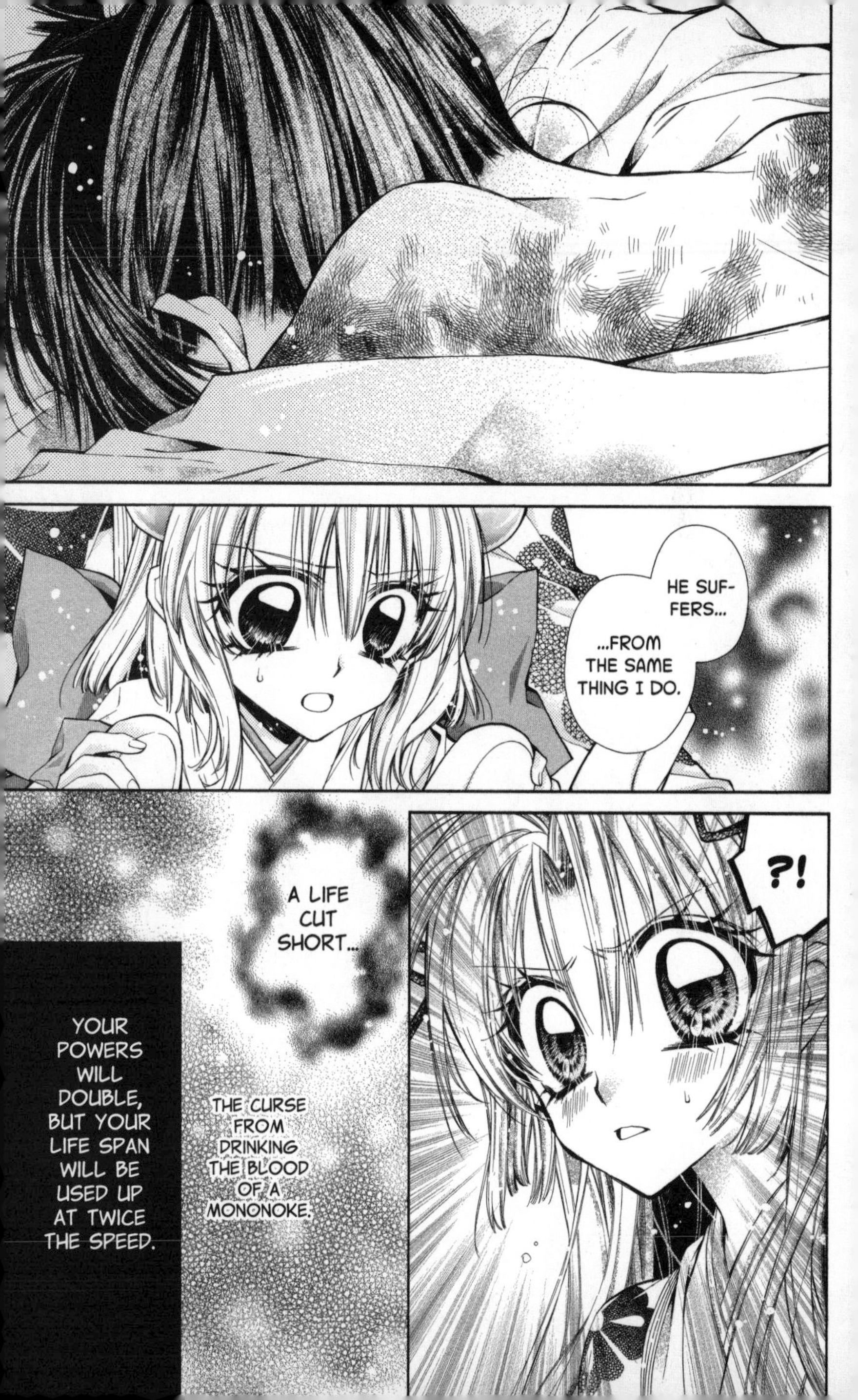
HE SUFFERS...
...FROM THE SAME THING I DO.
?!
A LIFE CUT SHORT...
THE CURSE FROM DRINKING THE BLOOD OF A MONONOKE.
YOUR POWERS WILL DOUBLE, BUT YOUR LIFE SPAN WILL BE USED UP AT TWICE THE SPEED.

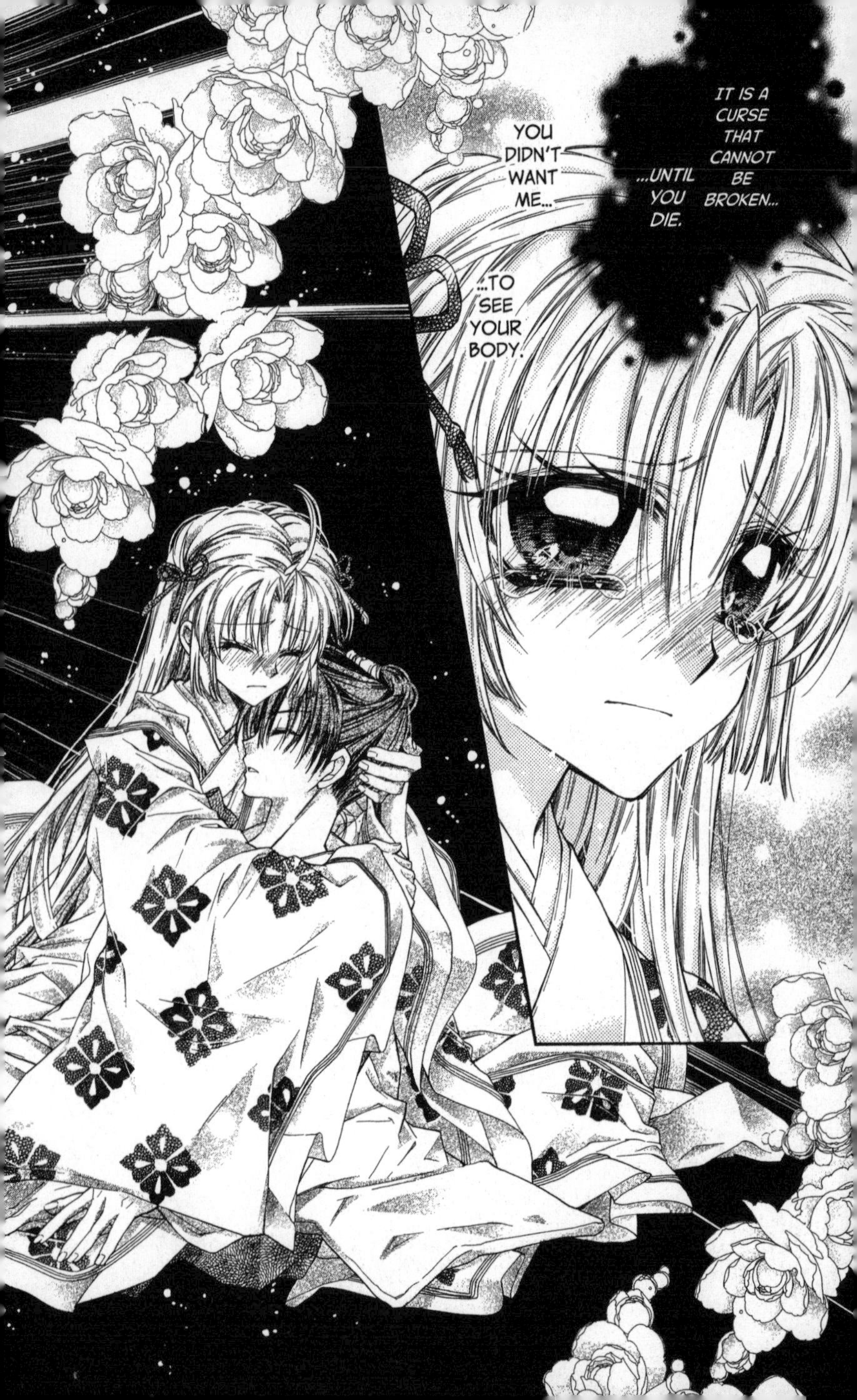
IT IS A CURSE THAT CANNOT BE BROKEN...
...UNTIL YOU DIE.
YOU DIDN'T WANT ME...
...TO SEE YOUR BODY.

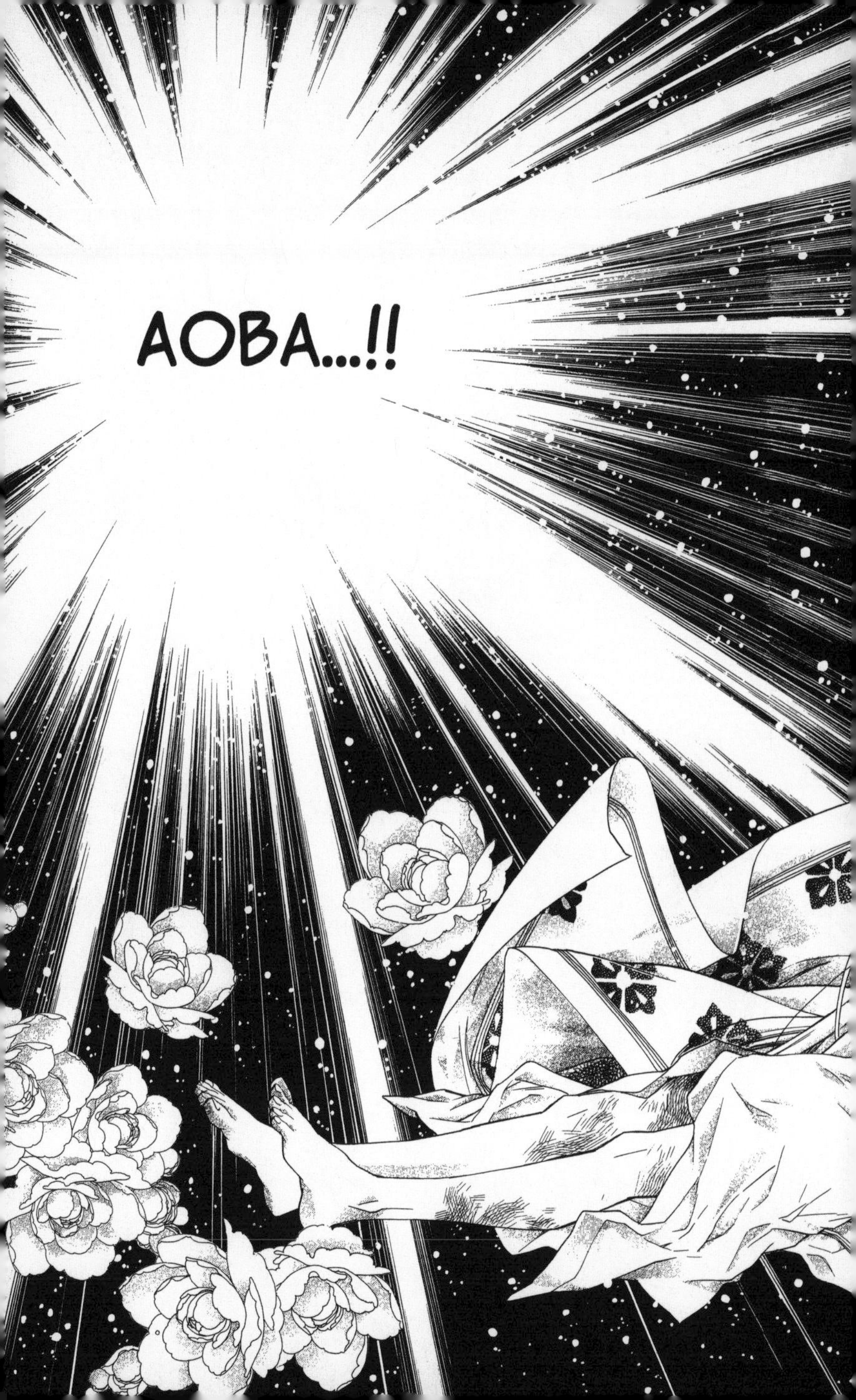
AOBA...!!

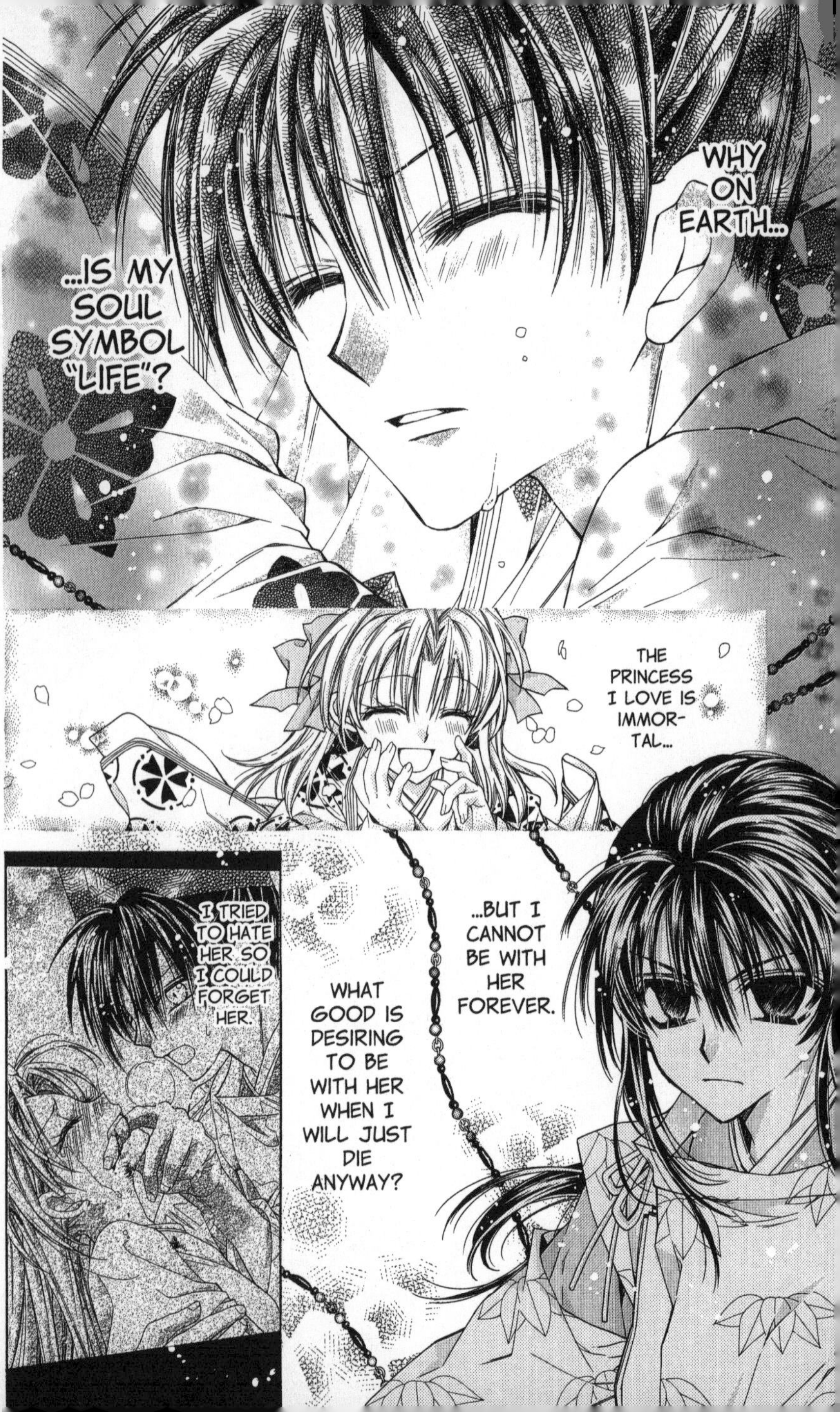
WHY ON EARTH...
...IS MY SOUL SYMBOL "LIFE"?
THE PRINCESS I LOVE IS IMMORTAL...
...BUT I CANNOT BE WITH HER FOREVER.
WHAT GOOD IS DESIRING TO BE WITH HER WHEN I WILL JUST DIE ANYWAY?
I TRIED TO HATE HER SO I COULD FORGET HER.

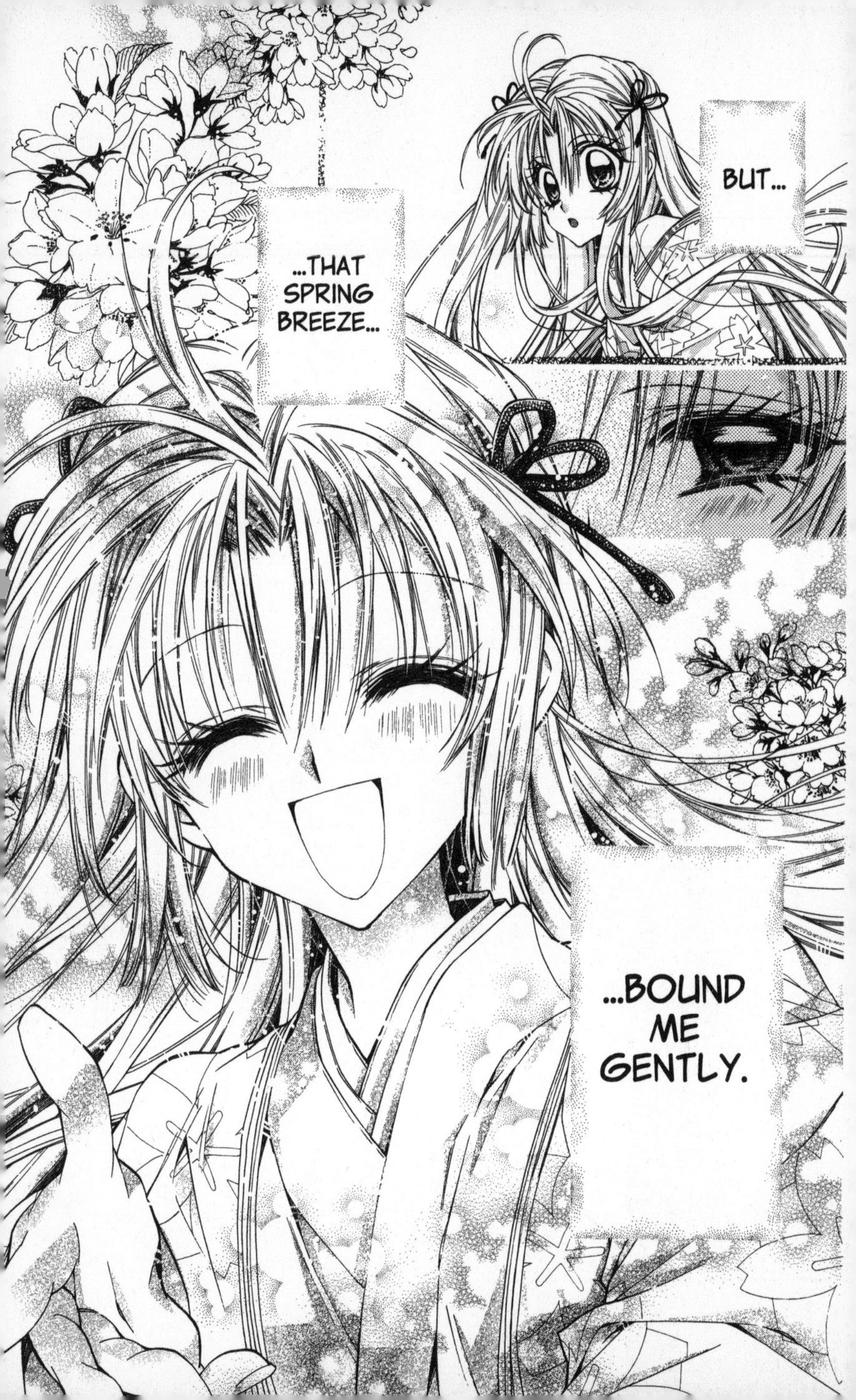
BUT...
...THAT SPRING BREEZE...
...BOUND ME GENTLY.

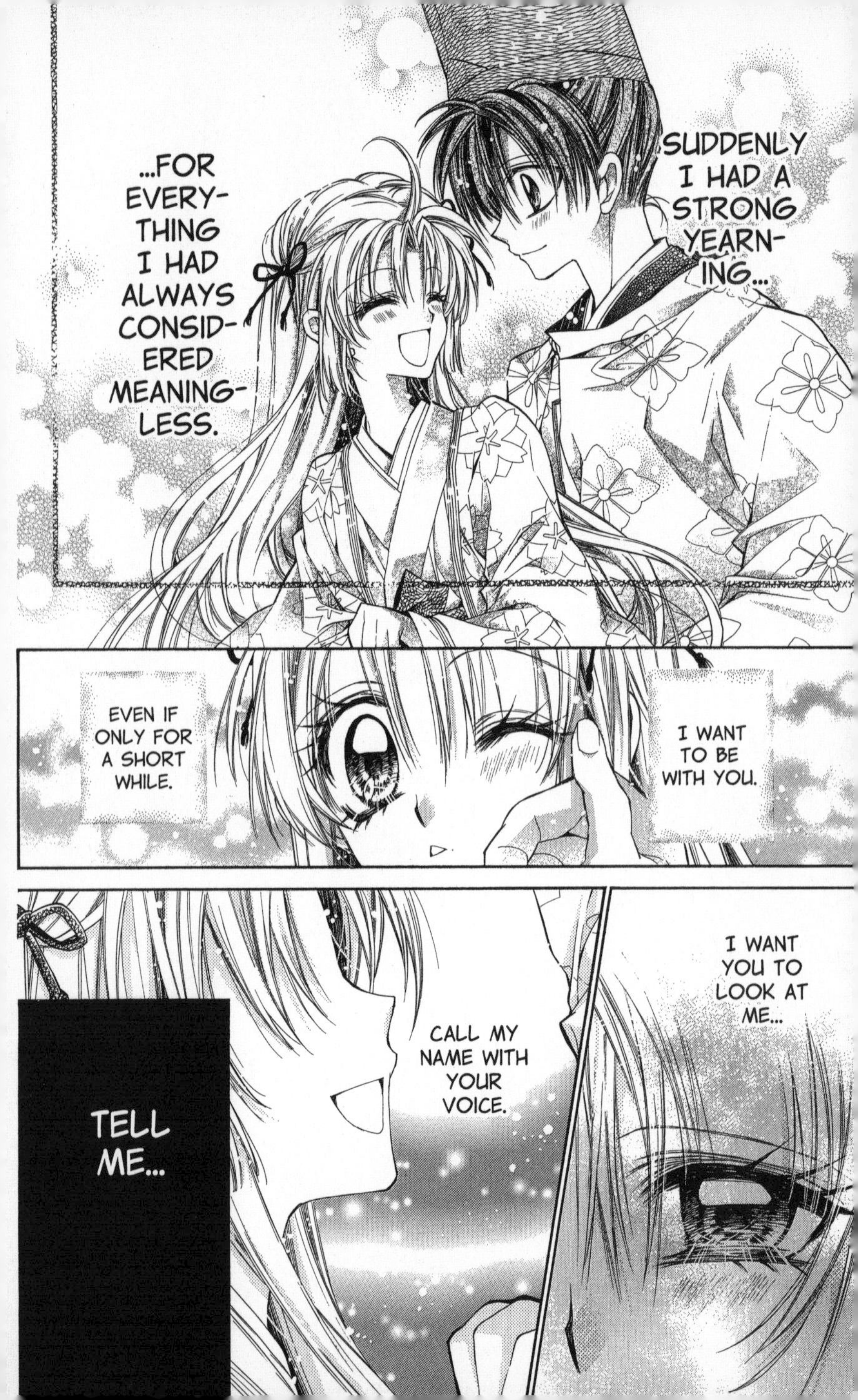
SUDDENLY I HAD A STRONG YEARNING...
...FOR EVERYTHING I HAD ALWAYS CONSIDERED MEANINGLESS.
I WANT TO BE WITH YOU.
EVEN IF ONLY FOR A SHORT WHILE.
I WANT YOU TO LOOK AT ME...
CALL MY NAME WITH YOUR VOICE.
TELL ME...

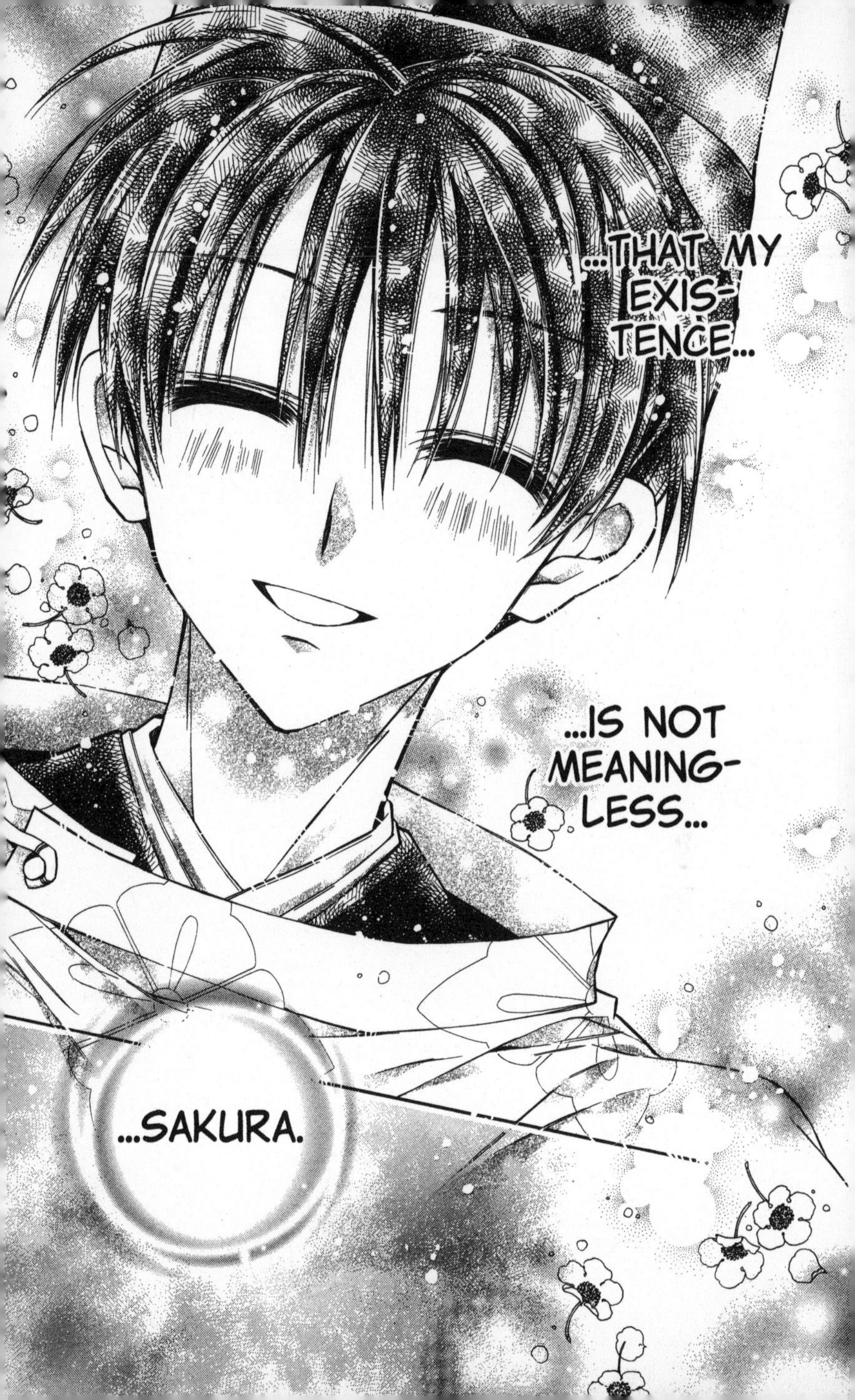
...THAT MY EXIS-TENCE...
...IS NOT MEANING-LESS...
...SAKURA.

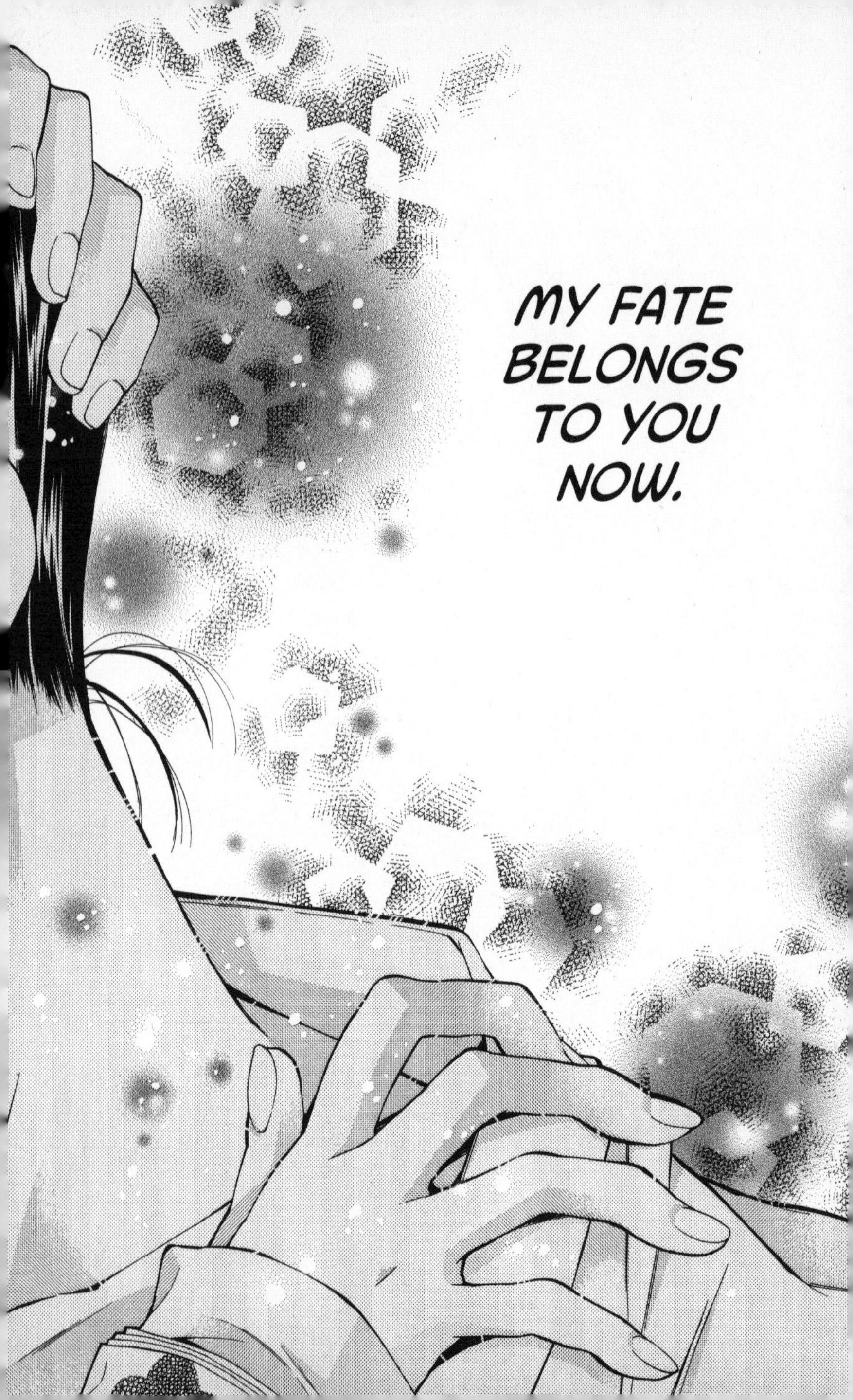
MY FATE BELONGS TO YOU NOW.

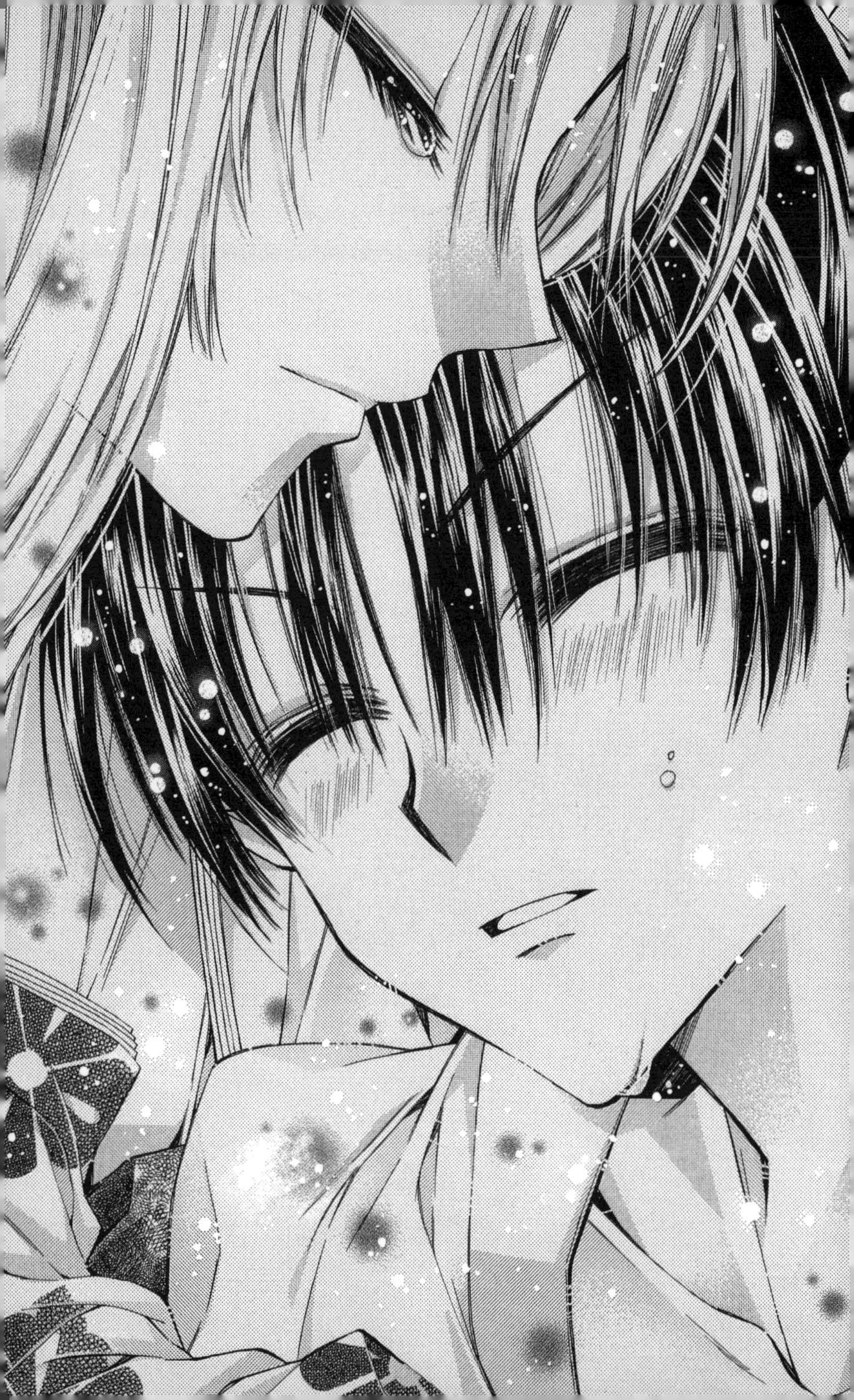

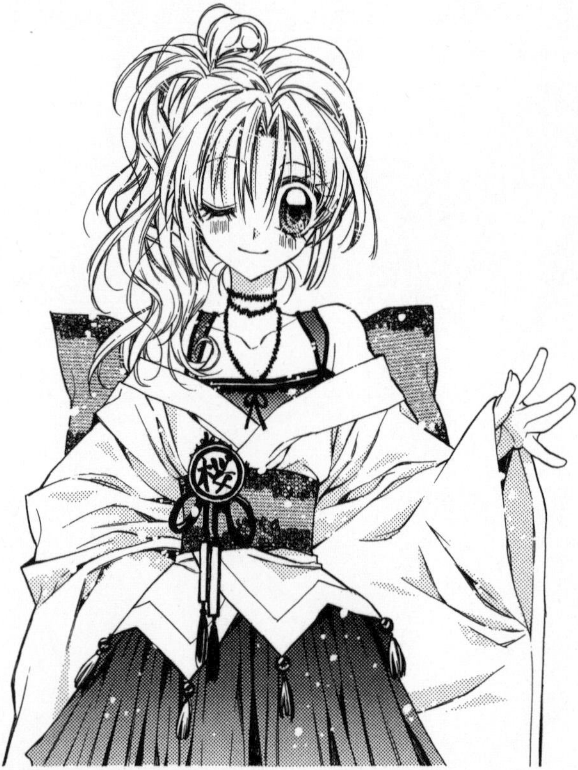
桜

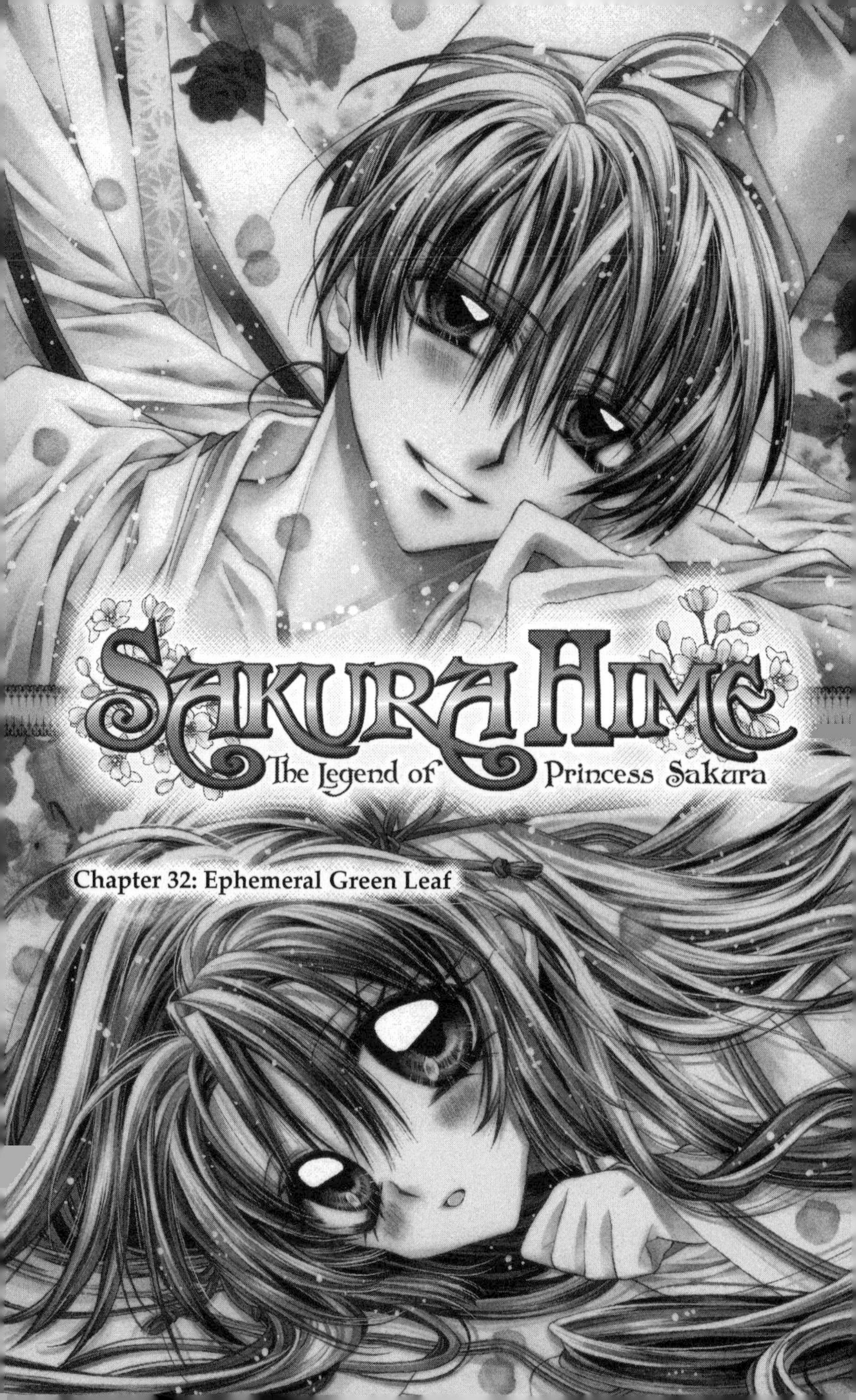
SAKURA HIME
The Legend of Princess Sakura
Chapter 32: Ephemeral Green Leaf

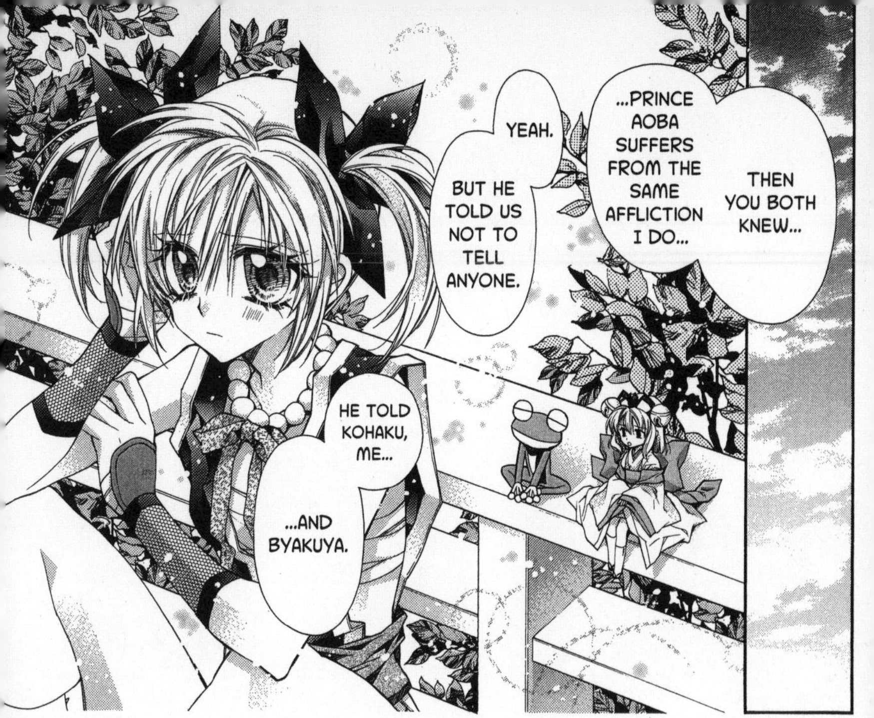
THEN YOU BOTH KNEW...
...PRINCE AOBA SUFFERS FROM THE SAME AFFLICTION I DO...
YEAH.
BUT HE TOLD US NOT TO TELL ANYONE.
HE TOLD KOHAKU, ME...
...AND BYAKUYA.

Chapter 32: Ephemeral Green Leaf

※I'm giving away the story.

After so long I got to draw Oumi and Ukyo in this chapter. It was so much fun!♥♥♥ (What? The Councilor? He was fun to draw too). Aoba seems so enlightened in this chapter, but I guess he's thought about it for a long time... PLIP

Aoba agrees without hesitation because he had already thought about it. I like it when Aoba and Sakura are getting along with a warm✿ feeling between them, so I enjoyed drawing the scene of them walking together.

The story starts to move rapidly again starting with this chapter. First, there's Shuri.✧ I must have been very happy he was in the chapter when I did the storyboard because my assistants told me how excited I was while I was working on the final draft. //// (Ah! Come to think of it, all my favorite characters have black hair!) I had Shuri wear new clothes and gave him a ponytail. What do you think? It's a pain to ink his hair... but I'll do it out of love.

You get to see you-know-who at the end. This was a chapter I had looked forward to doing for a long time. Enjoy!

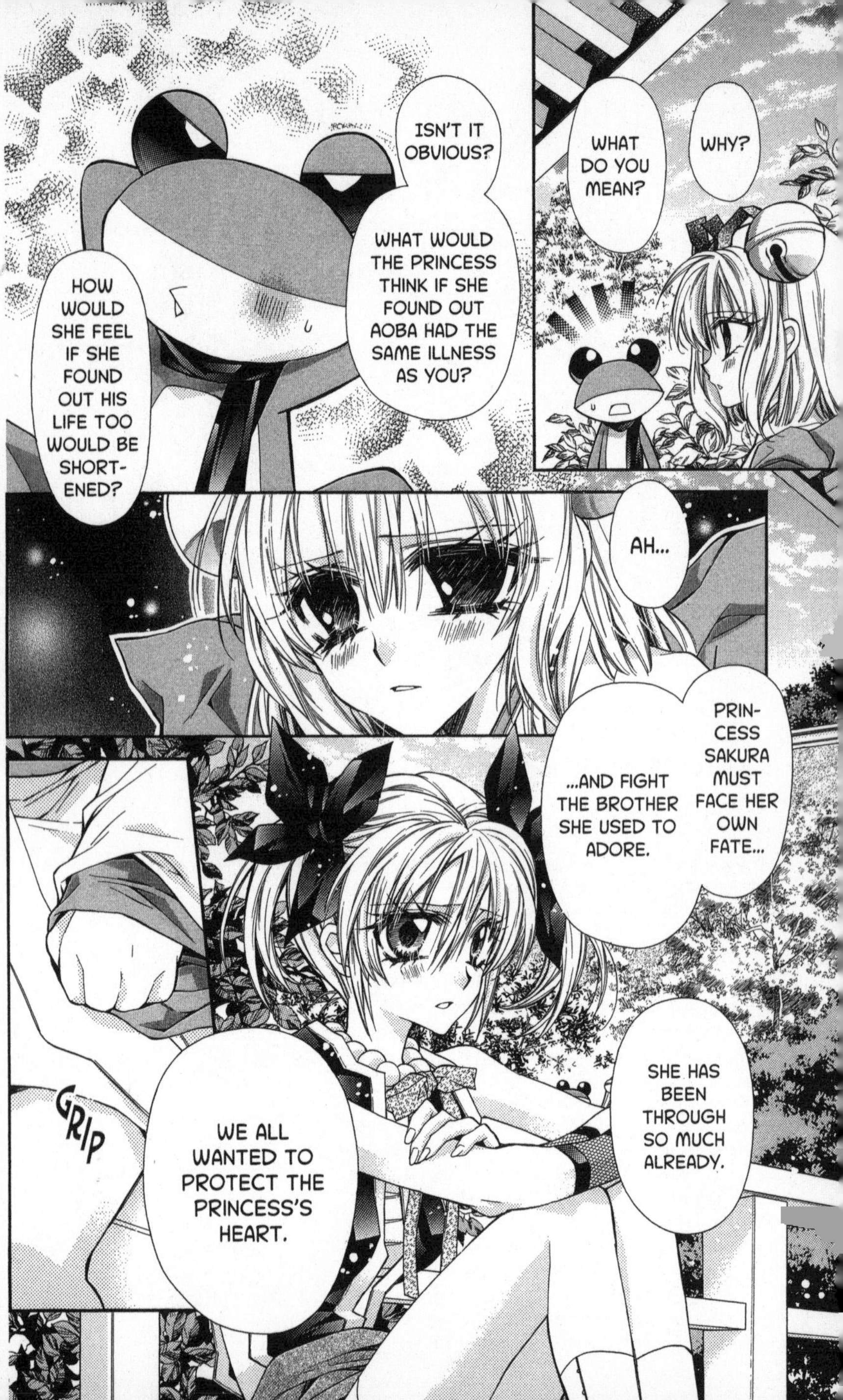
WHY?
WHAT DO YOU MEAN?
ISN'T IT OBVIOUS?
WHAT WOULD THE PRINCESS THINK IF SHE FOUND OUT AOBA HAD THE SAME ILLNESS AS YOU?
HOW WOULD SHE FEEL IF SHE FOUND OUT HIS LIFE TOO WOULD BE SHORT-ENED?
AH...
PRIN-CESS SAKURA MUST FACE HER OWN FATE...
...AND FIGHT THE BROTHER SHE USED TO ADORE.
SHE HAS BEEN THROUGH SO MUCH ALREADY.
WE ALL WANTED TO PROTECT THE PRINCESS'S HEART.
GRIP

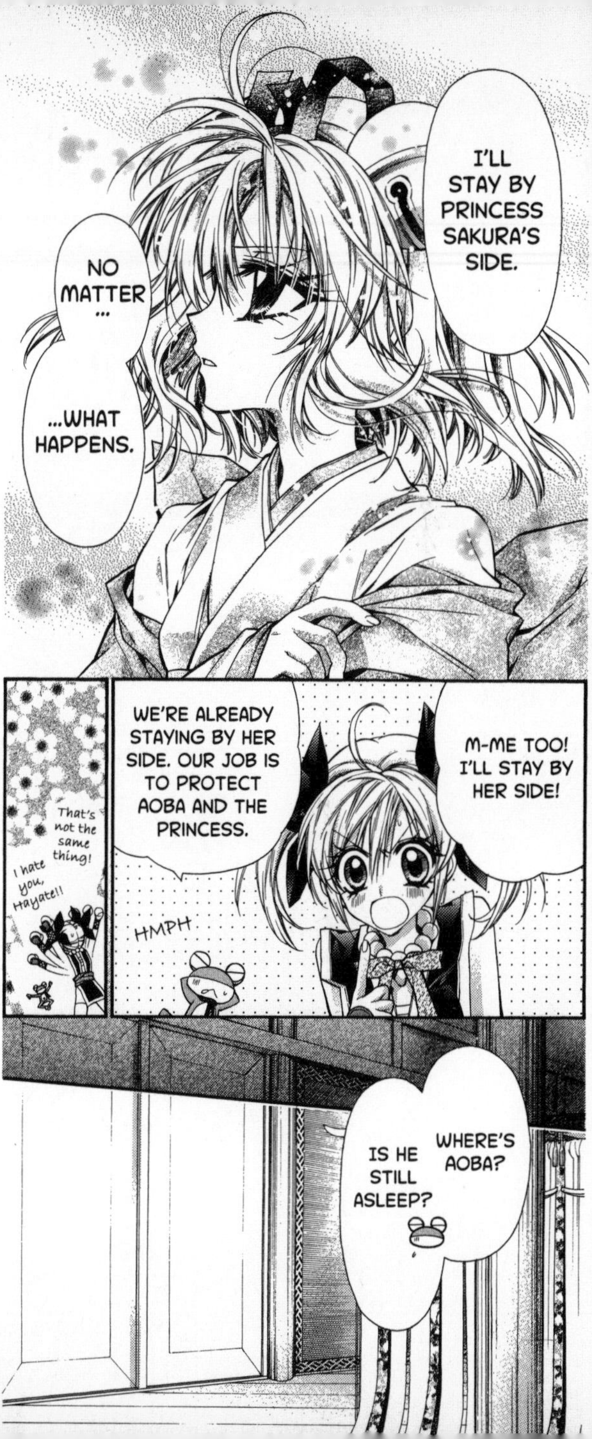
I'LL STAY BY PRINCESS SAKURA'S SIDE.
NO MATTER ...
...WHAT HAPPENS.
M-ME TOO! I'LL STAY BY HER SIDE!
WE'RE ALREADY STAYING BY HER SIDE. OUR JOB IS TO PROTECT AOBA AND THE PRINCESS.
HMPH
That's not the same thing!
I hate you, Hayate!!
WHERE'S AOBA?
IS HE STILL ASLEEP?

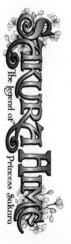

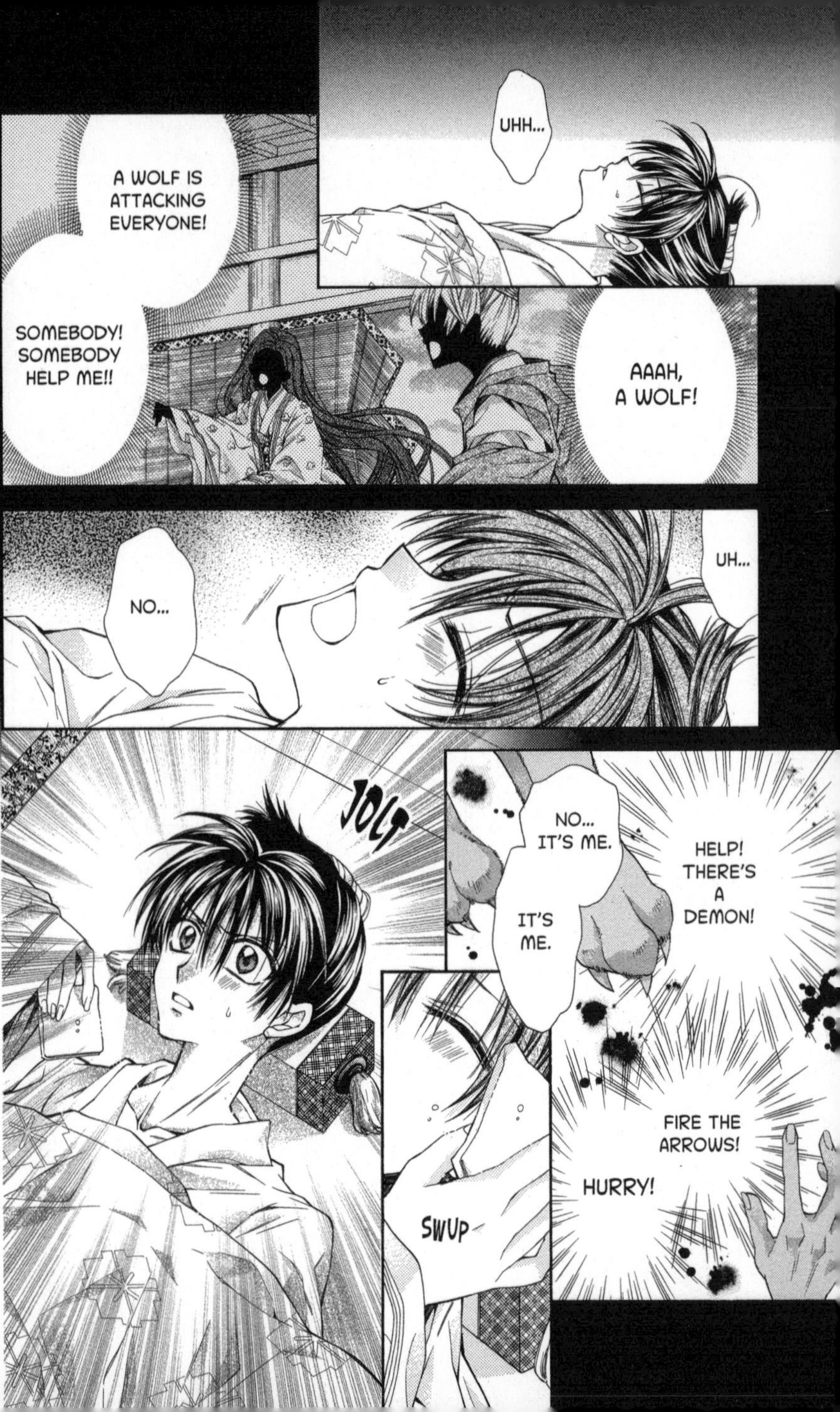
UHH...
AAAH, A WOLF!
A WOLF IS ATTACKING EVERYONE!
SOMEBODY! SOMEBODY HELP ME!!
UH...
NO...
HELP! THERE'S A DEMON!
NO... IT'S ME.
IT'S ME.
FIRE THE ARROWS!
HURRY!
SWUP
JOLT

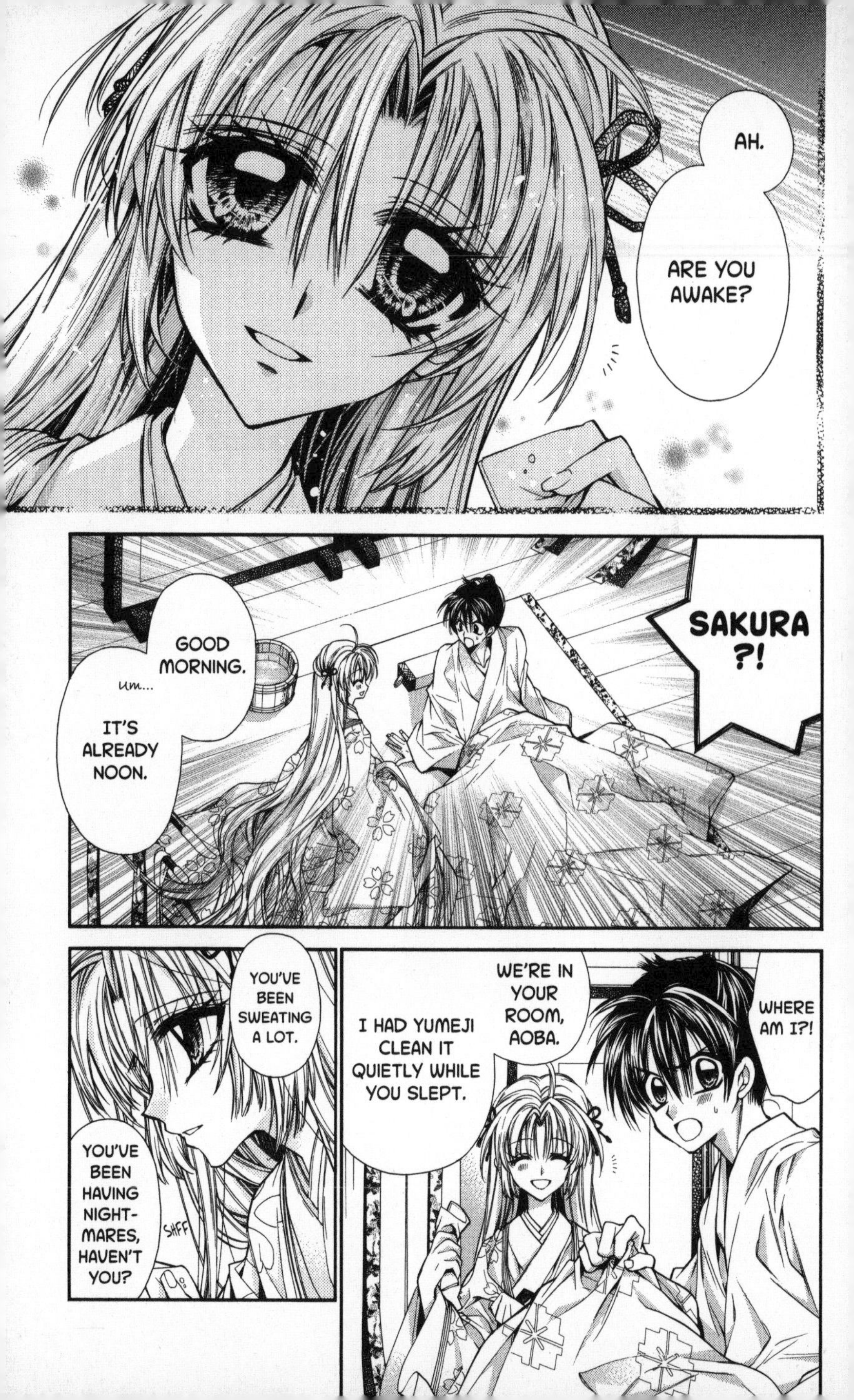
AH.
ARE YOU AWAKE?
SAKURA ?!
GOOD MORNING.
um...
IT'S ALREADY NOON.
WHERE AM I?!
WE'RE IN YOUR ROOM, AOBA.
I HAD YUMEJI CLEAN IT QUIETLY WHILE YOU SLEPT.
YOU'VE BEEN SWEATING A LOT.
YOU'VE BEEN HAVING NIGHT-MARES, HAVEN'T YOU?
SHFF

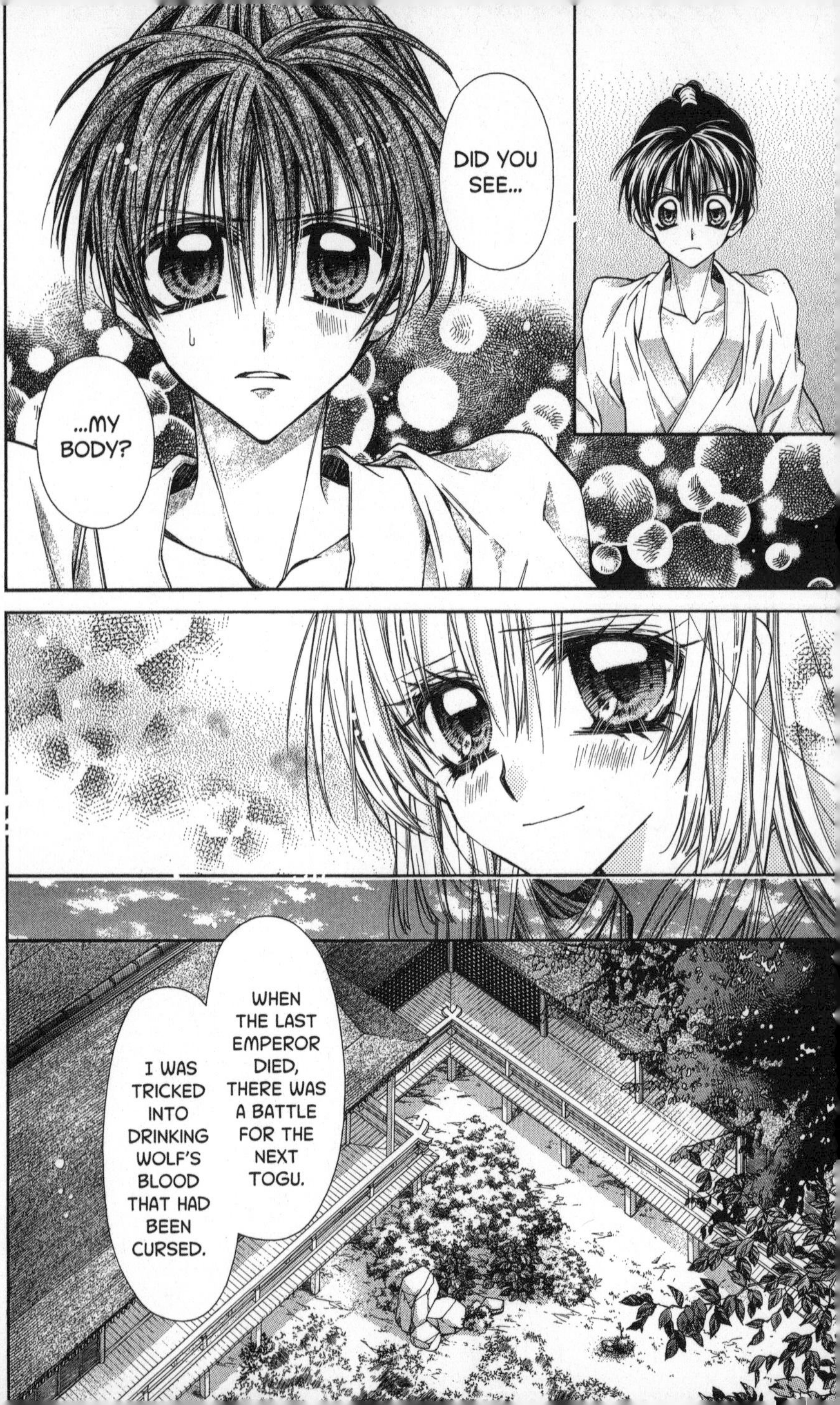
DID YOU SEE...
...MY BODY?
WHEN THE LAST EMPEROR DIED, THERE WAS A BATTLE FOR THE NEXT TOGU.
I WAS TRICKED INTO DRINKING WOLF'S BLOOD THAT HAD BEEN CURSED.

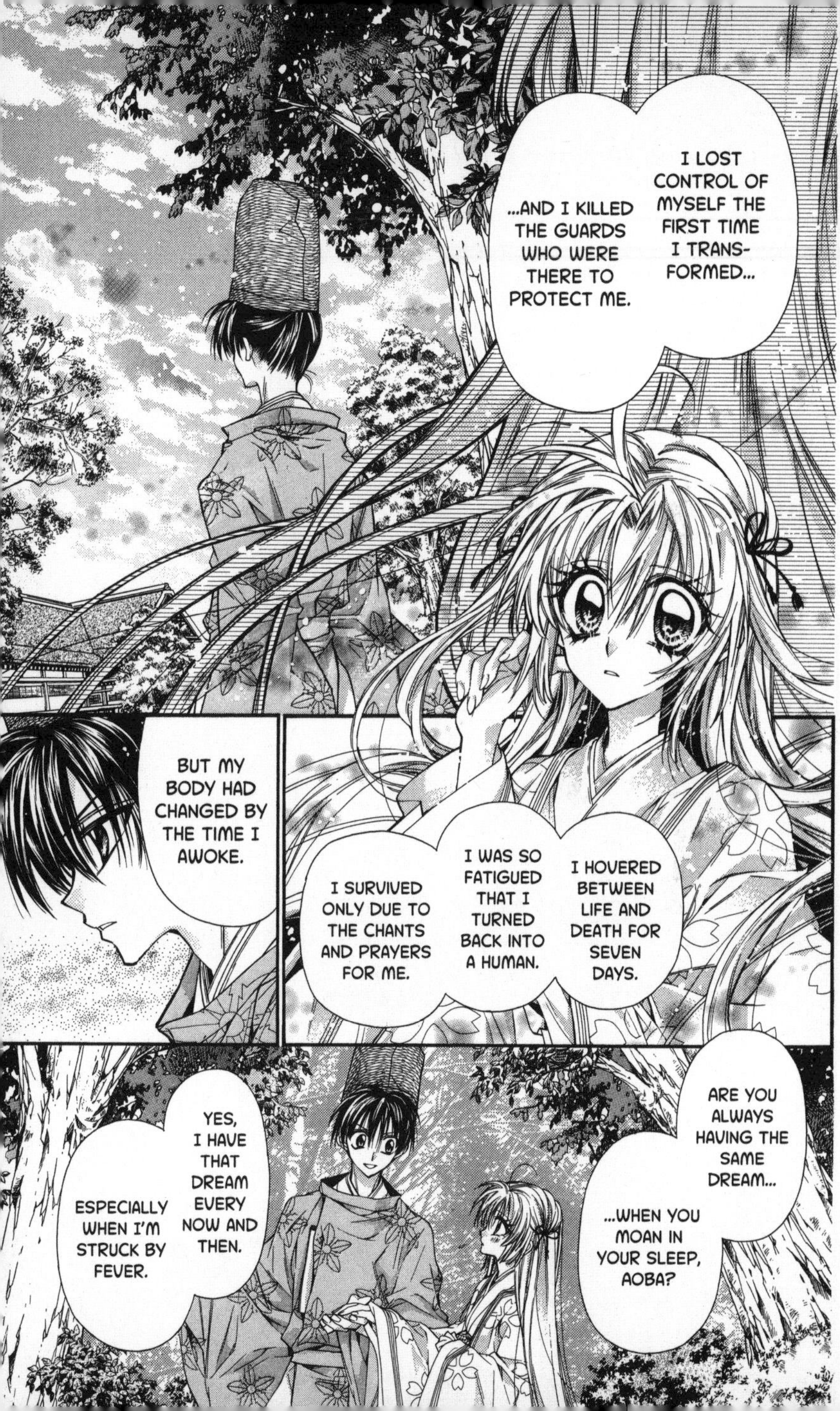
I LOST CONTROL OF MYSELF THE FIRST TIME I TRANS-FORMED...
...AND I KILLED THE GUARDS WHO WERE THERE TO PROTECT ME.
I HOVERED BETWEEN LIFE AND DEATH FOR SEVEN DAYS.
I WAS SO FATIGUED THAT I TURNED BACK INTO A HUMAN.
I SURVIVED ONLY DUE TO THE CHANTS AND PRAYERS FOR ME.
BUT MY BODY HAD CHANGED BY THE TIME I AWOKE.
ARE YOU ALWAYS HAVING THE SAME DREAM...
...WHEN YOU MOAN IN YOUR SLEEP, AOBA?
YES, I HAVE THAT DREAM EVERY NOW AND THEN.
ESPECIALLY WHEN I'M STRUCK BY FEVER.

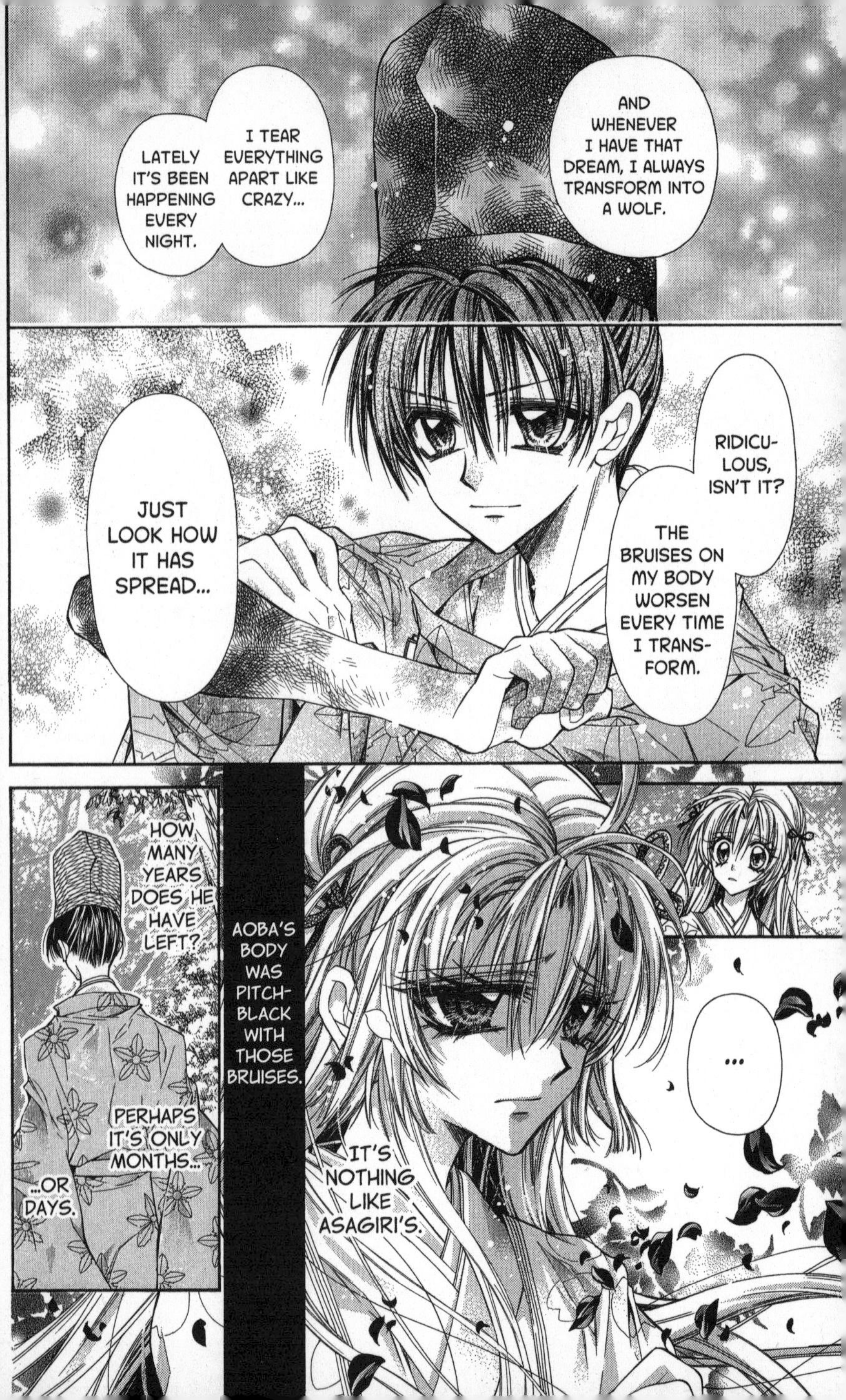
AND WHENEVER I HAVE THAT DREAM, I ALWAYS TRANSFORM INTO A WOLF.
I TEAR EVERYTHING APART LIKE CRAZY...
LATELY IT'S BEEN HAPPENING EVERY NIGHT.
RIDICU-LOUS, ISN'T IT?
THE BRUISES ON MY BODY WORSEN EVERY TIME I TRANS-FORM.
JUST LOOK HOW IT HAS SPREAD...
...
IT'S NOTHING LIKE ASAGIRI'S.
AOBA'S BODY WAS PITCH-BLACK WITH THOSE BRUISES.
HOW MANY YEARS DOES HE HAVE LEFT?
PERHAPS IT'S ONLY MONTHS...
...OR DAYS.

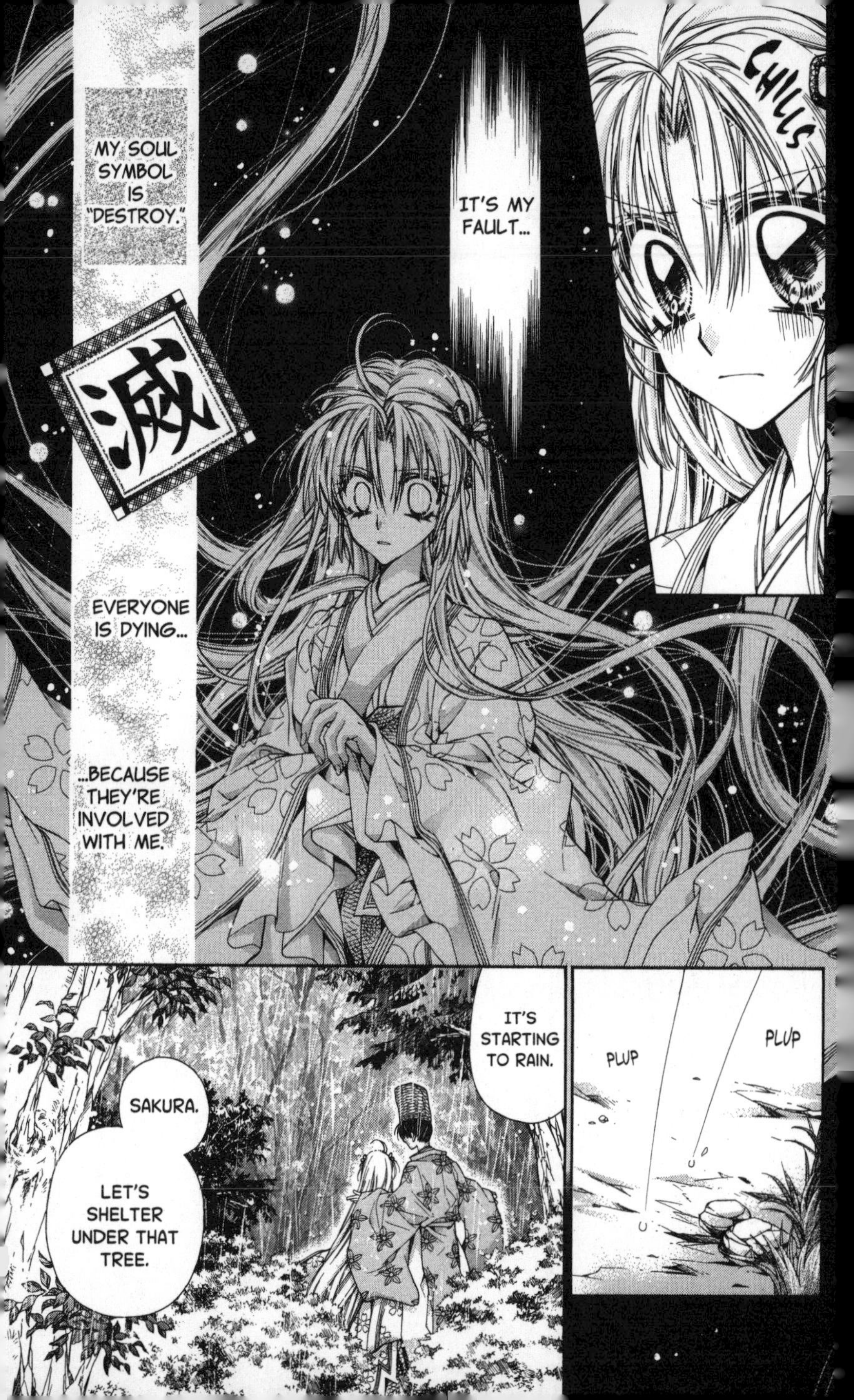
CHILLS
IT'S MY FAULT...
MY SOUL SYMBOL IS "DESTROY."
滅
EVERYONE IS DYING...
...BECAUSE THEY'RE INVOLVED WITH ME.
PLUP
PLUP
IT'S STARTING TO RAIN.
SAKURA.
LET'S SHELTER UNDER THAT TREE.

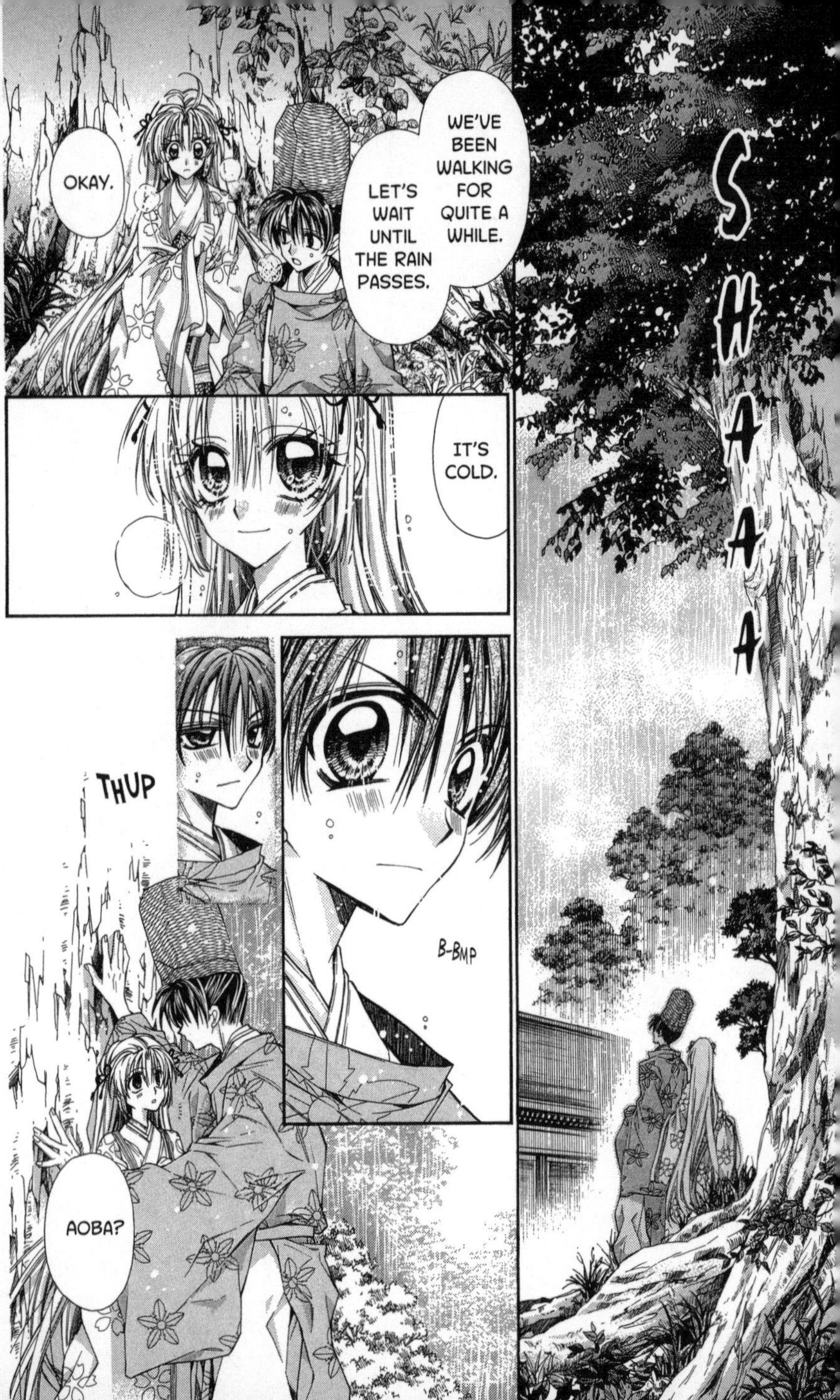
SHAAAA
WE'VE BEEN WALKING FOR QUITE A WHILE.
LET'S WAIT UNTIL THE RAIN PASSES.
OKAY.
IT'S COLD.
B-BMP
THUP
AOBA?

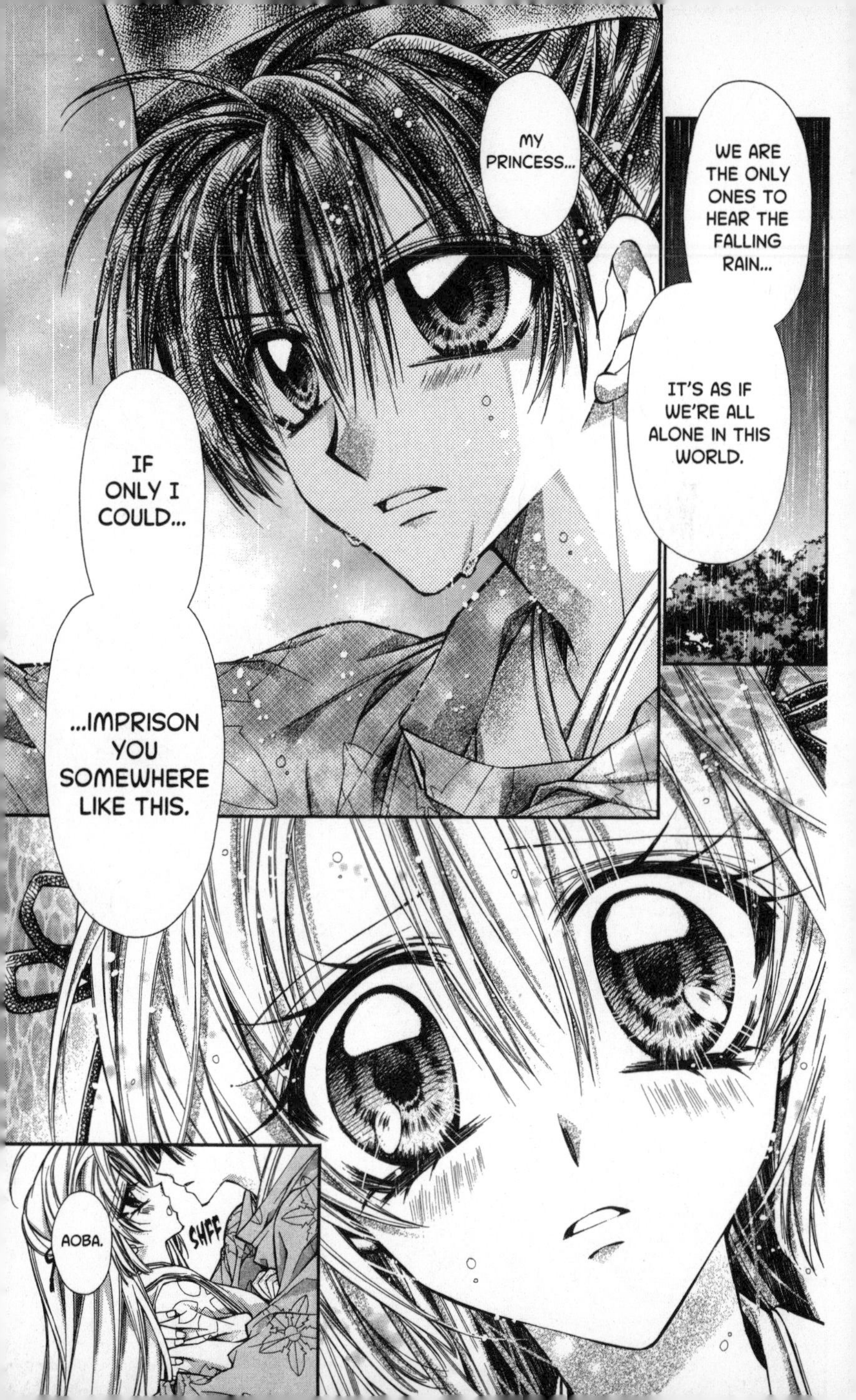
MY PRINCESS...
WE ARE THE ONLY ONES TO HEAR THE FALLING RAIN...
IT'S AS IF WE'RE ALL ALONE IN THIS WORLD.
IF ONLY I COULD...
...IMPRISON YOU SOMEWHERE LIKE THIS.
SHFF
AOBA.

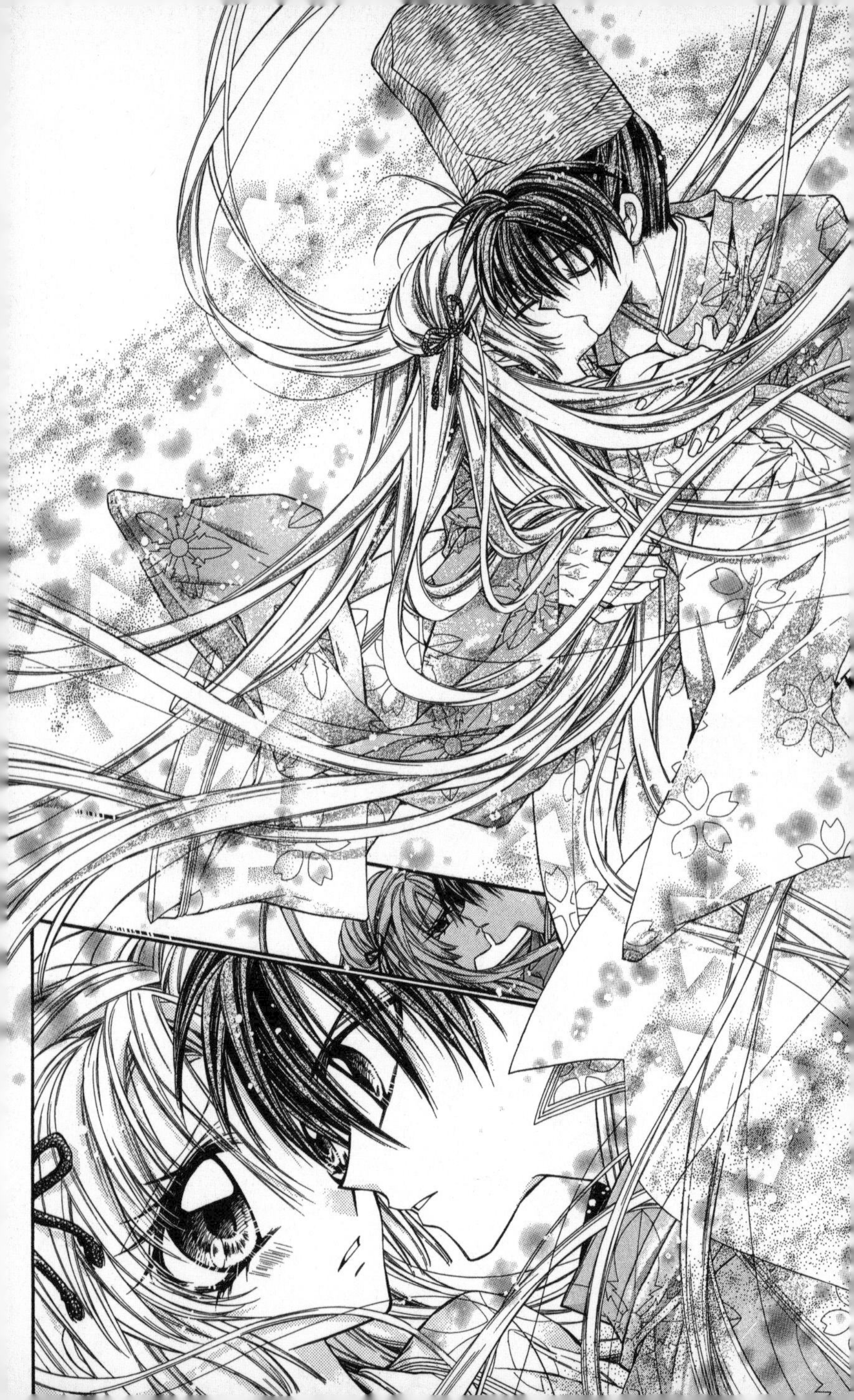

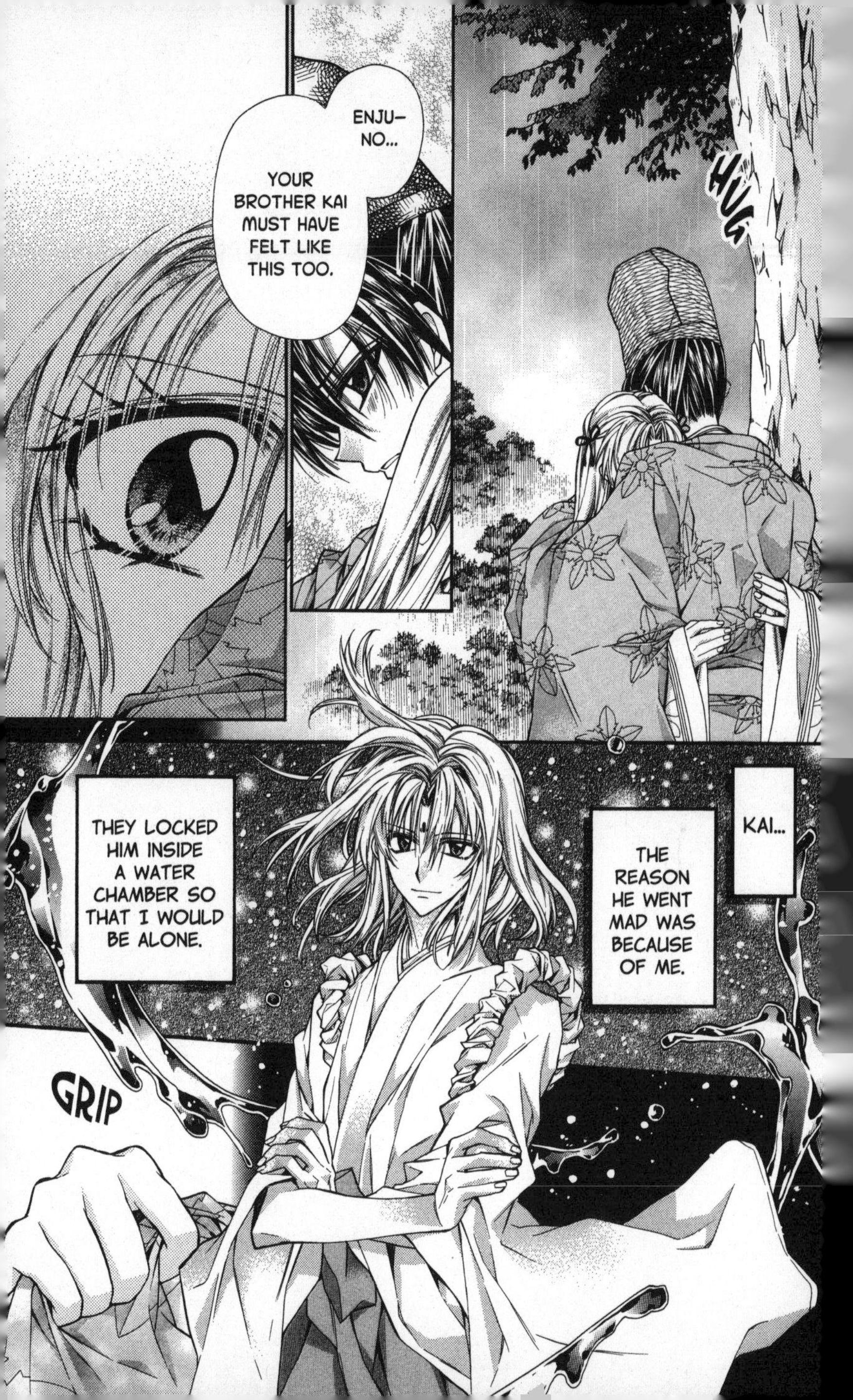
HUG
ENJU-NO...
YOUR BROTHER KAI MUST HAVE FELT LIKE THIS TOO.
KAI...
THE REASON HE WENT MAD WAS BECAUSE OF ME.
THEY LOCKED HIM INSIDE A WATER CHAMBER SO THAT I WOULD BE ALONE.
GRIP

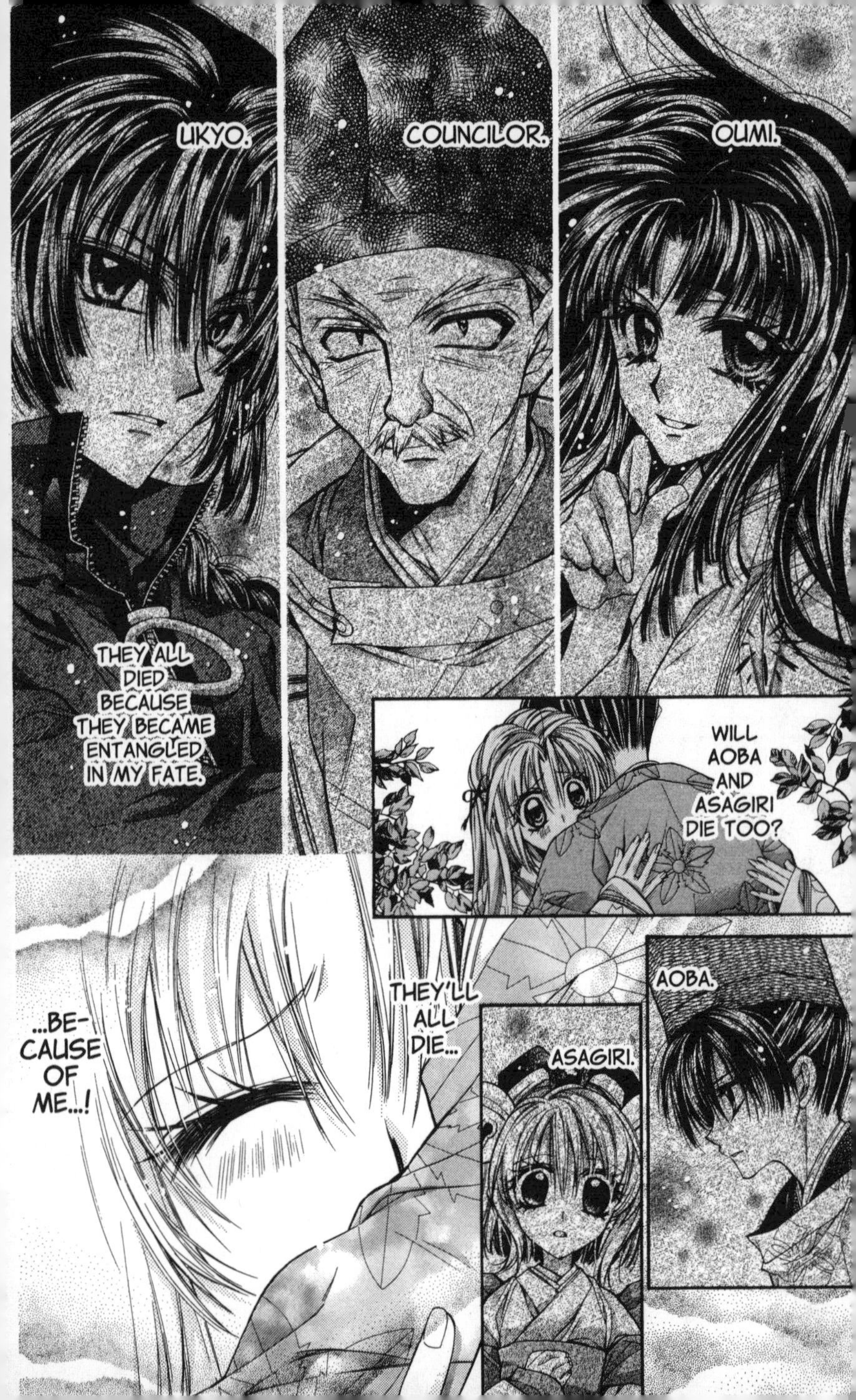
OUMI.
COUNCILOR.
UKYO.
THEY ALL DIED BECAUSE THEY BECAME ENTANGLED IN MY FATE.
WILL AOBA AND ASAGIRI DIE TOO?
AOBA.
ASAGIRI.
THEY'LL ALL DIE...
...BE-CAUSE OF ME...!

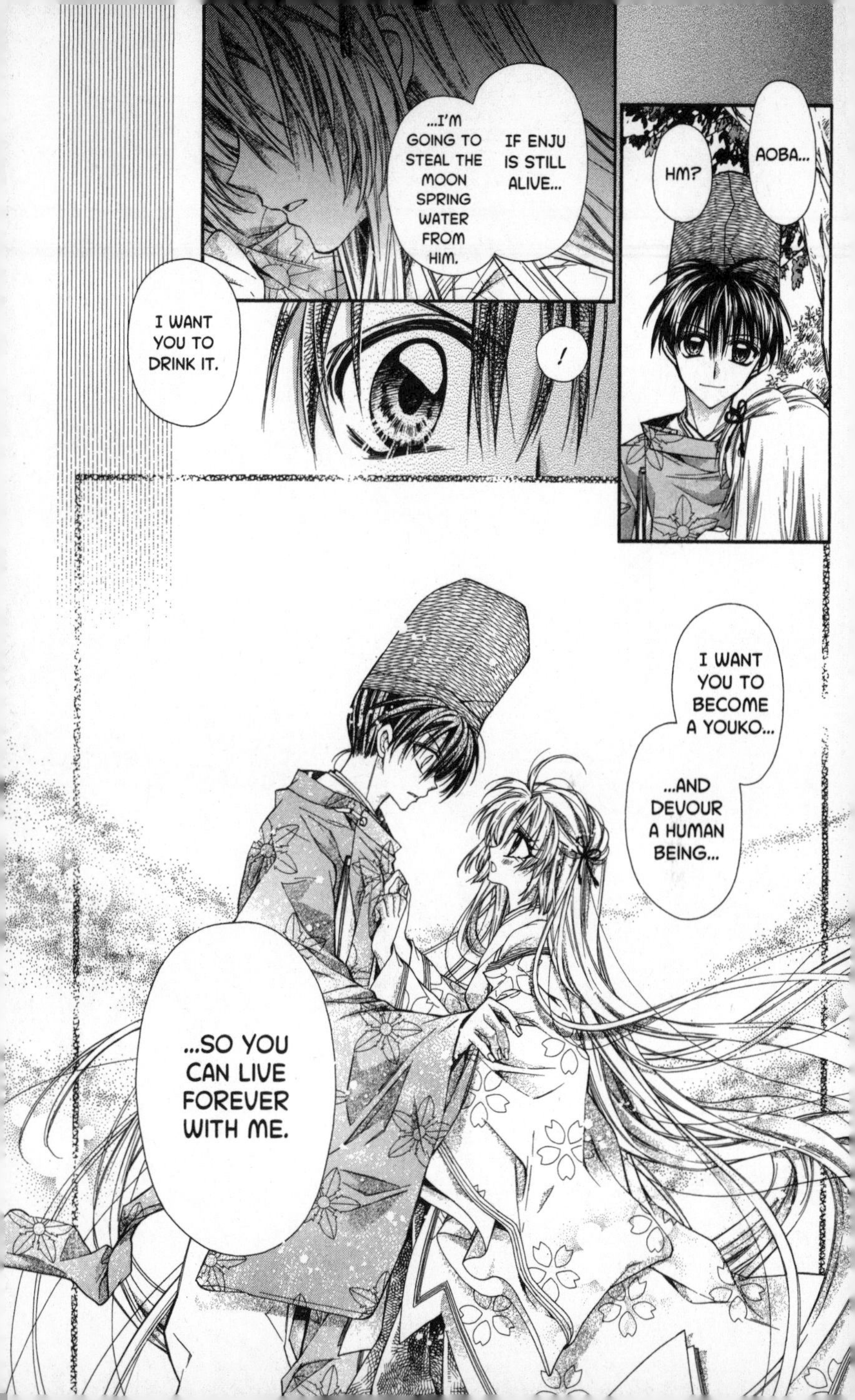
AOBA...
HM?
IF ENJU IS STILL ALIVE...
...I'M GOING TO STEAL THE MOON SPRING WATER FROM HIM.
!
I WANT YOU TO DRINK IT.
I WANT YOU TO BECOME A YOUKO...
...AND DEVOUR A HUMAN BEING...
...SO YOU CAN LIVE FOREVER WITH ME.

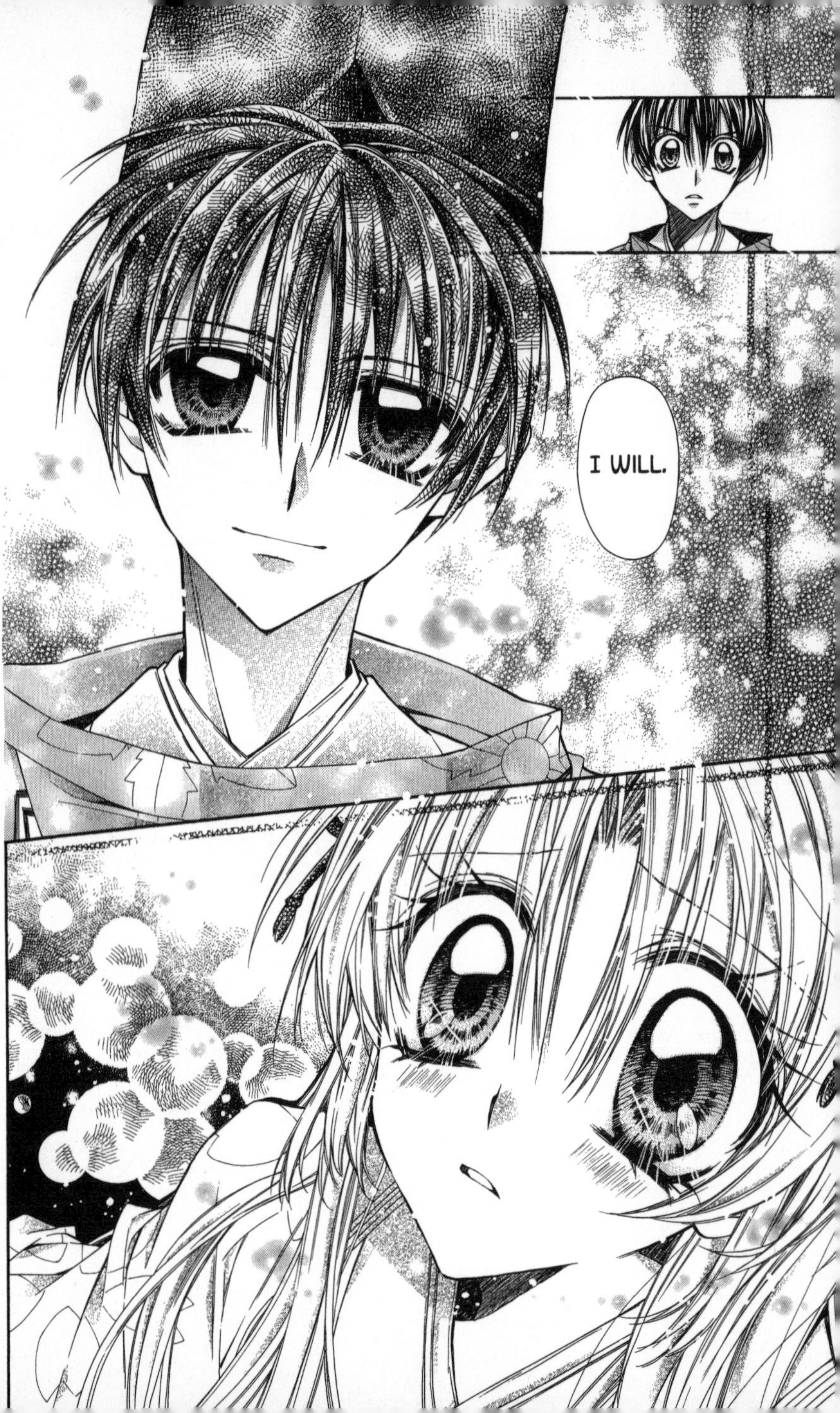
I WILL.

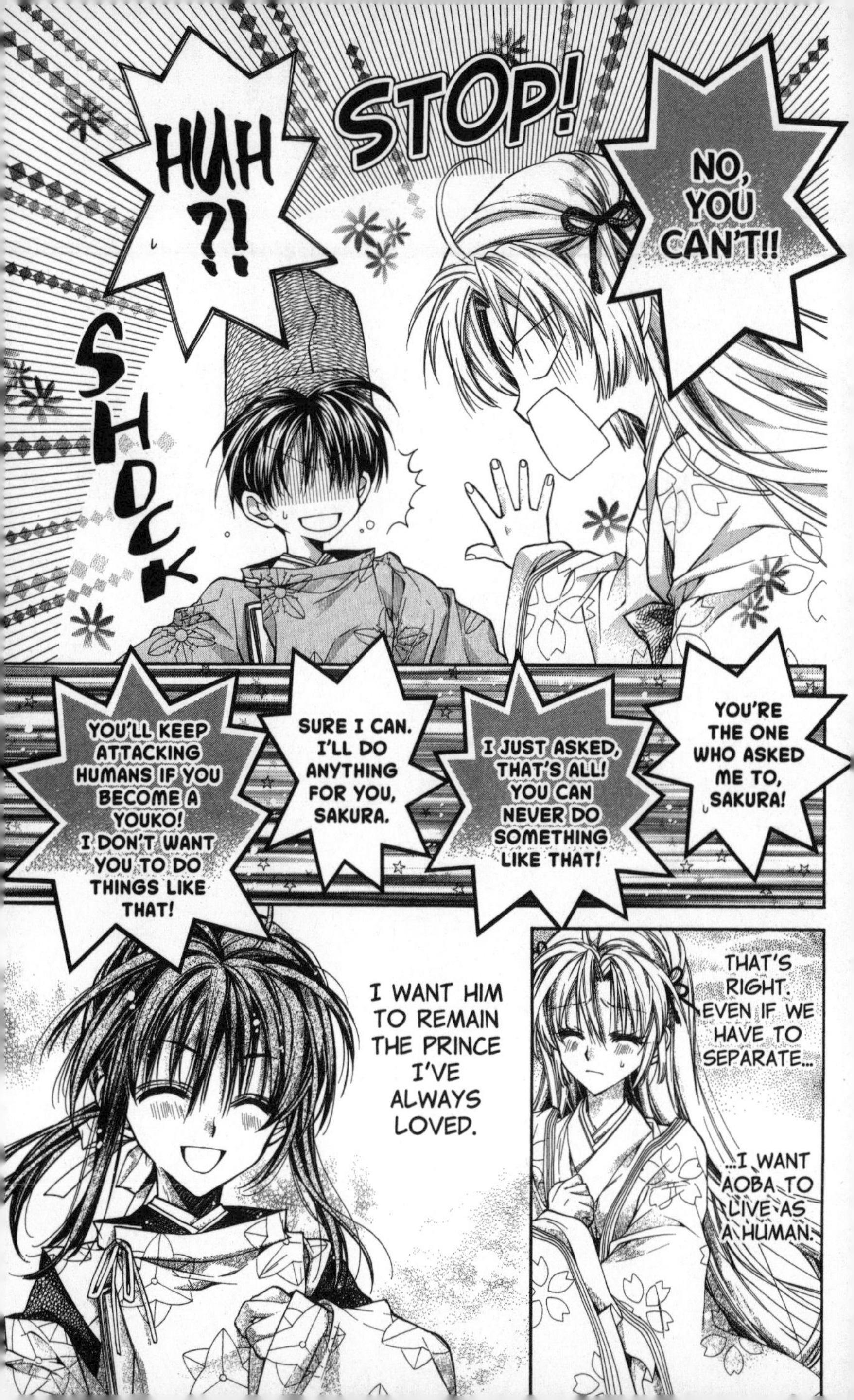
NO, YOU CAN'T!!
STOP!
HUH ?!
SHOCK
YOU'RE THE ONE WHO ASKED ME TO, SAKURA!
I JUST ASKED, THAT'S ALL! YOU CAN NEVER DO SOMETHING LIKE THAT!
SURE I CAN. I'LL DO ANYTHING FOR YOU, SAKURA.
YOU'LL KEEP ATTACKING HUMANS IF YOU BECOME A YOUKO! I DON'T WANT YOU TO DO THINGS LIKE THAT!
THAT'S RIGHT. EVEN IF WE HAVE TO SEPARATE...
...I WANT AOBA TO LIVE AS A HUMAN.
I WANT HIM TO REMAIN THE PRINCE I'VE ALWAYS LOVED.

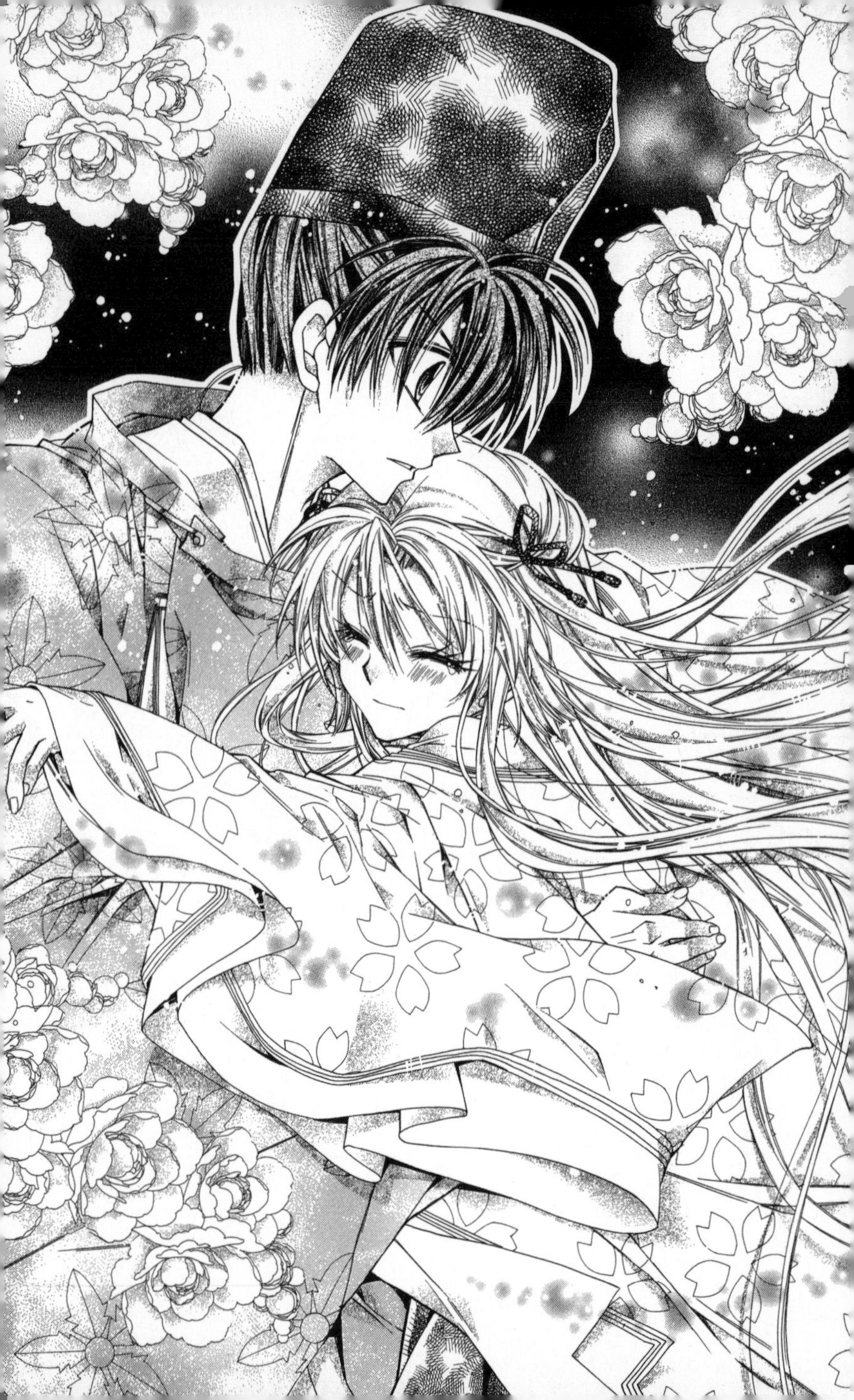

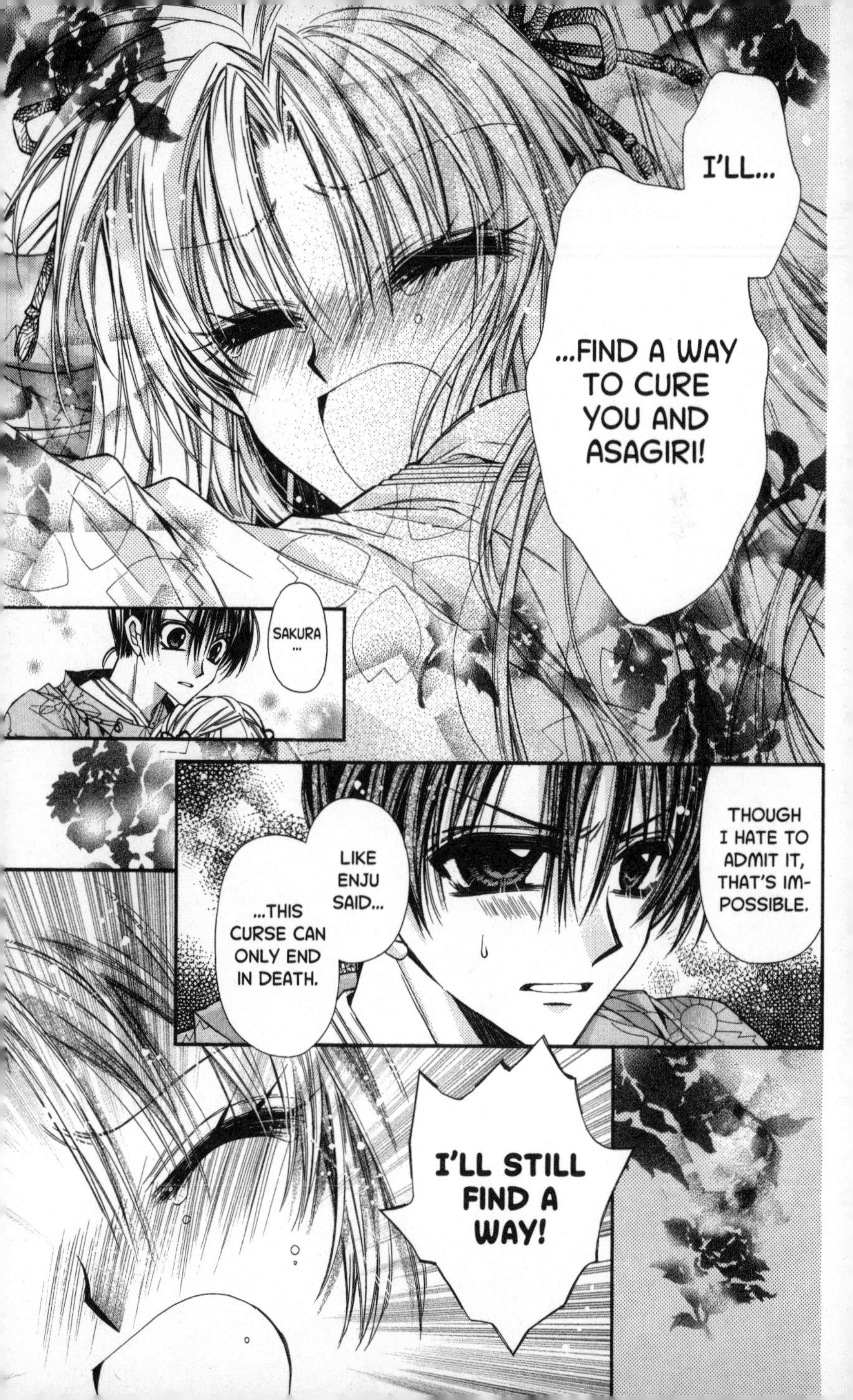
I'LL...
...FIND A WAY TO CURE YOU AND ASAGIRI!
SAKURA...
THOUGH I HATE TO ADMIT IT, THAT'S IM-POSSIBLE.
LIKE ENJU SAID...
...THIS CURSE CAN ONLY END IN DEATH.
I'LL STILL FIND A WAY!

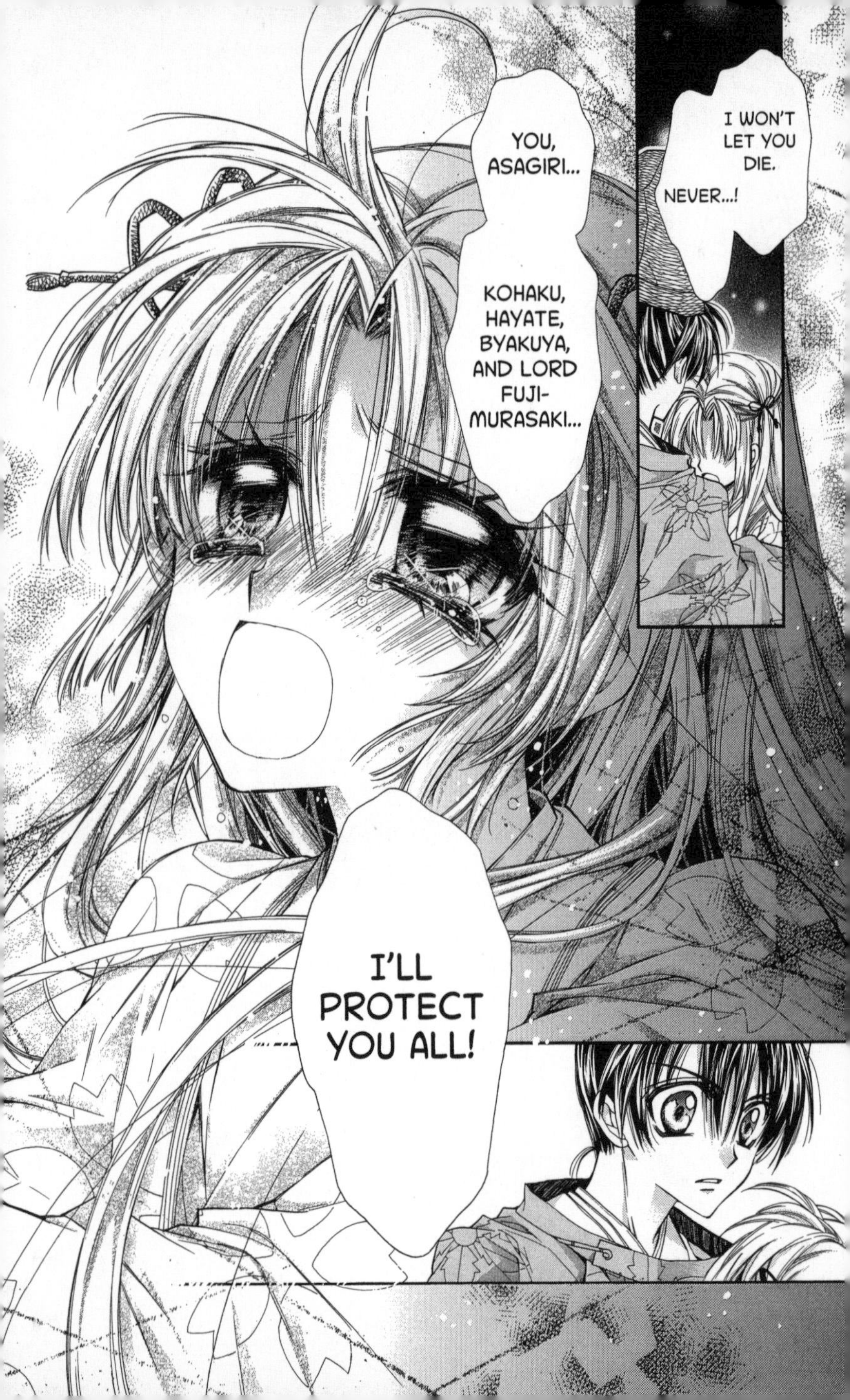
I WON'T LET YOU DIE.
NEVER...!
YOU, ASAGIRI...
KOHAKU, HAYATE, BYAKUYA, AND LORD FUJI-MURASAKI...
I'LL PROTECT YOU ALL!

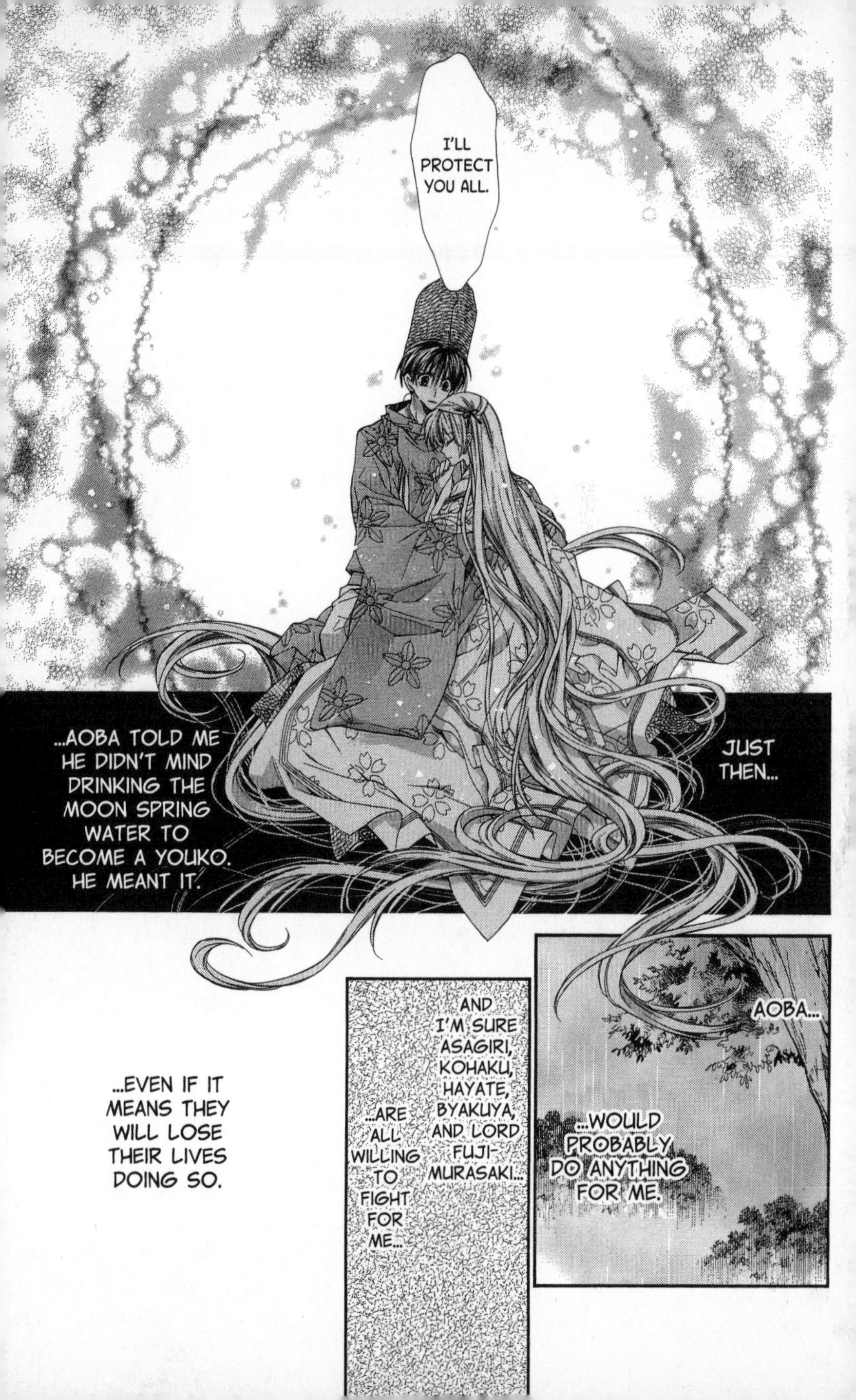
I'LL PROTECT YOU ALL.
JUST THEN...
...AOBA TOLD ME HE DIDN'T MIND DRINKING THE MOON SPRING WATER TO BECOME A YOUKO. HE MEANT IT.
AOBA...
...WOULD PROBABLY DO ANYTHING FOR ME.
AND I'M SURE ASAGIRI, KOHAKU, HAYATE, BYAKUYA, AND LORD FUJI-MURASAKI...
...ARE ALL WILLING TO FIGHT FOR ME...
...EVEN IF IT MEANS THEY WILL LOSE THEIR LIVES DOING SO.

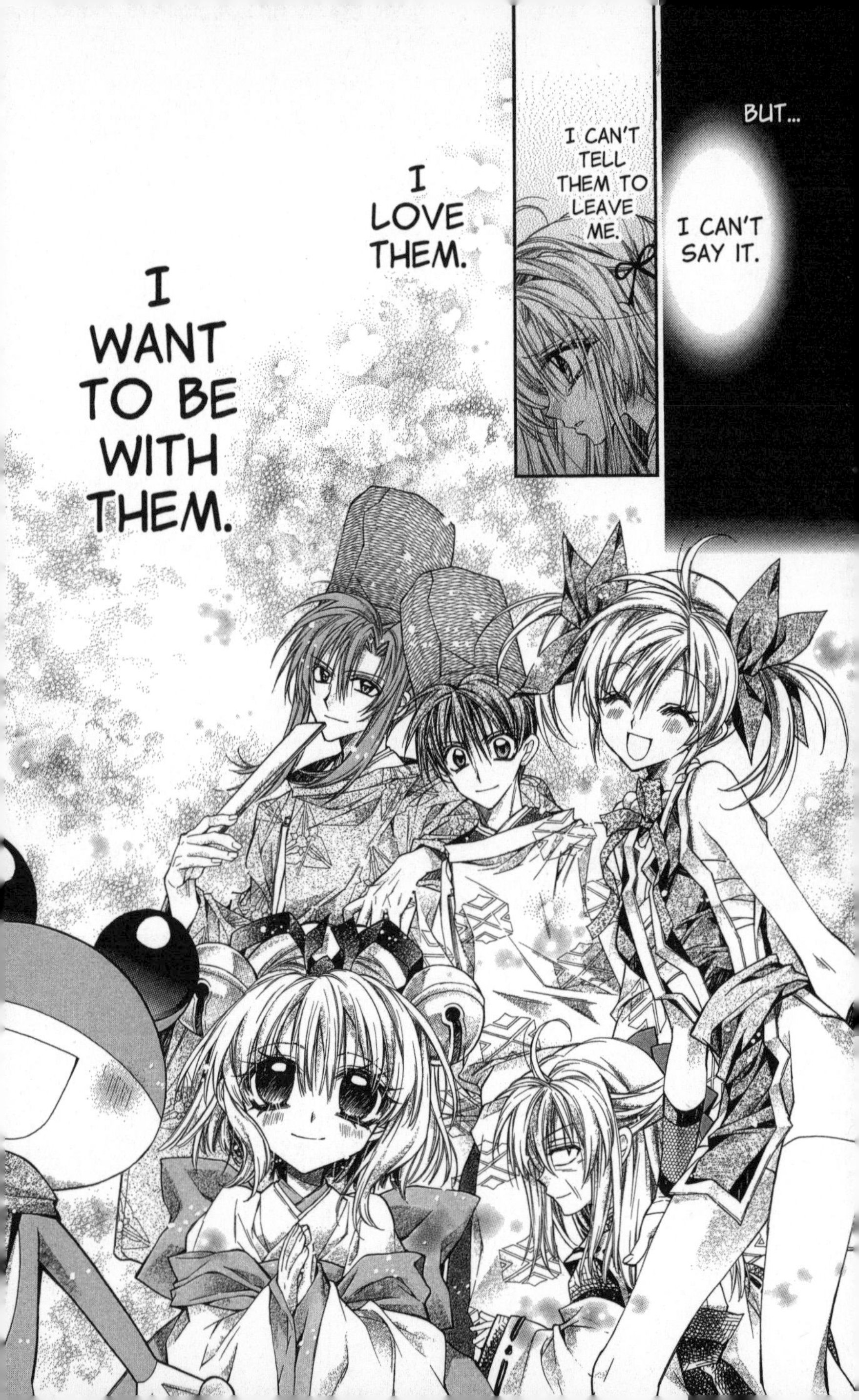
BUT...
I CAN'T SAY IT.
I CAN'T TELL THEM TO LEAVE ME.
I LOVE THEM.
I WANT TO BE WITH THEM.

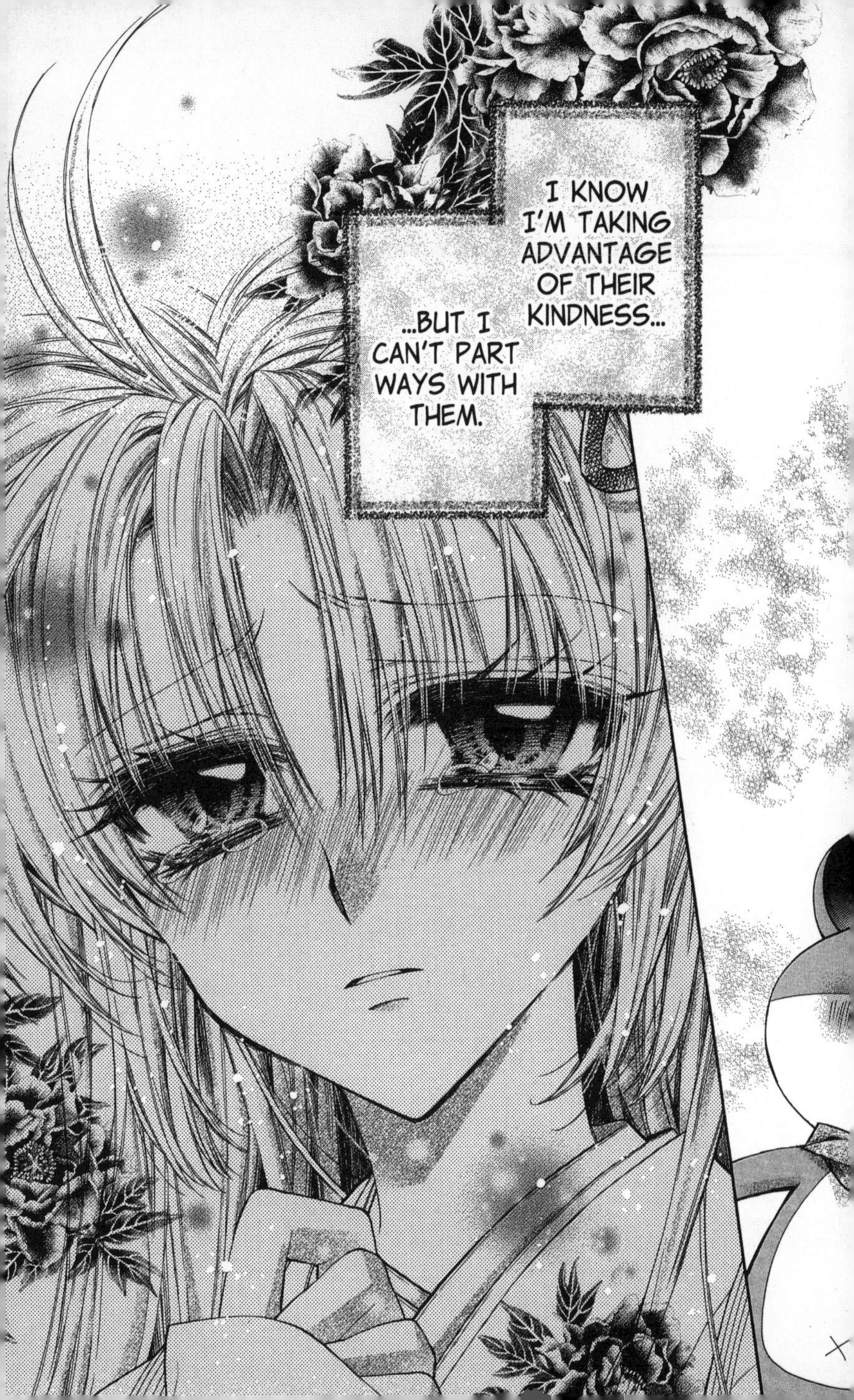
I KNOW I'M TAKING ADVANTAGE OF THEIR KINDNESS...
...BUT I CAN'T PART WAYS WITH THEM.

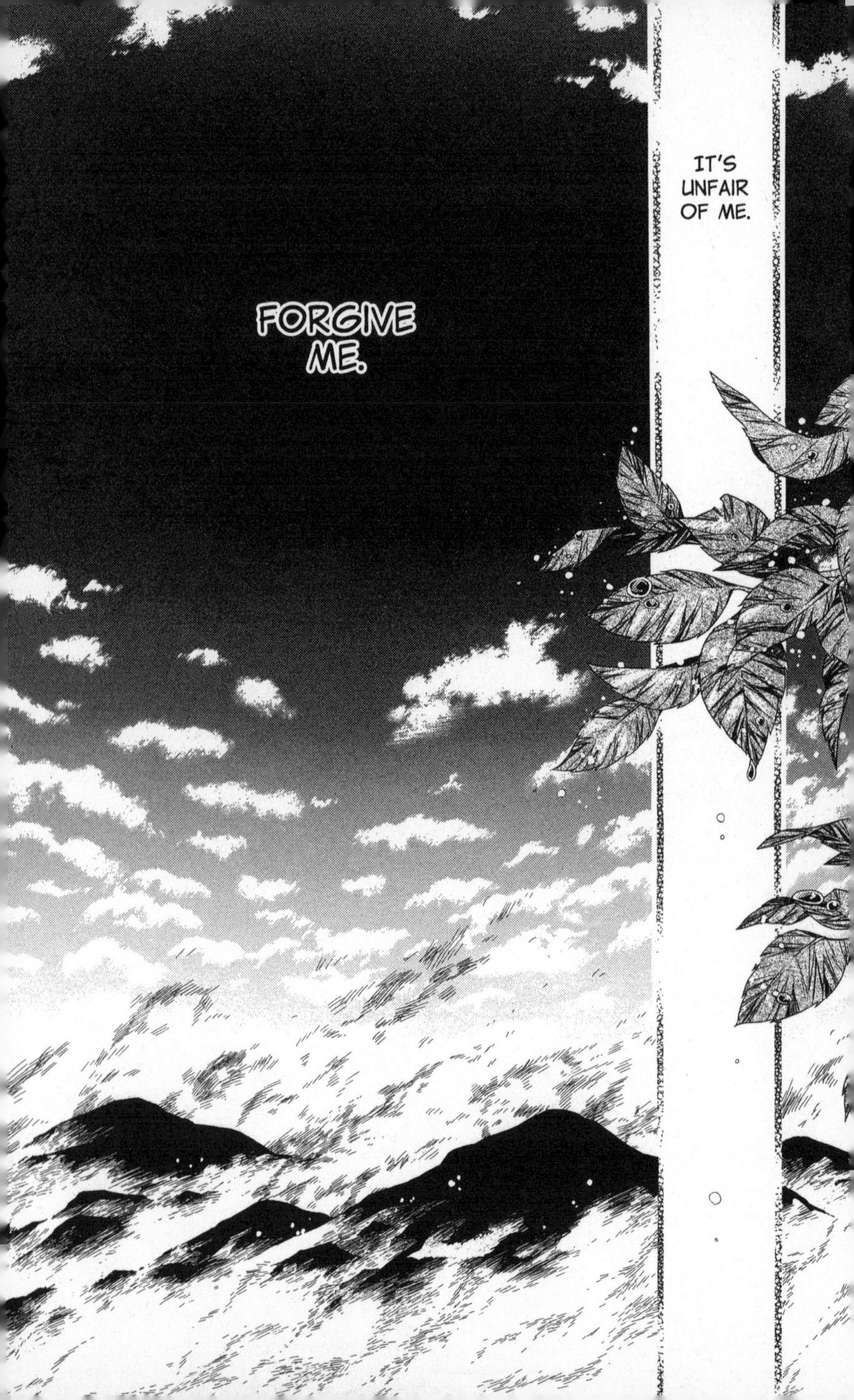
IT'S UNFAIR OF ME.
FORGIVE ME.

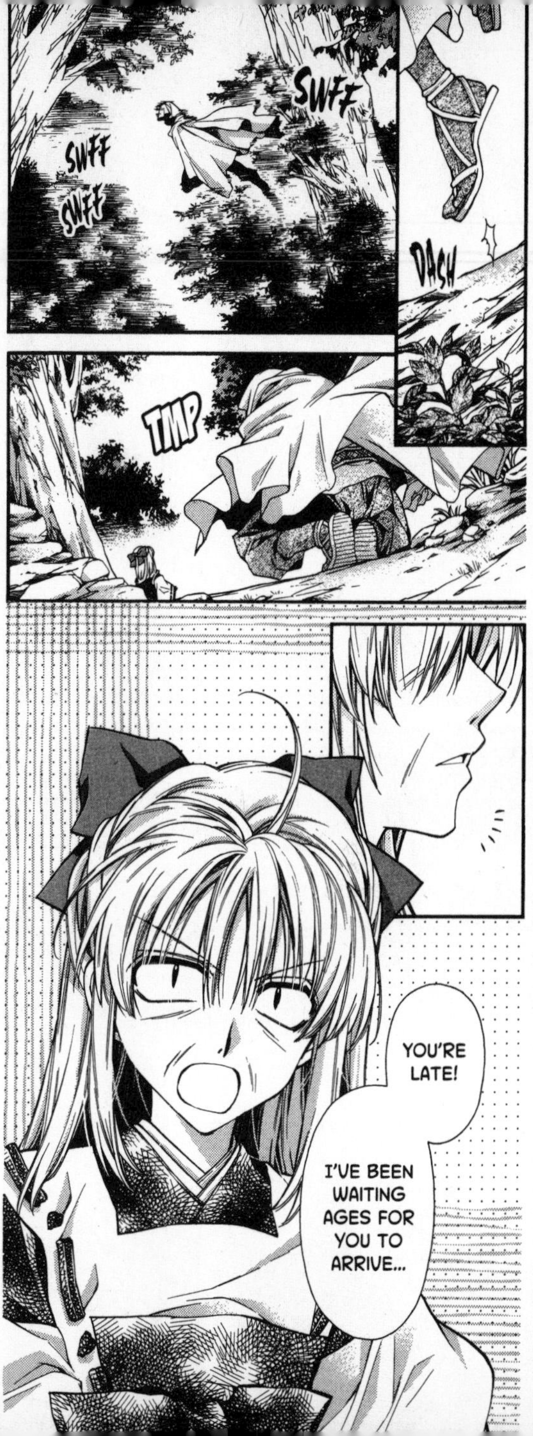
DASH
SWFF
SWFF
SWFF
TMP
YOU'RE LATE!
I'VE BEEN WAITING AGES FOR YOU TO ARRIVE...

FF TYPE-0

This is the game I'm hooked on right now! I've been playing Type-0 all the time! I cleared the game after roughly 40 hours. (I'm already on my second round right now.) The character I used was Ace and his level was around 51. (All the other characters were around level 25 to 37.)

The story is very simple until chapter 3—nothing much happens—but the story starts to move rapidly in chapter 4. The graphics are obviously pretty! The story is simple for an FF game, which I think is good.

My favorite characters are Kurasame and Setsuna. ✓ (Ace is the character I control, so I love him too of course.)

It was fun trying to aim for a Break Sight and Kill Sight, and I never used the Trinity Attack, War God, or Suzaku at all. (But I would like to see what they look like once.)

Oh! The theme song is sung by Bump of Chicken whom I love so much! "Zero" is such a great song!! You get to hear it during the opening movie too. It's a masterpiece.

I advise anybody with a PSP to play it!

You should buy a 4GB memory stick so you can install the game in the beginning. (That will shorten loading time.)

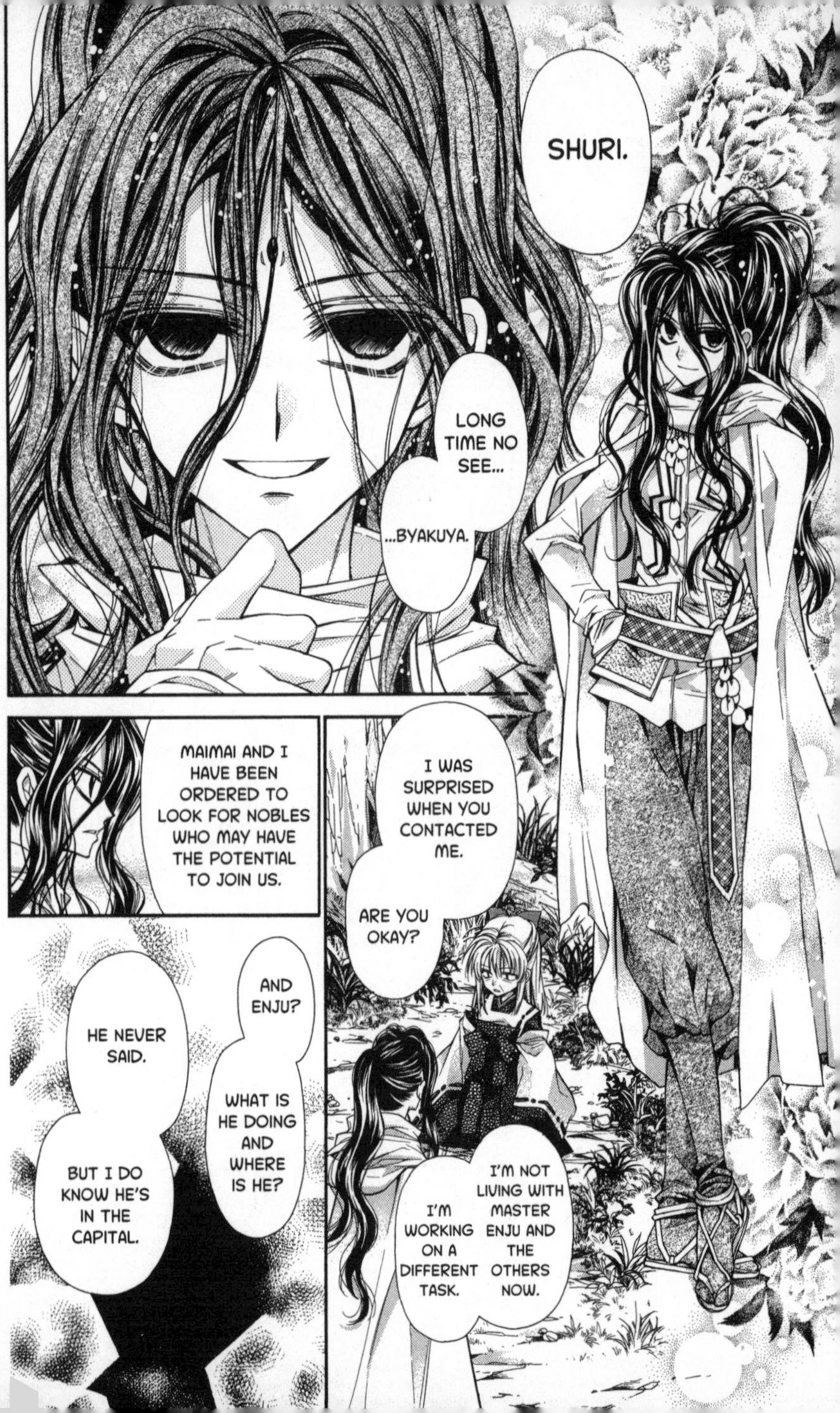
SHURI.
LONG TIME NO SEE...
...BYAKUYA.
I WAS SURPRISED WHEN YOU CONTACTED ME.
ARE YOU OKAY?
I'M NOT LIVING WITH MASTER ENJU AND THE OTHERS NOW.
I'M WORKING ON A DIFFERENT TASK.
MAIMAI AND I HAVE BEEN ORDERED TO LOOK FOR NOBLES WHO MAY HAVE THE POTENTIAL TO JOIN US.
AND ENJU?
WHAT IS HE DOING AND WHERE IS HE?
HE NEVER SAID.
BUT I DO KNOW HE'S IN THE CAPITAL.

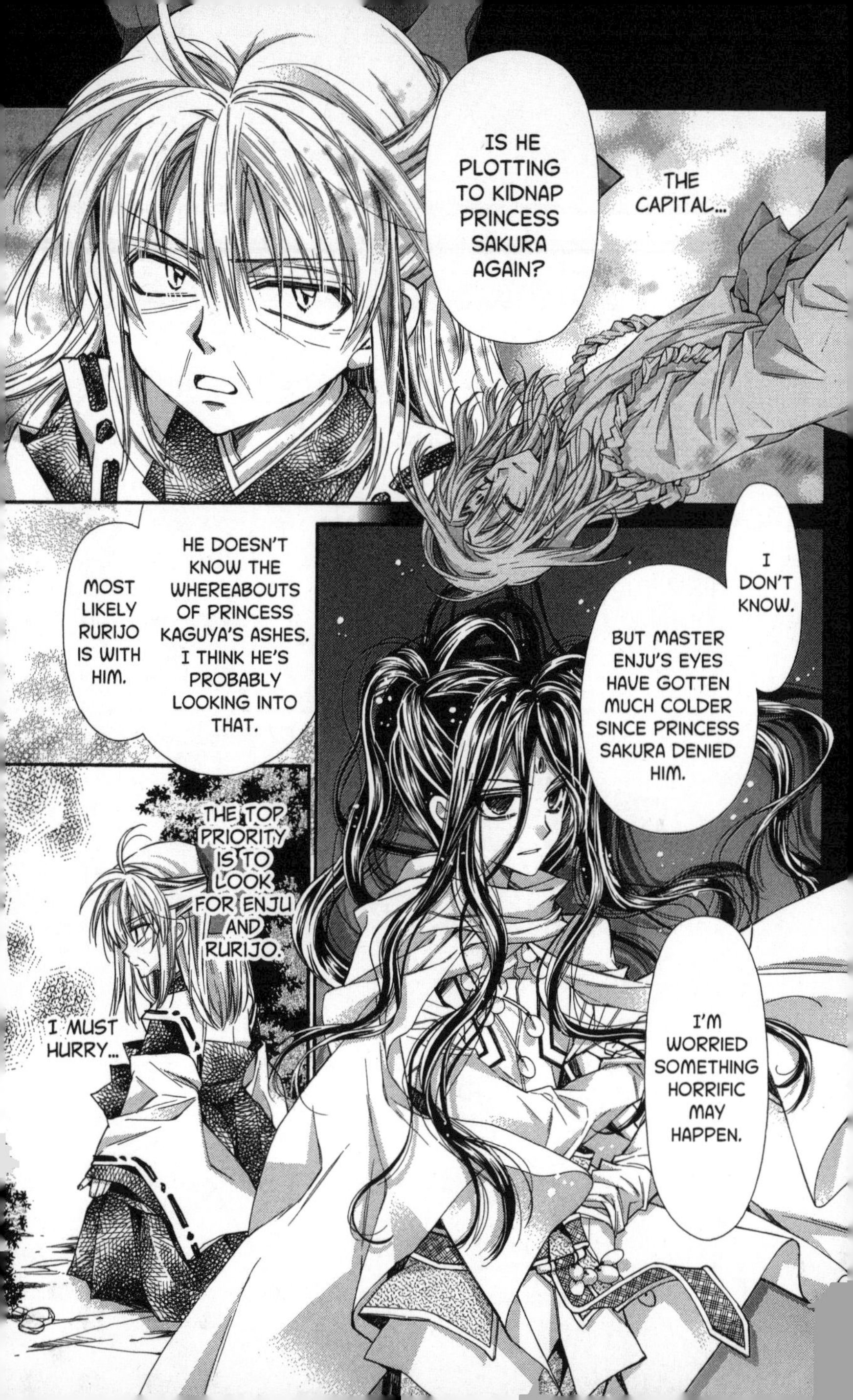
THE CAPITAL...
IS HE PLOTTING TO KIDNAP PRINCESS SAKURA AGAIN?
I DON'T KNOW.
BUT MASTER ENJU'S EYES HAVE GOTTEN MUCH COLDER SINCE PRINCESS SAKURA DENIED HIM.
I'M WORRIED SOMETHING HORRIFIC MAY HAPPEN.
HE DOESN'T KNOW THE WHEREABOUTS OF PRINCESS KAGUYA'S ASHES. I THINK HE'S PROBABLY LOOKING INTO THAT.
MOST LIKELY RURIJO IS WITH HIM.
THE TOP PRIORITY IS TO LOOK FOR ENJU AND RURIJO.
I MUST HURRY...

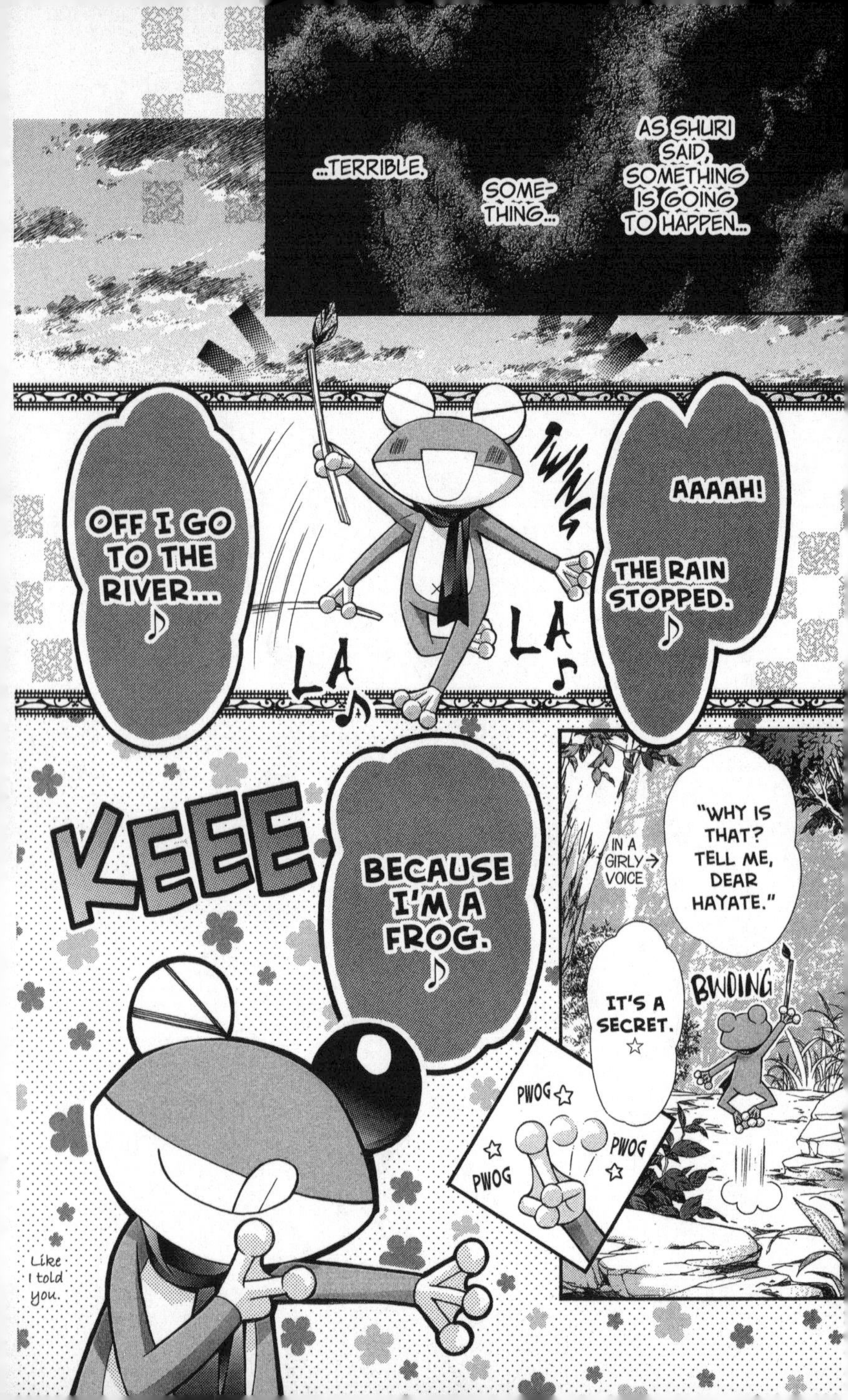
AS SHURI SAID, SOMETHING IS GOING TO HAPPEN...
SOME-THING...
...TERRIBLE.
AAAAH! THE RAIN STOPPED. ♪
TWING
LA ♪
LA ♪
OFF I GO TO THE RIVER... ♪
IN A GIRLY VOICE
"WHY IS THAT? TELL ME, DEAR HAYATE."
BWOING
IT'S A SECRET. ☆
PWOG ☆
PWOG ☆
☆ PWOG
BECAUSE I'M A FROG. ♪
KEEE
Like I told you.

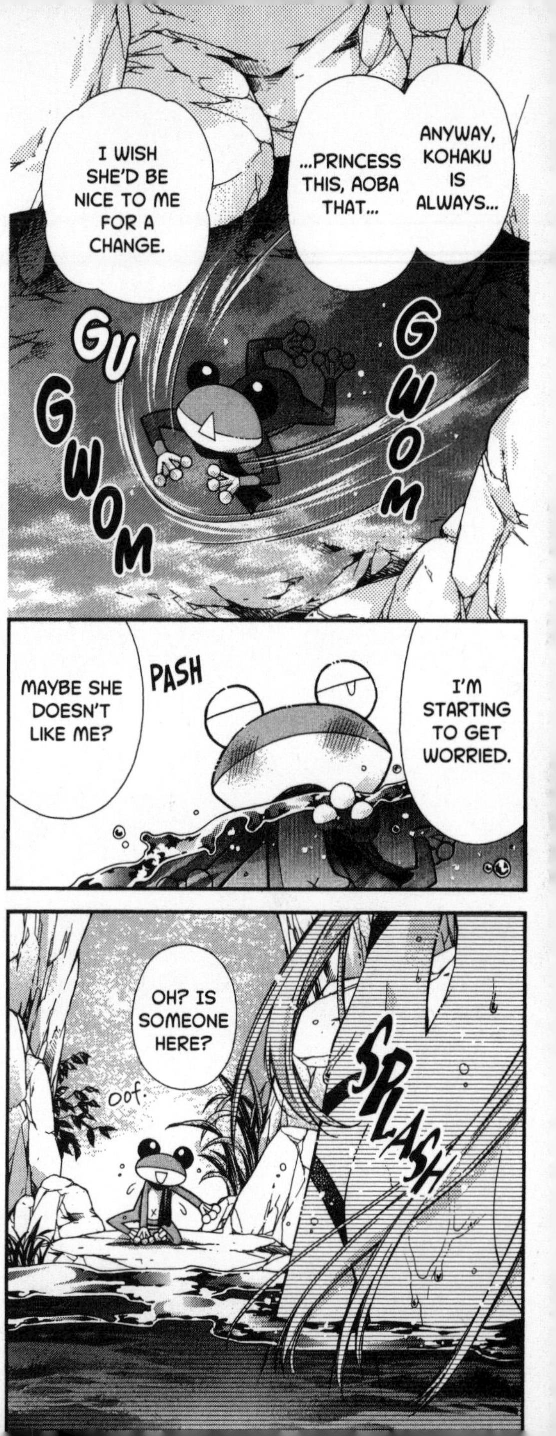
ANYWAY, KOHAKU IS ALWAYS...
...PRINCESS THIS, AOBA THAT...
I WISH SHE'D BE NICE TO ME FOR A CHANGE.
GWOM GWOM
GU GWOM
I'M STARTING TO GET WORRIED.
PASH
MAYBE SHE DOESN'T LIKE ME?
SPLASH
OH? IS SOMEONE HERE?
oof.

ANIME SONG: DJ LIVE

By the way, I did something called an "Anime Song: DJ Live" event the other day. Basically, I became the DJ and played lots of anime songs alongside video images! I hosted it with myco-chan whom I have known since she played Mitsuki in the *Full Moon* anime. But I stopped the music during the show! (laugh)

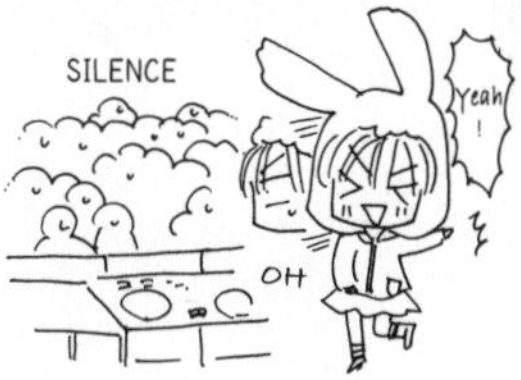
SILENCE
Yeah!
OH

Yeah, that was a big surprise. Total silence during a live set. //// I'm such a klutz.

Other than that, I sang a little bit with myco. It was great to see the moves of Hama-san and Saaya-san, the anime DJs. And I was enchanted by the fast movements of VJ Kitune-san who managed to play video images in perfect time to the music!

If you like anime songs please drop by to see the live performance. ♥ Let's scream and shout!

"Full Moon Sanctuary"
Blog and ticket information:
→ http://ameblo.jp/arina-myco

You can buy original goods with my illustrations there too!

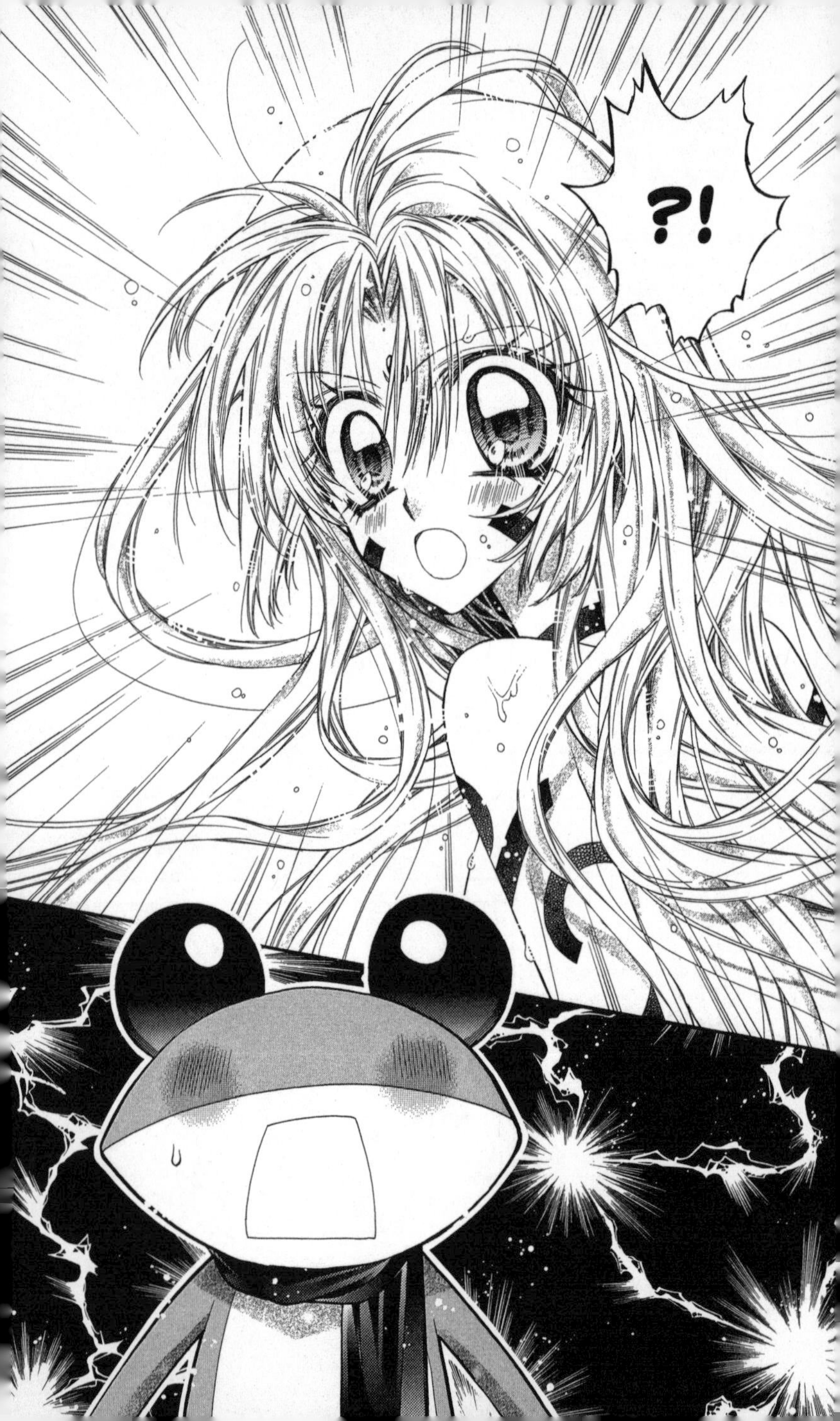
?!

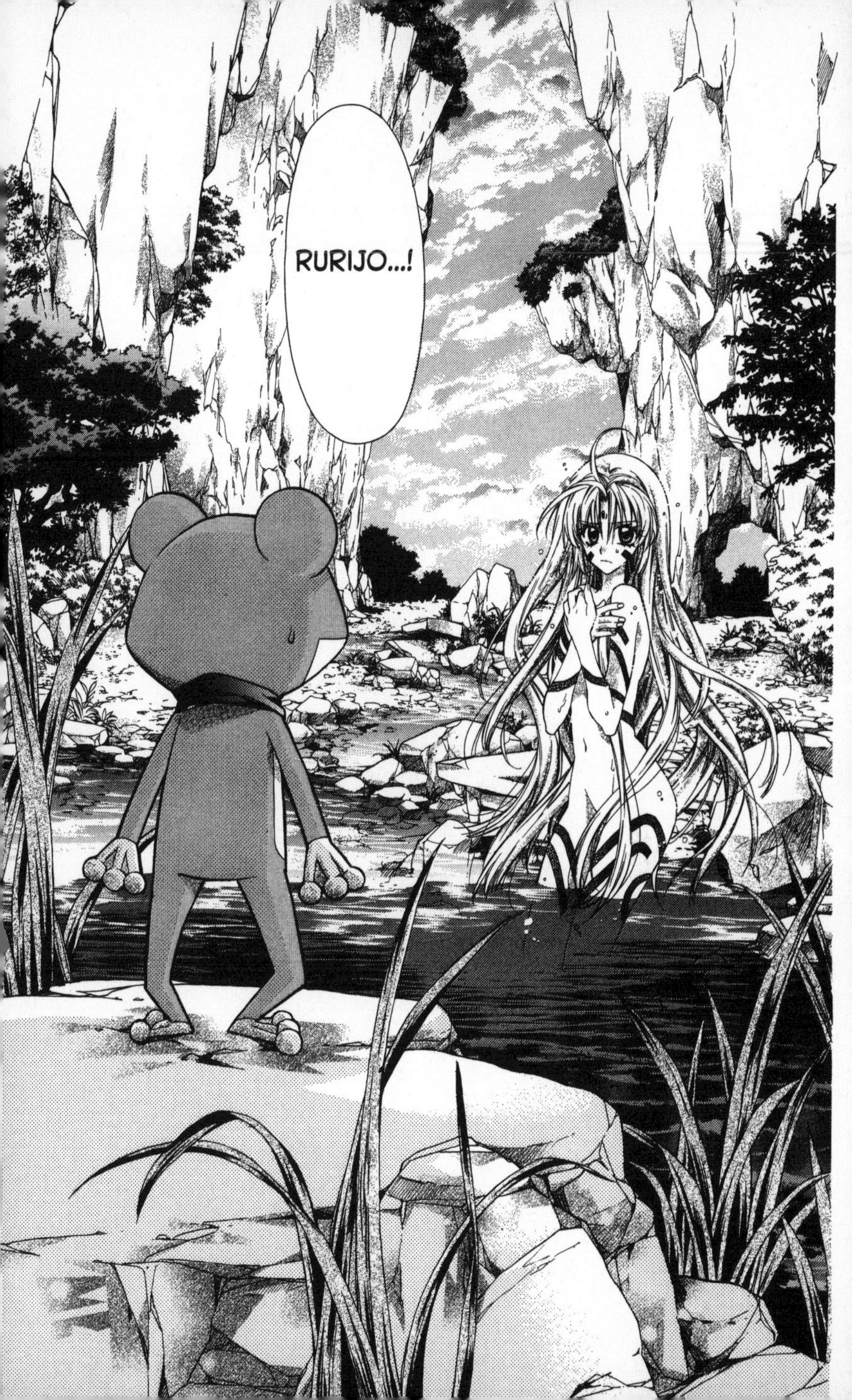
RURIJO...!

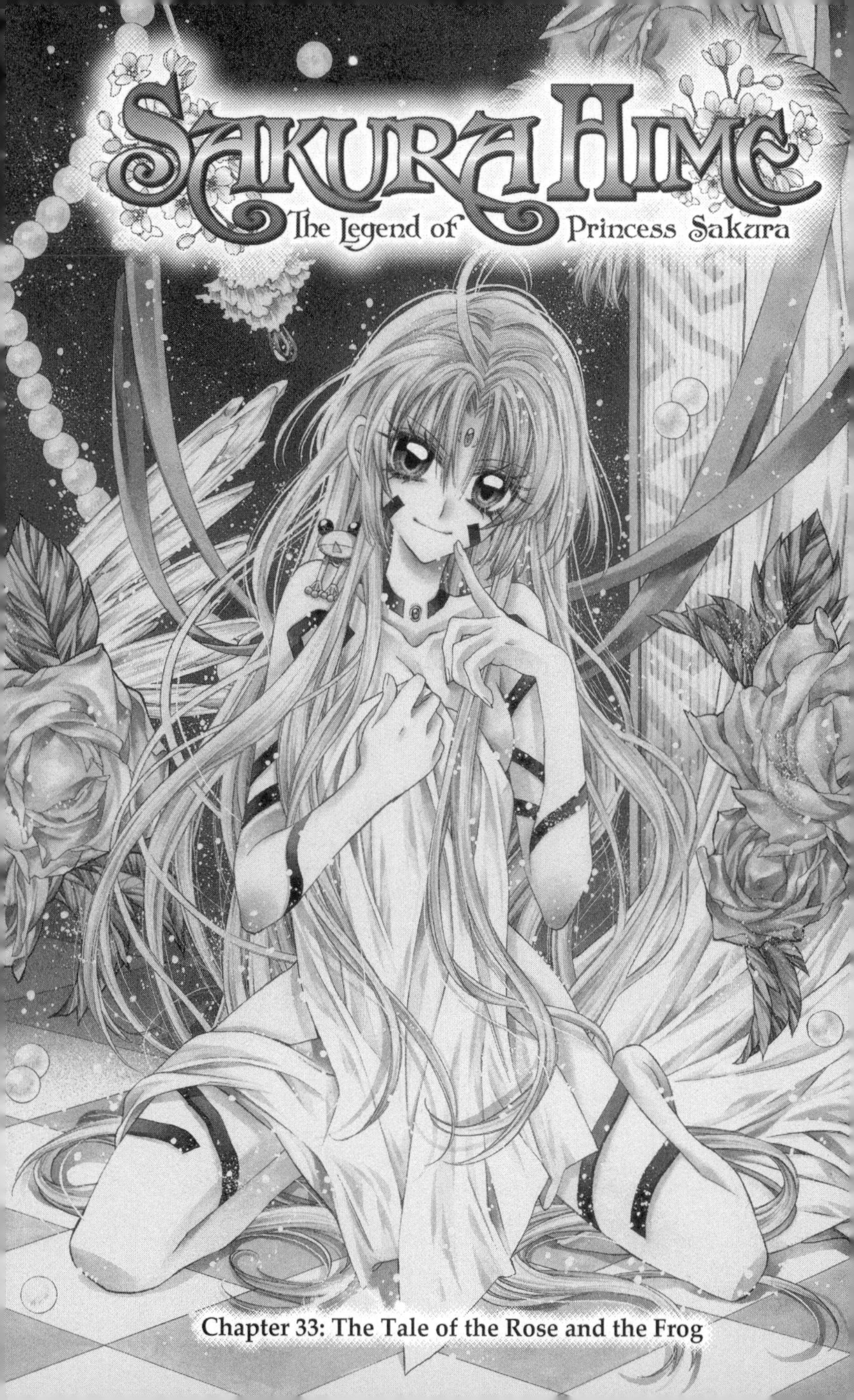
Sakura Hime
The Legend of Princess Sakura

Chapter 33: The Tale of the Rose and the Frog

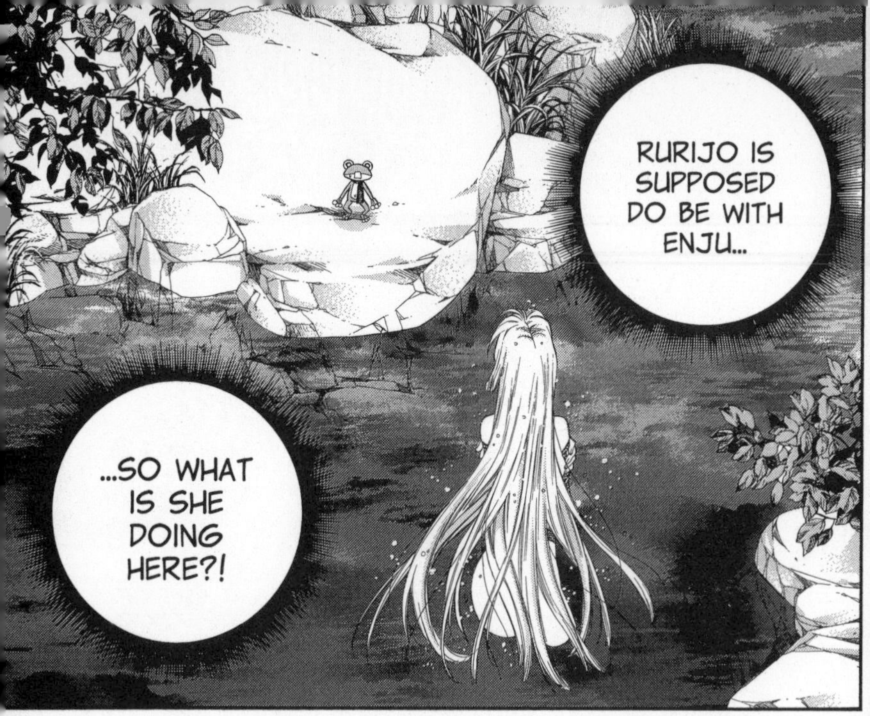
RURIJO IS SUPPOSED DO BE WITH ENJU...
...SO WHAT IS SHE DOING HERE?!

Chapter 33: The Tale of the Rose and the Frog

※ I'm giving away the story.

Up until the last minute I was wondering whether to go with "The Tale of the Frog and the Rose" instead, but I think this has a nicer balance. I see Rurijo as always being naked for some reason... I was a little embarrassed while I worked on this chapter. ////ˇ But this is how I see her, so I couldn't do anything about it. Rurijo lives by sucking the life force from other living creatures, so she can be heavily affected by the personality of whomever she is near. In this she starts to take on Hayate's traits: facial expressions, manner of speaking, etc.

I really wanted to draw this chapter, but the main character hardly comes into the story here. I did it with some doubts in my mind... I was glad when this chapter received a good response. >_< ;
(But I need to write chapters about Sakura too, of course.)

Nothing has happened between Hayate and Kohaku because this chapter was coming up. Well, let's see how things will turn out now.

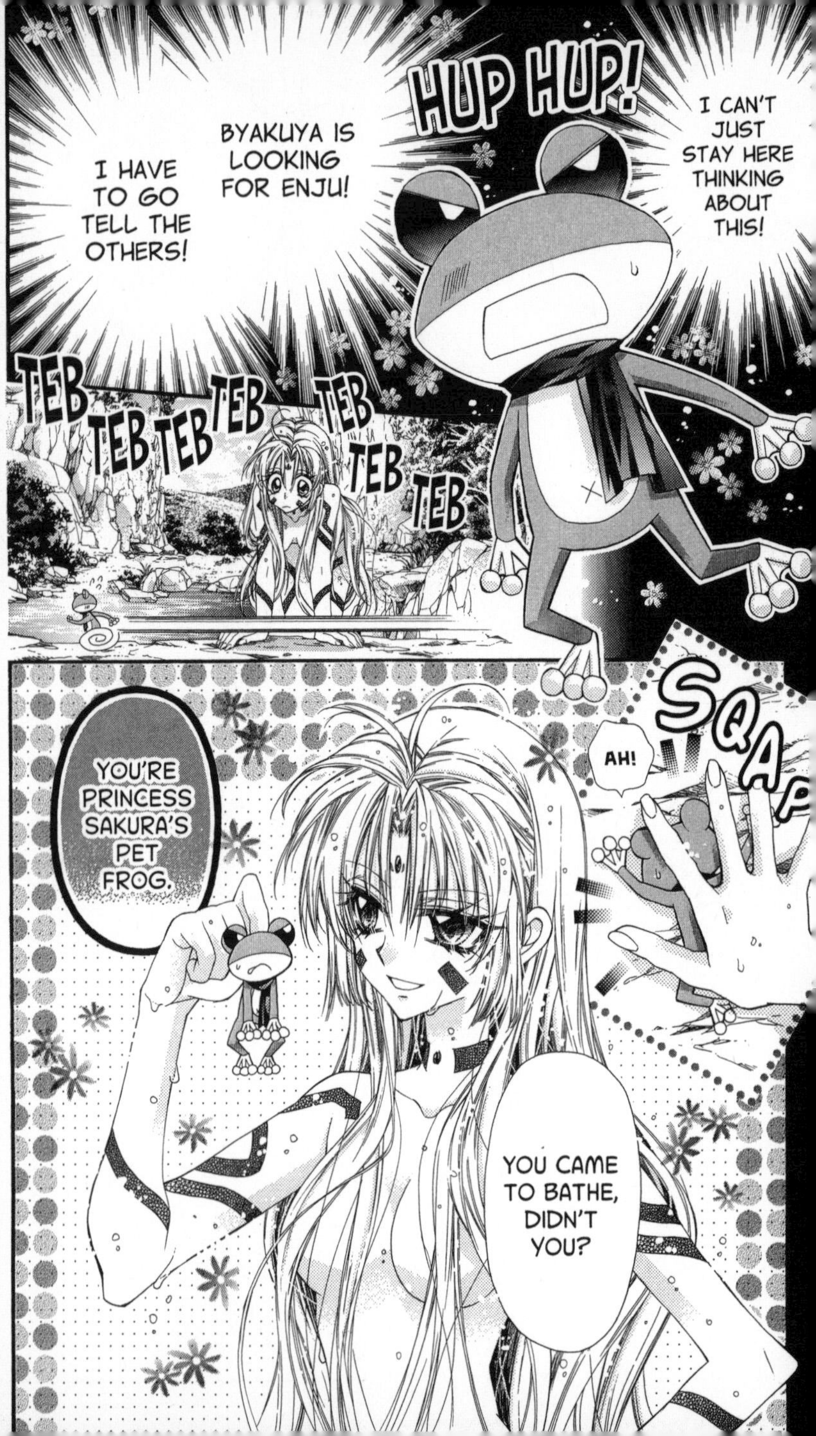
HUP HUP!
I CAN'T JUST STAY HERE THINKING ABOUT THIS!
BYAKUYA IS LOOKING FOR ENJU!
I HAVE TO GO TELL THE OTHERS!
TEB TEB TEB TEB TEB TEB TEB
SQAP
AH!
YOU'RE PRINCESS SAKURA'S PET FROG.
YOU CAME TO BATHE, DIDN'T YOU?

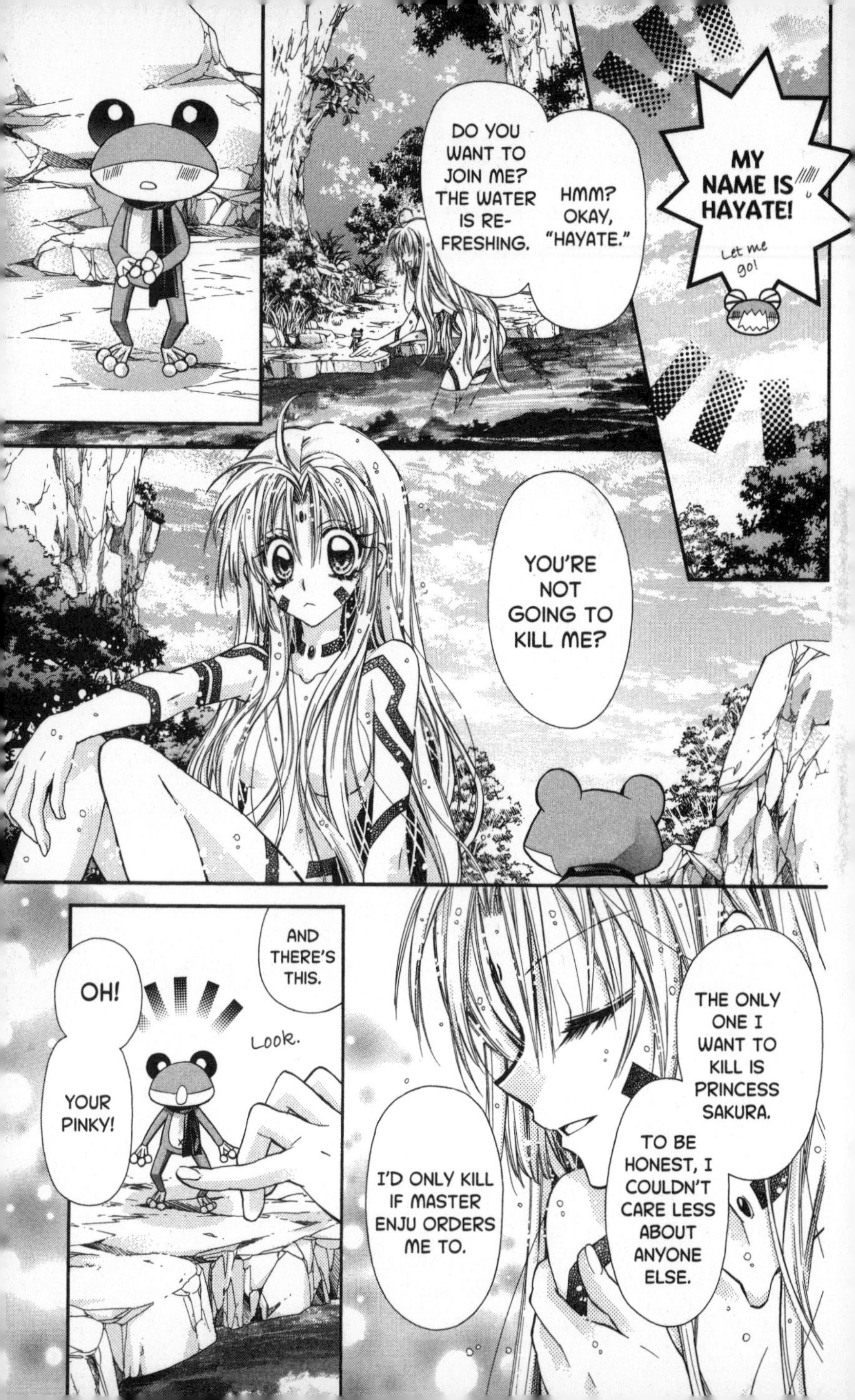
MY NAME IS HAYATE!
Let me go!
HMM? OKAY, "HAYATE."
DO YOU WANT TO JOIN ME? THE WATER IS RE-FRESHING.
YOU'RE NOT GOING TO KILL ME?
THE ONLY ONE I WANT TO KILL IS PRINCESS SAKURA.
TO BE HONEST, I COULDN'T CARE LESS ABOUT ANYONE ELSE.
I'D ONLY KILL IF MASTER ENJU ORDERS ME TO.
AND THERE'S THIS.
Look.
OH!
YOUR PINKY!

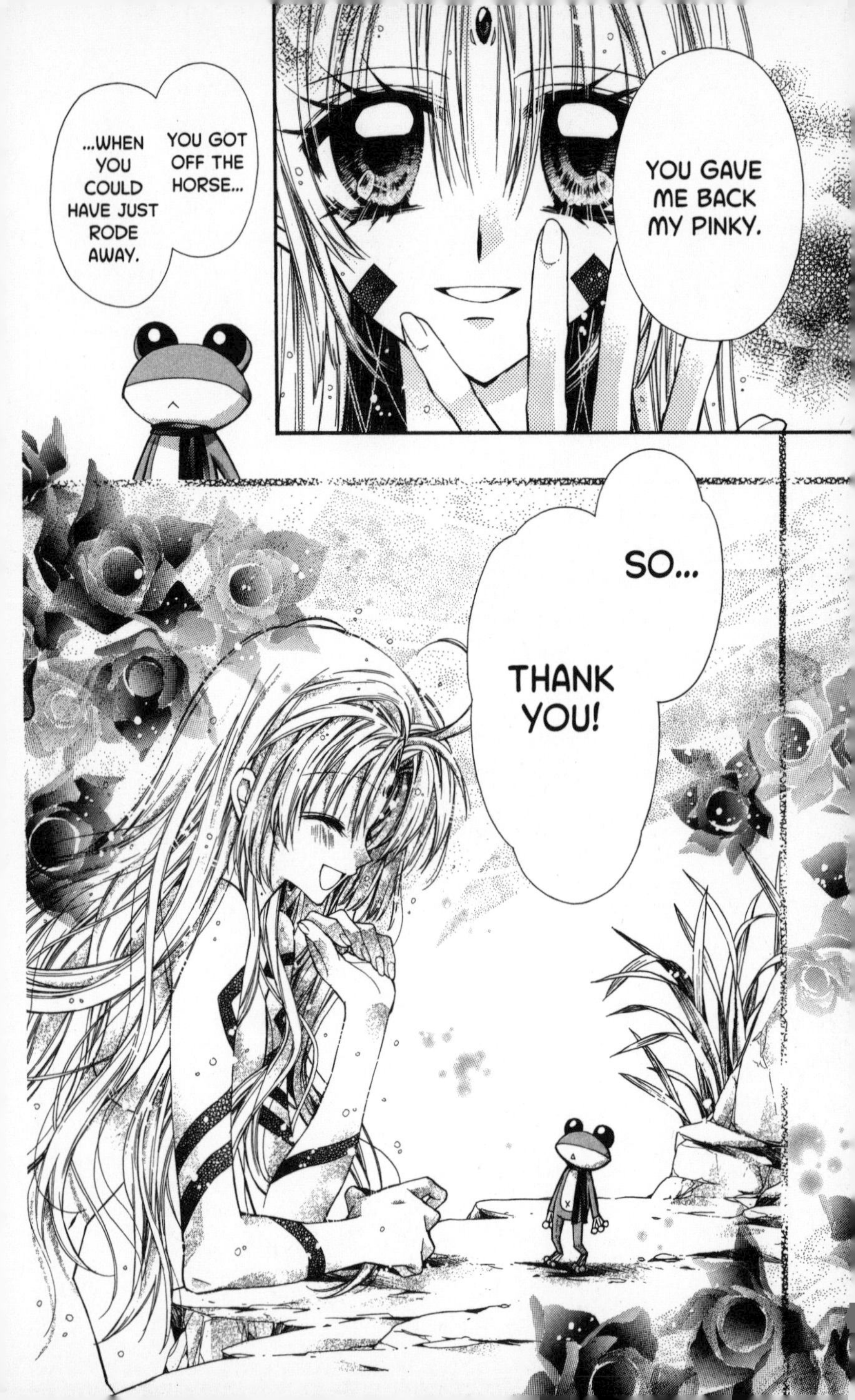
YOU GAVE ME BACK MY PINKY.
YOU GOT OFF THE HORSE... ...WHEN YOU COULD HAVE JUST RODE AWAY.
SO... THANK YOU!

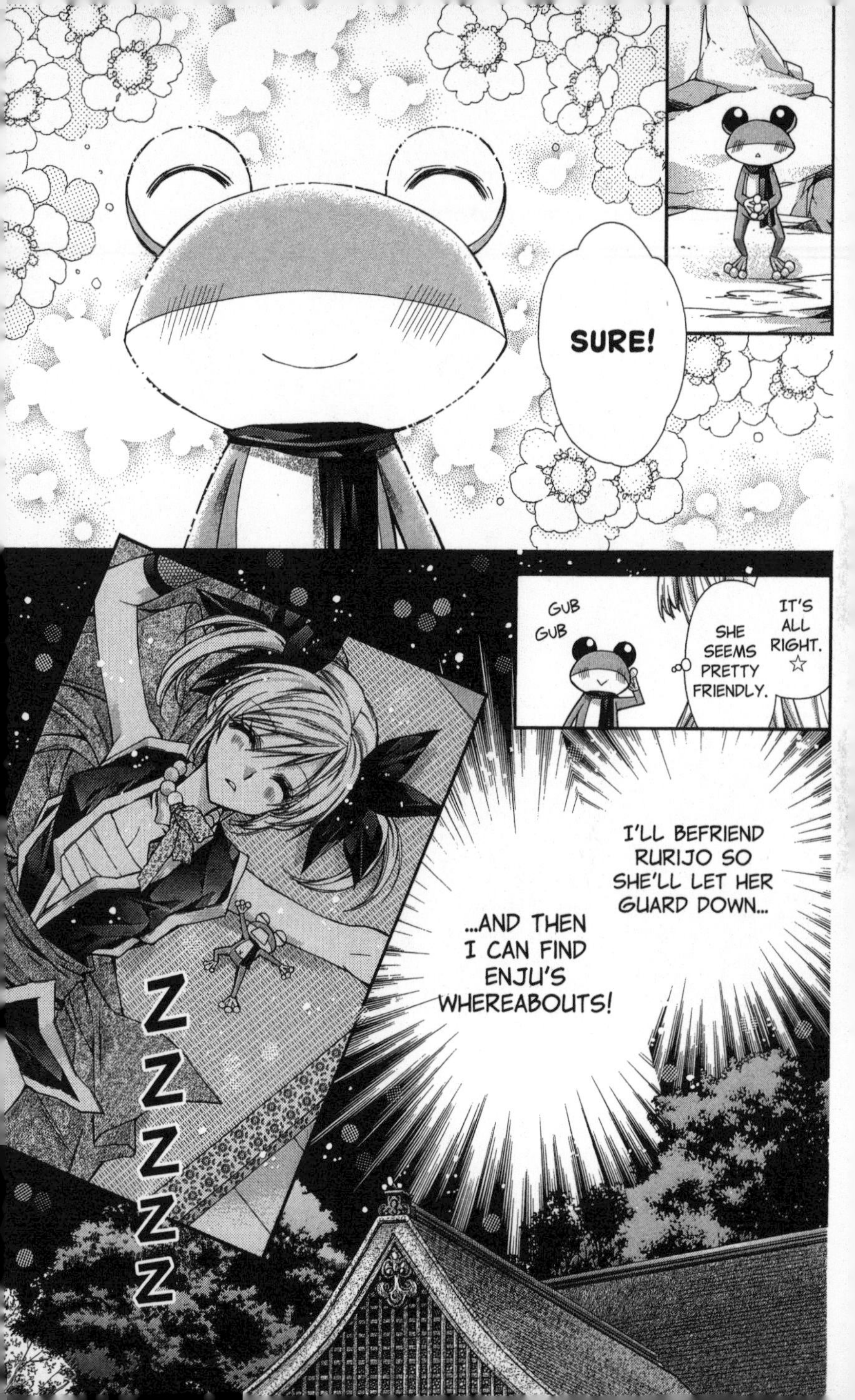
SURE!
IT'S ALL RIGHT. ☆
SHE SEEMS PRETTY FRIENDLY.
GUB GUB
I'LL BEFRIEND RURIJO SO SHE'LL LET HER GUARD DOWN...
...AND THEN I CAN FIND ENJU'S WHEREABOUTS!
ZZZZZ

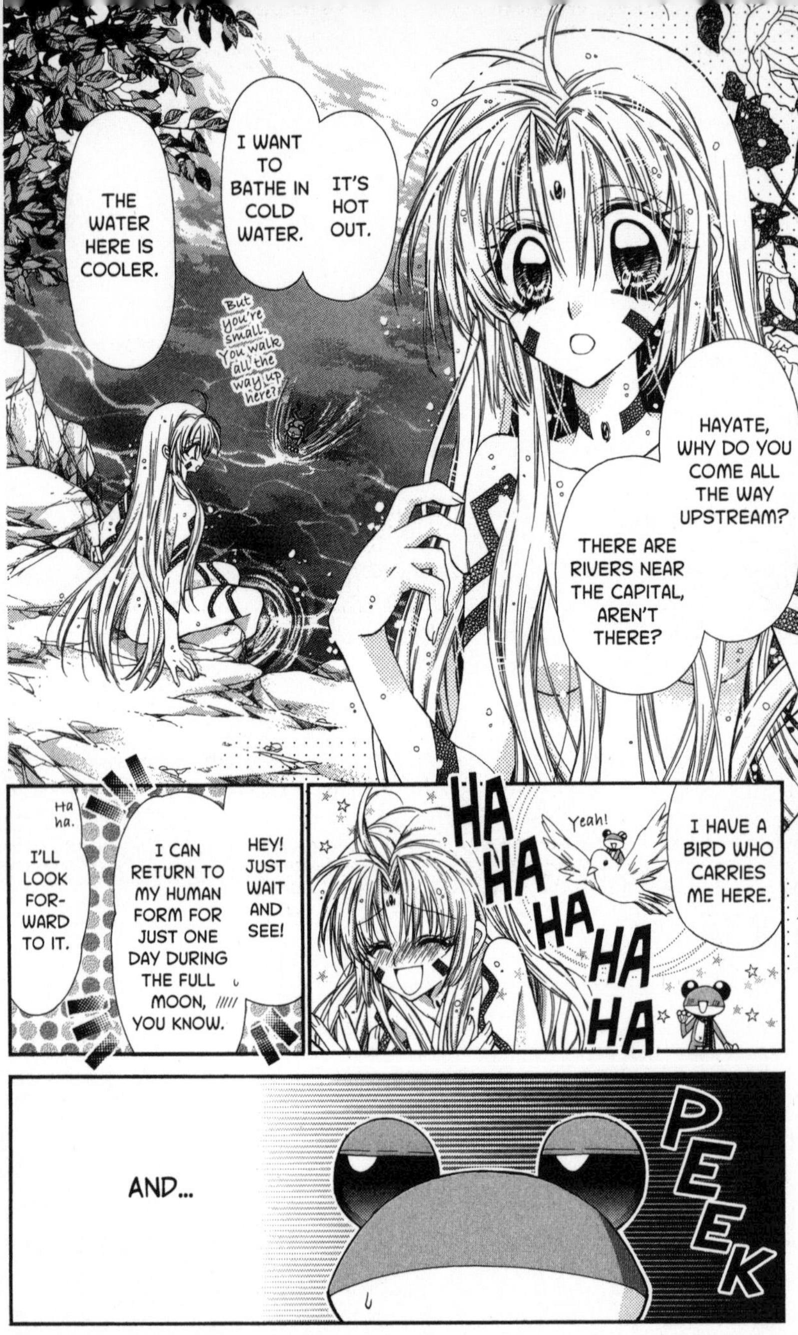
HAYATE, WHY DO YOU COME ALL THE WAY UPSTREAM?
THERE ARE RIVERS NEAR THE CAPITAL, AREN'T THERE?
IT'S HOT OUT.
I WANT TO BATHE IN COLD WATER.
THE WATER HERE IS COOLER.
But you're small. You walk all the way up here?
I HAVE A BIRD WHO CARRIES ME HERE.
Yeah!
HA HA HA HA HA HA
HEY! JUST WAIT AND SEE!
I CAN RETURN TO MY HUMAN FORM FOR JUST ONE DAY DURING THE FULL MOON, YOU KNOW.
Ha ha.
I'LL LOOK FOR-WARD TO IT.
PEEK
AND...

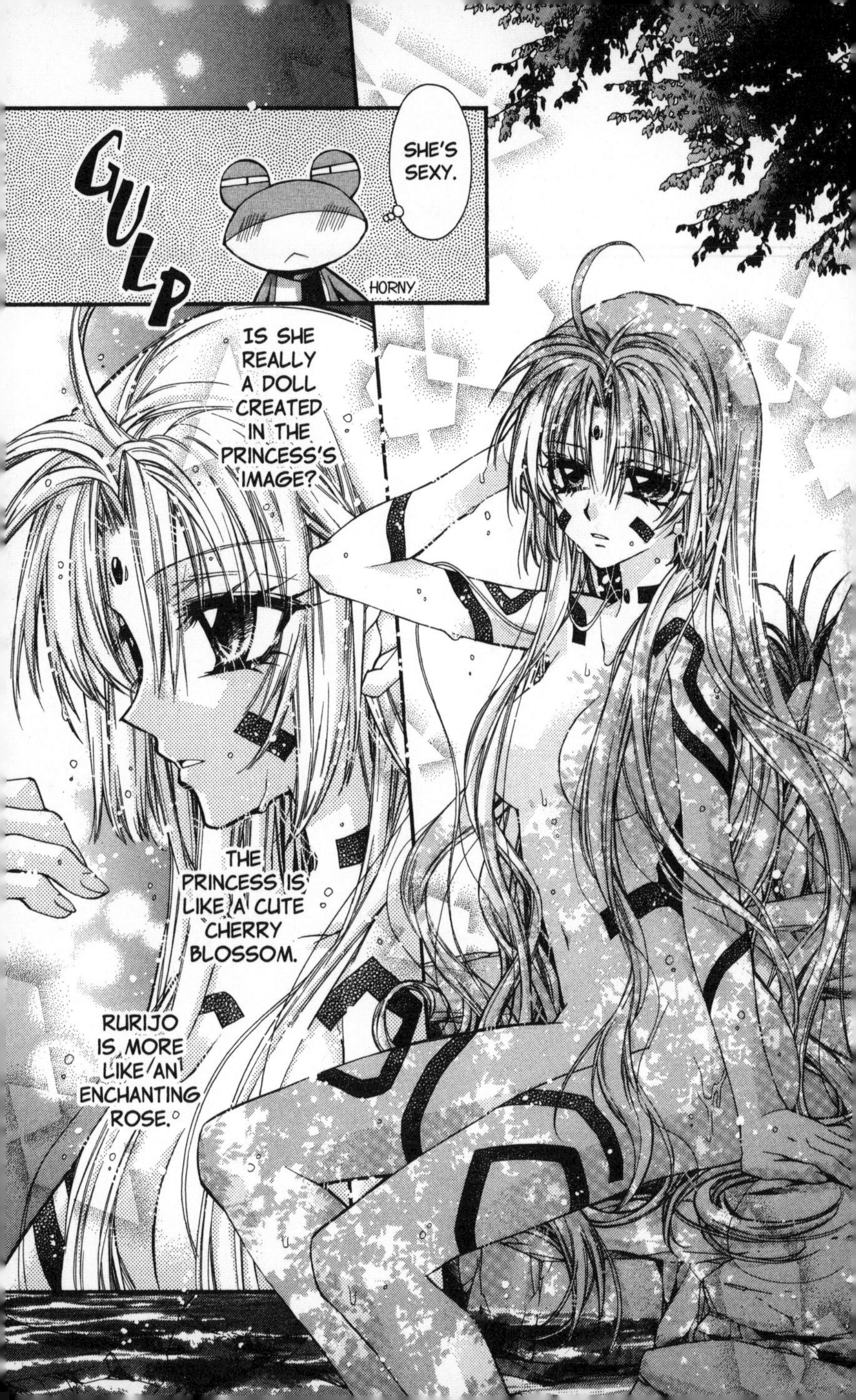
SHE'S SEXY.
GULP
HORNY
IS SHE REALLY A DOLL CREATED IN THE PRINCESS'S IMAGE?
THE PRINCESS IS LIKE A CUTE CHERRY BLOSSOM.
RURIJO IS MORE LIKE AN ENCHANTING ROSE.

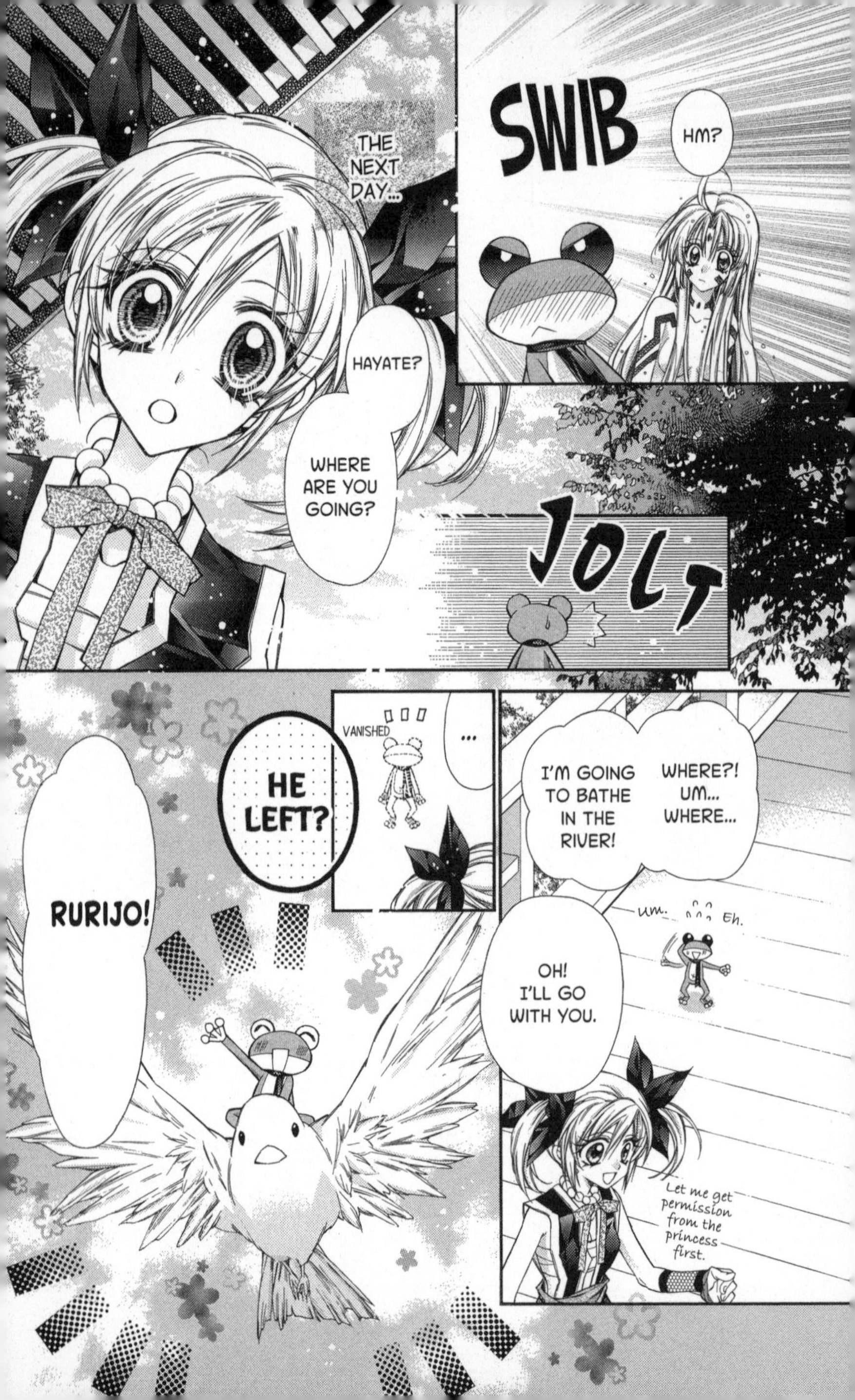
SWIB
HM?
JOLT
THE NEXT DAY...
HAYATE?
WHERE ARE YOU GOING?
WHERE?! UM... WHERE...
I'M GOING TO BATHE IN THE RIVER!
Um.
Eh.
OH! I'LL GO WITH YOU.
Let me get permission from the princess first.
...
VANISHED
HE LEFT?
RURIJO!

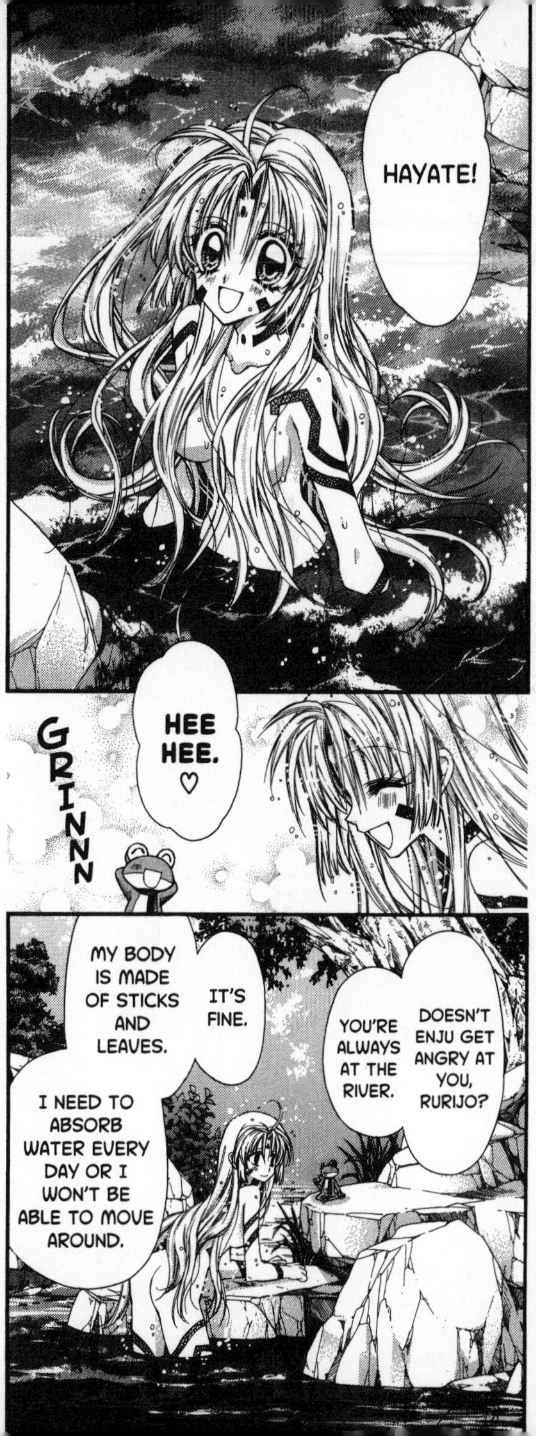
HAYATE!
HEE HEE. ♡
GRINNN
DOESN'T ENJU GET ANGRY AT YOU, RURIJO?
YOU'RE ALWAYS AT THE RIVER.
IT'S FINE.
MY BODY IS MADE OF STICKS AND LEAVES.
I NEED TO ABSORB WATER EVERY DAY OR I WON'T BE ABLE TO MOVE AROUND.

HOMEPAGE

By the way, I now have my own homepage!

This is it. ↓

http://tanemura-arina.com/

I'm hoping the staff and I will be able to host more events so I can interact with my fans more often. Please check the website for details.

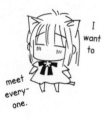

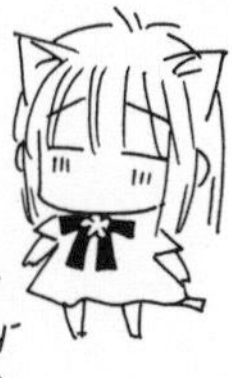
I want to meet everyone.

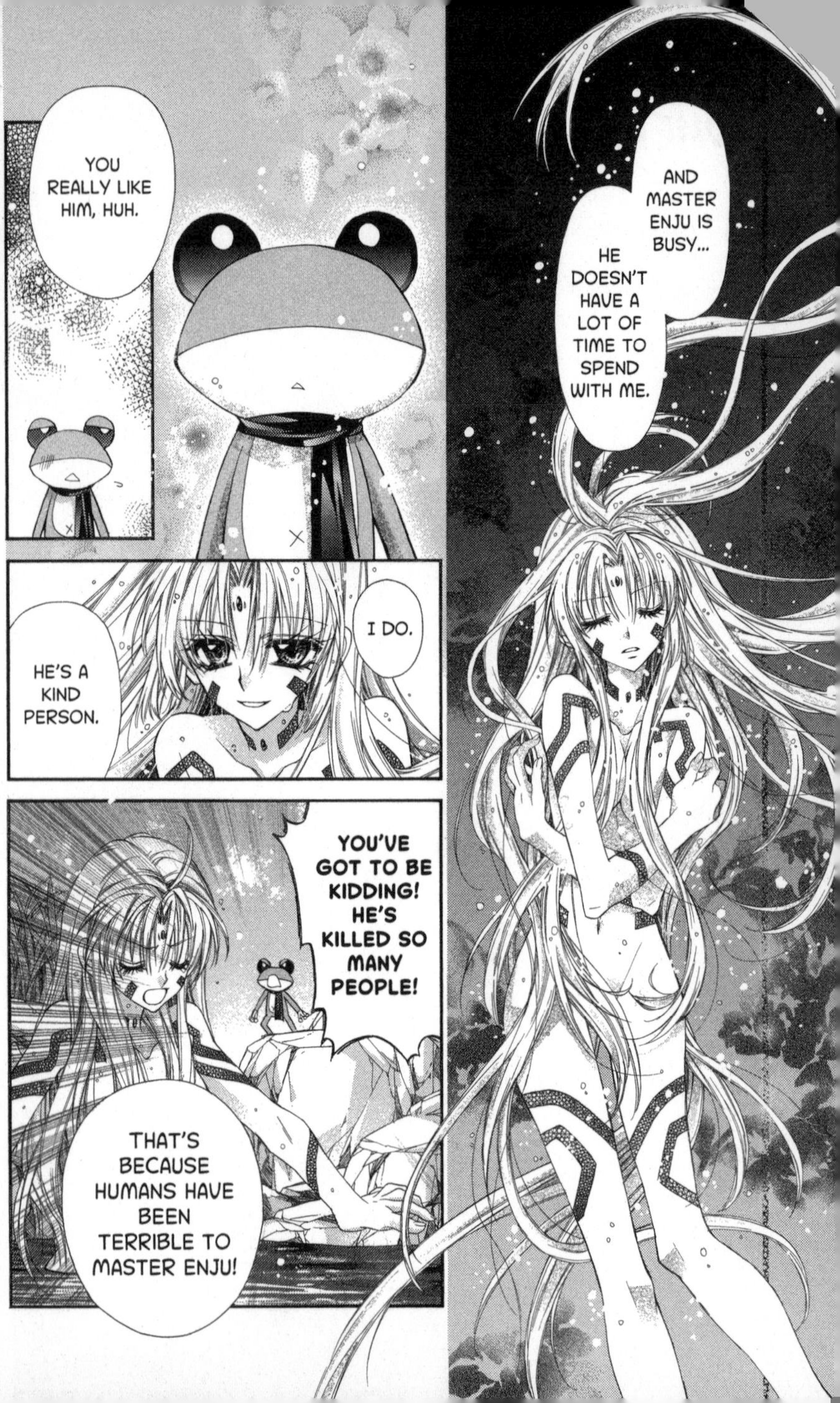
AND MASTER ENJU IS BUSY...
HE DOESN'T HAVE A LOT OF TIME TO SPEND WITH ME.
YOU REALLY LIKE HIM, HUH.
I DO.
HE'S A KIND PERSON.
YOU'VE GOT TO BE KIDDING! HE'S KILLED SO MANY PEOPLE!
THAT'S BECAUSE HUMANS HAVE BEEN TERRIBLE TO MASTER ENJU!

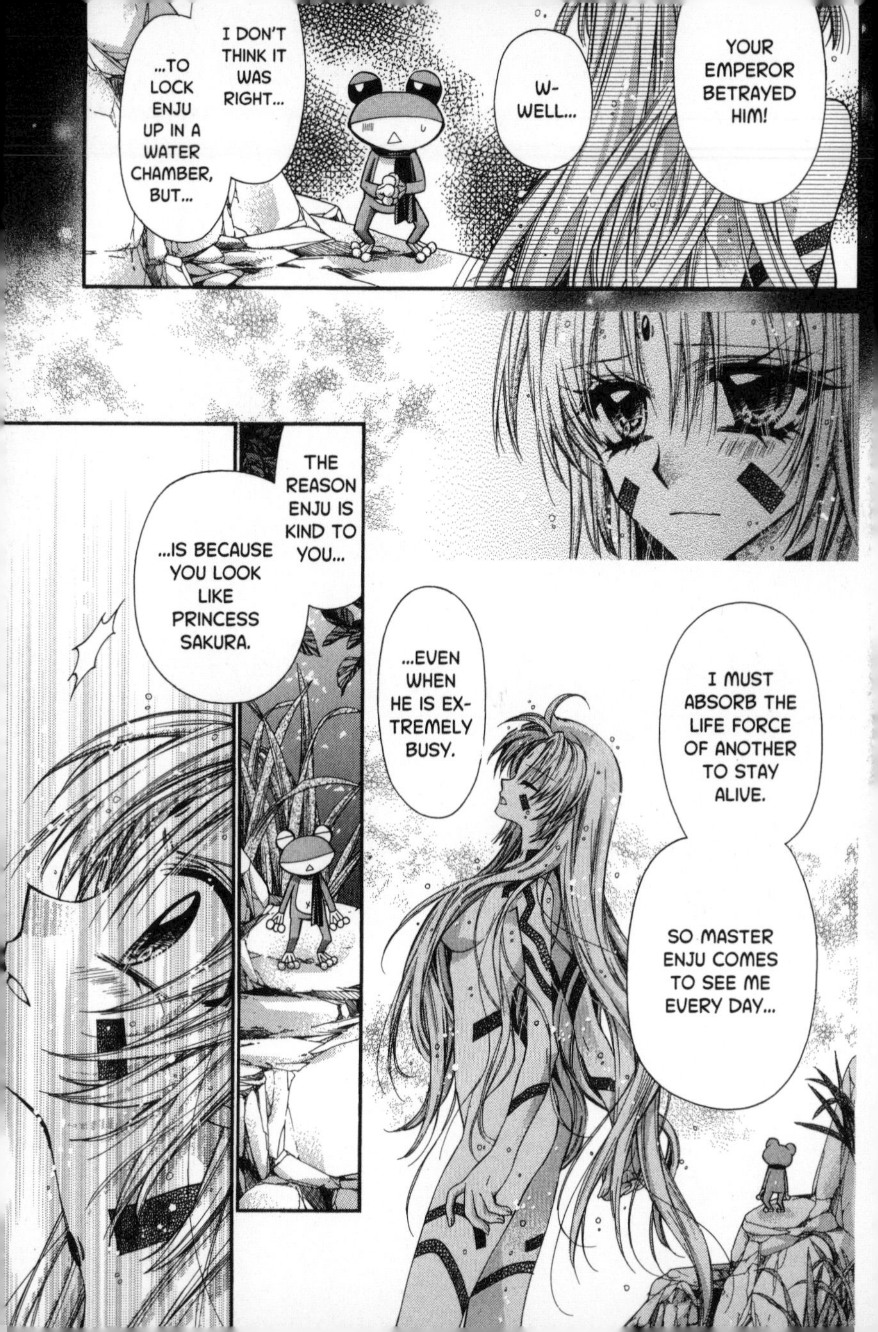
YOUR EMPEROR BETRAYED HIM!
W-WELL...
I DON'T THINK IT WAS RIGHT...
...TO LOCK ENJU UP IN A WATER CHAMBER, BUT...
I MUST ABSORB THE LIFE FORCE OF ANOTHER TO STAY ALIVE.
SO MASTER ENJU COMES TO SEE ME EVERY DAY...
...EVEN WHEN HE IS EXTREMELY BUSY.
THE REASON ENJU IS KIND TO YOU...
...IS BECAUSE YOU LOOK LIKE PRINCESS SAKURA.

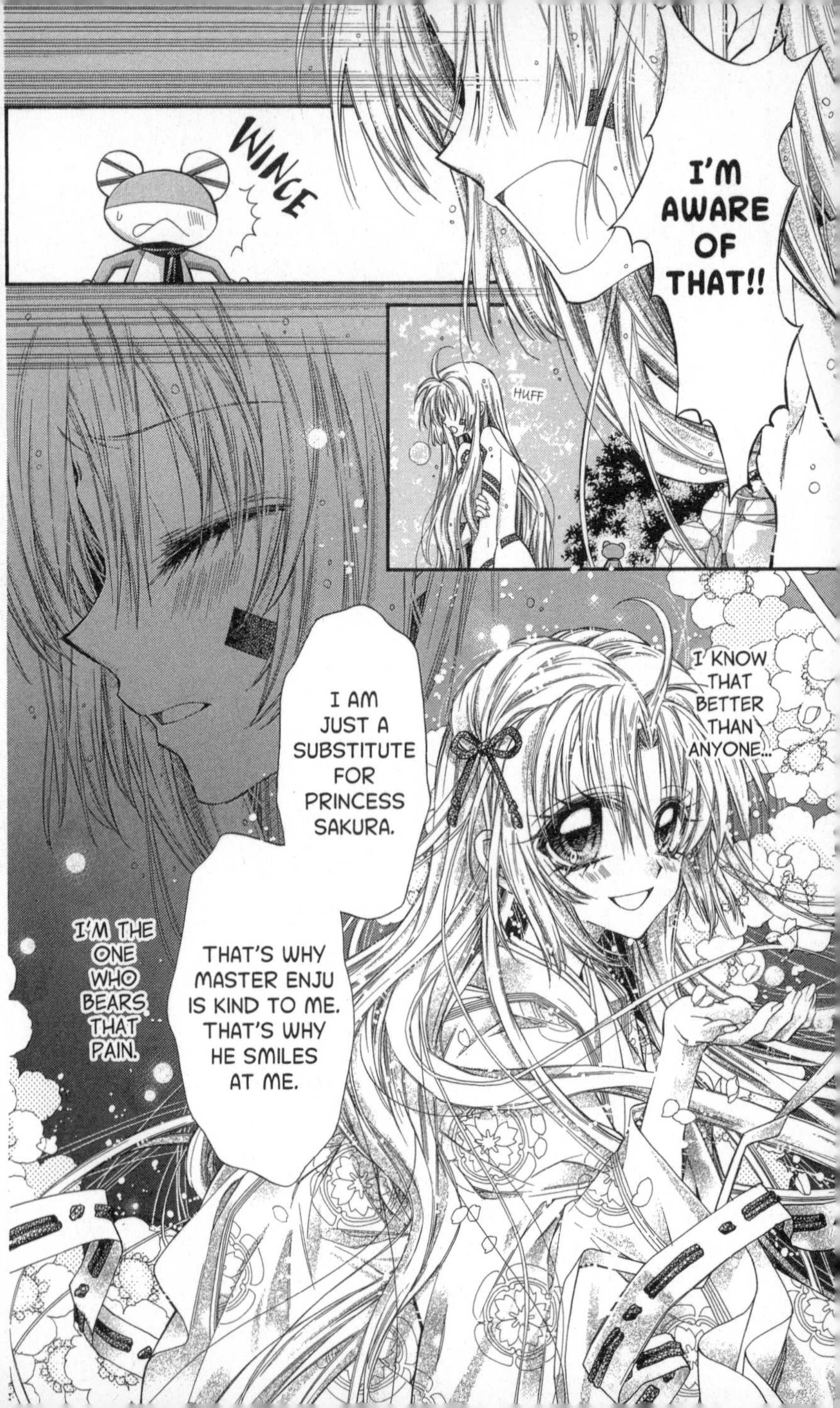
I'M AWARE OF THAT!!
WINCE
HUFF
I KNOW THAT BETTER THAN ANYONE...
I AM JUST A SUBSTITUTE FOR PRINCESS SAKURA.
THAT'S WHY MASTER ENJU IS KIND TO ME. THAT'S WHY HE SMILES AT ME.
I'M THE ONE WHO BEARS THAT PAIN.

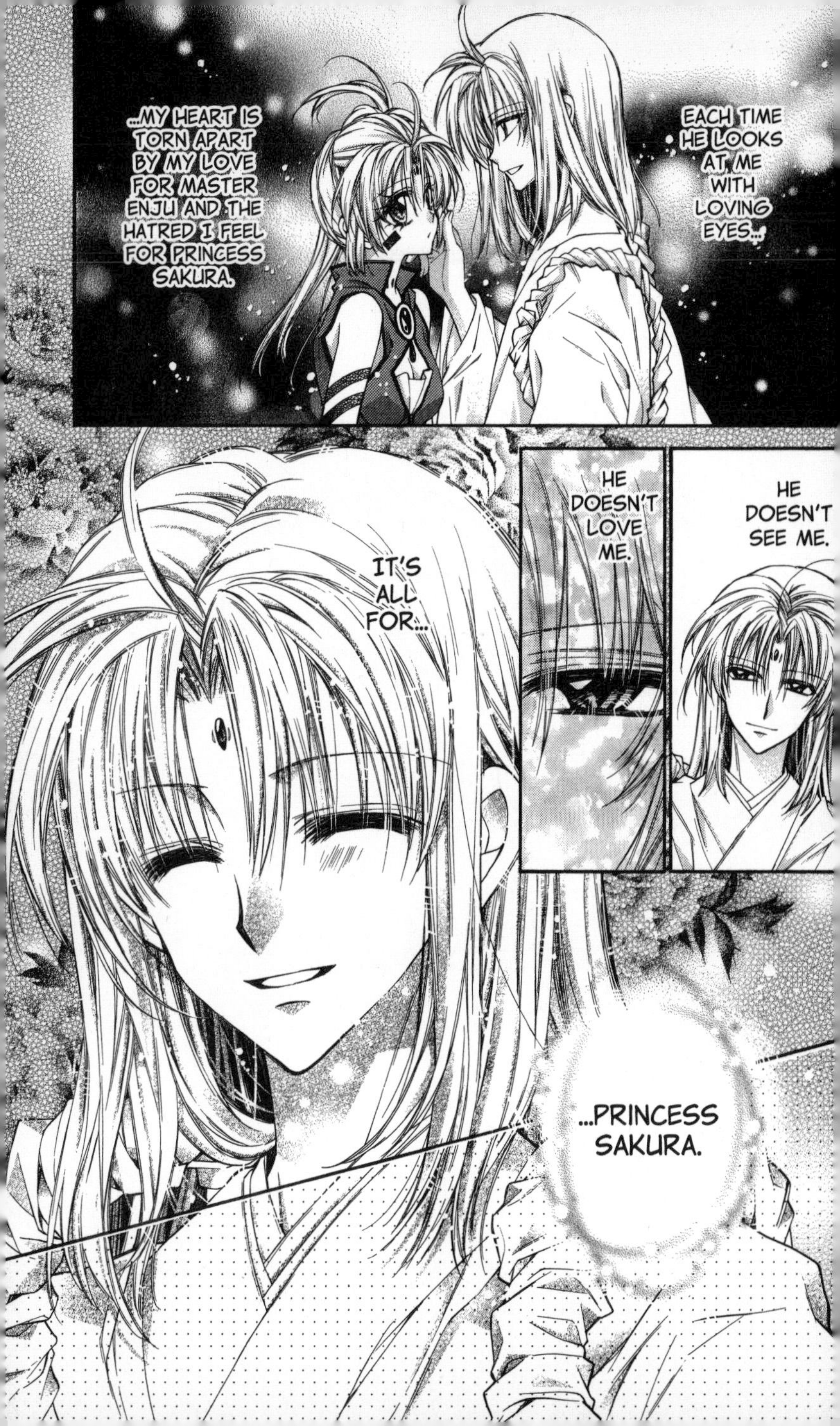
EACH TIME HE LOOKS AT ME WITH LOVING EYES...
...MY HEART IS TORN APART BY MY LOVE FOR MASTER ENJU AND THE HATRED I FEEL FOR PRINCESS SAKURA.
HE DOESN'T SEE ME.
HE DOESN'T LOVE ME.
IT'S ALL FOR...
...PRINCESS SAKURA.

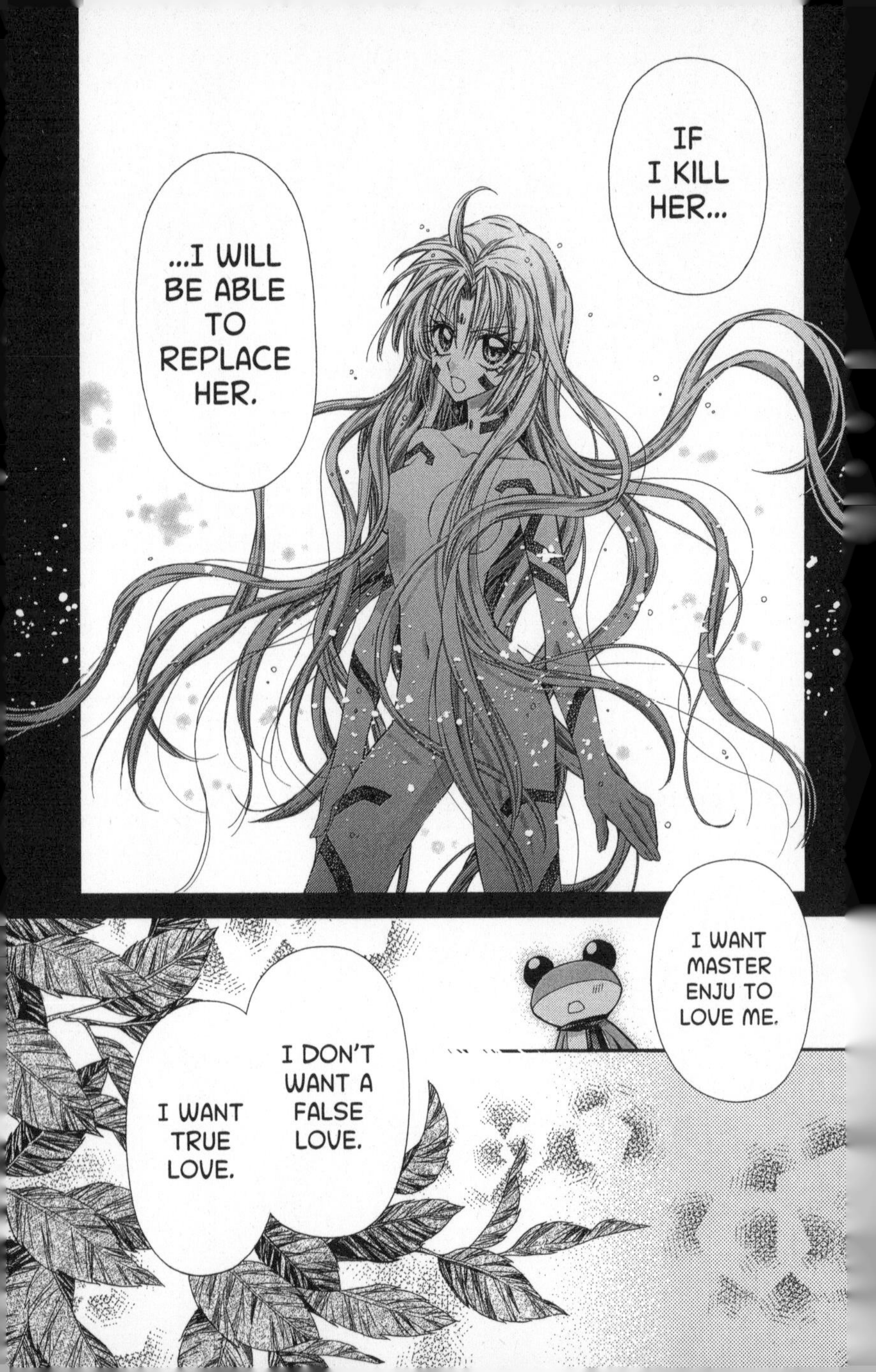
IF I KILL HER...
...I WILL BE ABLE TO REPLACE HER.
I WANT MASTER ENJU TO LOVE ME.
I DON'T WANT A FALSE LOVE.
I WANT TRUE LOVE.

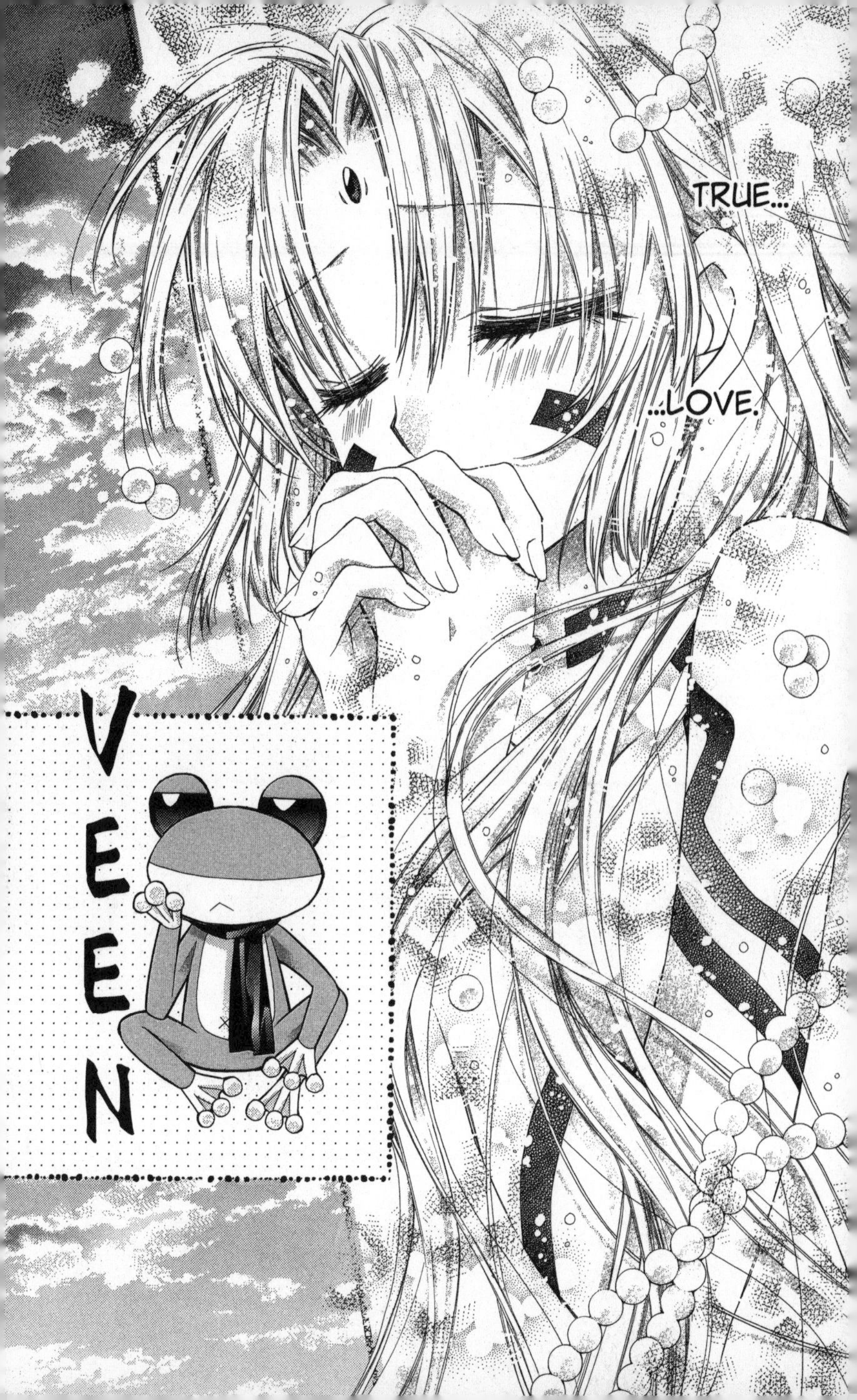
TRUE...
...LOVE.
VEEN

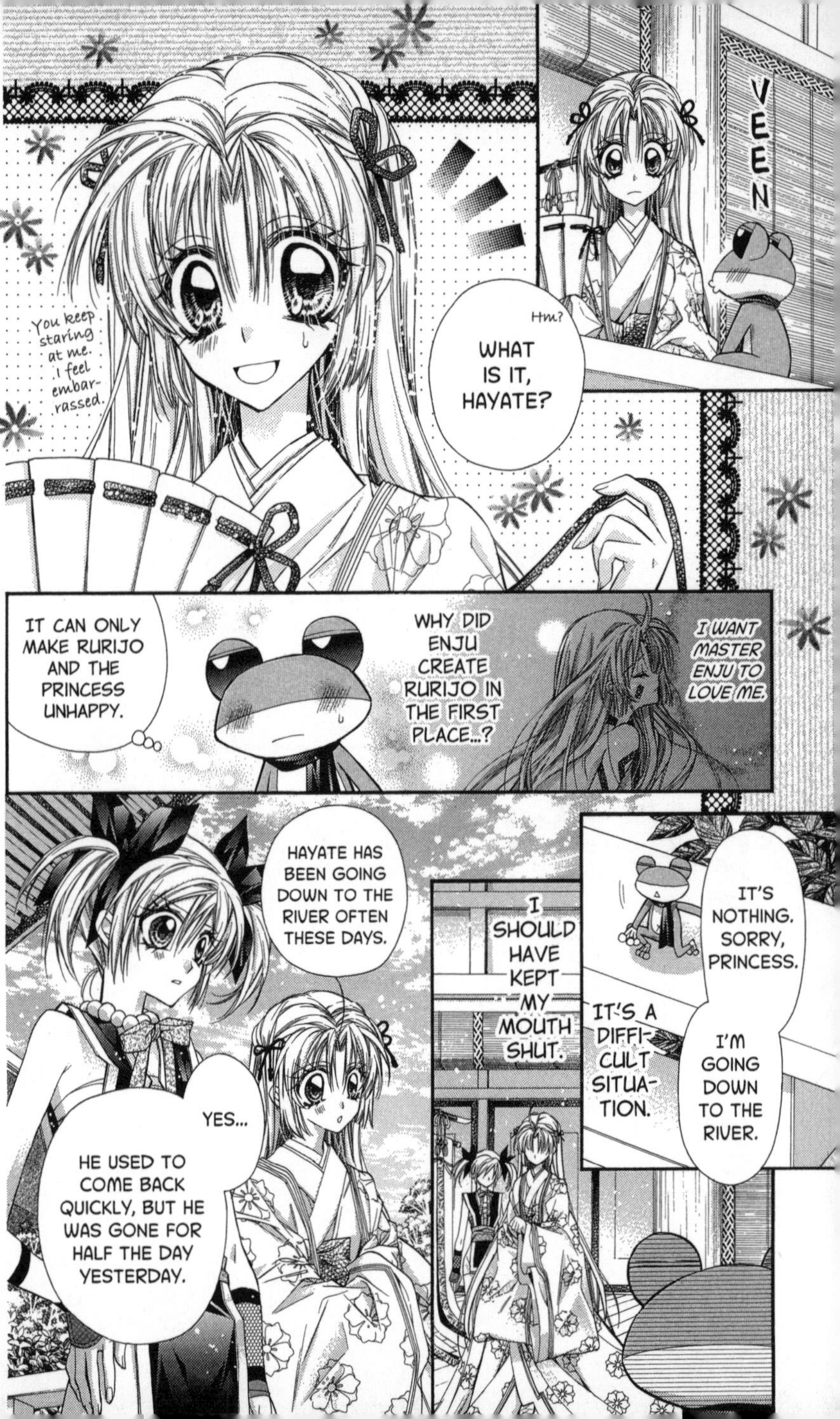
VEEN
Hm?
WHAT IS IT, HAYATE?
You keep staring at me. I feel embarrassed.
I WANT MASTER ENJU TO LOVE ME.
WHY DID ENJU CREATE RURIJO IN THE FIRST PLACE...?
IT CAN ONLY MAKE RURIJO AND THE PRINCESS UNHAPPY.
IT'S NOTHING. SORRY, PRINCESS.
I'M GOING DOWN TO THE RIVER.
IT'S A DIFFICULT SITUATION.
I SHOULD HAVE KEPT MY MOUTH SHUT.
HAYATE HAS BEEN GOING DOWN TO THE RIVER OFTEN THESE DAYS.
YES...
HE USED TO COME BACK QUICKLY, BUT HE WAS GONE FOR HALF THE DAY YESTERDAY.

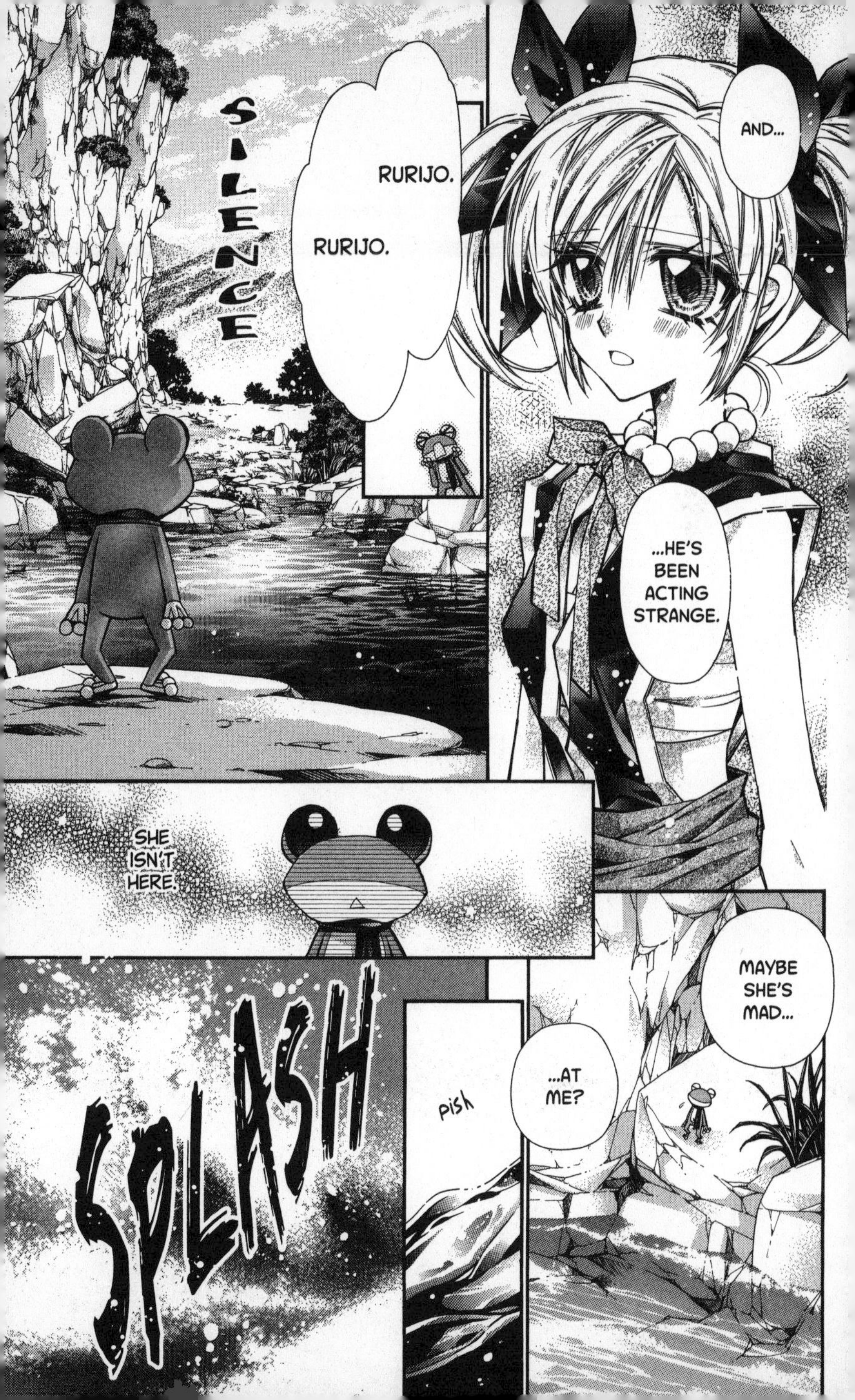
AND...
...HE'S BEEN ACTING STRANGE.
RURIJO.
RURIJO.
SILENCE
SHE ISN'T HERE.
MAYBE SHE'S MAD...
...AT ME?
pish
SPLASH

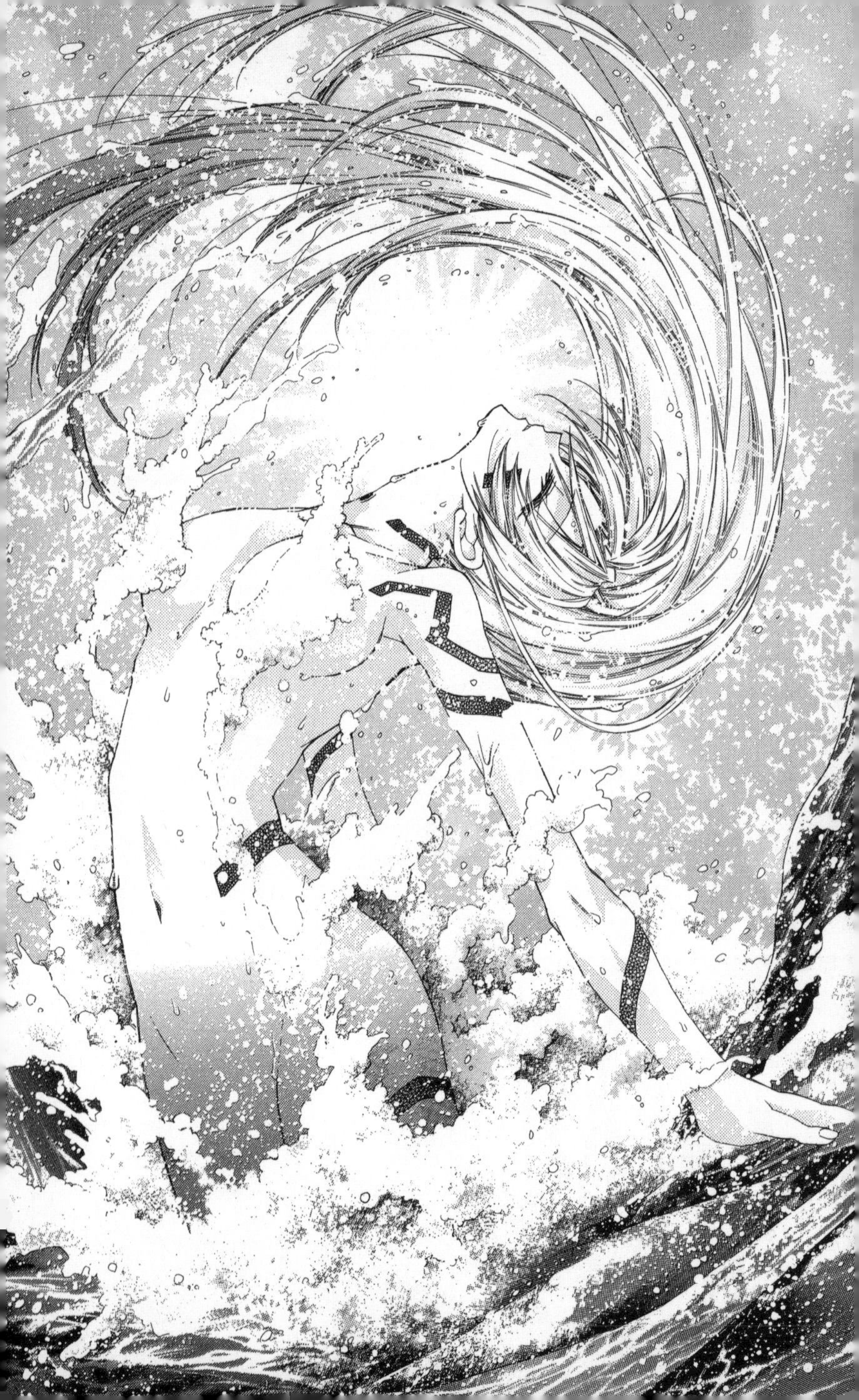

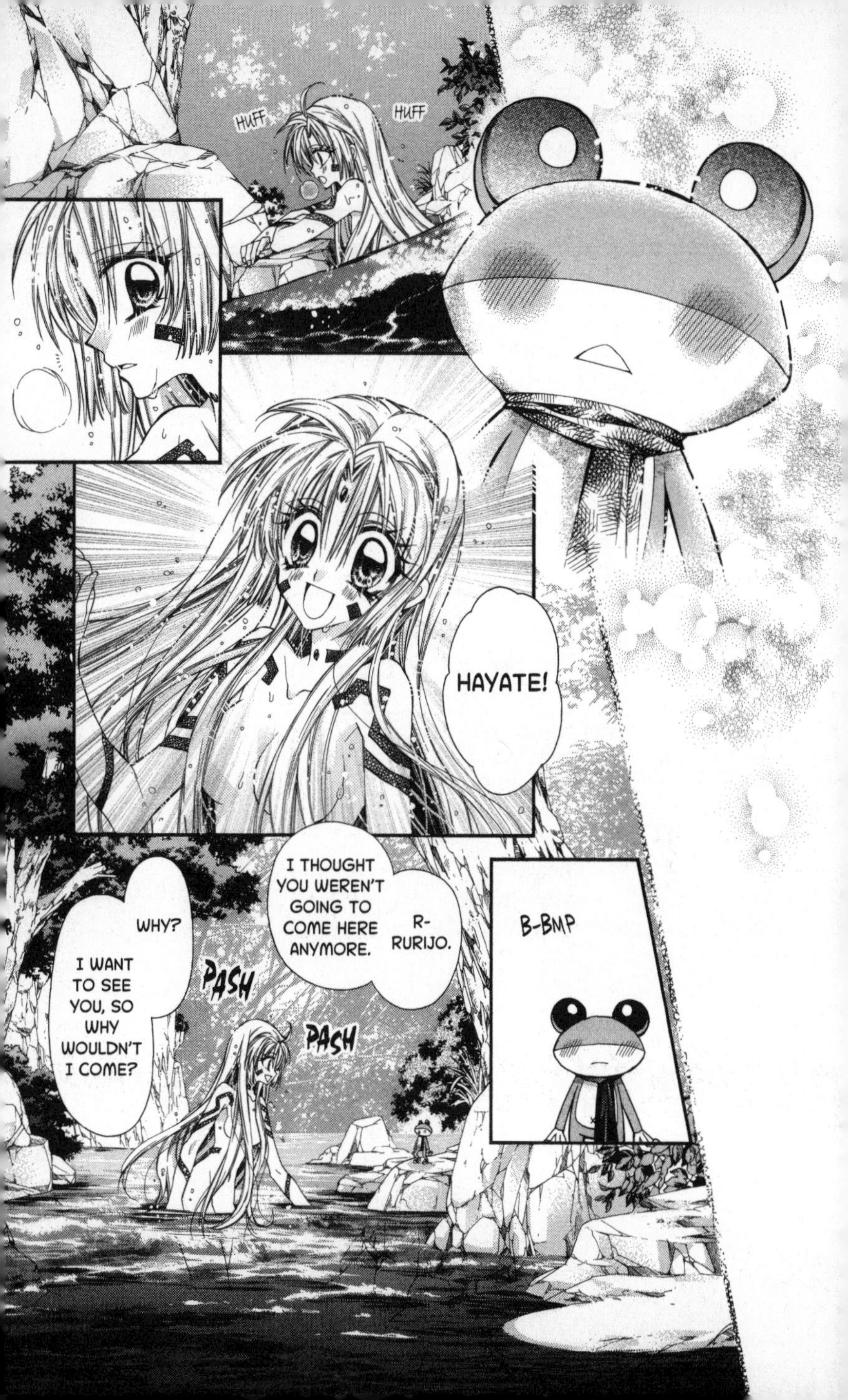
HUFF
HUFF
HAYATE!
B-BMP
R- RURIJO.
I THOUGHT YOU WEREN'T GOING TO COME HERE ANYMORE.
WHY?
I WANT TO SEE YOU, SO WHY WOULDN'T I COME?
PASH
PASH

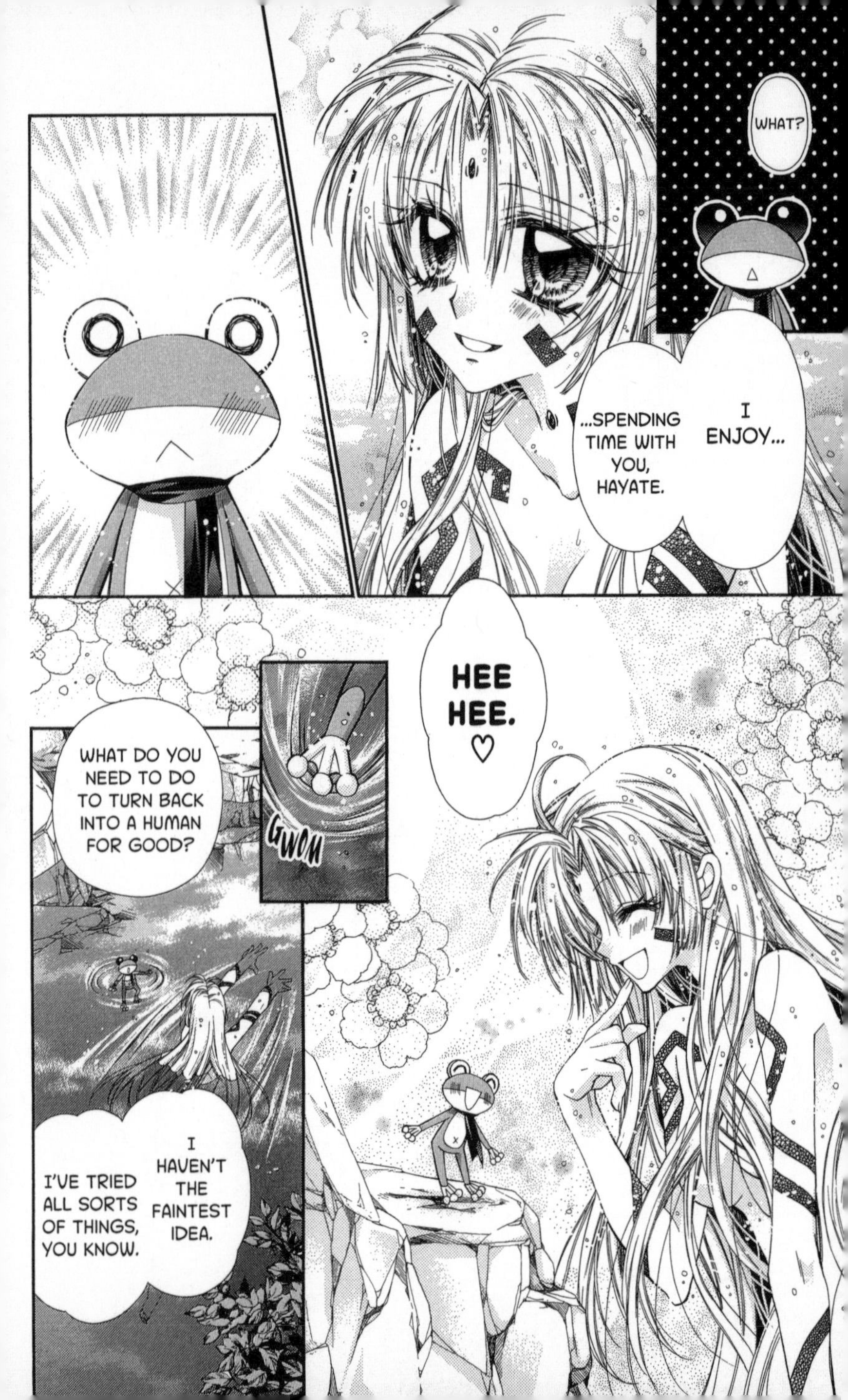
WHAT?
I ENJOY...
...SPENDING TIME WITH YOU, HAYATE.
HEE HEE. ♡
GWOM
WHAT DO YOU NEED TO DO TO TURN BACK INTO A HUMAN FOR GOOD?
I HAVEN'T THE FAINTEST IDEA.
I'VE TRIED ALL SORTS OF THINGS, YOU KNOW.

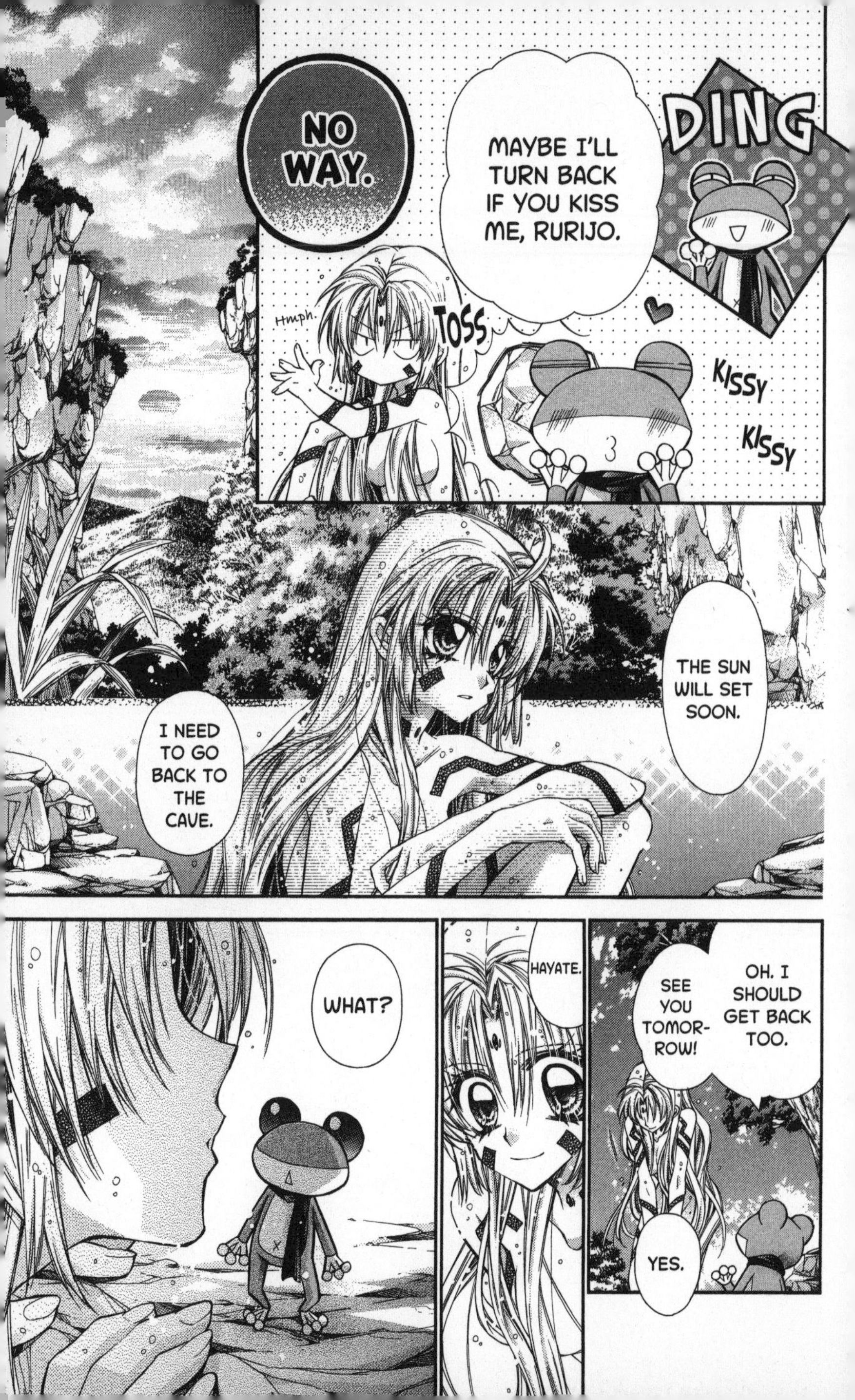
DING
MAYBE I'LL TURN BACK IF YOU KISS ME, RURIJO.
KISSY
KISSY
NO WAY.
TOSS
Hmph.
THE SUN WILL SET SOON.
I NEED TO GO BACK TO THE CAVE.
OH. I SHOULD GET BACK TOO.
SEE YOU TOMOR-ROW!
YES.
HAYATE.
WHAT?

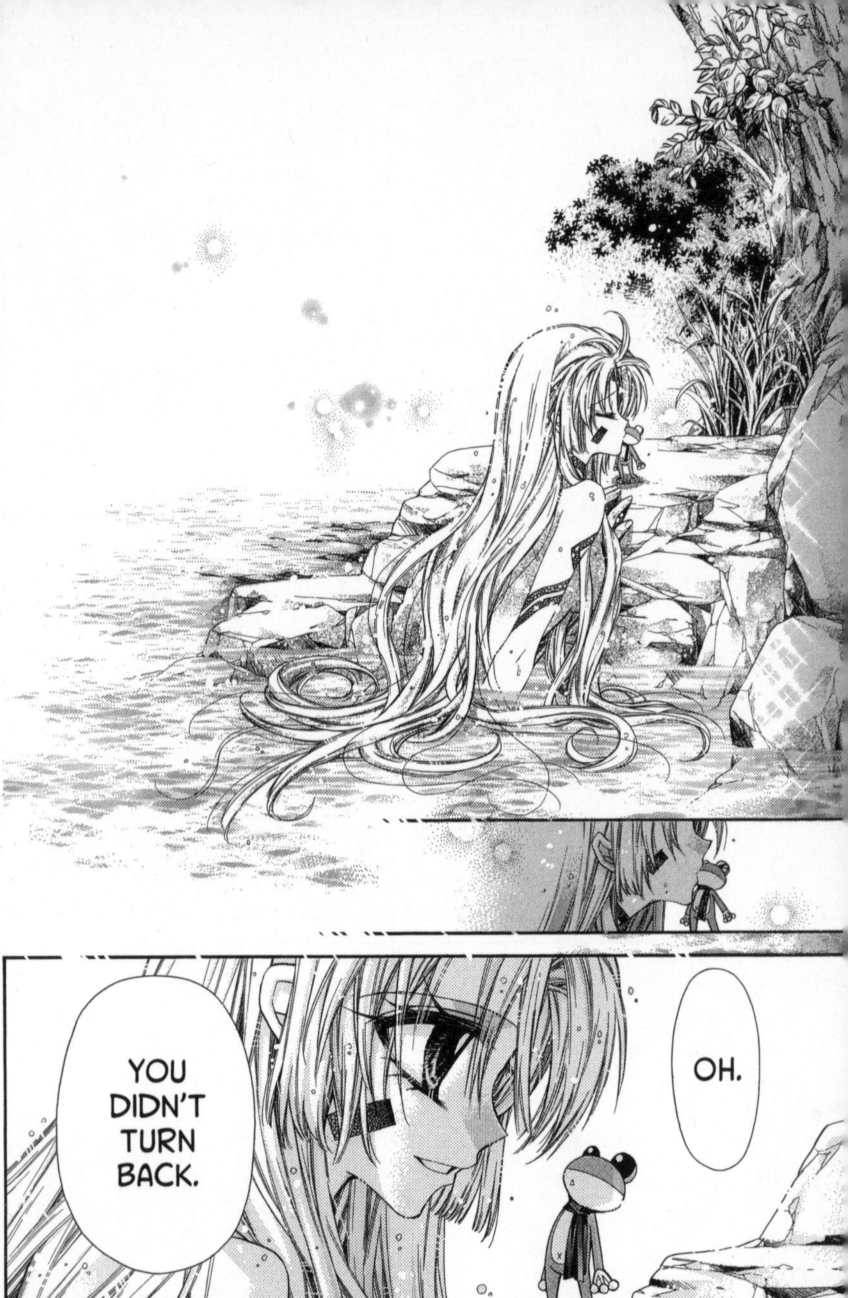
OH.
YOU DIDN'T TURN BACK.

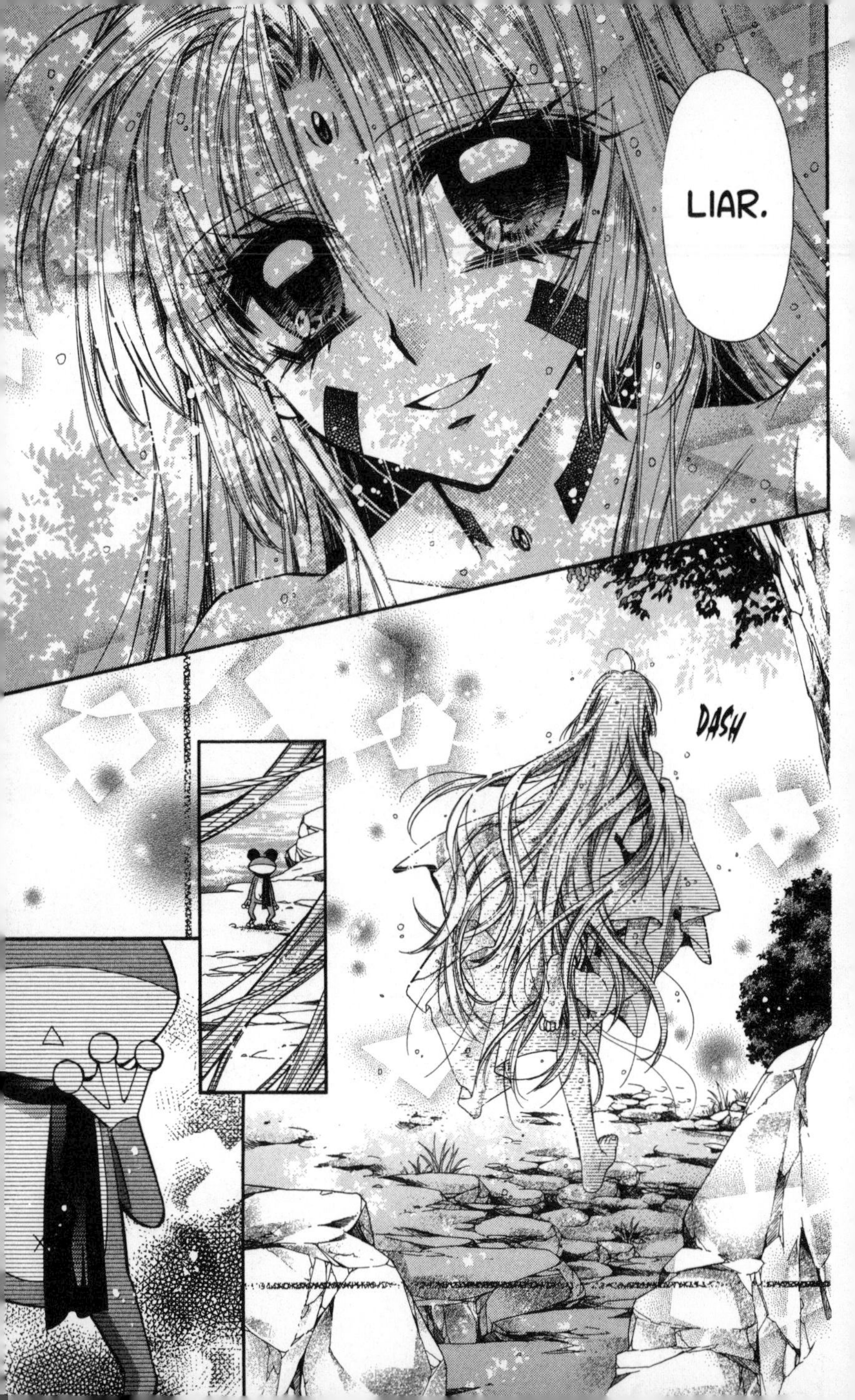
LIAR.
DASH

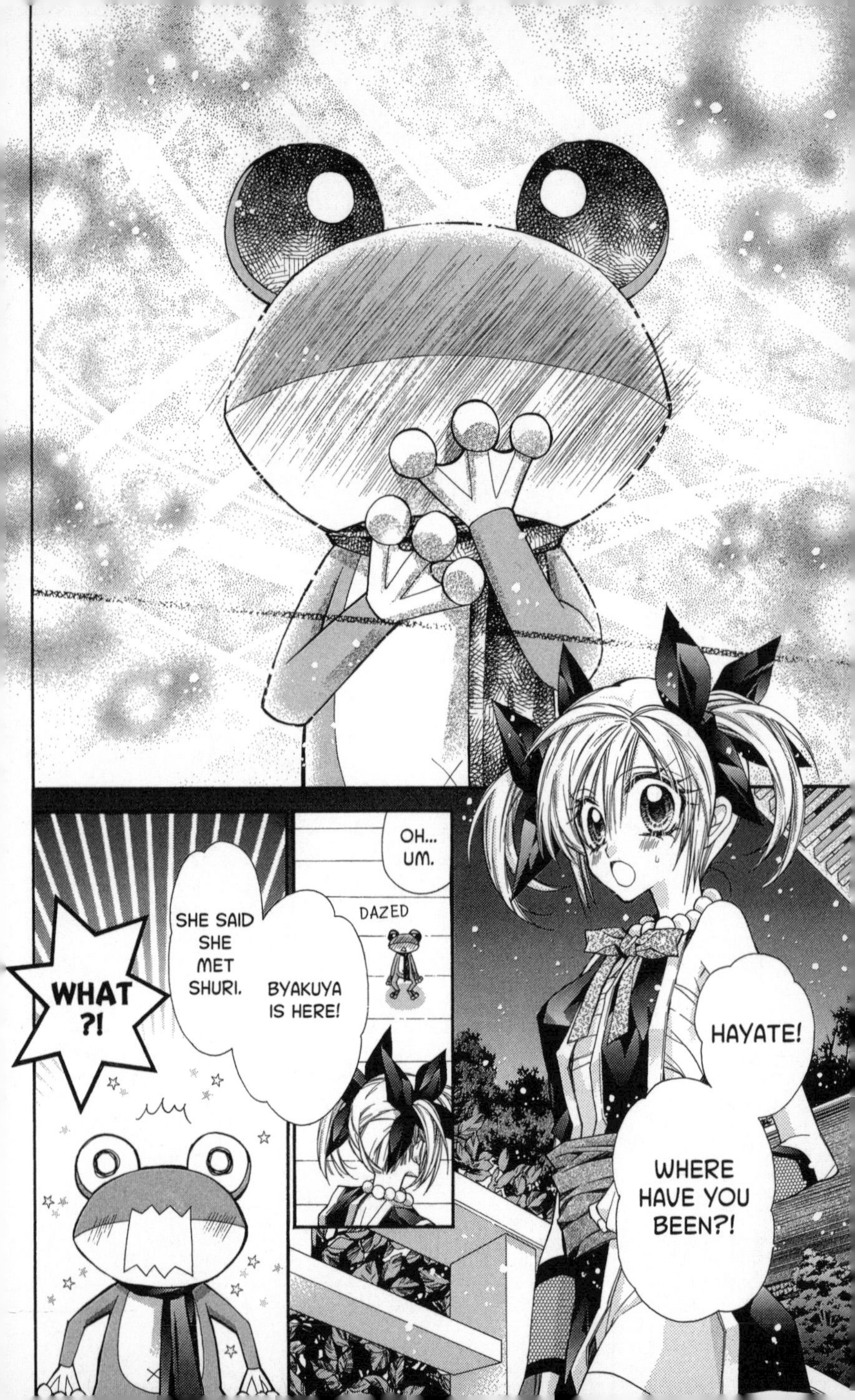
HAYATE!
WHERE HAVE YOU BEEN?!
OH... UM.
DAZED
BYAKUYA IS HERE!
SHE SAID SHE MET SHURI.
WHAT ?!

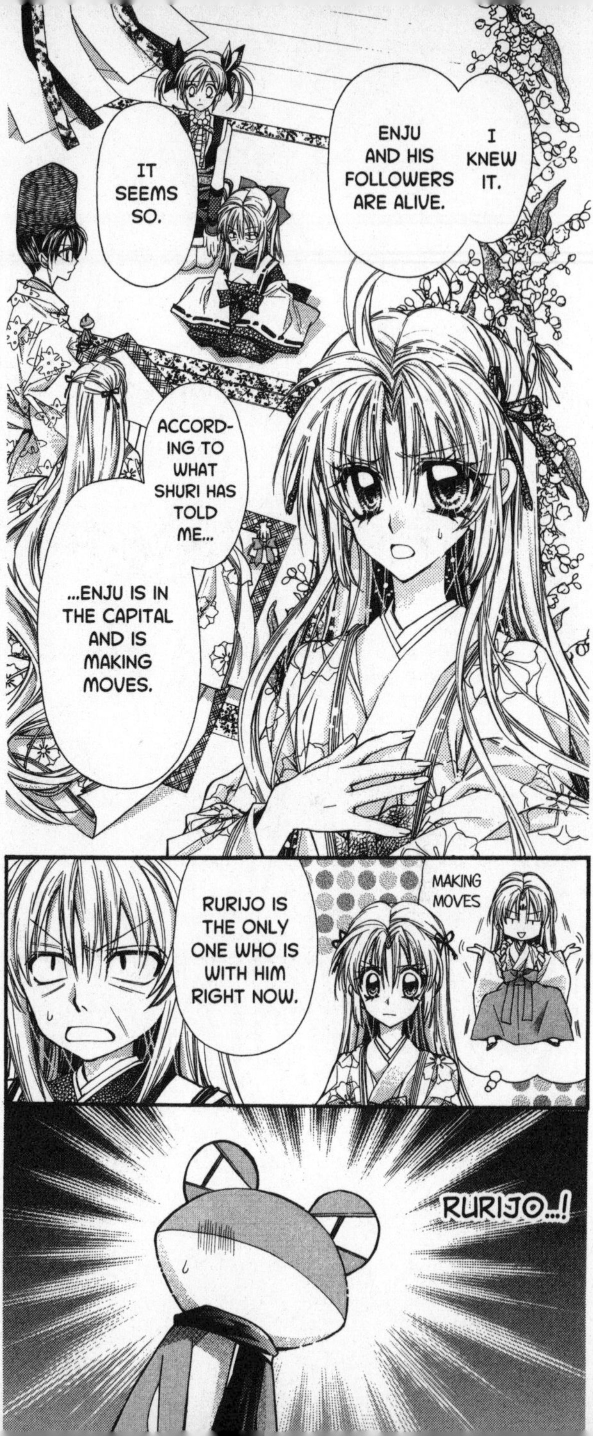
I KNEW IT.
ENJU AND HIS FOLLOWERS ARE ALIVE.
IT SEEMS SO.
ACCORDING TO WHAT SHURI HAS TOLD ME...
...ENJU IS IN THE CAPITAL AND IS MAKING MOVES.
MAKING MOVES
RURIJO IS THE ONLY ONE WHO IS WITH HIM RIGHT NOW.
RURIJO...!

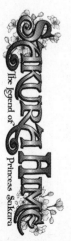

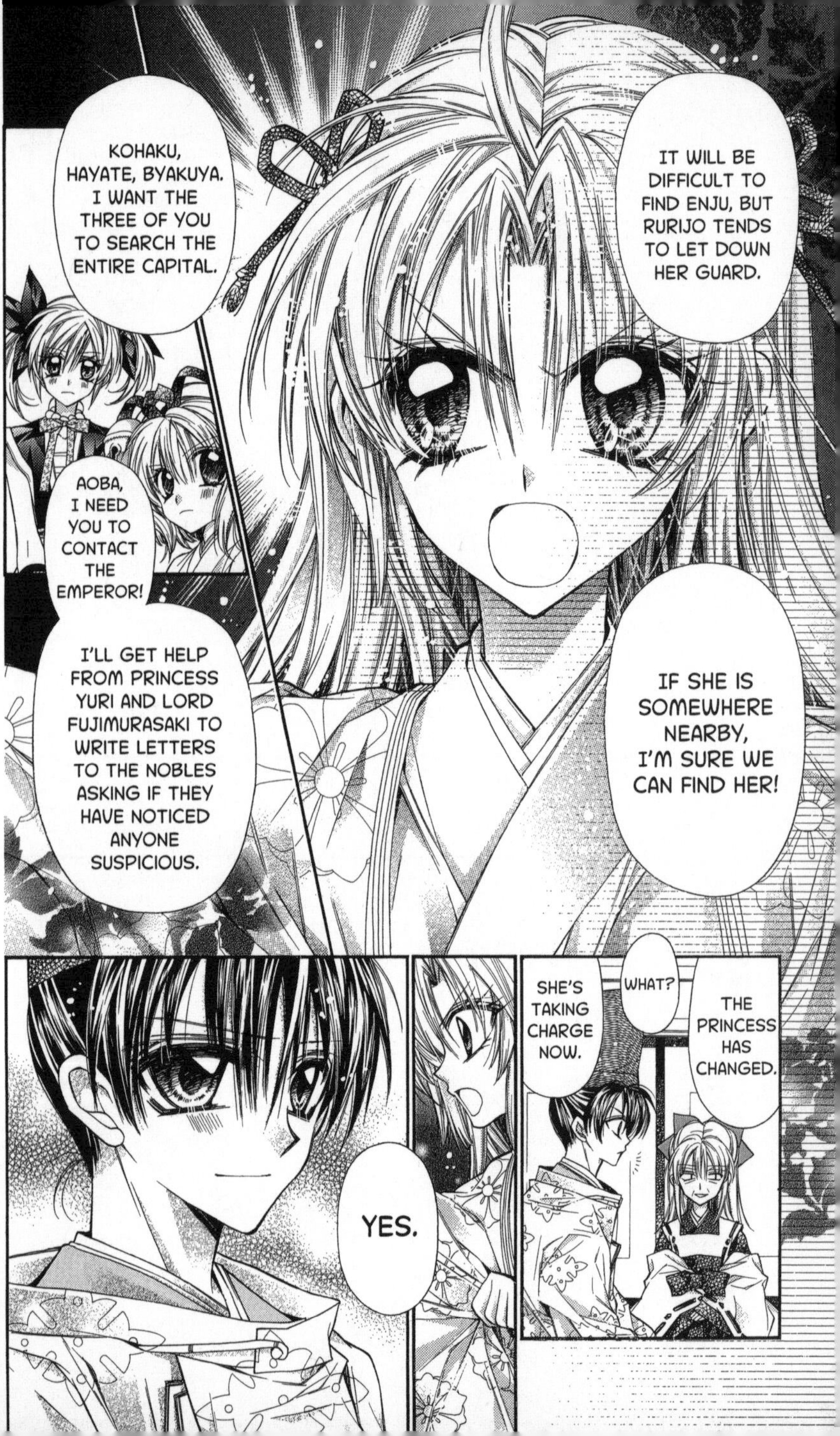
IT WILL BE DIFFICULT TO FIND ENJU, BUT RURIJO TENDS TO LET DOWN HER GUARD.
IF SHE IS SOMEWHERE NEARBY, I'M SURE WE CAN FIND HER!
KOHAKU, HAYATE, BYAKUYA. I WANT THE THREE OF YOU TO SEARCH THE ENTIRE CAPITAL.
AOBA, I NEED YOU TO CONTACT THE EMPEROR!
I'LL GET HELP FROM PRINCESS YURI AND LORD FUJIMURASAKI TO WRITE LETTERS TO THE NOBLES ASKING IF THEY HAVE NOTICED ANYONE SUSPICIOUS.
THE PRINCESS HAS CHANGED.
WHAT?
SHE'S TAKING CHARGE NOW.
YES.

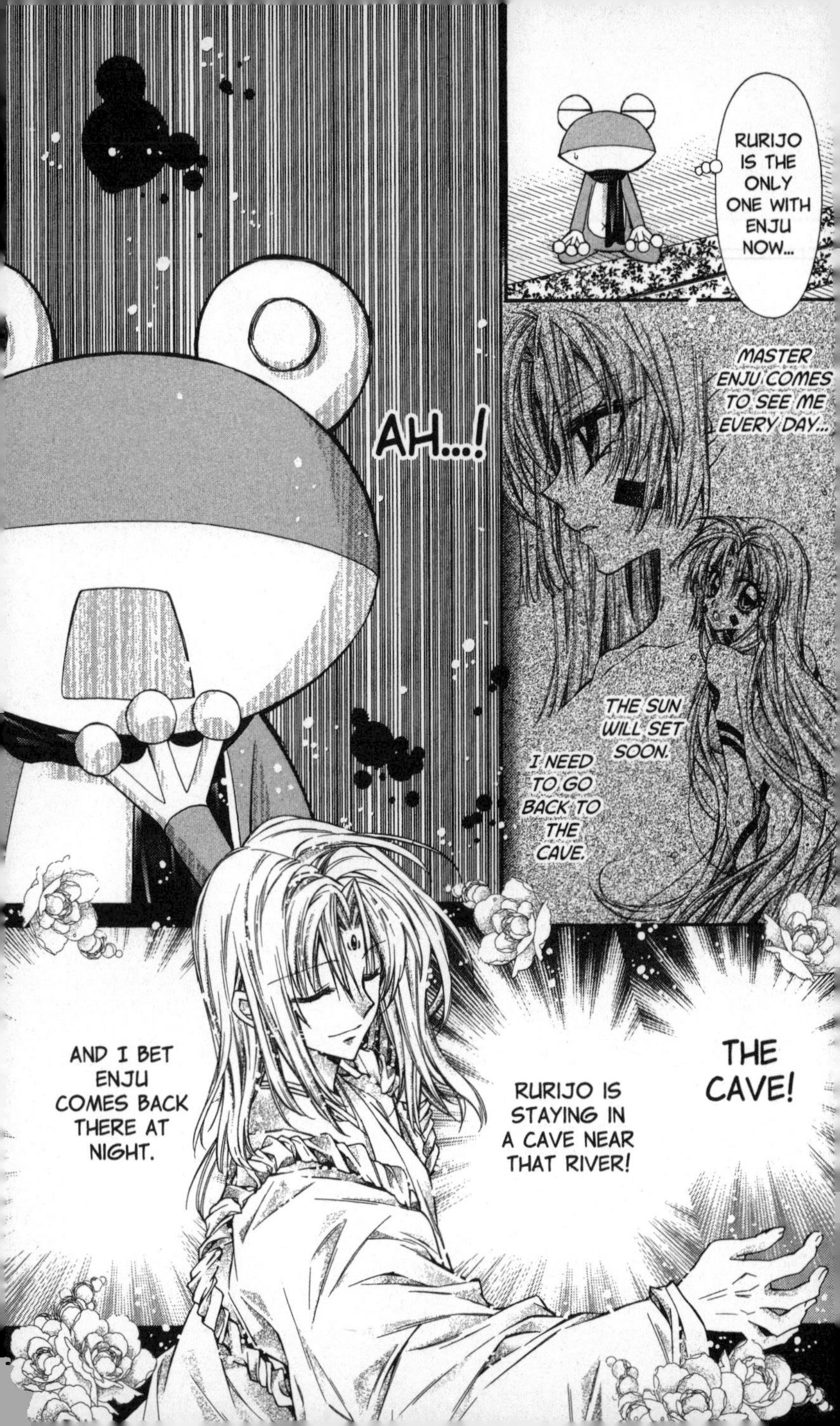
RURIJO IS THE ONLY ONE WITH ENJU NOW...
MASTER ENJU COMES TO SEE ME EVERY DAY...
THE SUN WILL SET SOON.
I NEED TO GO BACK TO THE CAVE.
AH...!
THE CAVE!
RURIJO IS STAYING IN A CAVE NEAR THAT RIVER!
AND I BET ENJU COMES BACK THERE AT NIGHT.

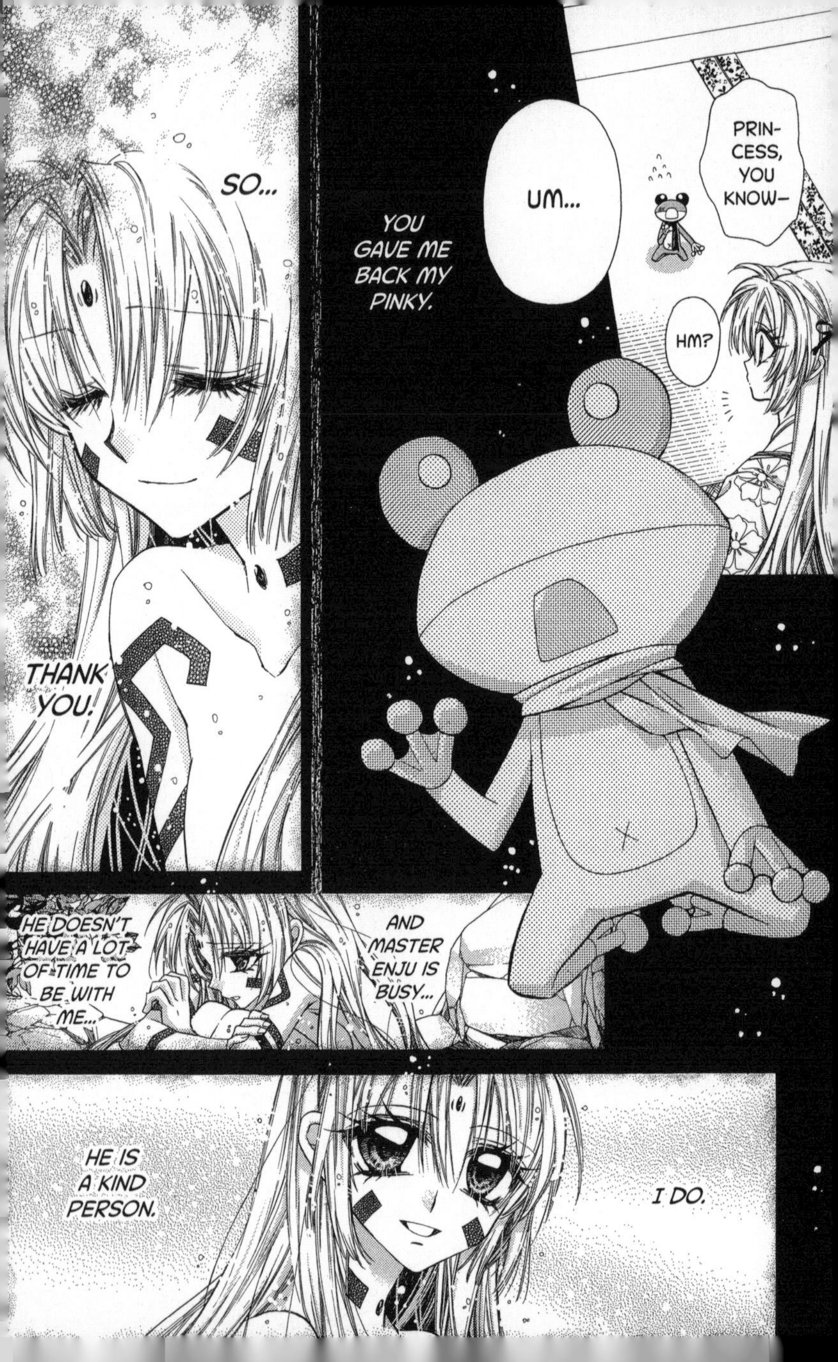
PRIN-CESS, YOU KNOW—
UM...
HM?
YOU GAVE ME BACK MY PINKY.
SO...
THANK YOU.
AND MASTER ENJU IS BUSY...
HE DOESN'T HAVE A LOT OF TIME TO BE WITH ME...
I DO.
HE IS A KIND PERSON.

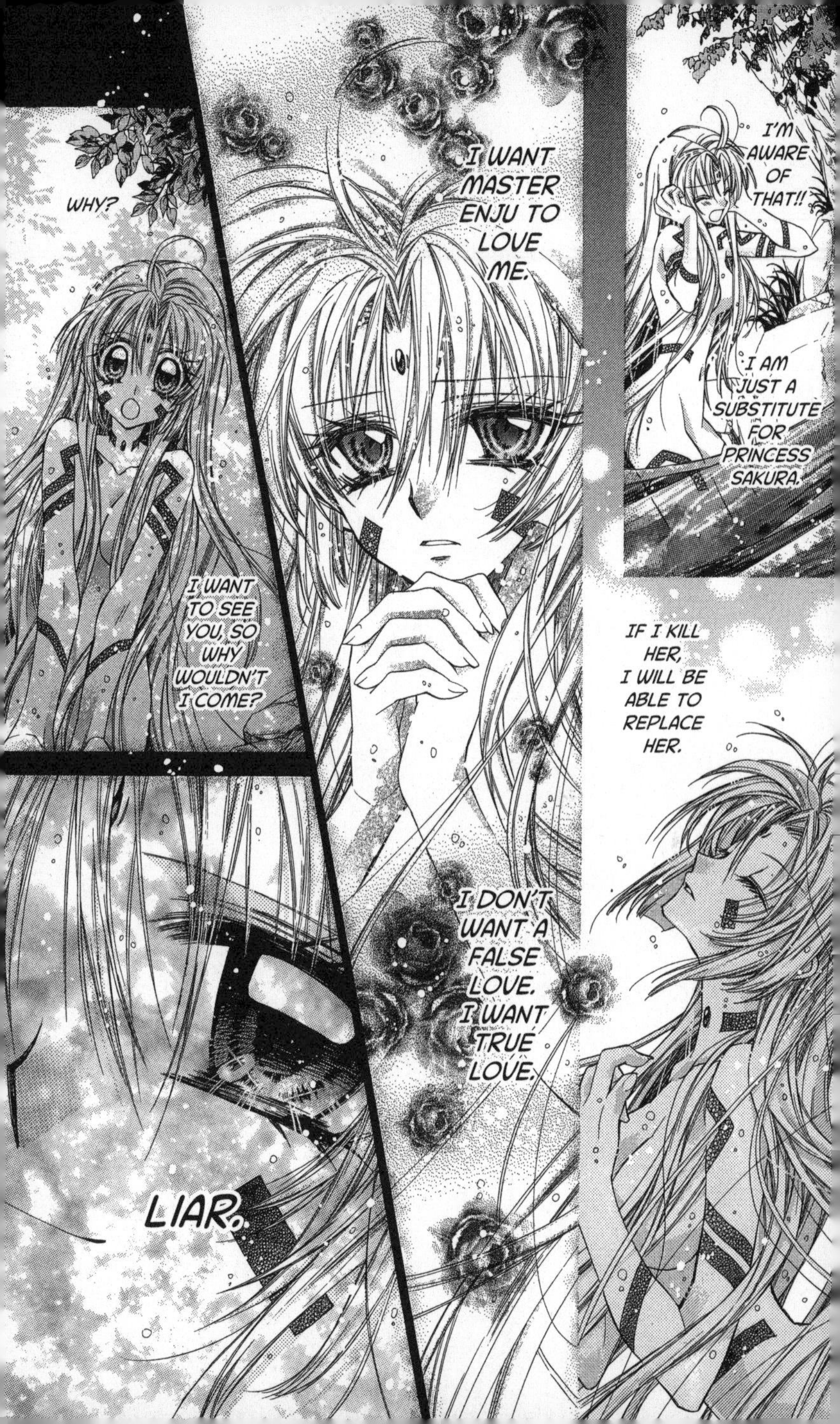
I'M AWARE OF THAT!!
I AM JUST A SUBSTITUTE FOR PRINCESS SAKURA.
IF I KILL HER, I WILL BE ABLE TO REPLACE HER.
I WANT MASTER ENJU TO LOVE ME.
I DON'T WANT A FALSE LOVE. I WANT TRUE LOVE.
WHY?
I WANT TO SEE YOU, SO WHY WOULDN'T I COME?
LIAR.

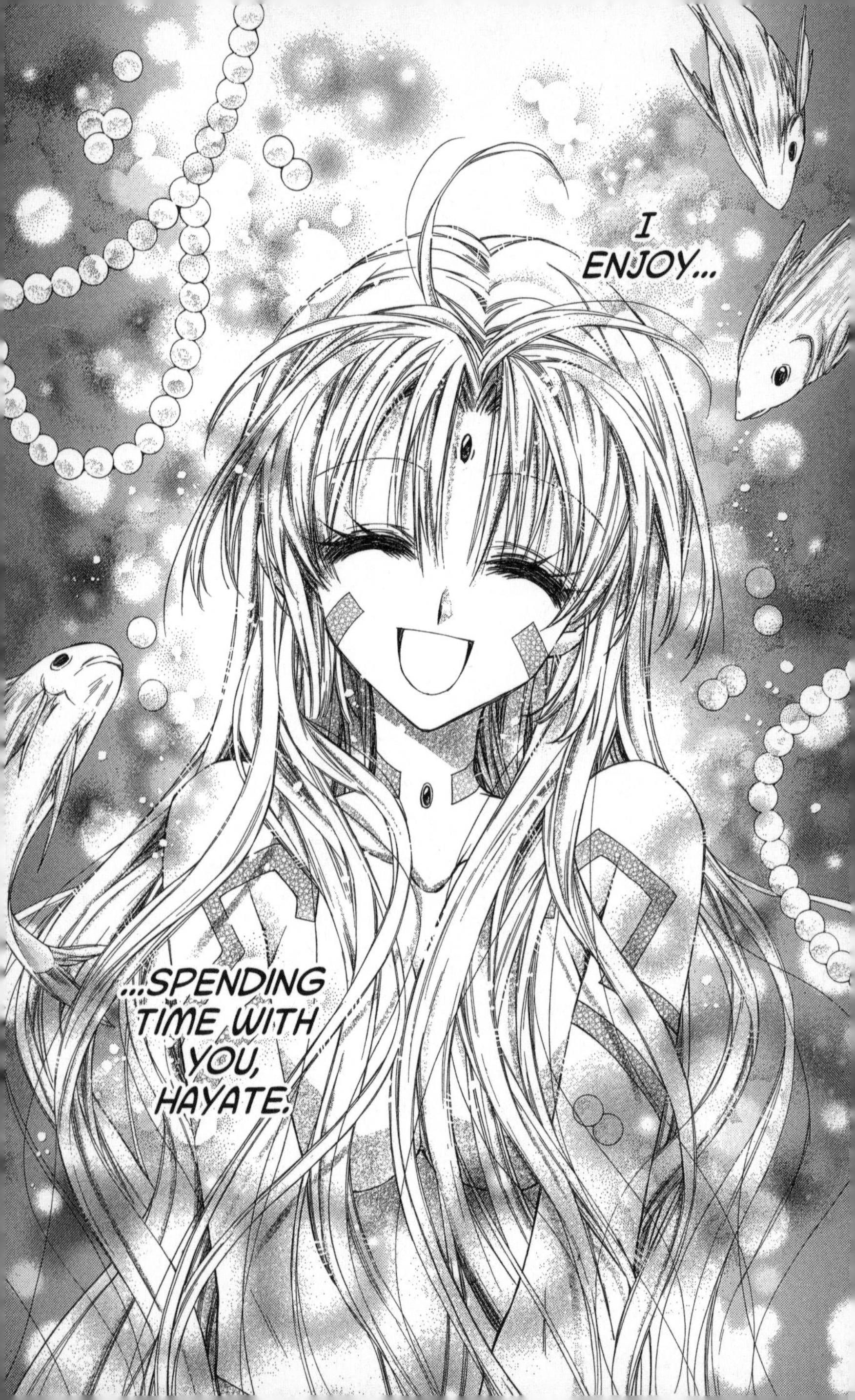
I ENJOY...
...SPENDING TIME WITH YOU, HAYATE.

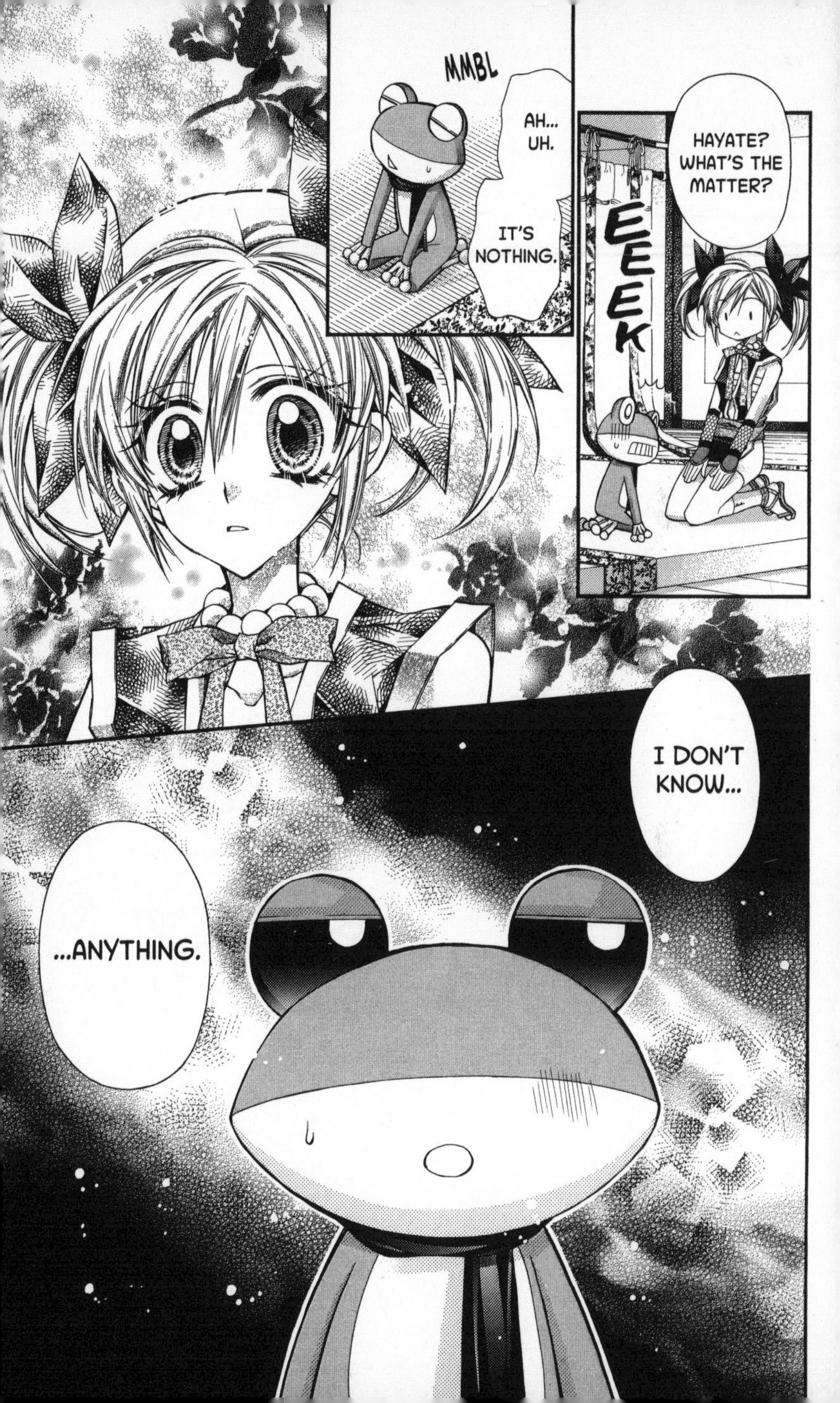
HAYATE? WHAT'S THE MATTER?
EEEK
MMBL
AH... UH.
IT'S NOTHING.
I DON'T KNOW...
...ANYTHING.

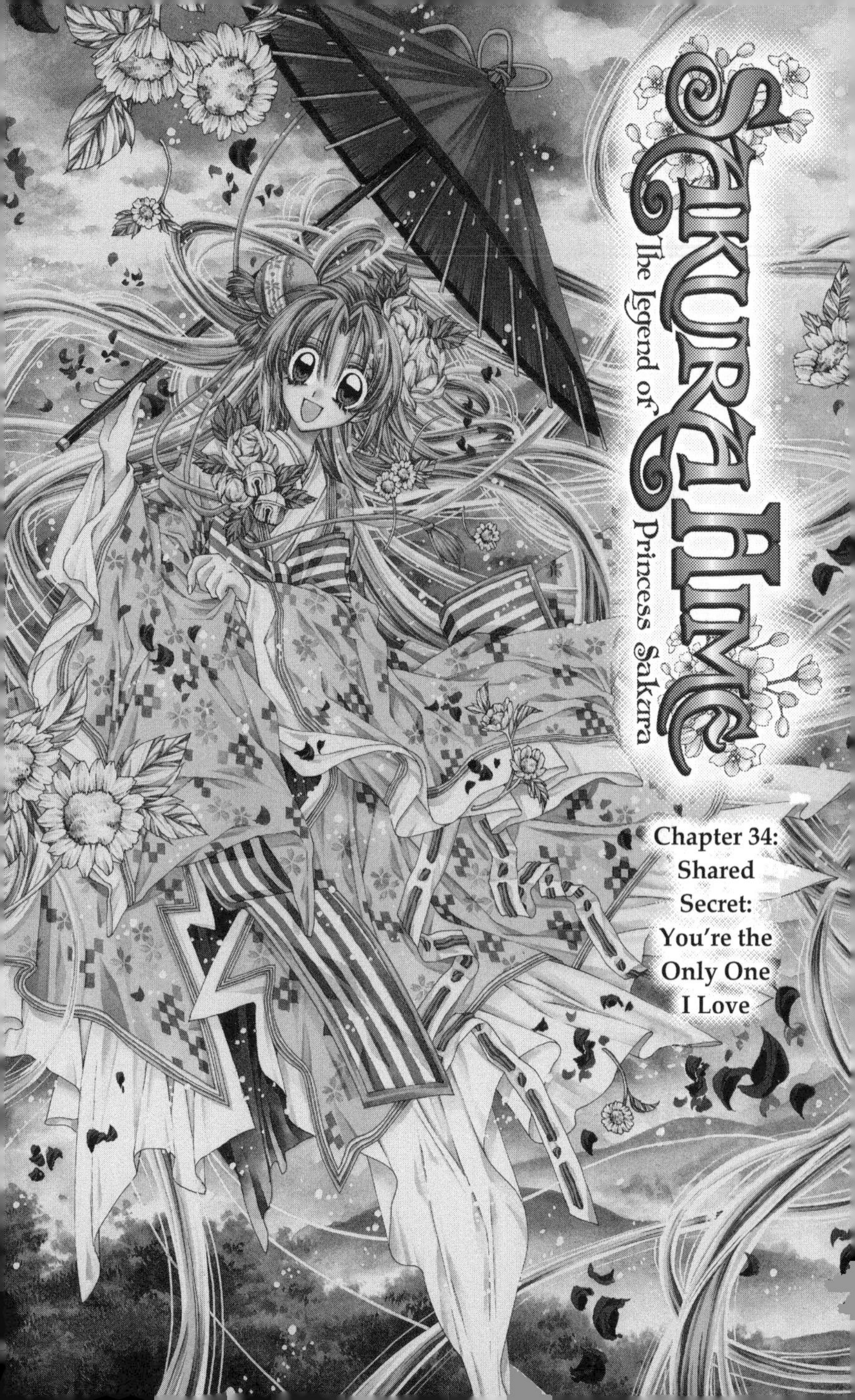
Sakura Hime
The Legend of Princess Sakura
Chapter 34:
Shared Secret: You're the Only One I Love

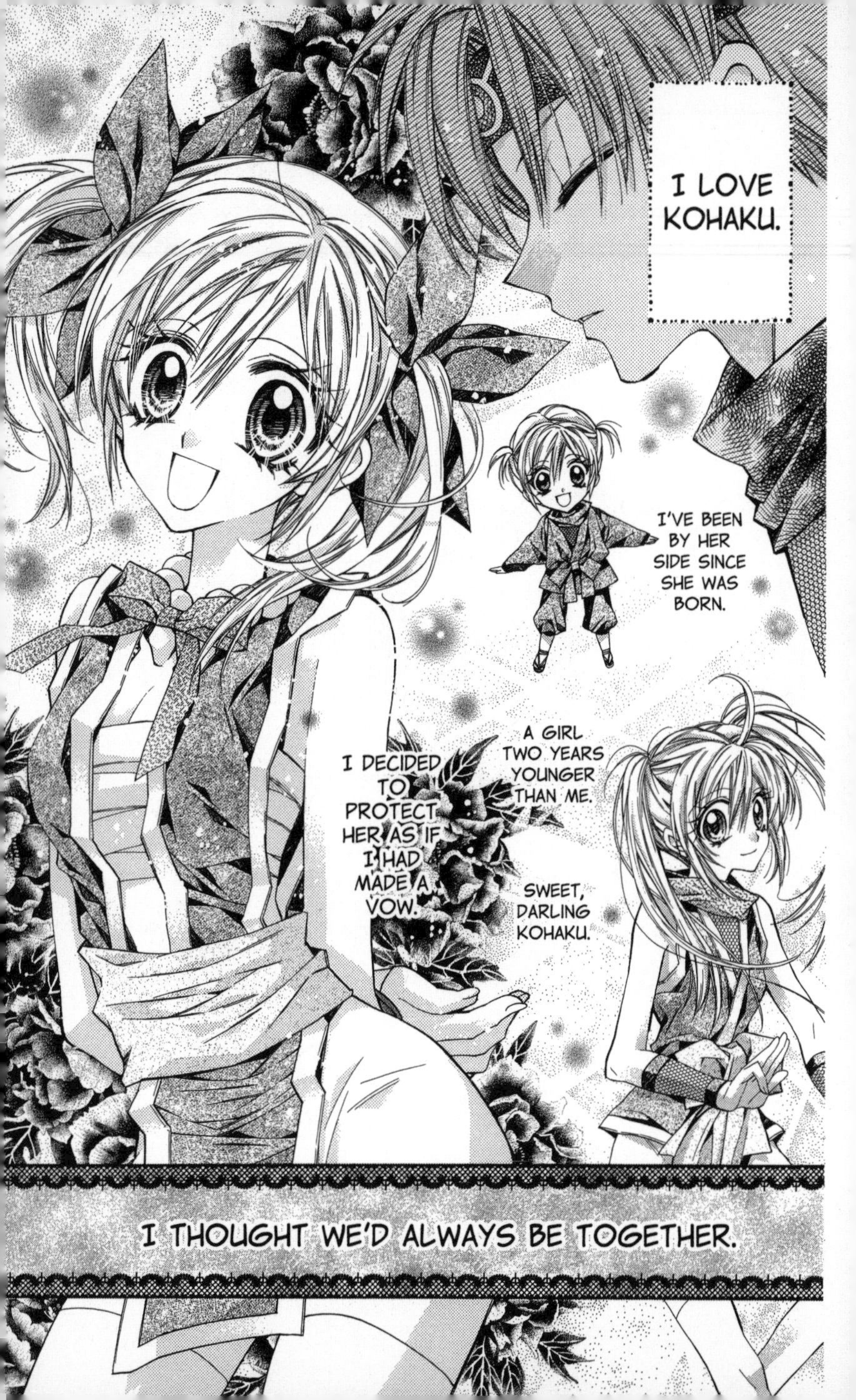
I LOVE KOHAKU.
I'VE BEEN BY HER SIDE SINCE SHE WAS BORN.
A GIRL TWO YEARS YOUNGER THAN ME.
SWEET, DARLING KOHAKU.
I DECIDED TO PROTECT HER AS IF I HAD MADE A VOW.
I THOUGHT WE'D ALWAYS BE TOGETHER.

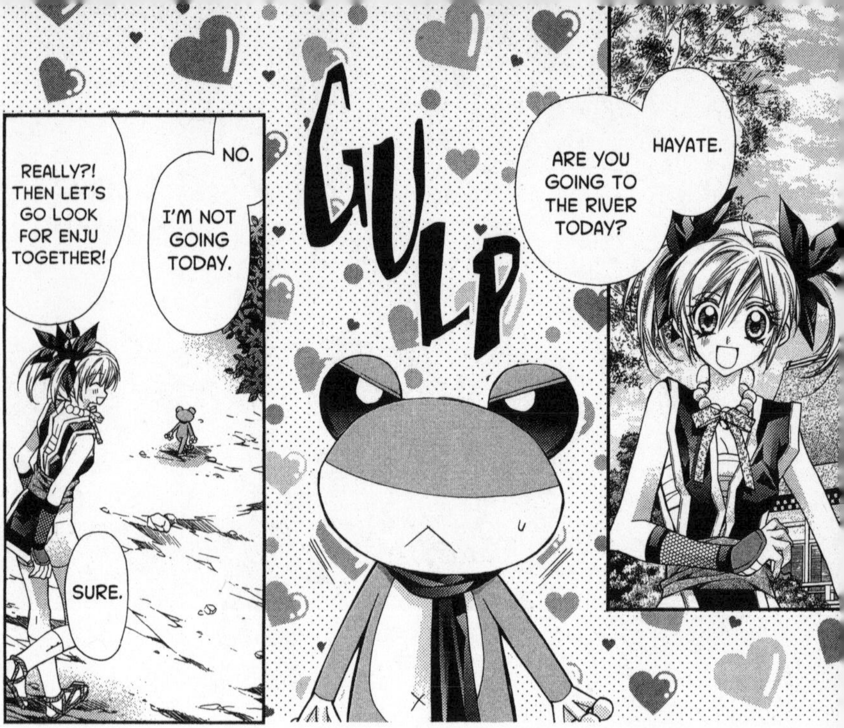

Chapter 34: Shared Secret: You're the Only One I Love

※ I'm giving away the story.

I had a series in *Margaret* when I was working on this arc. Three final drafts were due per month (four if I include the essay in *Cobalt*). But frog Hayate was so easy to draw, and naked Rurijo was easy for both me and my assistants. (←Because there isn't much room for screentones). I thought, "I might just be able to get through this...?!" Then I ended up with this chapter! I do the inking for the human Hayate myself, and the assistants paste his screentones, so he takes more time than any other character. But there was nothing I could do about it. This is the way the story turned out. (I'm the one who created it!) (laugh) So we all cried when we were working on this chapter. (laugh)

A duplicate of the chapter title page illustration was created for my exhibition as well. ♥ It's Princess Sakura flying with an umbrella in the setting sun... It doesn't sound very interesting if I put it into words, but it is one of my favorite illustrations. When I finished the inking, I thought it didn't look the way I had imagined it, so I was surprised how it turned out after I colored it. You can't tell what the final illustration will look like until it's complete.

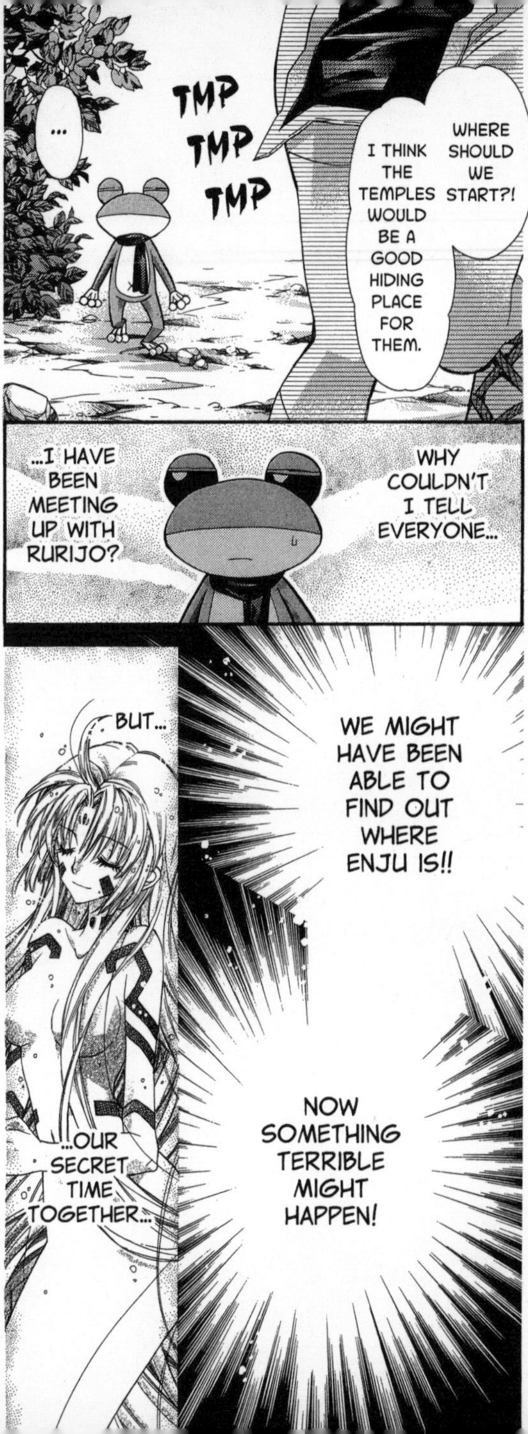
WHERE SHOULD WE START?!
I THINK THE TEMPLES WOULD BE A GOOD HIDING PLACE FOR THEM.
TMP TMP TMP
...
WHY COULDN'T I TELL EVERYONE...
...I HAVE BEEN MEETING UP WITH RURIJO?
WE MIGHT HAVE BEEN ABLE TO FIND OUT WHERE ENJU IS!!
NOW SOMETHING TERRIBLE MIGHT HAPPEN!
BUT...
...OUR SECRET TIME TOGETHER...

THANK YOU

Thank you very much for reading this! I hope I will see you again in volume 10 of *Sakura Hime*, which is coming out next month in Japan. ♪

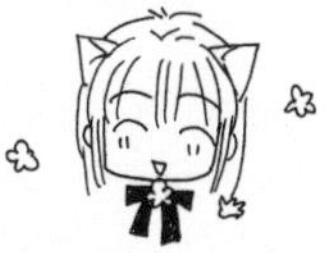

Special Thanks

Nakame
Momo-chan

Sakakura-san	Matsun
Hii-chan	Yogurt-chan
Kobata-san	Icchi
Miichi	Ikurun
Kogo-san	Mari
Rena-san	Naho Minami-tan
Tomi-chan	Hino-san

Ammonite, Inc.
Shueisha
Ribon Editorial Department

Kawatani Design

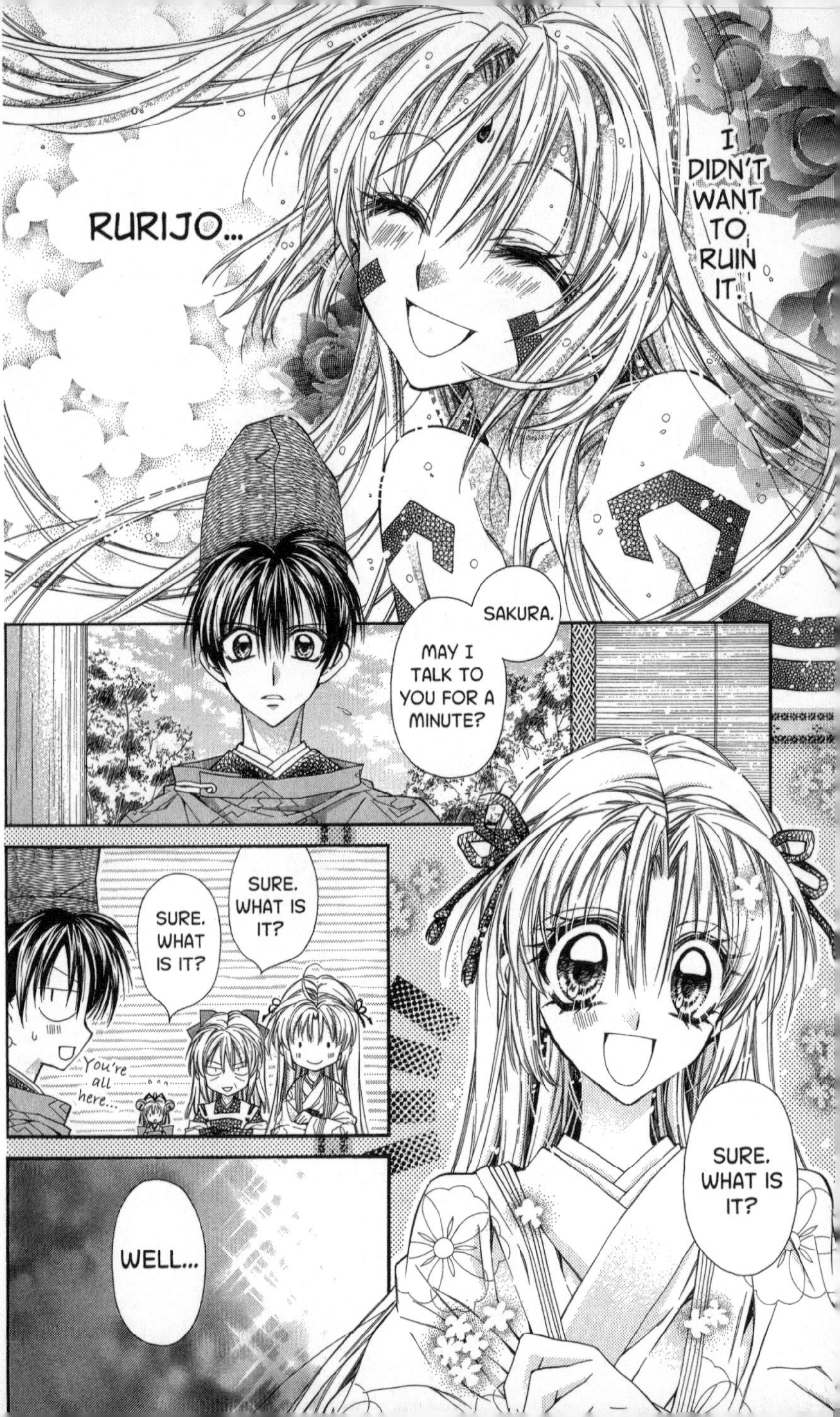

I DIDN'T WANT TO RUIN IT.
RURIJO...
SAKURA.
MAY I TALK TO YOU FOR A MINUTE?
SURE. WHAT IS IT?
SURE. WHAT IS IT?
SURE. WHAT IS IT?
You're all here...
WELL...

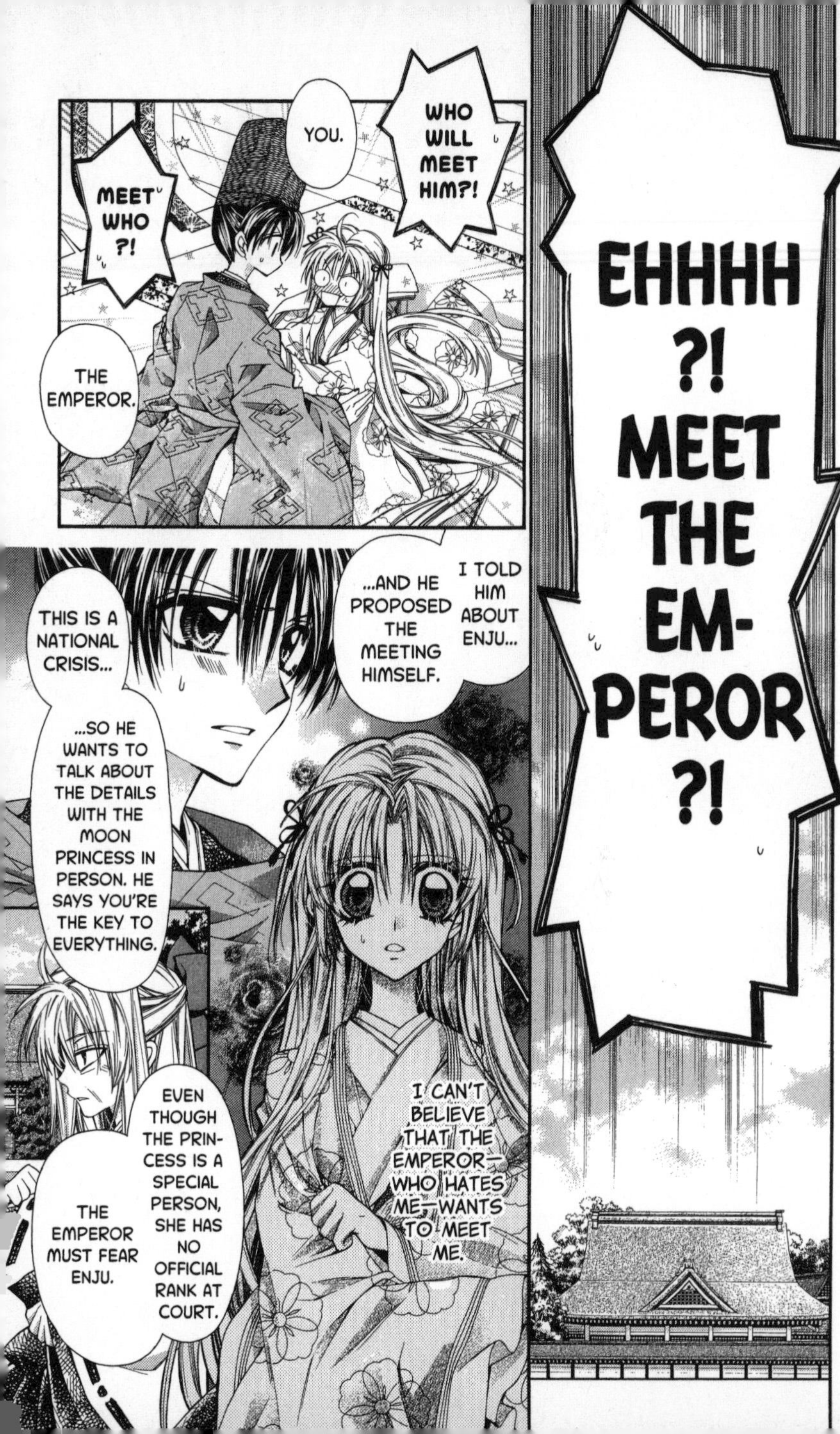
EHHHH ?! MEET THE EM-PEROR ?!
WHO WILL MEET HIM?!
YOU.
MEET WHO ?!
THE EMPEROR.
I TOLD HIM ABOUT ENJU...
...AND HE PROPOSED THE MEETING HIMSELF.
THIS IS A NATIONAL CRISIS...
...SO HE WANTS TO TALK ABOUT THE DETAILS WITH THE MOON PRINCESS IN PERSON. HE SAYS YOU'RE THE KEY TO EVERYTHING.
I CAN'T BELIEVE THAT THE EMPEROR—WHO HATES ME—WANTS TO MEET ME.
EVEN THOUGH THE PRIN-CESS IS A SPECIAL PERSON, SHE HAS NO OFFICIAL RANK AT COURT.
THE EMPEROR MUST FEAR ENJU.

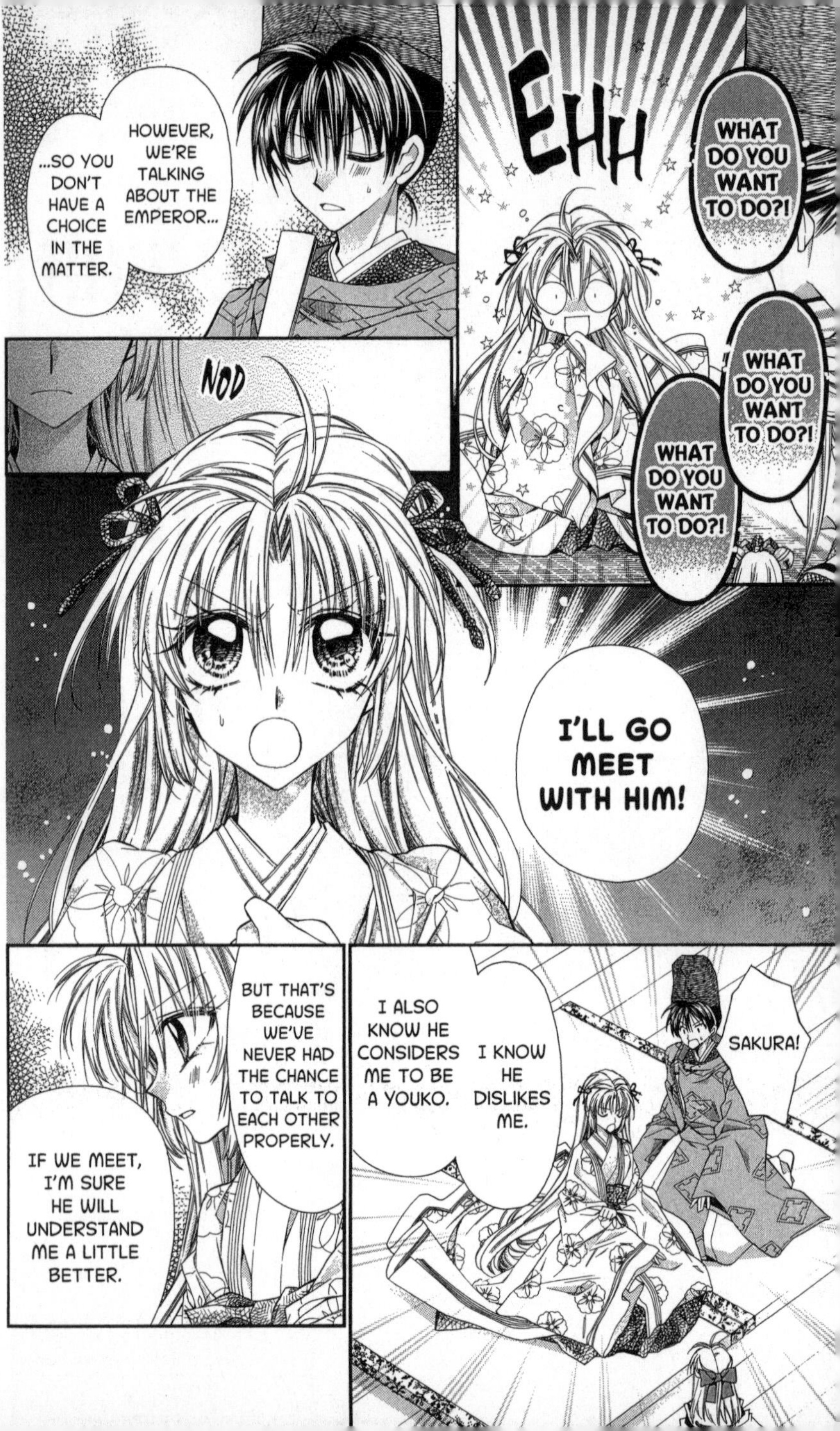
EHH
WHAT DO YOU WANT TO DO?!
WHAT DO YOU WANT TO DO?!
WHAT DO YOU WANT TO DO?!
HOWEVER, WE'RE TALKING ABOUT THE EMPEROR...
...SO YOU DON'T HAVE A CHOICE IN THE MATTER.
NOD
I'LL GO MEET WITH HIM!
SAKURA!
I KNOW HE DISLIKES ME.
I ALSO KNOW HE CONSIDERS ME TO BE A YOUKO.
BUT THAT'S BECAUSE WE'VE NEVER HAD THE CHANCE TO TALK TO EACH OTHER PROPERLY.
IF WE MEET, I'M SURE HE WILL UNDERSTAND ME A LITTLE BETTER.

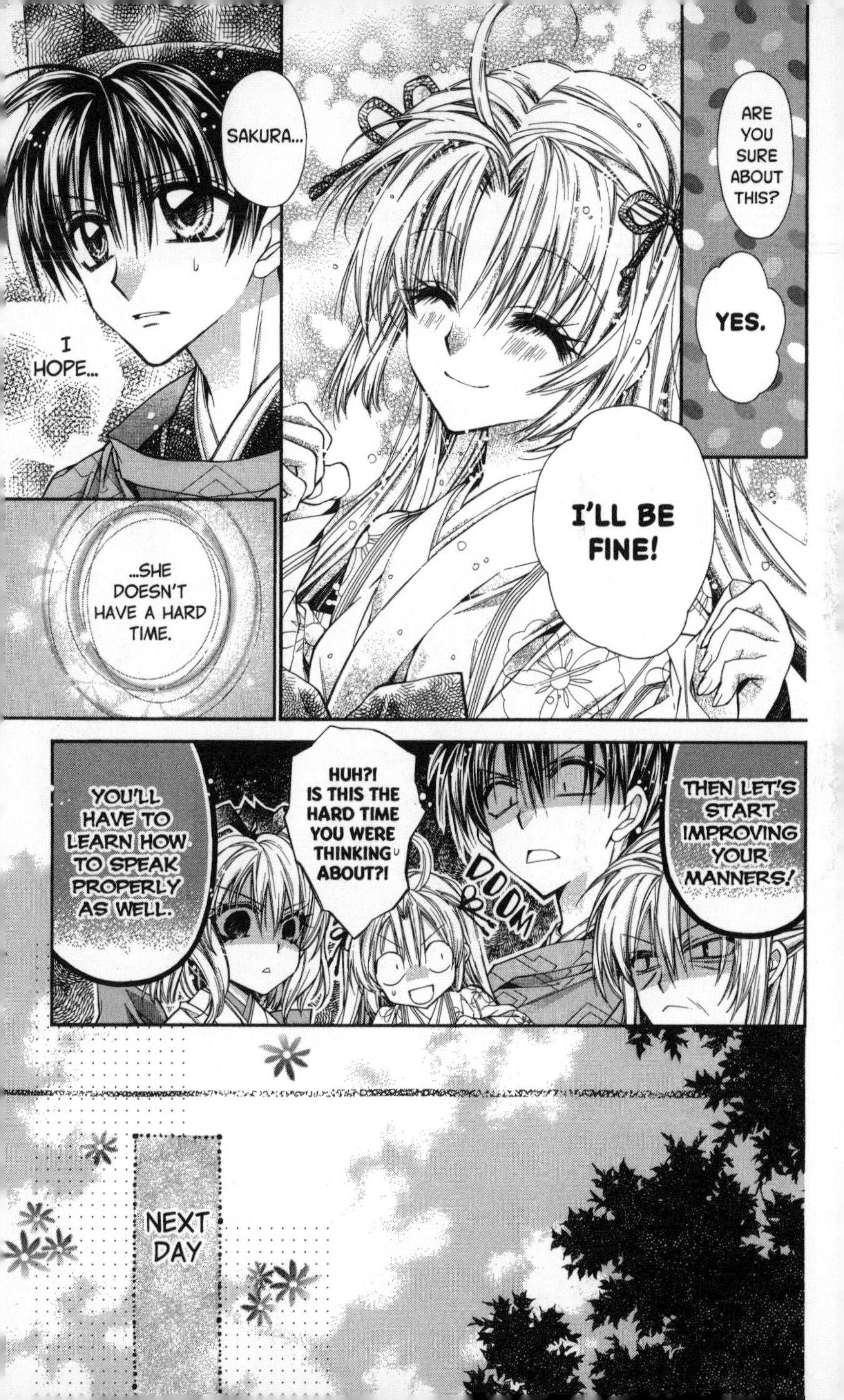
ARE YOU SURE ABOUT THIS?
YES.
I'LL BE FINE!
SAKURA...
I HOPE...
...SHE DOESN'T HAVE A HARD TIME.
THEN LET'S START IMPROVING YOUR MANNERS!
DOOM
HUH?! IS THIS THE HARD TIME YOU WERE THINKING ABOUT?!
YOU'LL HAVE TO LEARN HOW TO SPEAK PROPERLY AS WELL.
NEXT DAY

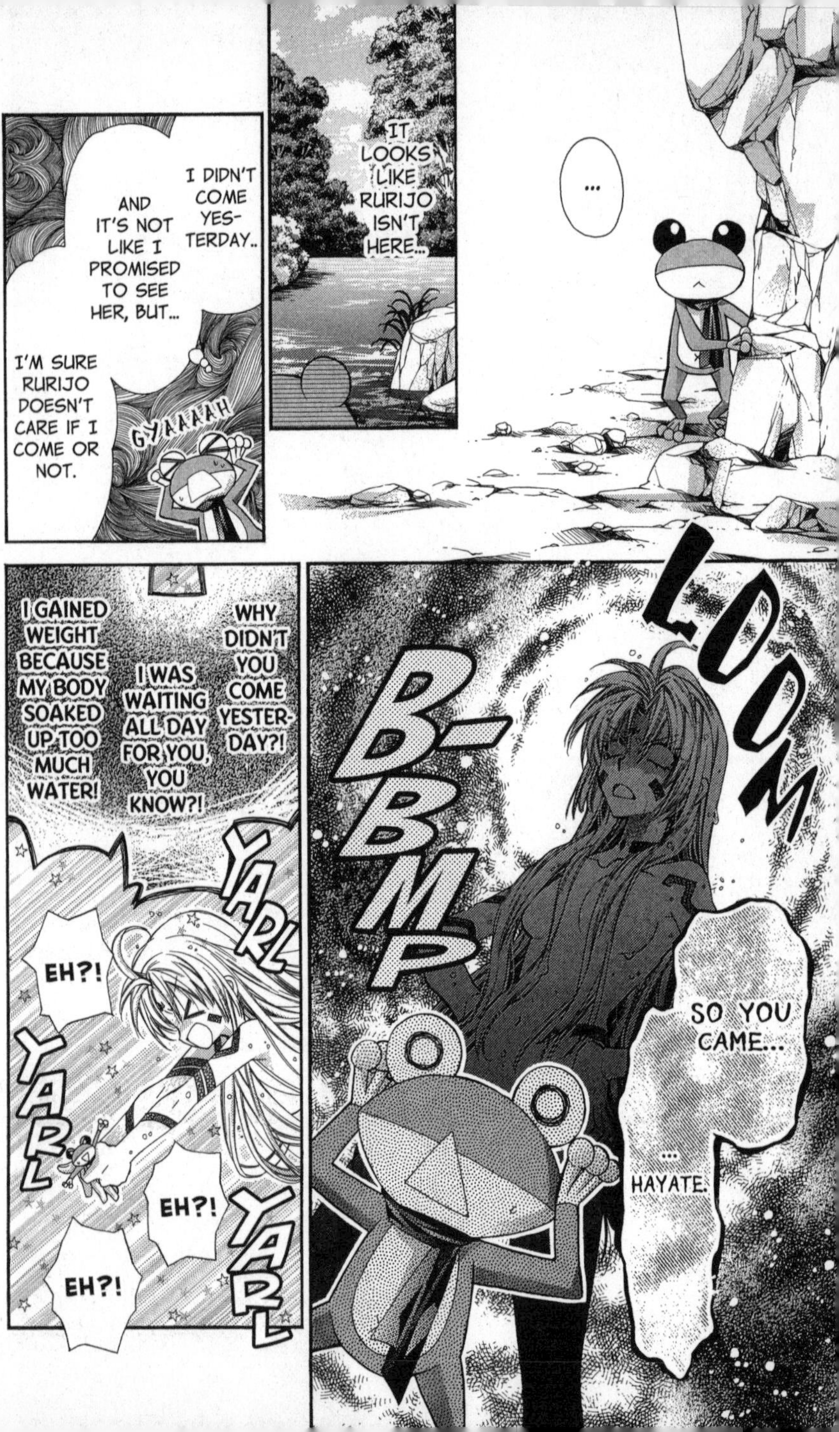
...
IT LOOKS LIKE RURIJO ISN'T HERE...
I DIDN'T COME YES-TERDAY..
AND IT'S NOT LIKE I PROMISED TO SEE HER, BUT...
I'M SURE RURIJO DOESN'T CARE IF I COME OR NOT.
GYAAAAH
LOOM
B-BMP
SO YOU CAME...
... HAYATE.
WHY DIDN'T YOU COME YESTER-DAY?!
I WAS WAITING ALL DAY FOR YOU, YOU KNOW?!
I GAINED WEIGHT BECAUSE MY BODY SOAKED UP TOO MUCH WATER!
YARL
EH?!
YARL
EH?!
YARL
EH?!

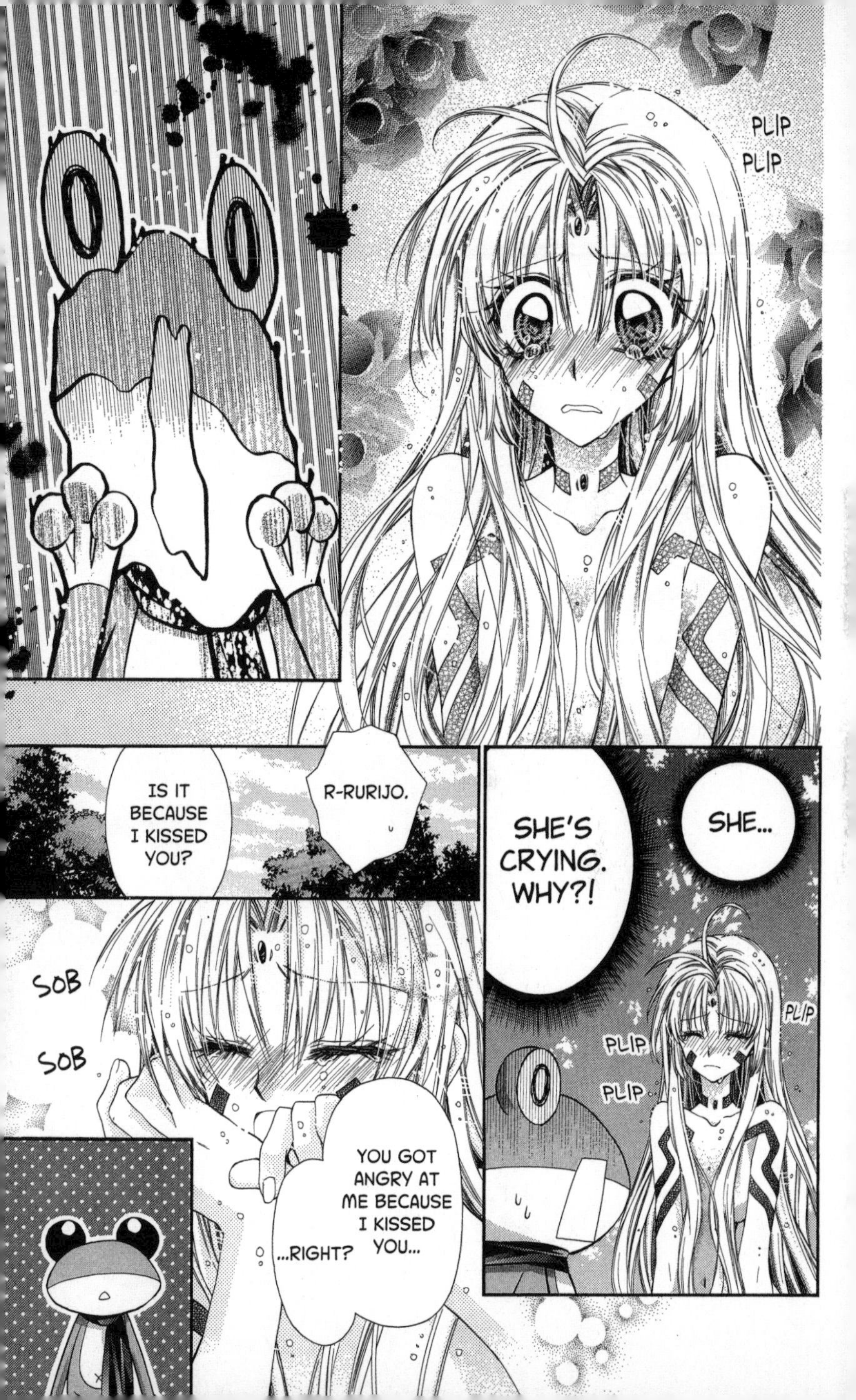
PLIP
PLIP
SHE...
SHE'S CRYING. WHY?!
PLIP
PLIP
PLIP
R-RURIJO.
IS IT BECAUSE I KISSED YOU?
YOU GOT ANGRY AT ME BECAUSE I KISSED YOU...
...RIGHT?
SOB
SOB

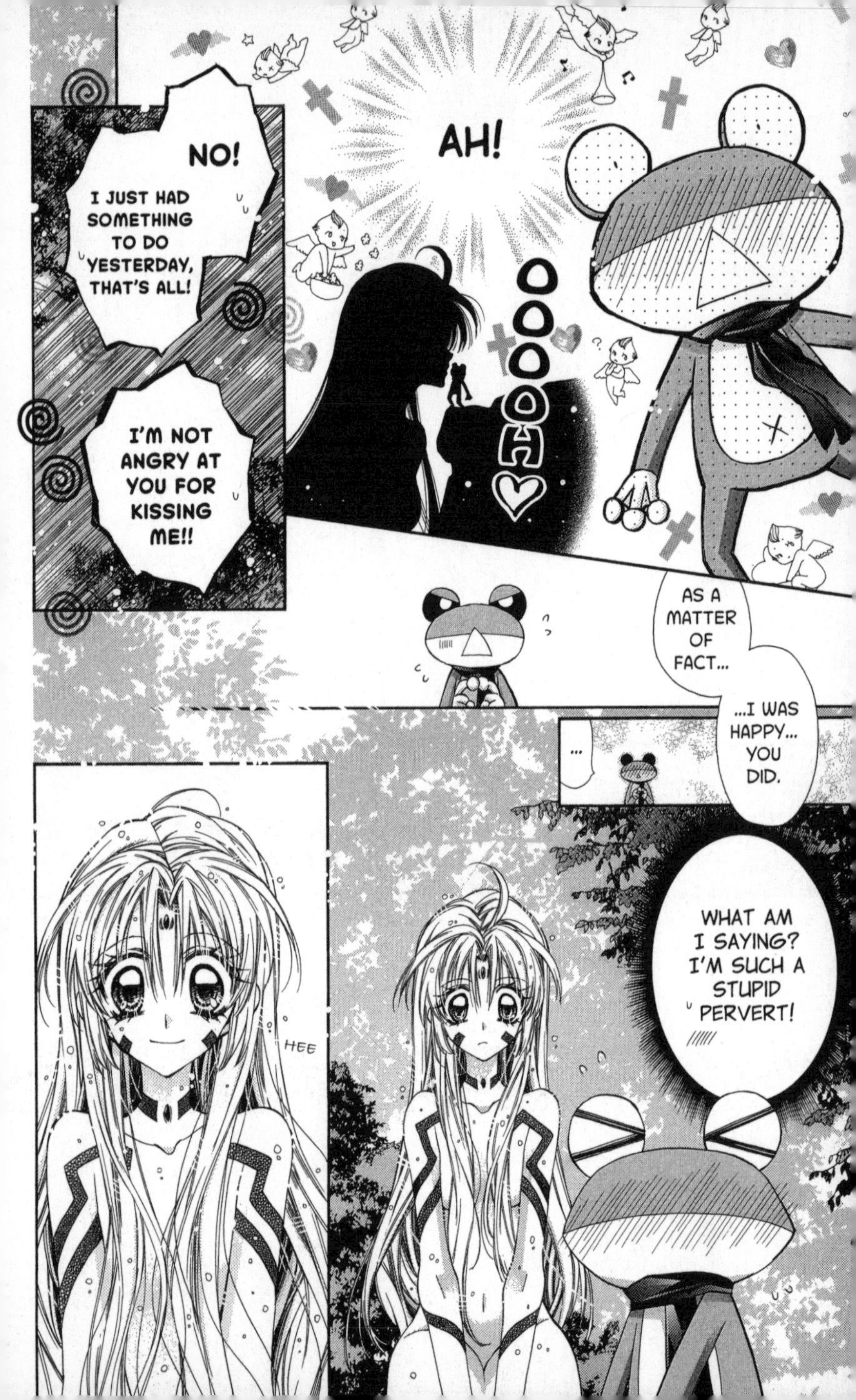
AH!
OOOOOH♥
NO!
I JUST HAD SOMETHING TO DO YESTERDAY, THAT'S ALL!
I'M NOT ANGRY AT YOU FOR KISSING ME!!
AS A MATTER OF FACT...
...I WAS HAPPY... YOU DID.
...
WHAT AM I SAYING? I'M SUCH A STUPID PERVERT!
HEE

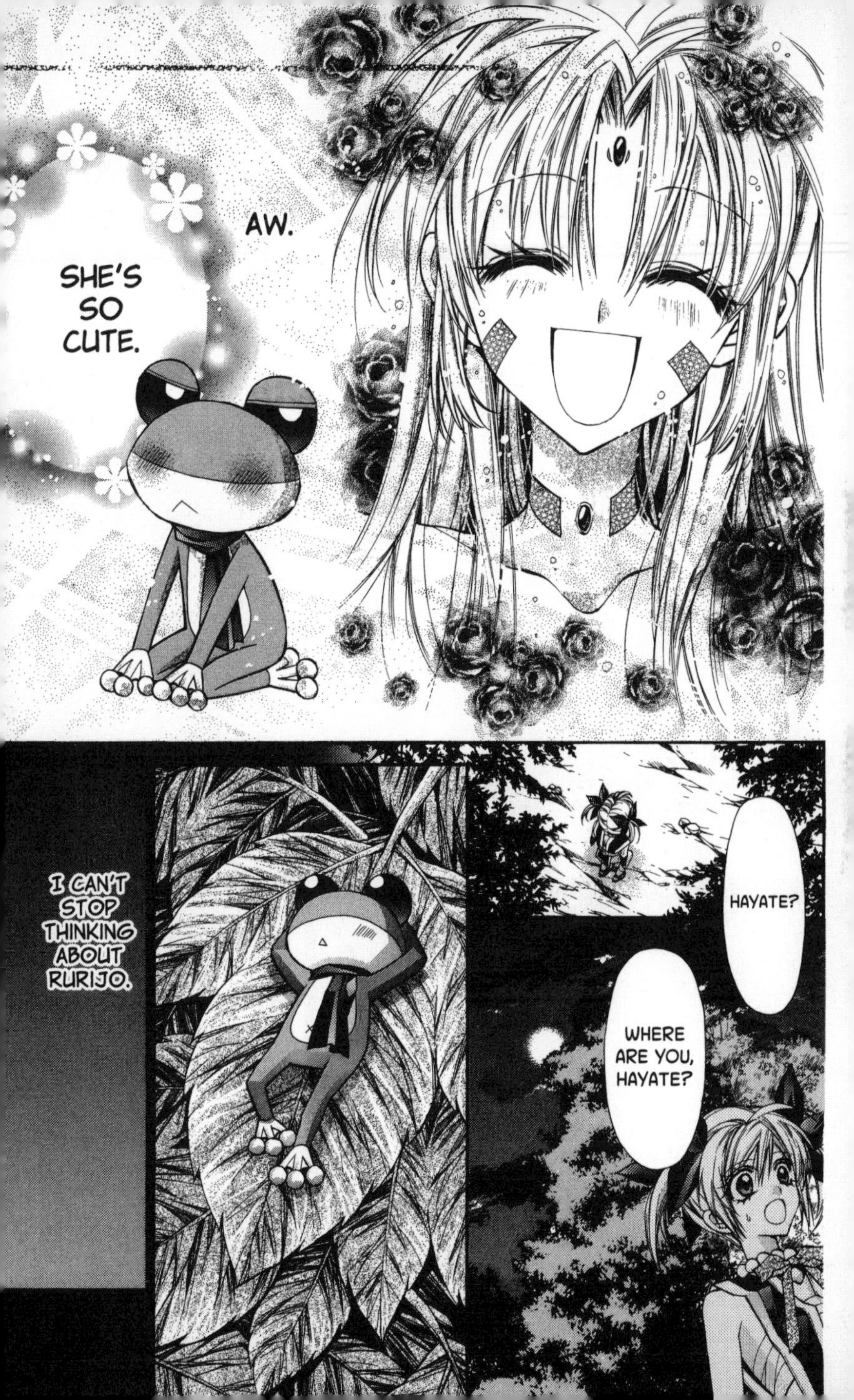
AW.
SHE'S SO CUTE.
HAYATE?
WHERE ARE YOU, HAYATE?
I CAN'T STOP THINKING ABOUT RURIJO.

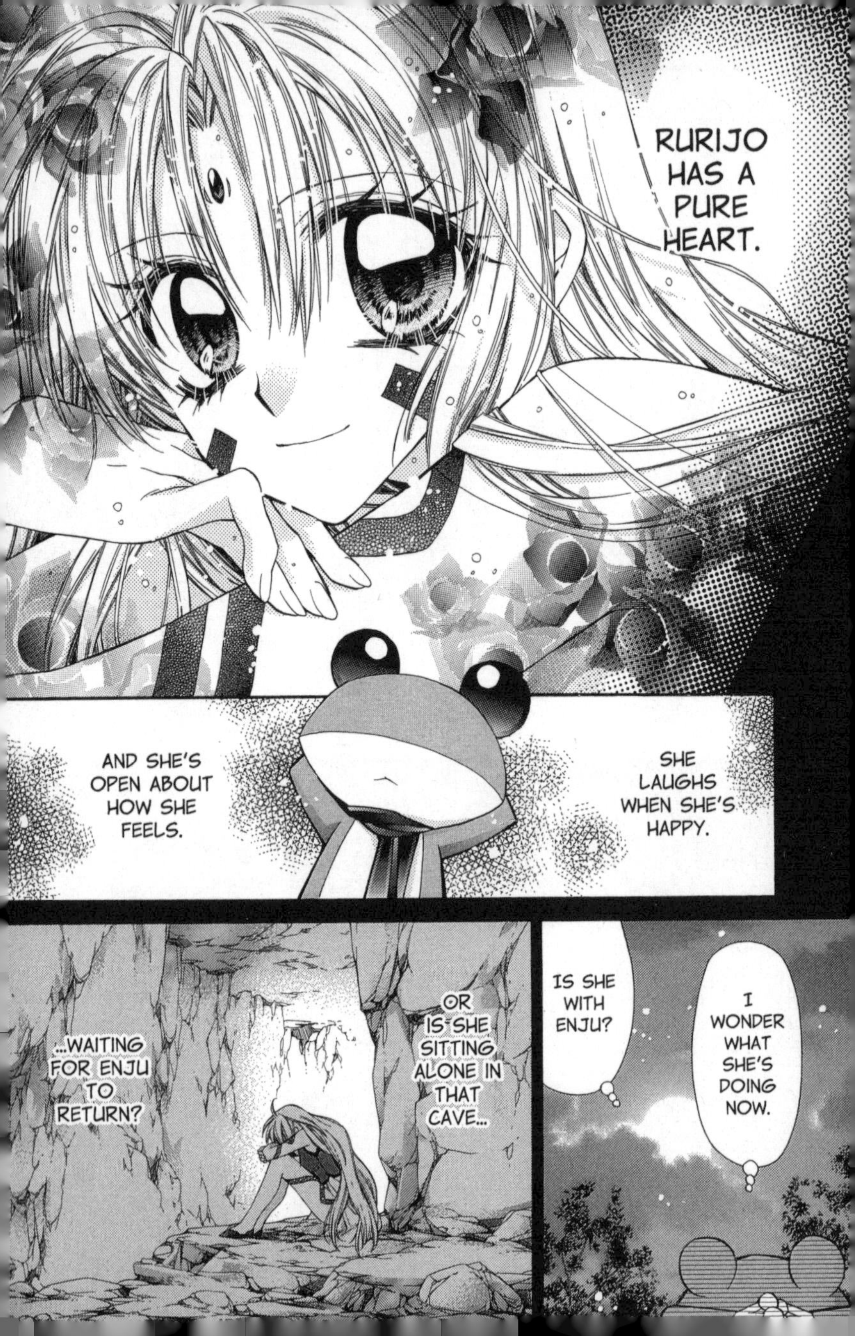
RURIJO HAS A PURE HEART.
SHE LAUGHS WHEN SHE'S HAPPY.
AND SHE'S OPEN ABOUT HOW SHE FEELS.
I WONDER WHAT SHE'S DOING NOW.
IS SHE WITH ENJU?
OR IS SHE SITTING ALONE IN THAT CAVE...
...WAITING FOR ENJU TO RETURN?

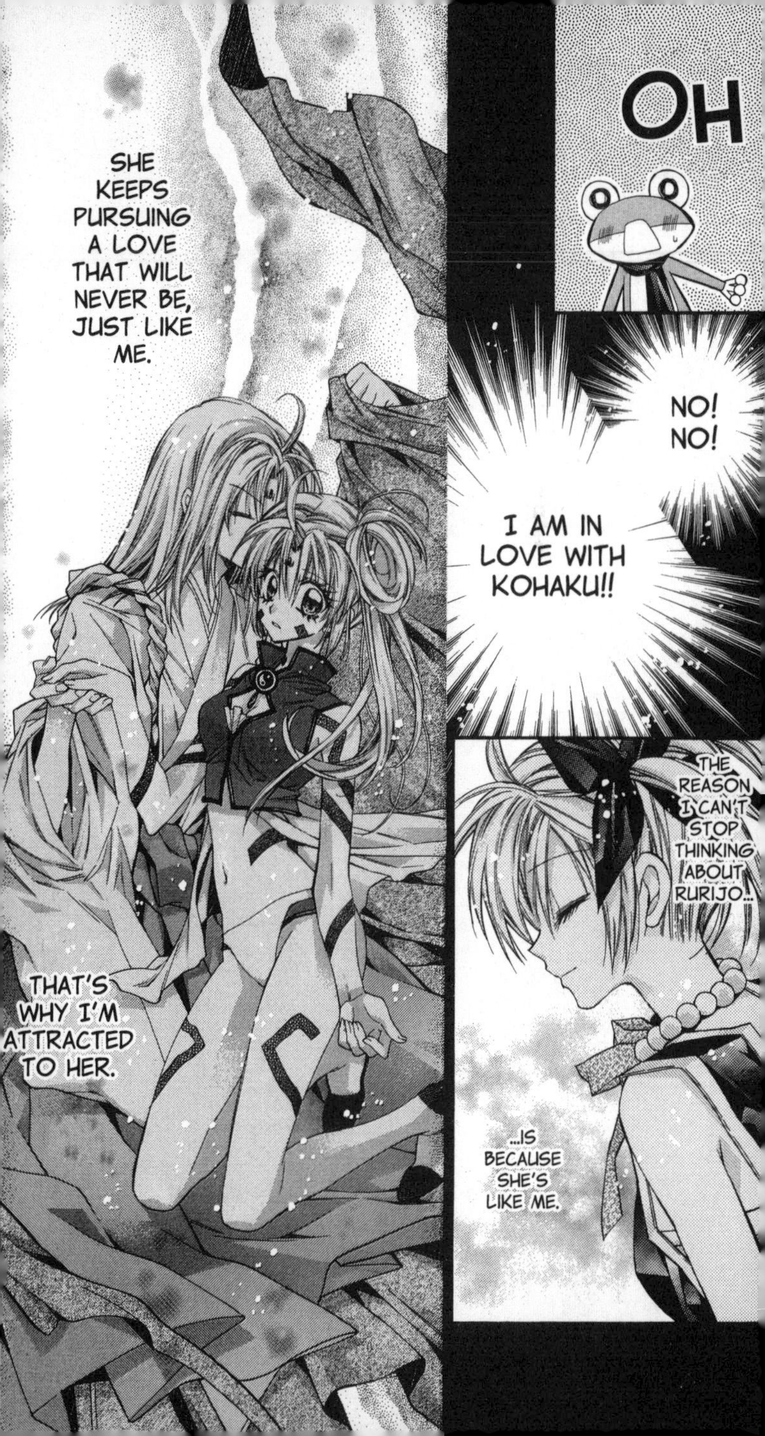
OH
NO! NO!
I AM IN LOVE WITH KOHAKU!!
THE REASON I CAN'T STOP THINKING ABOUT RURIJO...
...IS BECAUSE SHE'S LIKE ME.
SHE KEEPS PURSUING A LOVE THAT WILL NEVER BE, JUST LIKE ME.
THAT'S WHY I'M ATTRACTED TO HER.

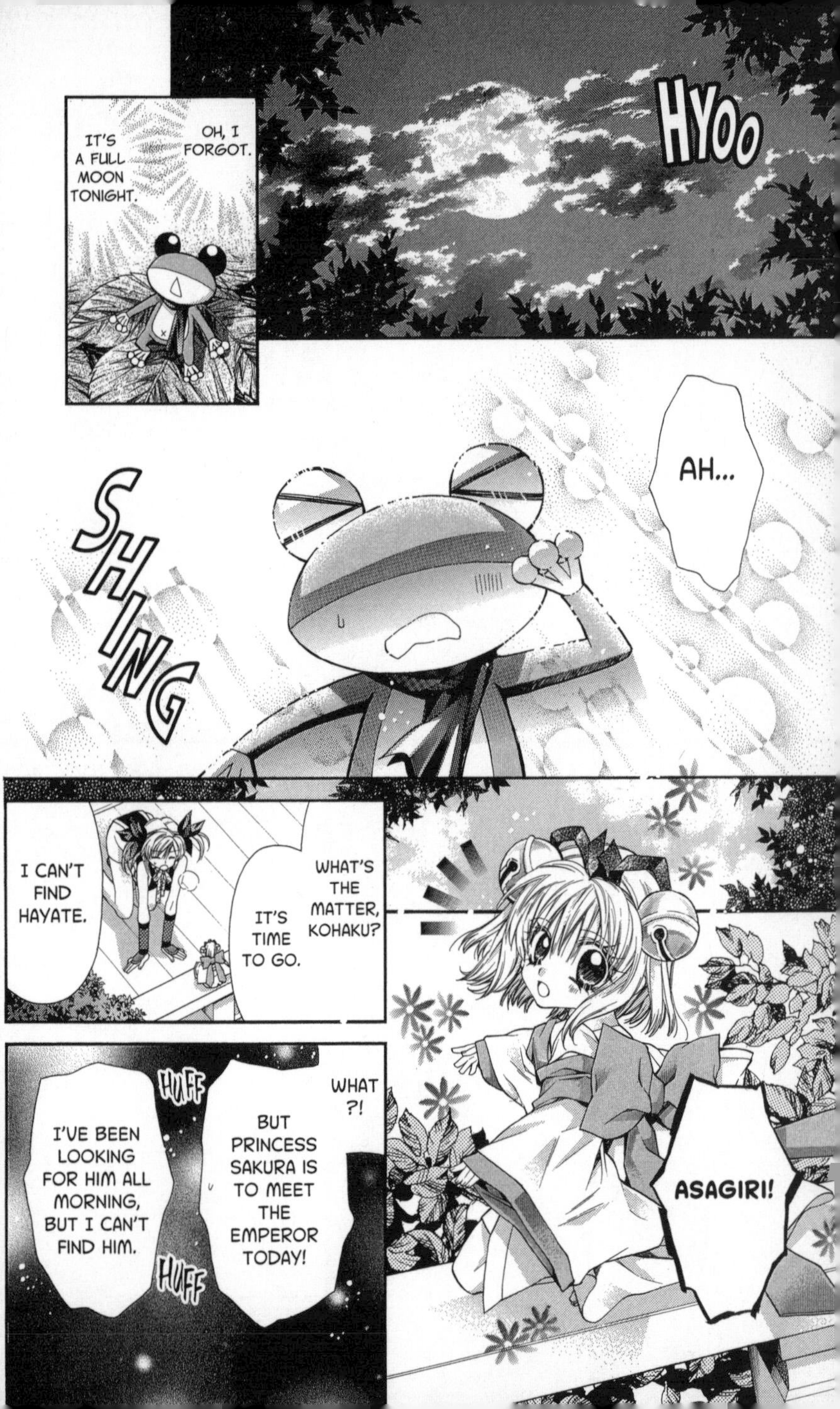
HYOO
OH, I FORGOT.
IT'S A FULL MOON TONIGHT.
AH...
SHING
ASAGIRI!
WHAT'S THE MATTER, KOHAKU?
IT'S TIME TO GO.
I CAN'T FIND HAYATE.
WHAT?!
BUT PRINCESS SAKURA IS TO MEET THE EMPEROR TODAY!
HUFF
I'VE BEEN LOOKING FOR HIM ALL MORNING, BUT I CAN'T FIND HIM.
HUFF

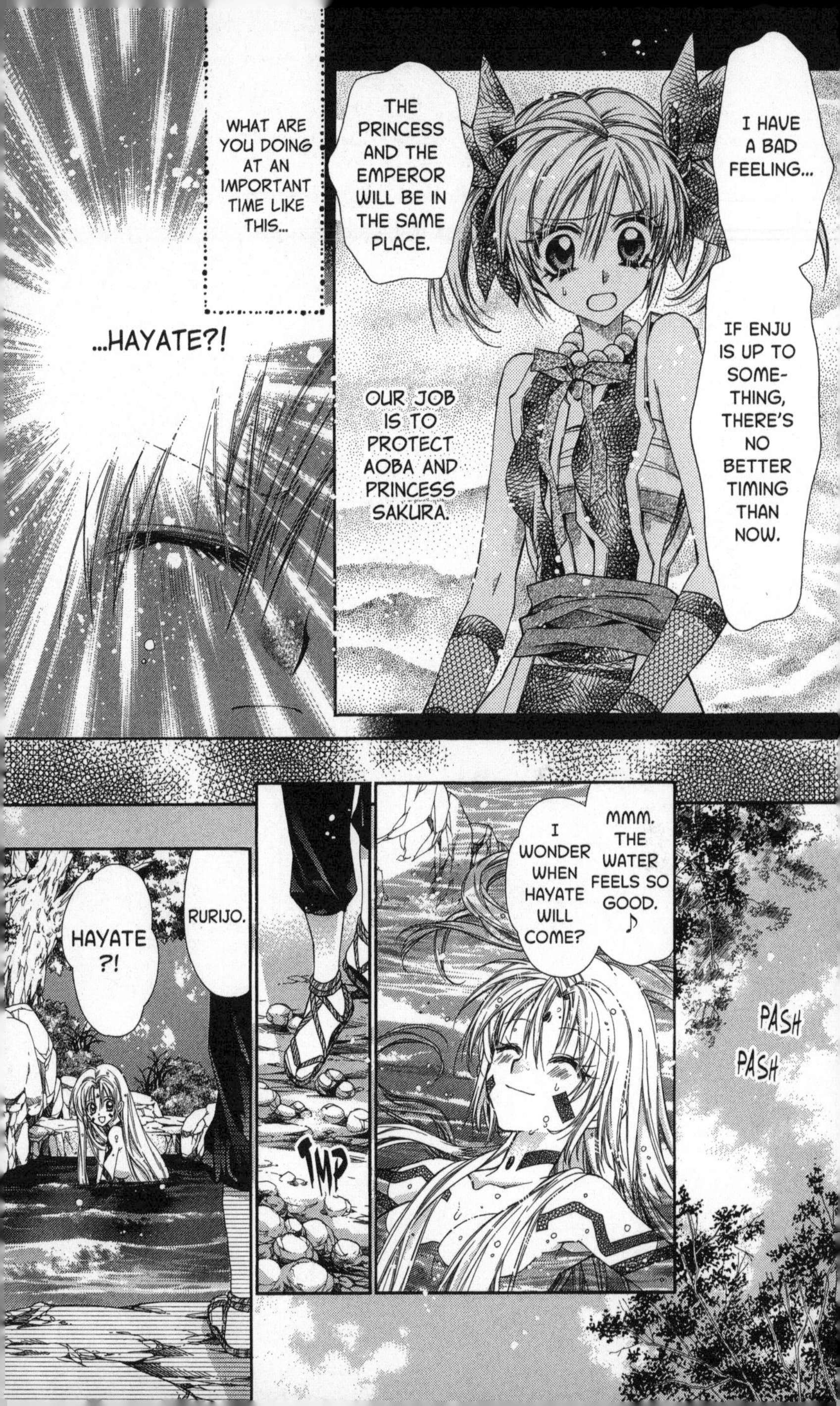
I HAVE A BAD FEELING...
THE PRINCESS AND THE EMPEROR WILL BE IN THE SAME PLACE.
IF ENJU IS UP TO SOMETHING, THERE'S NO BETTER TIMING THAN NOW.
OUR JOB IS TO PROTECT AOBA AND PRINCESS SAKURA.
WHAT ARE YOU DOING AT AN IMPORTANT TIME LIKE THIS...
...HAYATE?!
PASH
PASH
MMM. THE WATER FEELS SO GOOD. ♪
I WONDER WHEN HAYATE WILL COME?
TMP
RURIJO.
HAYATE ?!

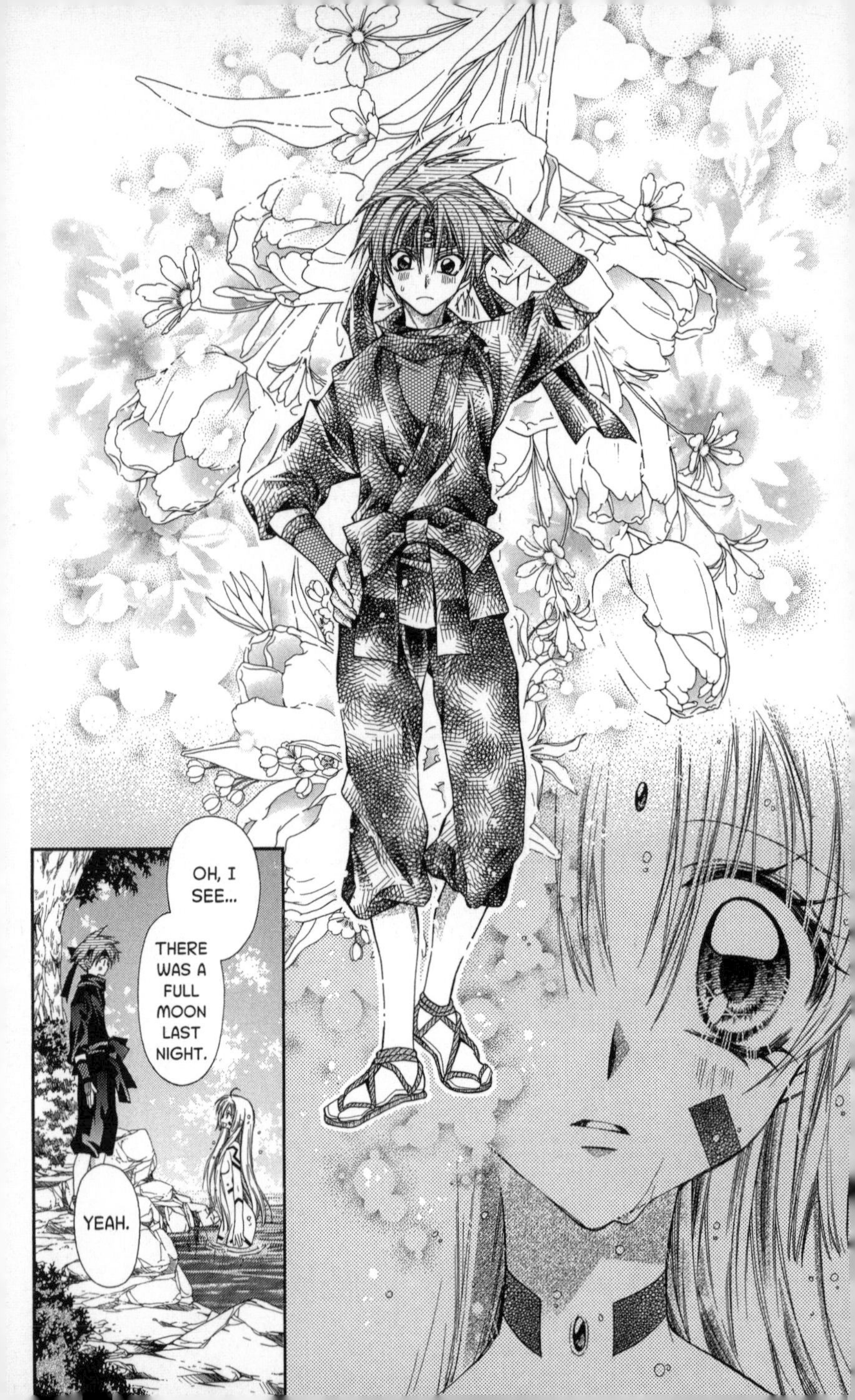
OH, I SEE...
THERE WAS A FULL MOON LAST NIGHT.
YEAH.

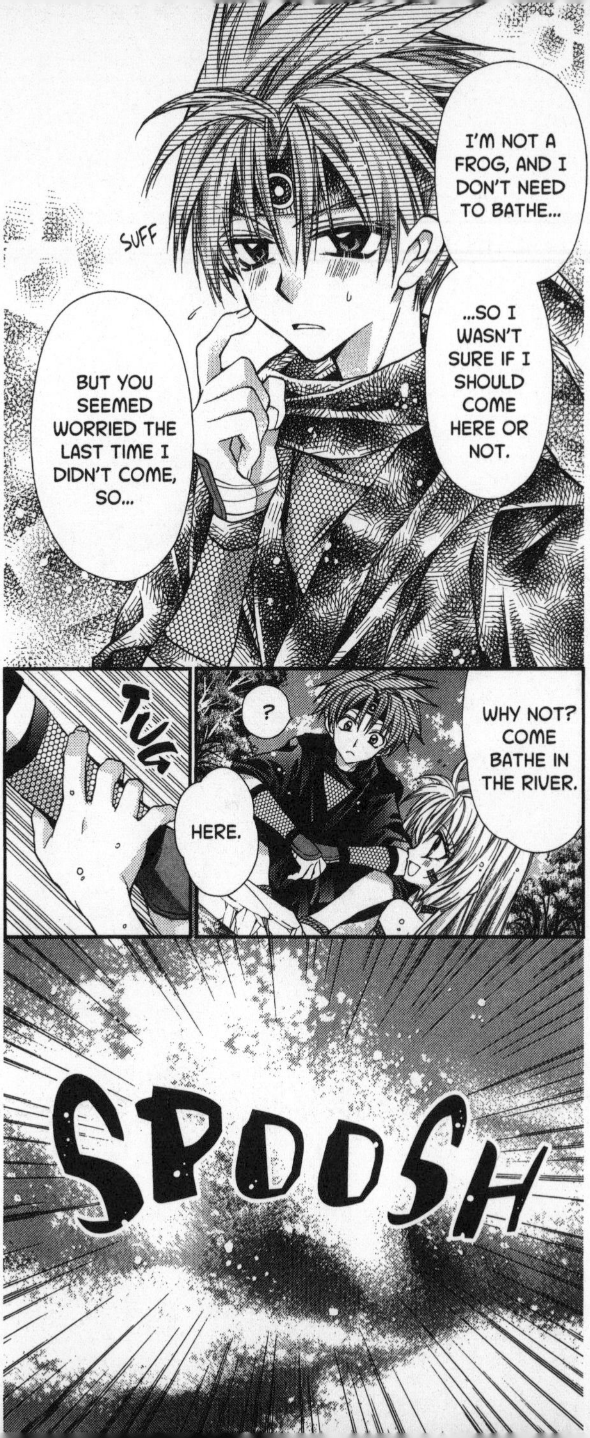
I'M NOT A FROG, AND I DON'T NEED TO BATHE...
...SO I WASN'T SURE IF I SHOULD COME HERE OR NOT.
SUFF
BUT YOU SEEMED WORRIED THE LAST TIME I DIDN'T COME, SO...
WHY NOT? COME BATHE IN THE RIVER.
?
HERE.
TUG
SPOOSH

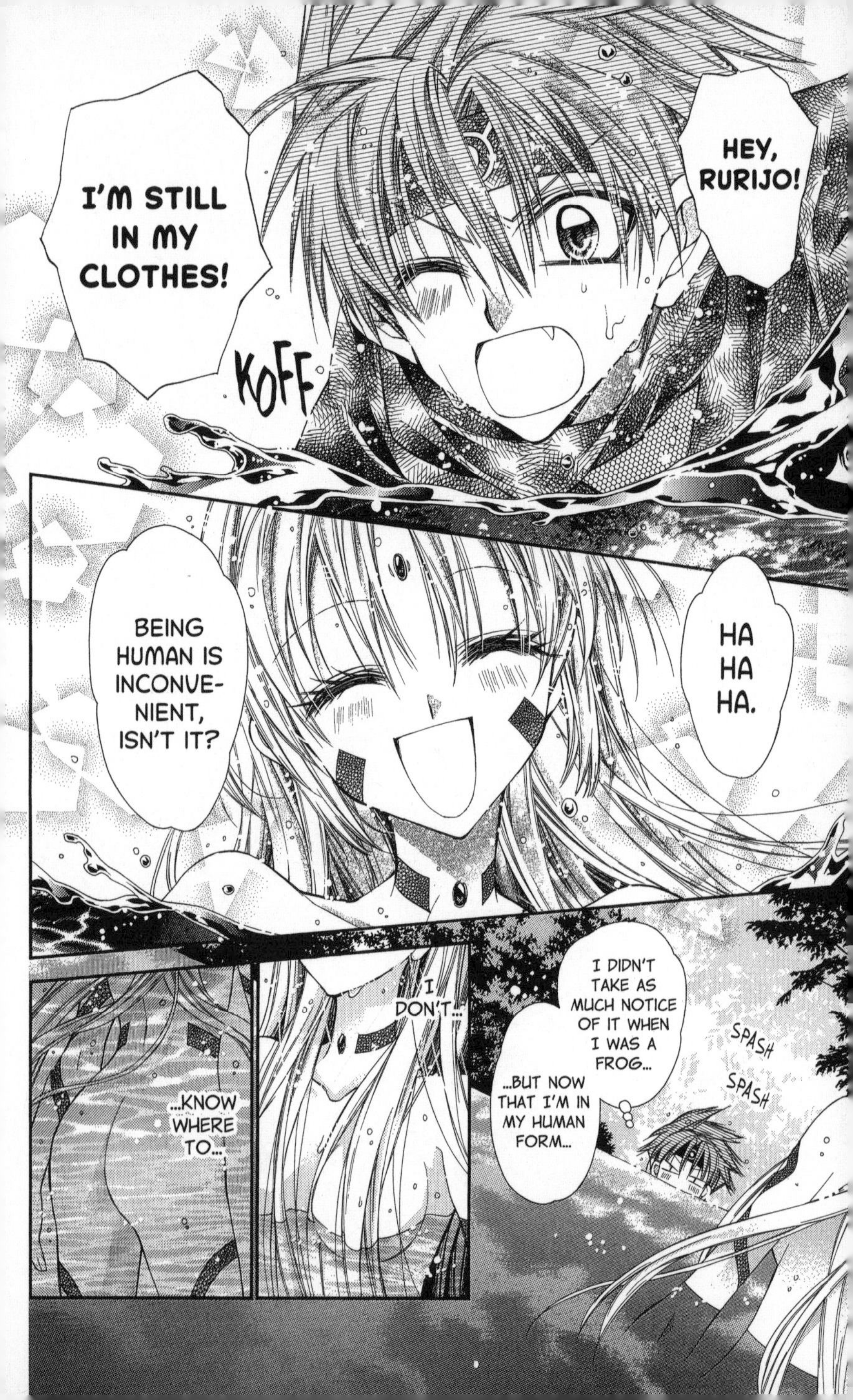
HEY, RURIJO!
KOFF
I'M STILL IN MY CLOTHES!
HA HA HA.
BEING HUMAN IS INCONVENIENT, ISN'T IT?
SPASH
SPASH
I DIDN'T TAKE AS MUCH NOTICE OF IT WHEN I WAS A FROG...
...BUT NOW THAT I'M IN MY HUMAN FORM...
I DON'T...
...KNOW WHERE TO...

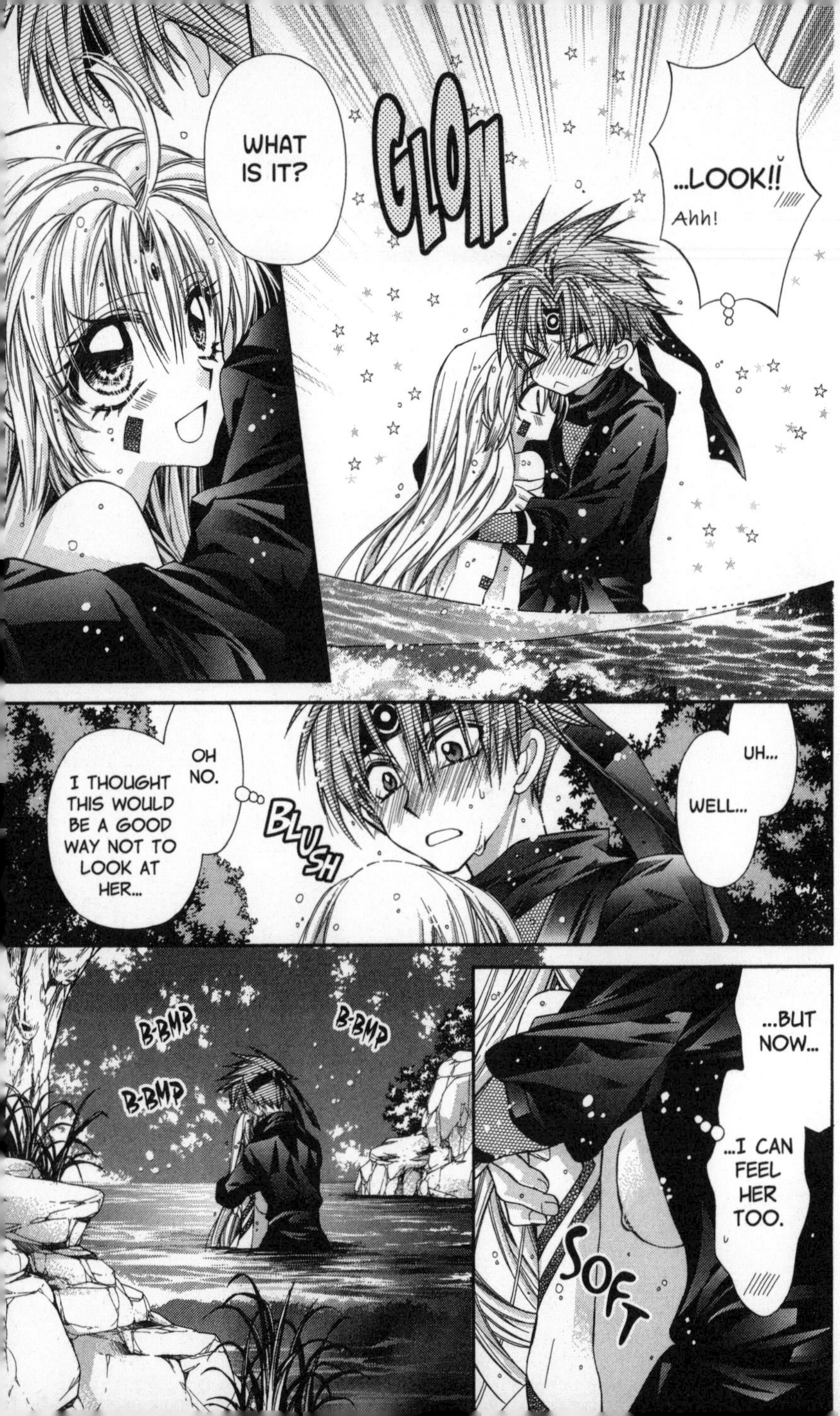
...LOOK!!
Ahh!
GLOMM
WHAT IS IT?
UH...
WELL...
OH NO.
I THOUGHT THIS WOULD BE A GOOD WAY NOT TO LOOK AT HER...
BLUSH
...BUT NOW...
...I CAN FEEL HER TOO.
SOFT
B-BMP
B-BMP
B-BMP

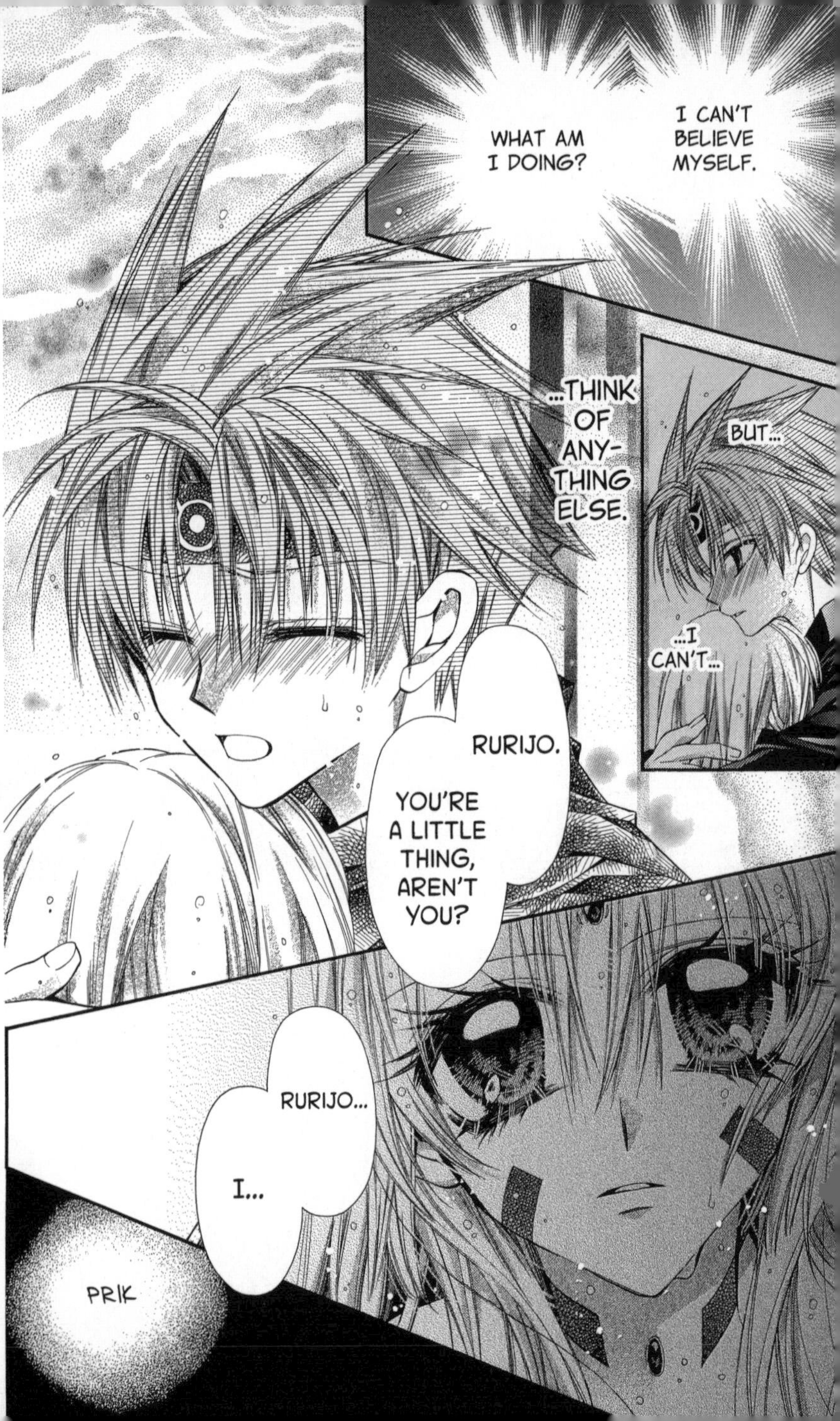
I CAN'T BELIEVE MYSELF.
WHAT AM I DOING?
BUT...
...I CAN'T...
...THINK OF ANY-THING ELSE.
RURIJO.
YOU'RE A LITTLE THING, AREN'T YOU?
RURIJO...
I...
PRIK

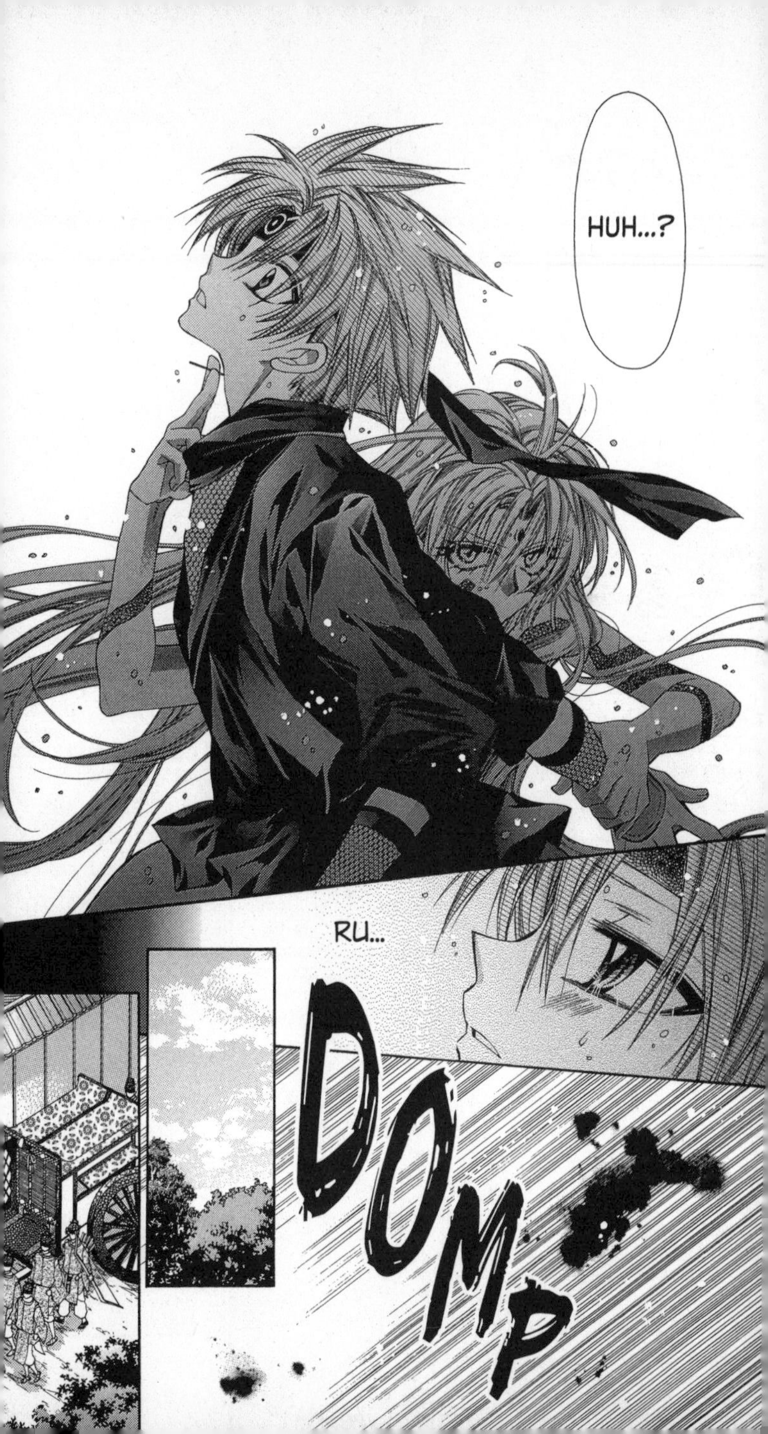
HUH...?
RU...
DOMP

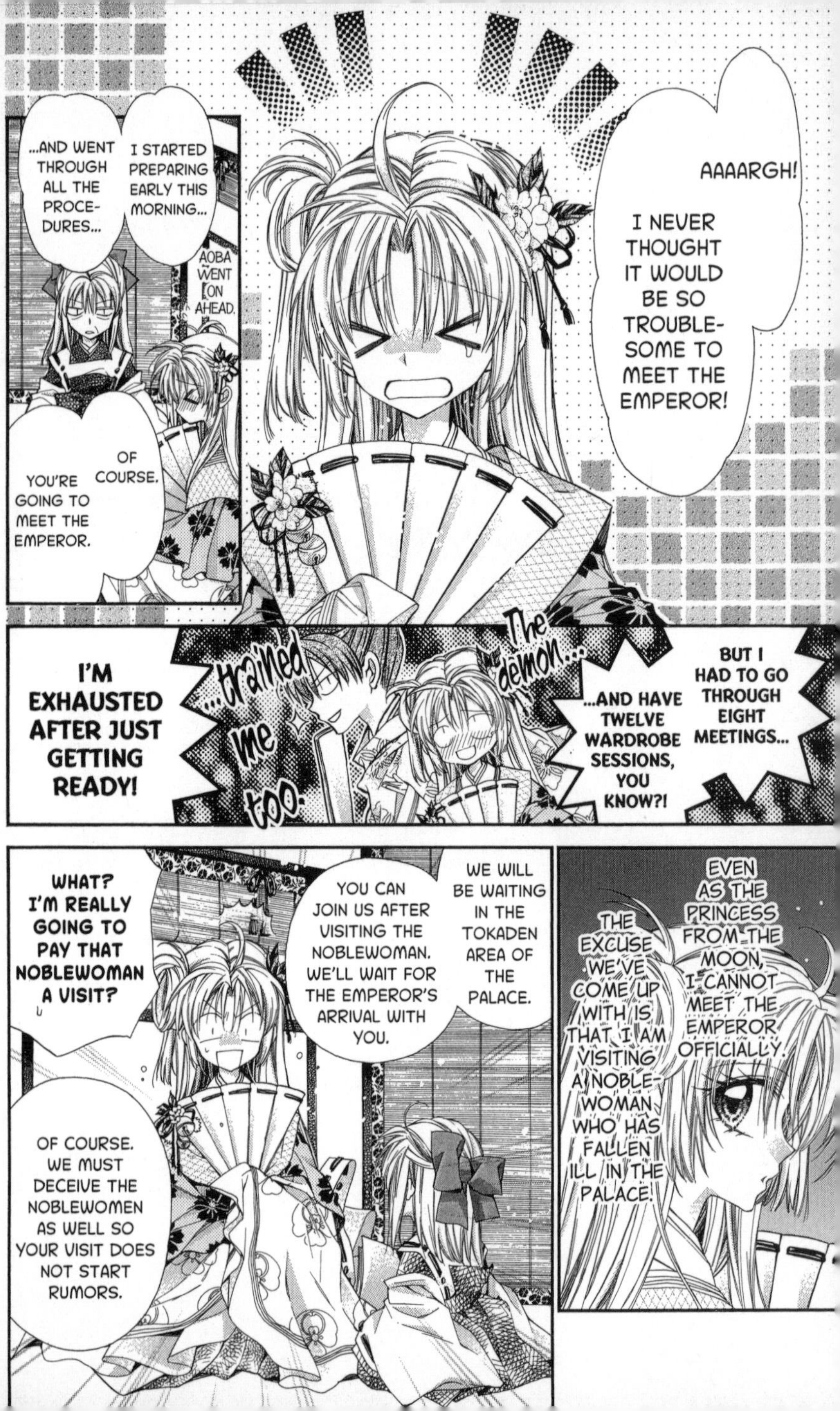

I STARTED PREPARING EARLY THIS MORNING...
...AND WENT THROUGH ALL THE PROCEDURES...
AOBA WENT ON AHEAD.
OF COURSE. YOU'RE GOING TO MEET THE EMPEROR.
AAAARGH!
I NEVER THOUGHT IT WOULD BE SO TROUBLESOME TO MEET THE EMPEROR!
BUT I HAD TO GO THROUGH EIGHT MEETINGS...
...AND HAVE TWELVE WARDROBE SESSIONS, YOU KNOW?!
The demon...
...trained me too.
I'M EXHAUSTED AFTER JUST GETTING READY!
EVEN AS THE PRINCESS FROM THE MOON, I CANNOT MEET THE EMPEROR OFFICIALLY.
THE EXCUSE WE'VE COME UP WITH IS THAT I AM VISITING A NOBLEWOMAN WHO HAS FALLEN ILL IN THE PALACE.
WE WILL BE WAITING IN THE TOKADEN AREA OF THE PALACE.
YOU CAN JOIN US AFTER VISITING THE NOBLEWOMAN. WE'LL WAIT FOR THE EMPEROR'S ARRIVAL WITH YOU.
WHAT? I'M REALLY GOING TO PAY THAT NOBLEWOMAN A VISIT?
OF COURSE. WE MUST DECEIVE THE NOBLEWOMEN AS WELL SO YOUR VISIT DOES NOT START RUMORS.

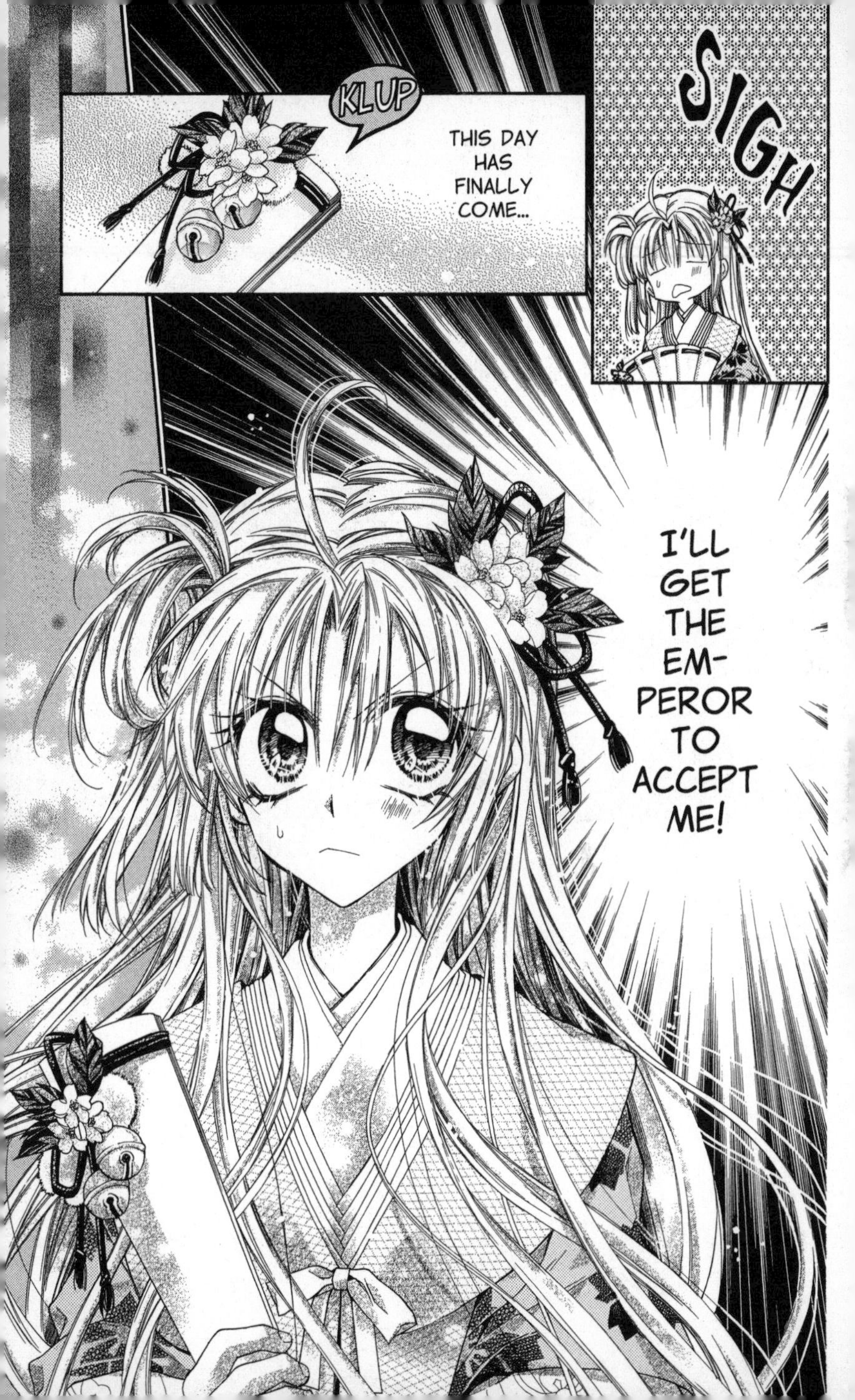
SIGH
KLUP
THIS DAY HAS FINALLY COME...
I'LL GET THE EM-PEROR TO ACCEPT ME!

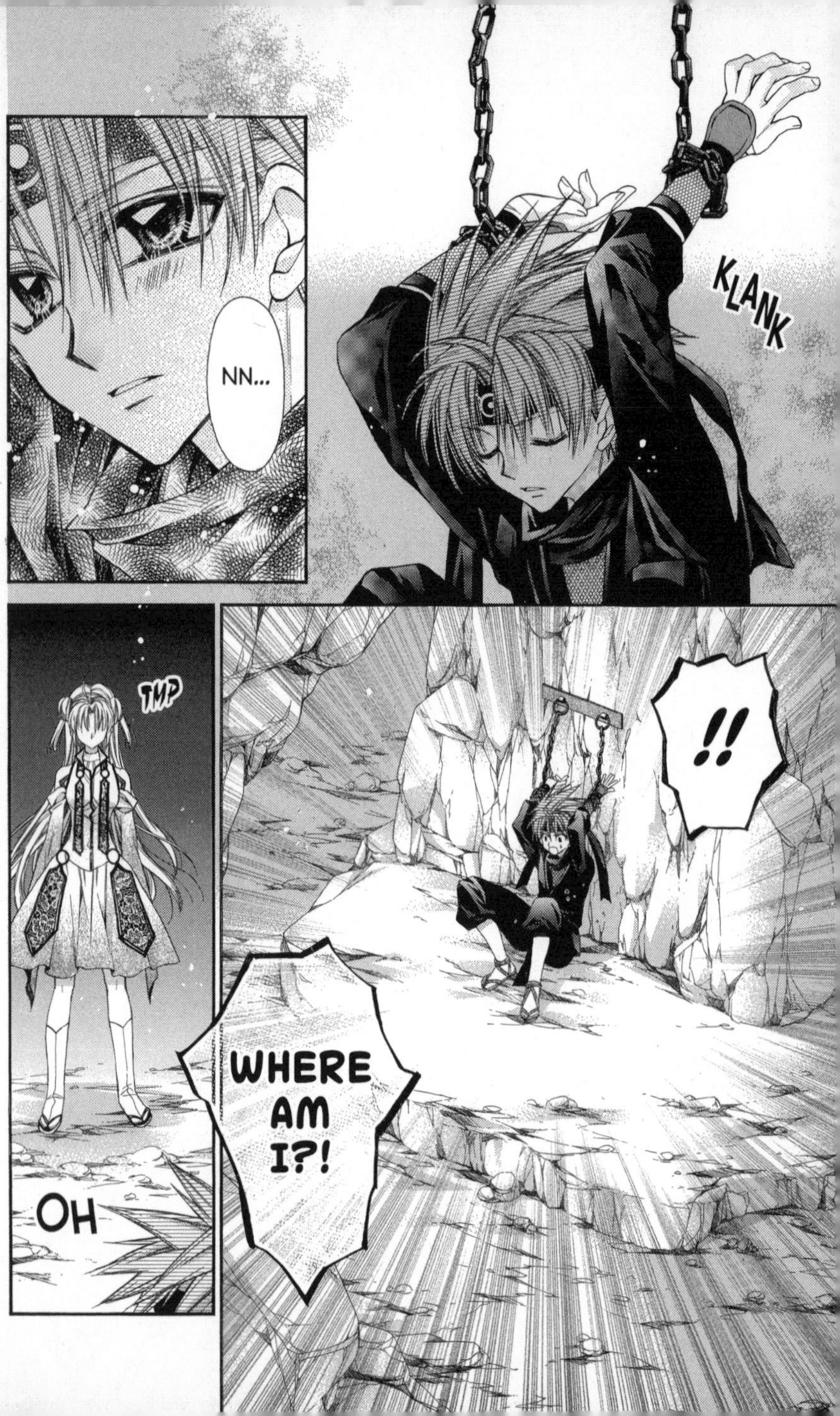
KLANK
NN...
!!
WHERE AM I?!
TMP
OH

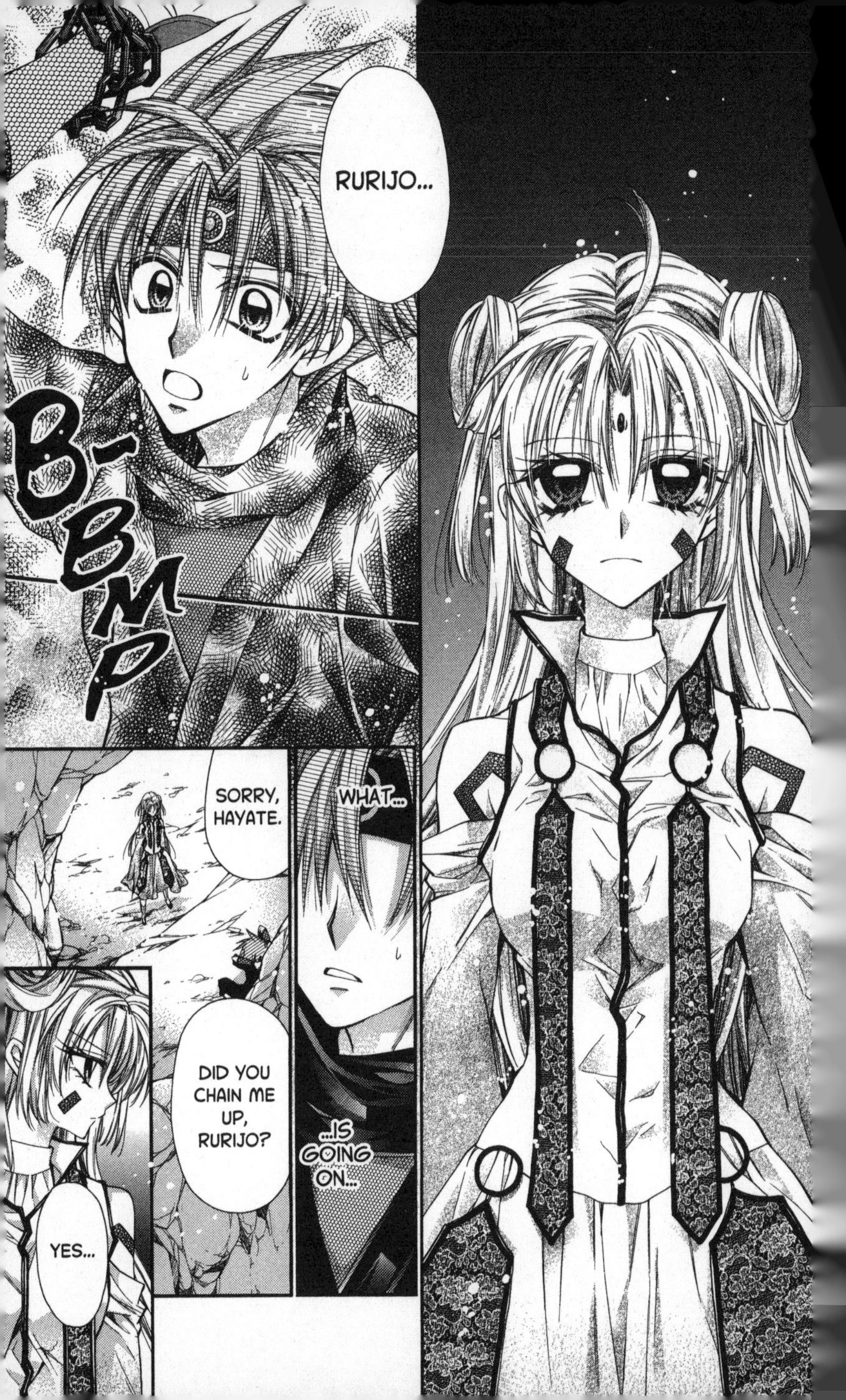
RURIJO...
B-BUMP
WHAT...
...IS GOING ON...
SORRY, HAYATE.
DID YOU CHAIN ME UP, RURIJO?
YES...

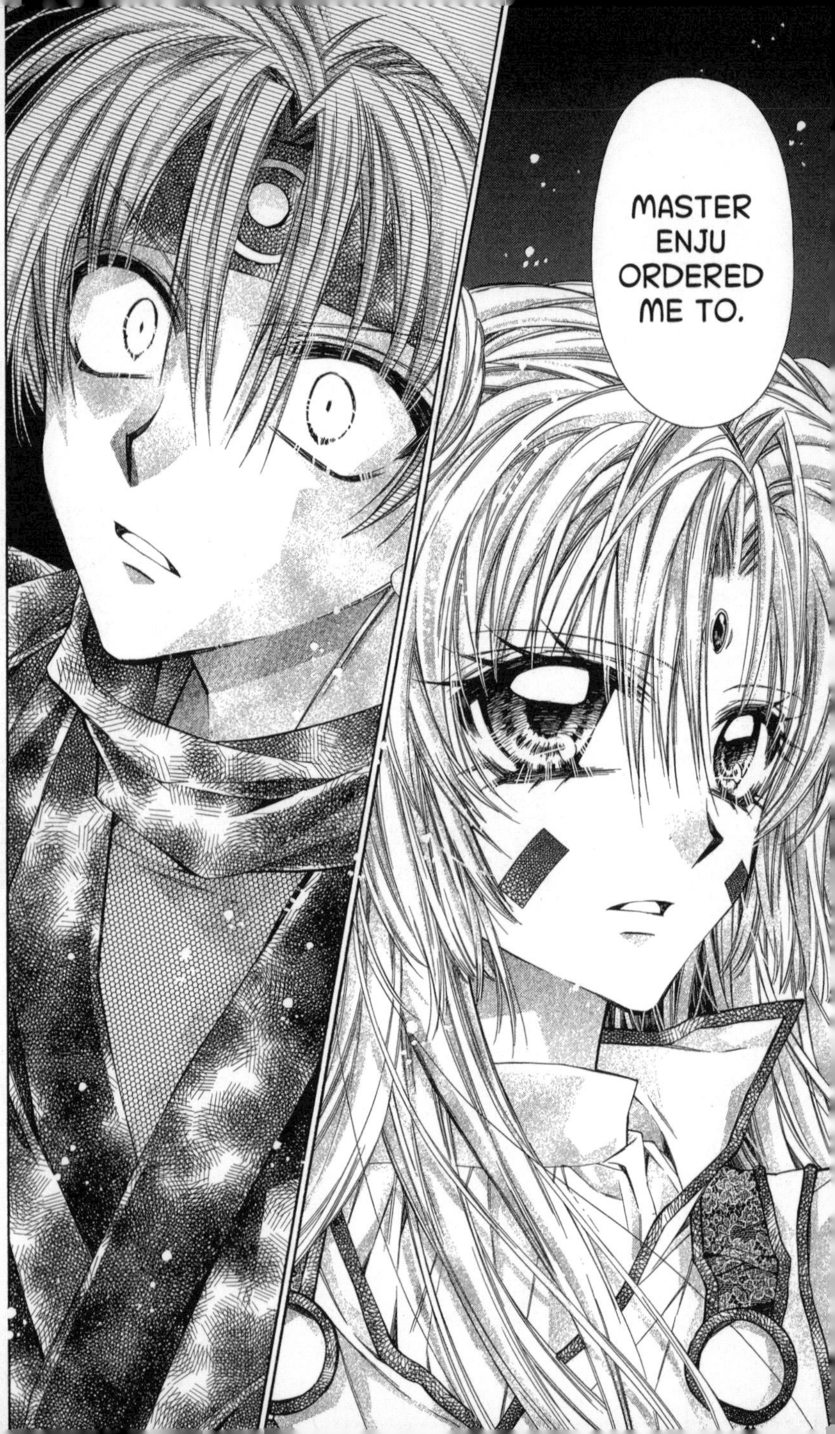
MASTER ENJU ORDERED ME TO.

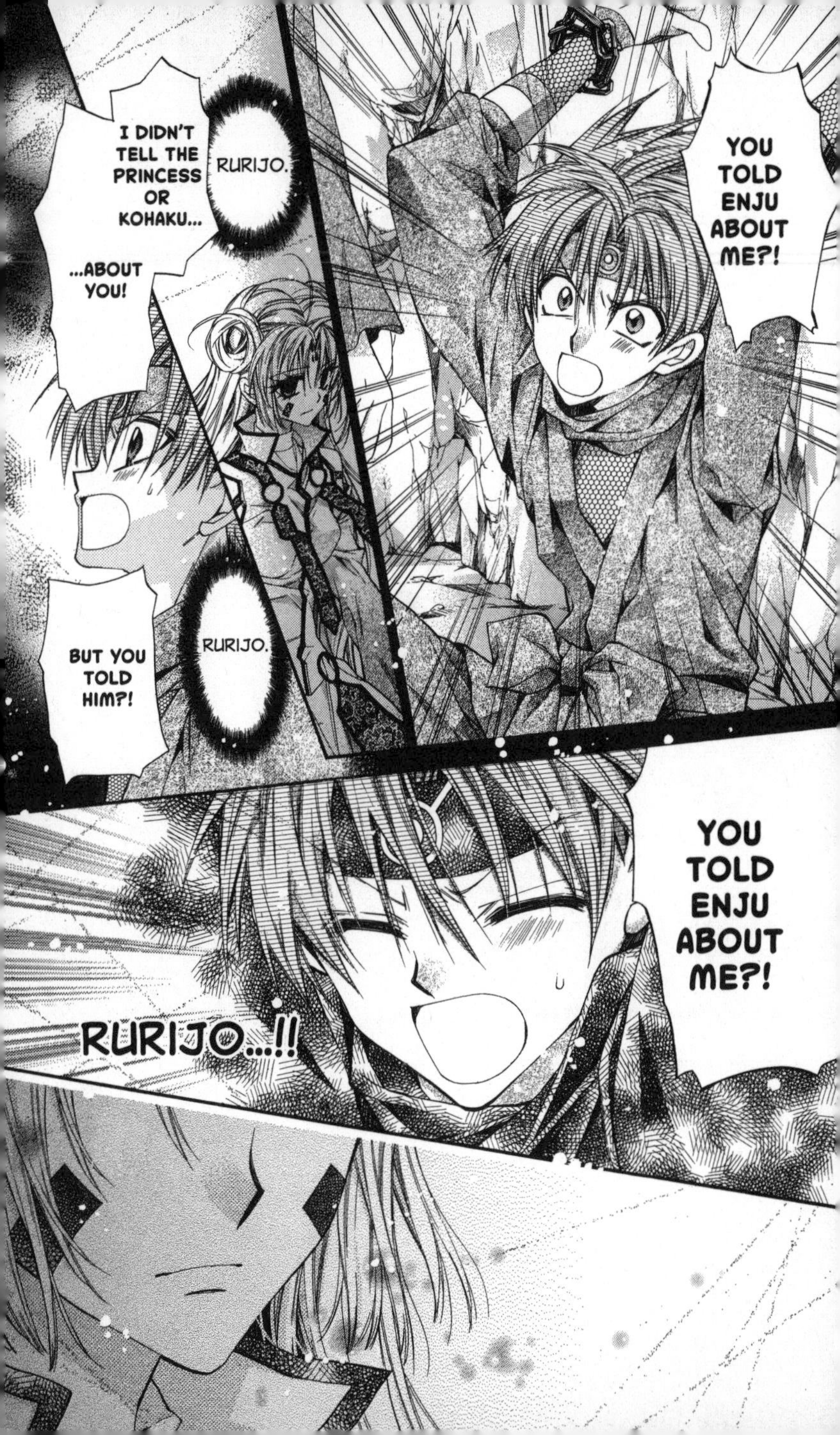
YOU TOLD ENJU ABOUT ME?!
RURIJO.
I DIDN'T TELL THE PRINCESS OR KOHAKU...
...ABOUT YOU!
RURIJO.
BUT YOU TOLD HIM?!
YOU TOLD ENJU ABOUT ME?!
RURIJO...!!

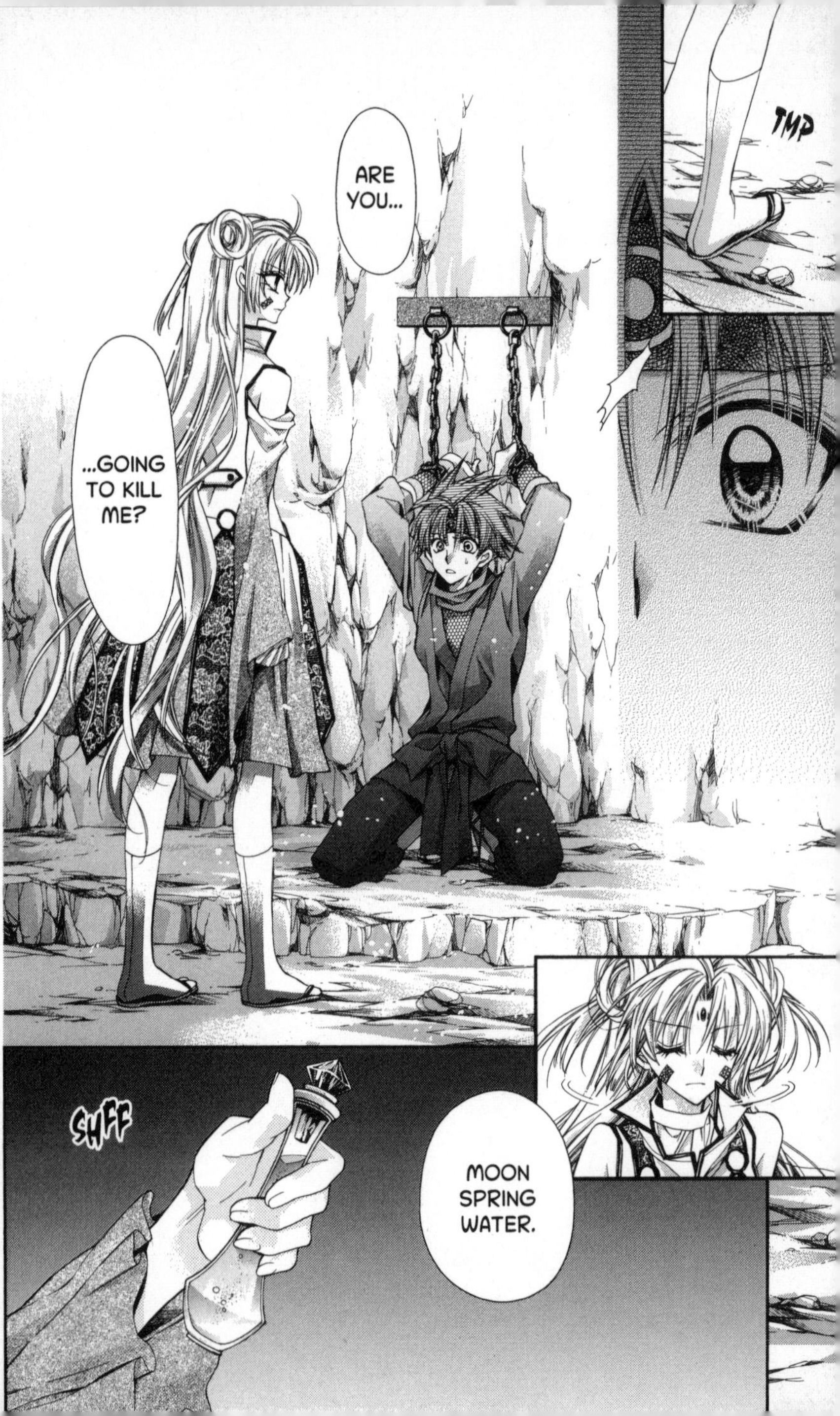
TMP
ARE YOU...
...GOING TO KILL ME?
MOON SPRING WATER.
SHFF

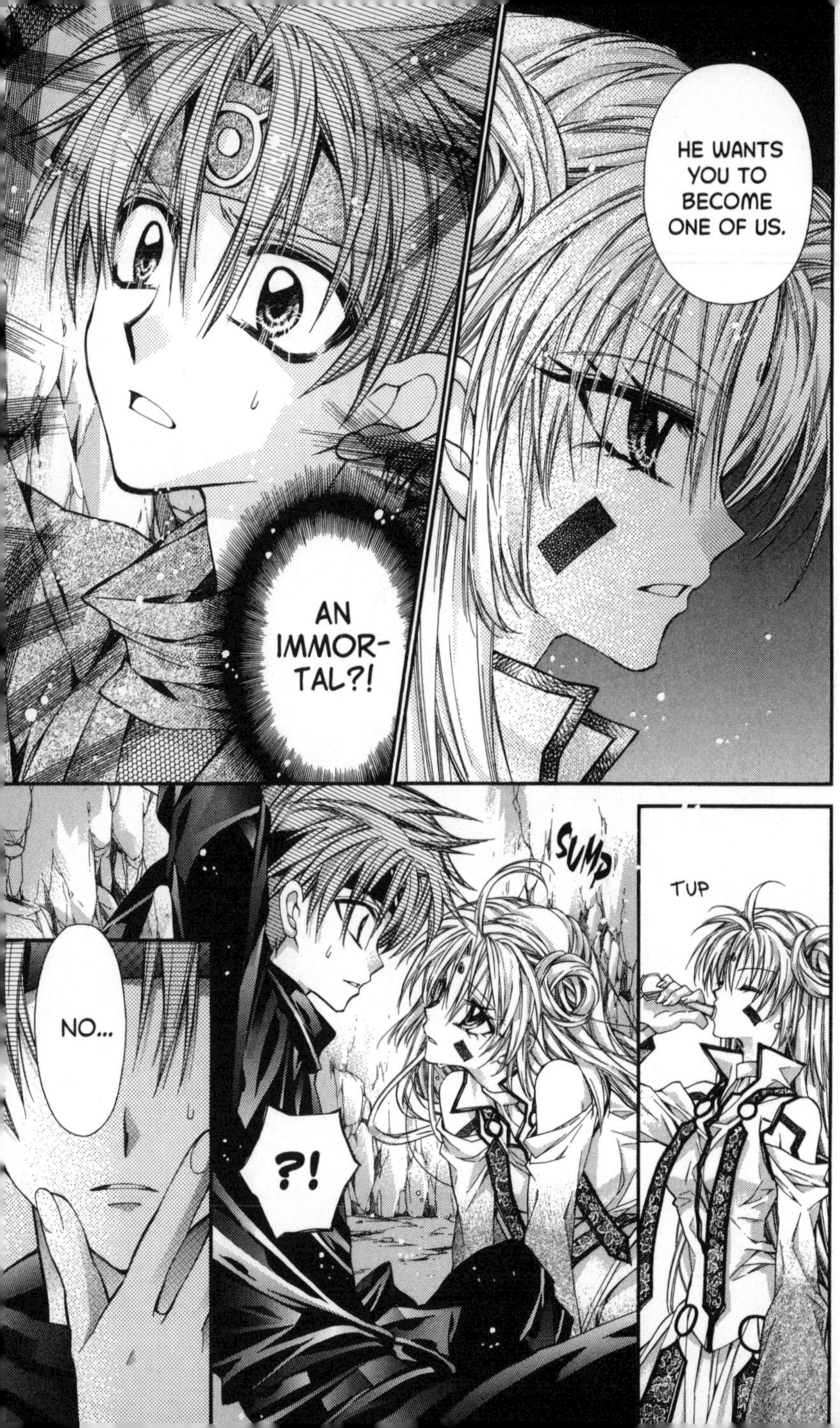
HE WANTS YOU TO BECOME ONE OF US.
AN IMMORTAL?!
TUP
SUMP
?!
NO...

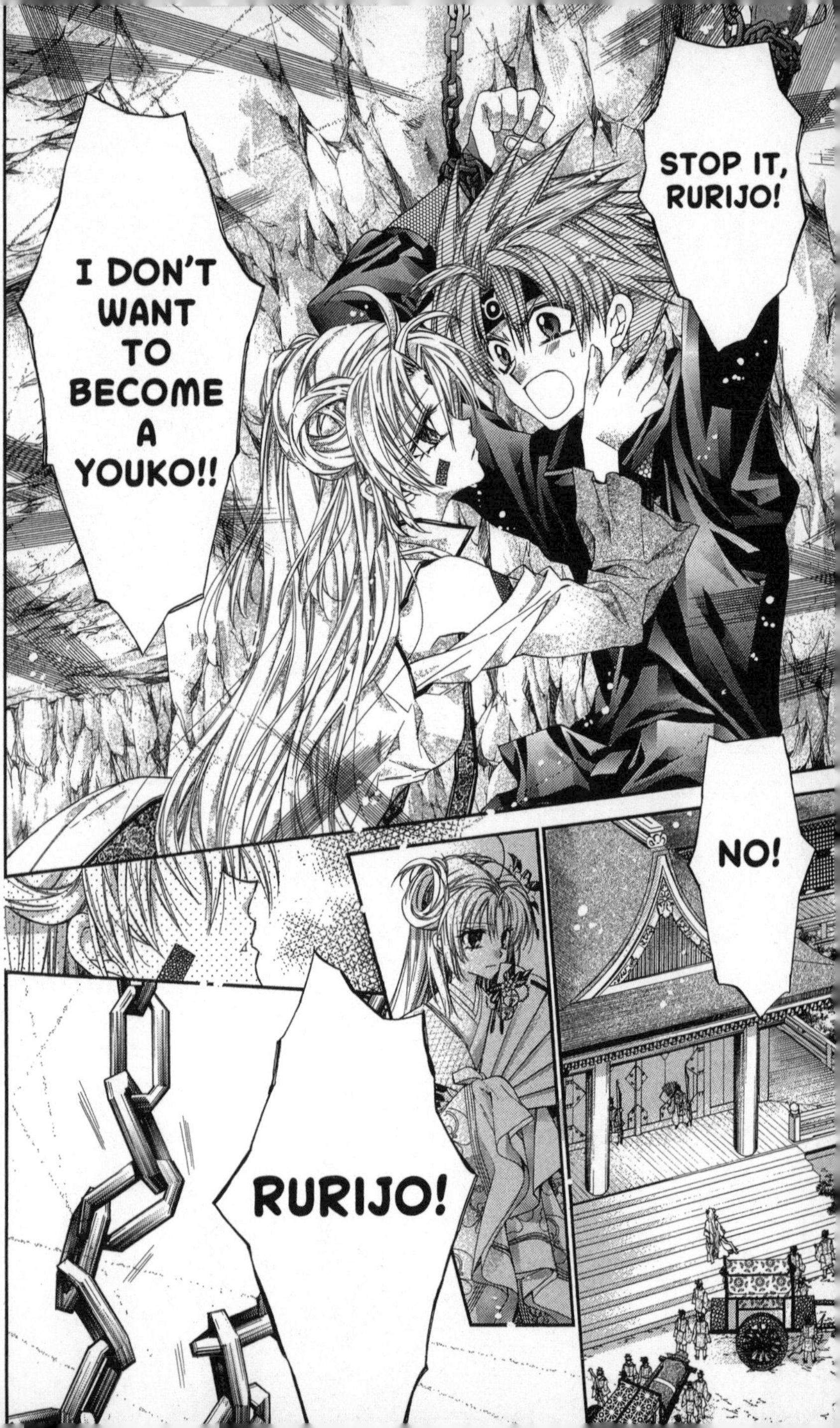
STOP IT, RURIJO!
I DON'T WANT TO BECOME A YOUKO!!
NO!
RURIJO!

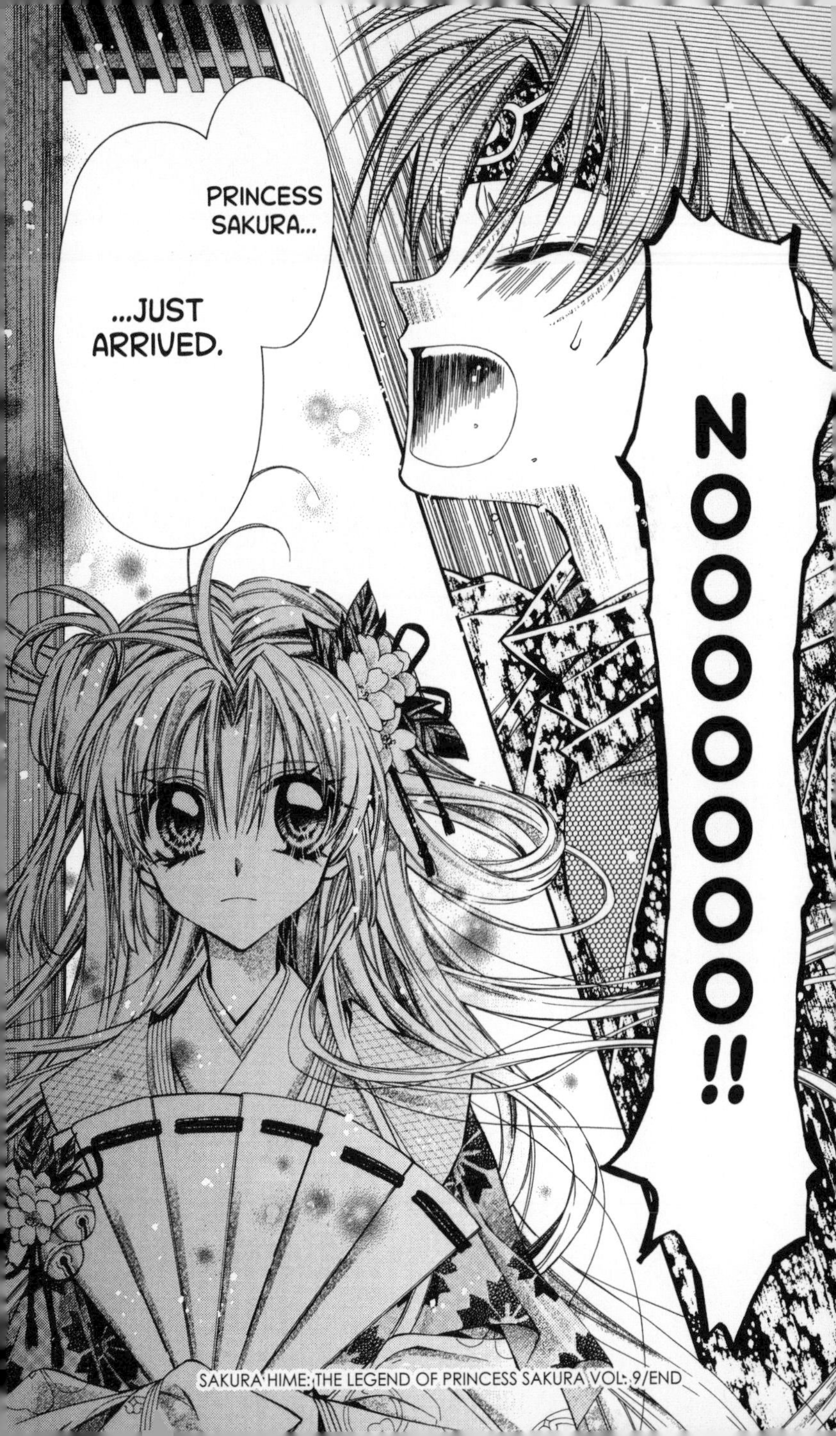
PRINCESS SAKURA...
...JUST ARRIVED.
NOOOOOO!!
SAKURA HIME: THE LEGEND OF PRINCESS SAKURA VOL. 9/END

Sakura Hime
The Legend of Princess Sakura

BONUS FUNNIES

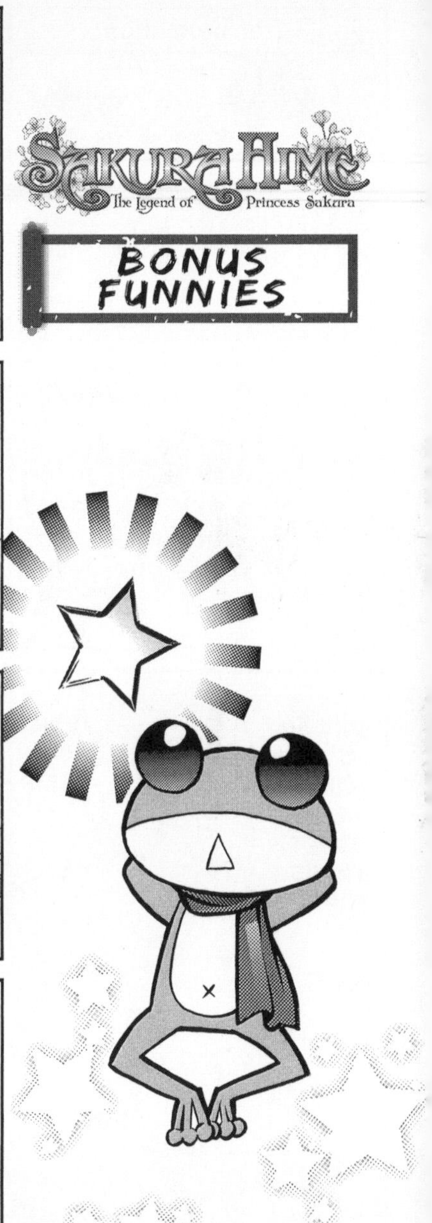

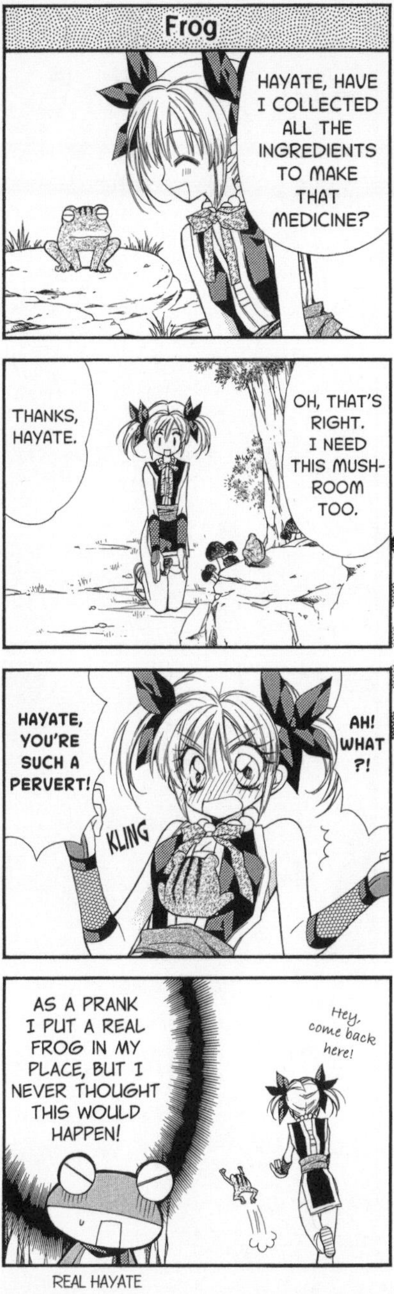
Frog
HAYATE, HAVE I COLLECTED ALL THE INGREDIENTS TO MAKE THAT MEDICINE?
OH, THAT'S RIGHT. I NEED THIS MUSH-ROOM TOO.
THANKS, HAYATE.
AH! WHAT ?!
HAYATE, YOU'RE SUCH A PERVERT!
KLING
Hey, come back here!
AS A PRANK I PUT A REAL FROG IN MY PLACE, BUT I NEVER THOUGHT THIS WOULD HAPPEN!
REAL HAYATE

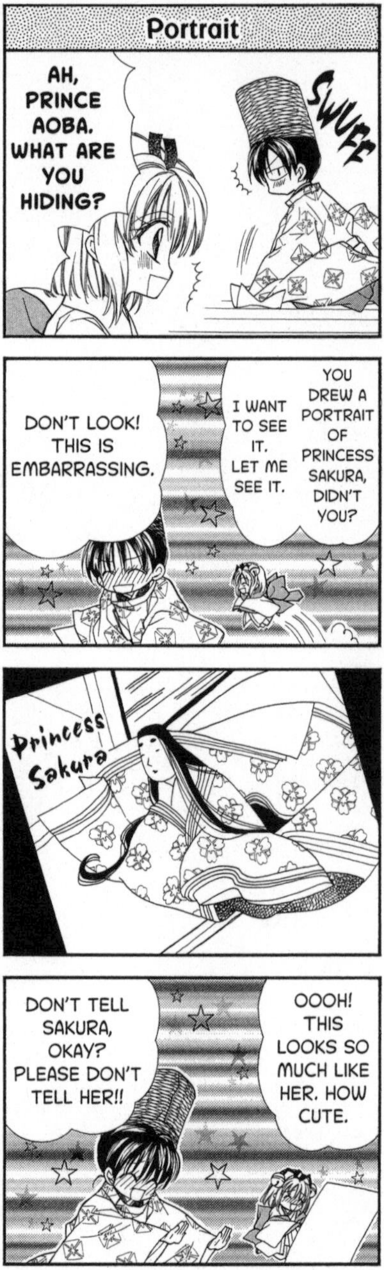
Portrait
AH, PRINCE AOBA. WHAT ARE YOU HIDING?
SWUFF
YOU DREW A PORTRAIT OF PRINCESS SAKURA, DIDN'T YOU?
I WANT TO SEE IT. LET ME SEE IT.
DON'T LOOK! THIS IS EMBARRASSING.
Princess Sakura
OOOH! THIS LOOKS SO MUCH LIKE HER. HOW CUTE.
DON'T TELL SAKURA, OKAY? PLEASE DON'T TELL HER!!

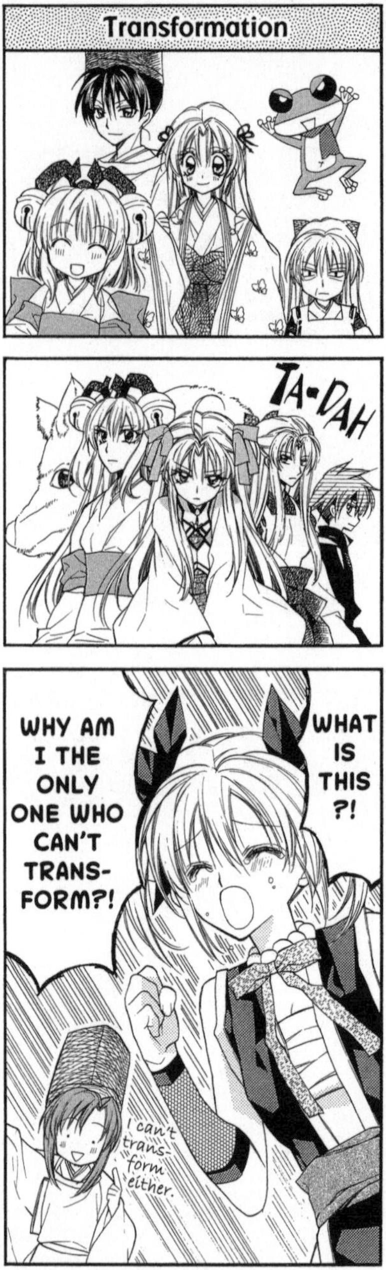
Transformation
TA-DAH
WHAT IS THIS?!
WHY AM I THE ONLY ONE WHO CAN'T TRANS-FORM?!
I can't trans-form either.

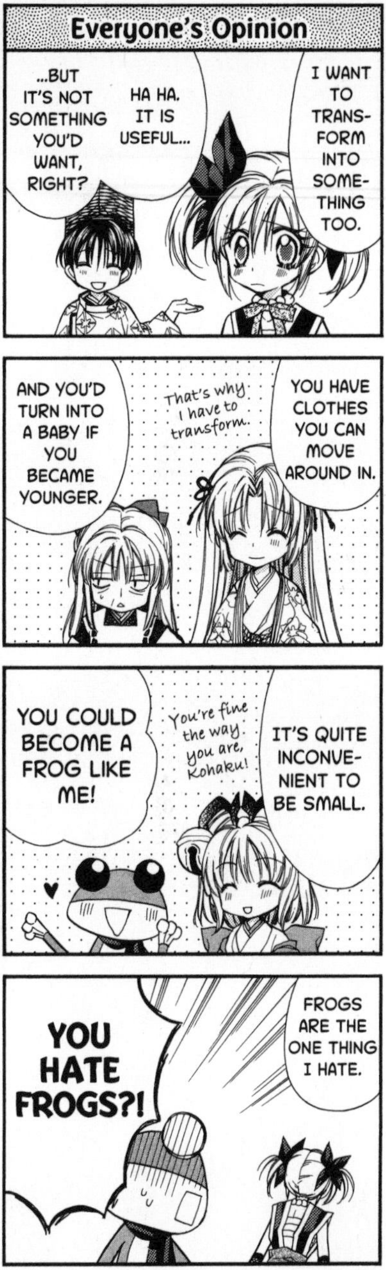
Everyone's Opinion
I WANT TO TRANSFORM INTO SOMETHING TOO.
HA HA. IT IS USEFUL...
...BUT IT'S NOT SOMETHING YOU'D WANT, RIGHT?
YOU HAVE CLOTHES YOU CAN MOVE AROUND IN.
That's why I have to transform.
AND YOU'D TURN INTO A BABY IF YOU BECAME YOUNGER.
IT'S QUITE INCONVENIENT TO BE SMALL.
You're fine the way you are, Kohaku!
YOU COULD BECOME A FROG LIKE ME!
FROGS ARE THE ONE THING I HATE.
YOU HATE FROGS?!

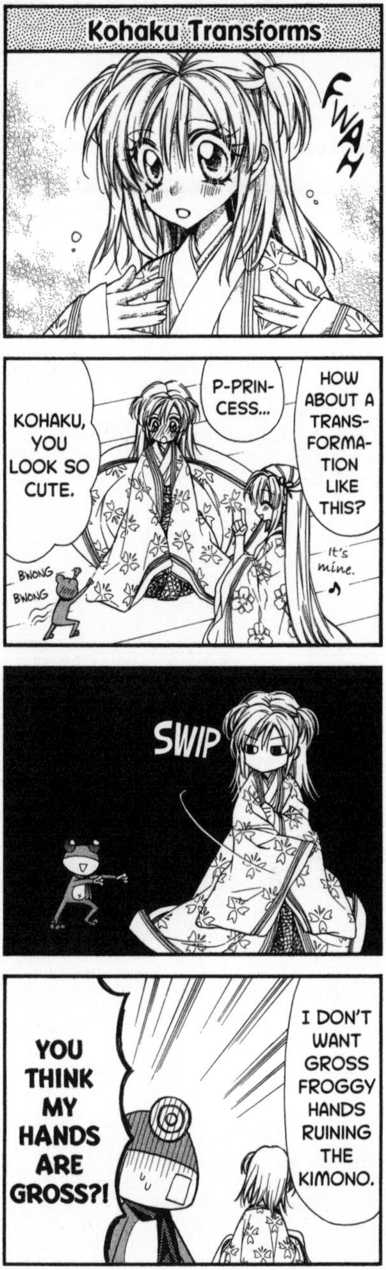
Kohaku Transforms
FWAH
HOW ABOUT A TRANSFORMATION LIKE THIS?
P-PRINCESS...
KOHAKU, YOU LOOK SO CUTE.
It's mine. ♪
BWONG BWONG
SWIP
I DON'T WANT GROSS FROGGY HANDS RUINING THE KIMONO.
YOU THINK MY HANDS ARE GROSS?!

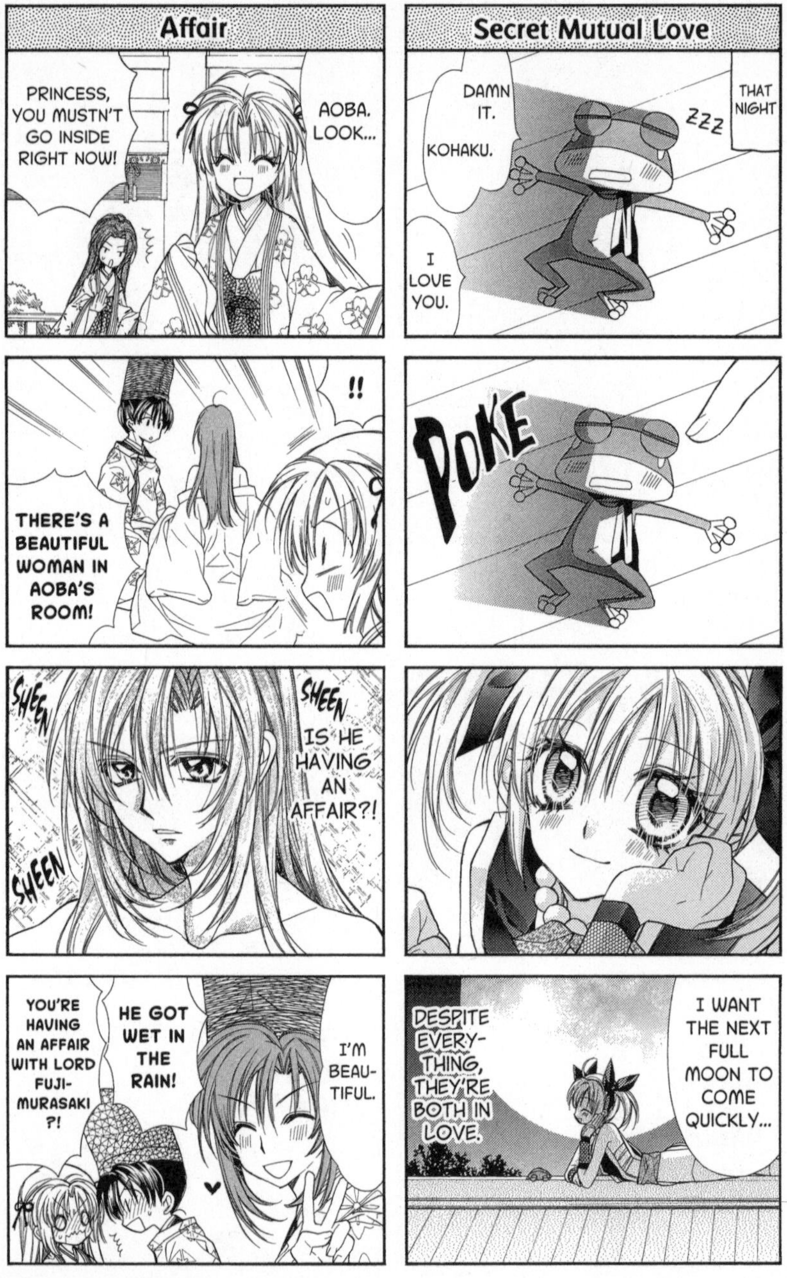
Secret Mutual Love
THAT NIGHT
ZZZ
DAMN IT.
KOHAKU.
I LOVE YOU.
POKE
I WANT THE NEXT FULL MOON TO COME QUICKLY...
DESPITE EVERYTHING, THEY'RE BOTH IN LOVE.
Affair
AOBA. LOOK...
PRINCESS, YOU MUSTN'T GO INSIDE RIGHT NOW!
!!
THERE'S A BEAUTIFUL WOMAN IN AOBA'S ROOM!
SHEEN
IS HE HAVING AN AFFAIR?!
SHEEN
SHEEN
I'M BEAUTIFUL.
HE GOT WET IN THE RAIN!
YOU'RE HAVING AN AFFAIR WITH LORD FUJIMURASAKI ?!

The next two pages were illustrated by my super assistants. ♪ Yogurt-chan is a kind and caring girl who loves cats. Matsun is an amazing girl who can handle any favor I ask of her even though she's still young! These two get along very well at the studio. ❀

Congratulations on the publication of volume 9!!

Nice to meet you, I'm Yogurt, the assistant. I'm in charge of pasting screentones. ♪ I like all the characters in *Sakura Hime* but my favorites are Princess Sakura and Aoba.☆ I'm so happy to be able to work on a series I love so much. I'll always be a fan of this series.

☆ Yogurt ☆

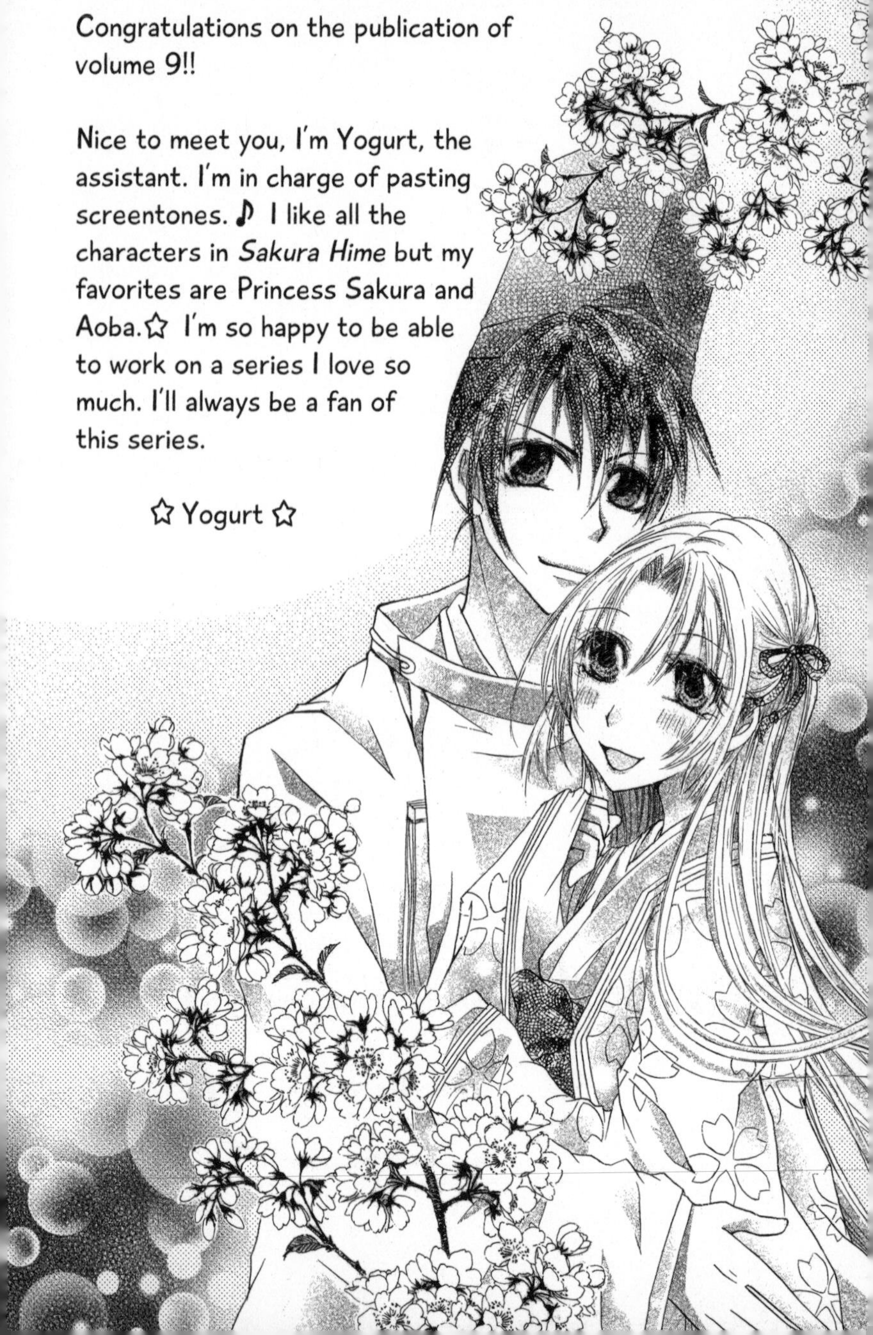

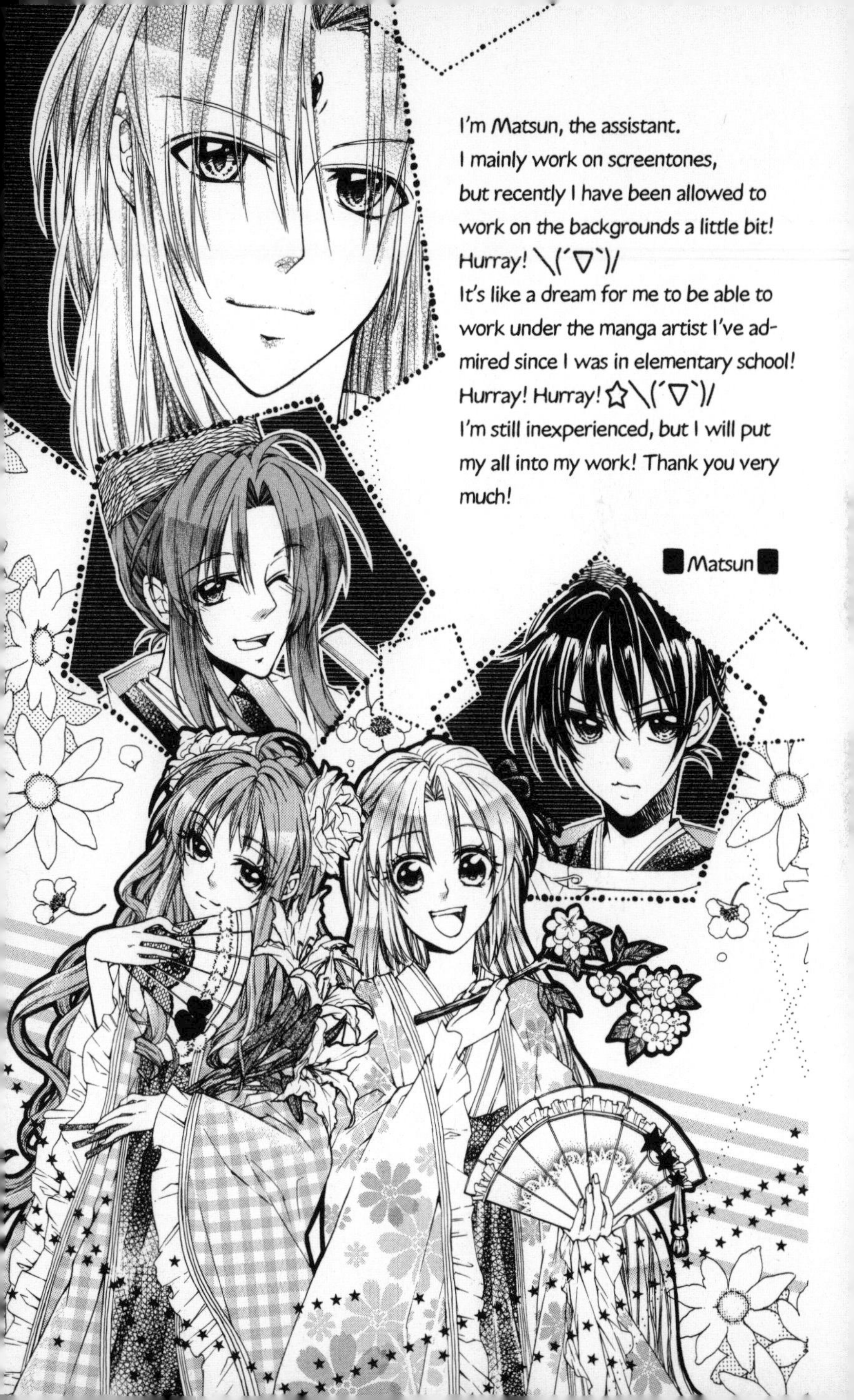

I'm Matsun, the assistant.
I mainly work on screentones, but recently I have been allowed to work on the backgrounds a little bit!
Hurray! \(´▽`)/
It's like a dream for me to be able to work under the manga artist I've admired since I was in elementary school!
Hurray! Hurray! ☆\(´▽`)/
I'm still inexperienced, but I will put my all into my work! Thank you very much!

■Matsun■

ARINA TANEMURA

Aoba's secret is revealed and a new arc begins in this volume. Rurijo is my favorite character, so I enjoyed drawing her story with Hayate. Frog Hayate is very easy to draw and adds a nice change to the artwork, so he is a very good character, though he suddenly becomes a very troublesome one once he turns human. I was in tears from all his black ink and screentones in the second half of the arc. You are going to see many chapters centered around specific characters for a while, but please continue to support the series! I'll see you in the next volume.

Arina Tanemura began her manga career in 1996 when her short stories debuted in *Ribon* magazine. She gained fame with the 1997 publication of *I•O•N*, and ever since her debut Tanemura has been a major force in shojo manga with popular series *Kamikaze Kaito Jeanne*, *Time Stranger Kyoko*, *Full Moon*, and *The Gentlemen's Alliance †*. Both *Kamikaze Kaito Jeanne* and *Full Moon* have been adapted into animated TV series.

Sakura Hime: The Legend of Princess Sakura
Volume 9
Shojo Beat Edition

STORY AND ART BY
Arina Tanemura

Translation & Adaptation/Tetsuichiro Miyaki
Touch-up Art & Lettering/Inori Fukuda Trant
Design/Sam Elzway
Editor/Nancy Thistlethwaite

SAKURA-HIME KADEN © 2008 by Arina Tanemura
All rights reserved.
First published in Japan in 2008 by SHUEISHA Inc., Tokyo.
English translation rights arranged by SHUEISHA Inc.

The rights of the author(s) of the work(s) in this publication
to be so identified have been asserted in accordance with the
Copyright, Designs and Patents Act 1988. A CIP catalogue
record for this book is available from the British Library.

The stories, characters and incidents mentioned in this
publication are entirely fictional.

Printed in the U.S.A.

Published by VIZ Media, LLC
P.O. Box 77010
San Francisco, CA 94107

10 9 8 7 6 5 4 3 2 1
First printing, December 2012

www.shojobeat.com
www.viz.com

SURPRISE!

You may be reading the wrong way!

It's true: In keeping with the original Japanese comic format, this book reads from right to left—so action, sound effects, and word balloons are completely reversed. This preserves the orientation of the original artwork—plus, it's fun! Check out the diagram shown here to get the hang of things, and then turn to the other side of the book to get started!

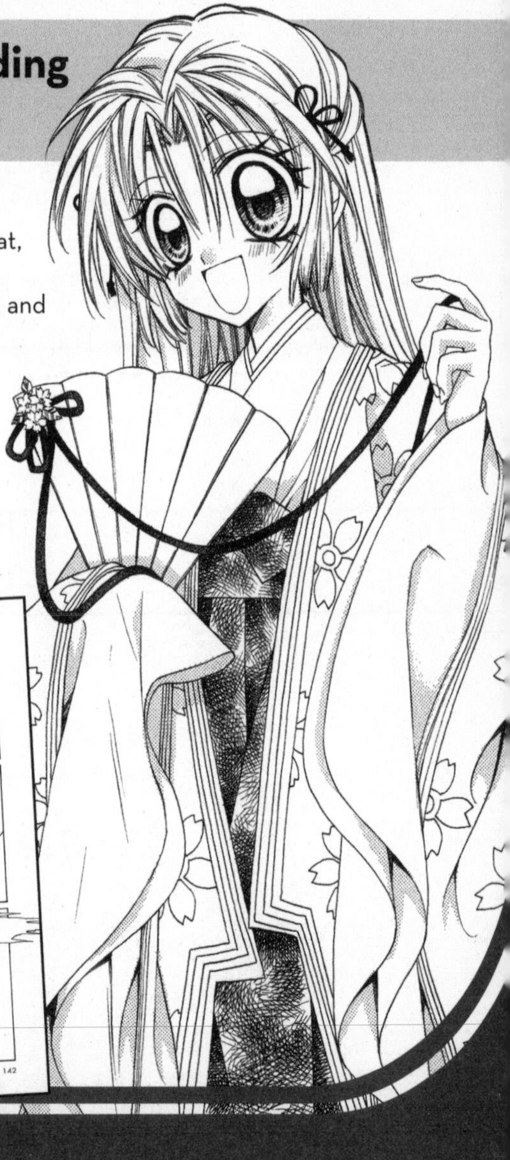

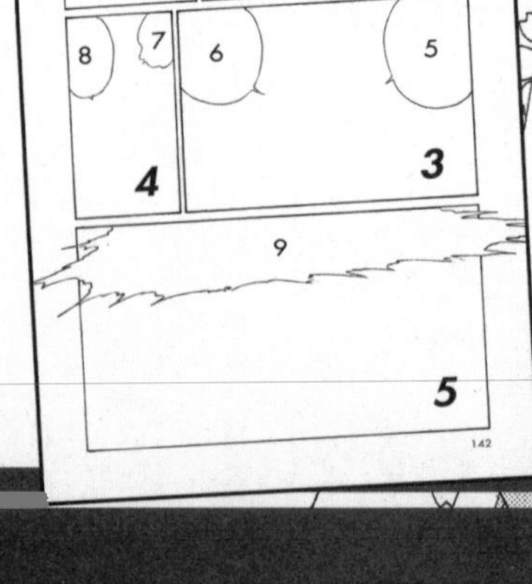
1
2
1
3
4
2
5
6
3
7
8
4
9
5
142

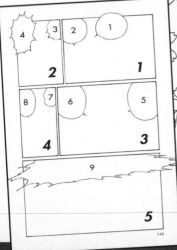